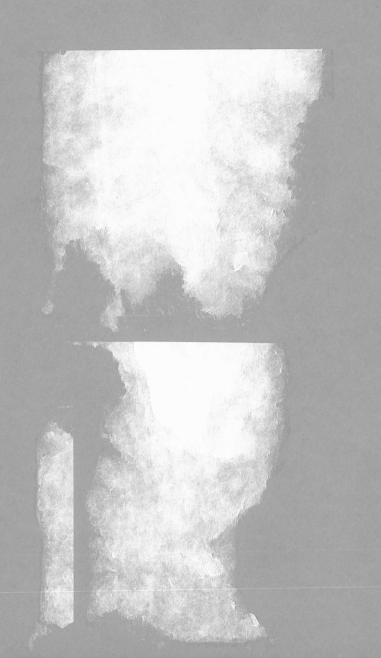

OTHER BOOKS BY ROBERT D. BALLARD

NONFICTION

The Lost Ships of Guadalcanal (with Rick Archbold)
Discovery of the Bismarck (with Rick Archbold)
Discovery of the Titanic (with Rick Archbold)

FICTION

Bright Shark (with Tony Chiu)

EXPLORATIONS

EXPLORATIONS

My Quest for Adventure and Discovery Under the Sea

ROBERT D. BALLARD, PH.D.

with Malcolm McConnell

HYPERION
New York

Library of Congress Cataloging-in-Publication Data

Ballard, Robert D.
    Explorations : my quest for adventure and discovery under the sea
/ by Robert D. Ballard with Malcolm McConnell.—1st ed.
        p.   cm.

    ISBN 0-7868-6042-1
    1. Ballard, Robert D.   2. Oceanographers—United States—
Biography.   I. McConnell, Malcolm.   II. Title.
GC30.B35A3   1995
930.1'02804'092—dc20   94–48507
                                                                CIP
    [B]
FIRST EDITION

10 9 8 7 6 5 4 3 2 1

To the three most important women in my life;
my wife, Barbara, my mother, Harriett,
and my sister, Nancy Ann.

PROLOGUE

April 10, 1963, 0750 Hours

Thresher spiraled slowly down toward the cold, black abyss.

Lieutenant Commander Wes Harvey, captain of America's newest nuclear attack submarine, watched the needle of the depth gauge creep across the dial face.

Quartermaster Jackie Gunter sat beside Harvey in the control room, gripping the UQC underwater acoustic phone. Gunter called their escort vessel, *Skylark*, steaming unseen above them on the gray surface of the Atlantic, 240 miles east of Cape Cod.

"Starting deep dive."

"Roger," *Skylark*'s reply echoed in the speaker.

On this second day of sea trials, following an overhaul at Portsmouth Naval Shipyard, *Thresher* had crossed the Georges Bank where the shallows did not permit deep dives. Now they were over the continental rise with a bottom depth of 8,500 feet.

Thresher, the lead ship of the world's most advanced class of nuclear-powered attack submarines, was back in her native element, hundreds of feet beneath the surface. And she was diving deeper, all the way down to her rated test depth of 1,000 feet.

The submarine's nuclear propulsion system meant *Thresher* was now independent of Earth's atmosphere. She no longer needed to surface and breathe to charge her batteries as did the older submarines of World War II. Her huge single screw could drive *Thresher* at speeds in excess of 35 knots. The submarine displaced more than 4,000 tons of seawater and was almost 300 feet long. It was bigger and faster than the destroyers that had hunted the puny U-boats of World War II.

The cold war was in its third decade. The Soviet Union had new types of nuclear submarines under construction. Their November Class attack sub was already prowling the world's oceans, and *Thresher,* the first of its own revolutionary class of fast, deep-diving attack subs, was designed to defeat this Soviet undersea menace. It was imperative that the lead vessel pass its sea tests so that construction of its sister ships could proceed quickly. The imperatives of wartime—hot or cold— could not be ignored.

At 0810 hours Chief Gunter reported to *Skylark.* "We are now at four hundred feet and checking for leaks."

The planesman slid back his yoke and the vessel turned in a slow circular course, its bow angling like the hand of a clock from north to east to south. One hundred twenty-nine men, including civilian shipyard workers, inspected every inch of exposed piping, every vulnerable valve and hatch seal.

Thirty minutes later they were certain there were no leaks. But the pressure on *Thresher*'s hull remained a silent, unseen menace, mounting inexorably with depth.

For every 33 feet, the pressure of seawater increases by one atmosphere. At 400 feet, the weight of water on *Thresher*'s hull was almost 14 atmospheres, 200 pounds per square inch. Engineers had established the vessel's test depth of 1,000 feet by calculating many complex factors. Although the welded hull could withstand immense pressures, the hull was pierced by periscopes, access hatches, and torpedo tubes.

The engineers had also established the depth limit below which *Thresher* would definitely not survive. This terminal point bore the the ominous name "crush depth." For *Thresher,* it was 1,500 feet.

"Proceed to test depth," Captain Harvey ordered Lieutenant John Smarz, *Thresher*'s diving officer.

"Test depth, aye aye, sir," Lieutenant Smarz replied.

Chief Gunter called *Skylark*. "Proceeding to test depth." It was 0900 hours.

The deck beneath Wes Harvey's feet angled more steeply, bow down. The hull groaned and creaked as packing glands and hatch seals compressed within the invisible vise jaws of sea pressure.

Wes Harvey was descending at slow speed, *Thresher*'s turbines idling at a fraction of their rated 18,000 horsepower. He was a skilled and prudent young officer, confident of his ship and crew but keenly aware of the relentless, unforgiving menace that surrounded them.

At 0910 hours, *Thresher* glided through 900 feet. Although the sub had no portholes, every man on board knew they had left the world of warmth and sunlight far above. Here the water was eternally cold, unriled by surface storms. No sunlight had ever penetrated these depths. The frames creaked; contracting bulkheads muttered dully.

The crew and yard technicians searched for any sign of weakness or failure. The submarine crept along at 5 knots, the curved blades of its huge single screw turning slowly in the black water.

In a few minutes, when Wes Harvey and his officers were sure the hull integrity had been well tested, he would order increased speed, allowing the vessel to acquire momentum. Then the planesman would raise the bow, and *Thresher*, its screw driven by the powerful nuclear-fed turbines, would soar like a bulbous airplane back to safer depths.

The conventional means of surfacing by blowing seawater from ballast tanks with compressed air was not a practical option at these great depths, where extreme pressure would overpower the deballasting system. *Thresher* could not survive this deep unless it "flew" forward. If the vessel stalled, it would sink inexorably past crush depth.

Taking submarines to this razor's edge required both courage and audacity.

The compartments reported no unusual leaks, no failed seals or valves.

Quartermaster Jackie Gunter was about to respond to *Skylark*'s request for a communications check. He never had the chance.

An explosive clap, like a rifle shot, rang through the hull. In the auxiliary machinery room, just aft of the reactor compartment, a narrow seawater pipe had burst at a vulnerable silver-brazed joint. As the frantic sailors rushed toward the noise, they were engulfed in a cloying, icy mist. The water spraying from the pipe at more than 500 pounds per square inch was instantly atomized, cloaking the compartment in a chill, briny fog. This cold steam condensed on bulkheads and decks, saturating one of *Thresher*'s two redundant master electrical panels, the port main bus. The circuit breakers were grounded and tripped. The panel went dead.

Crewmen worked with frantic speed to limit the damage. Submariners drilled ceaselessly for such emergencies.

"Shut the main seawater valves."

This would relieve the pressure on the burst pipe joint.

"Shift loads to starboard bus."

Electrical power was now fed through the redundant starboard master junction panel.

But the brief drop in power had triggered the nuclear reactor's automatic safety devices. Graphite control rods dropped into the core, damping the nuclear reaction. This automatic reactor "scram" deprived the turbines of steam.

"Reactor scram. Secure all unnecessary electrical loads."

The humming air conditioning went silent; sailors shut down unneeded equipment. In the control room, an engineman engaged the sub's battery-powered auxiliary electric propulsion system.

It was 0912 hours.

Thresher drifted forward, its wide propeller driven slowly by the weak electric motor.

When word came that the leak had been isolated, Wes Harvey ordered the engineers to restart the reactor. But it would take a full seven minutes for the renewed fission reaction to produce steam for the turbines. Harvey could not wait that long at this depth.

"Full rise on the planes," he ordered. "Maximum up-angle."

He hoped the submarine's momentum was sufficient to permit a slow climb to a safe depth.

The men in the control room felt the deck tilt as the bow rose. But then the speed gauge unwound from 3 knots to zero, no headway.

It was 0913 hours. The ship had stalled. *Thresher* slipped gently backward—its bow still optimistically raised toward the surface—deeper, past its test depth.

The reactor would produce steam again in five minutes.

It was essential to lighten the ship by deballasting.

"Blow all main ballast tanks. Blow safety. Blow negative."

No sooner had Harvey's orders been acknowledged than the shriek of compressed air unleashed into the ballast tanks howled through the ship. But given the unyielding laws of thermodynamics, the attempt to blow tanks at this depth was futile. Ice instantly formed on the tank screens that protected the air valves from debris, blocking the air stream.

Lieutenant Commander Wes Harvey took the underwater phone and called *Skylark*.

"Experiencing minor difficulty. Have positive up-angle," he shouted over the roar of the compressed air valves. "Attempting to blow."

More than 1,000 feet above the stricken submarine, *Skylark* steamed in a slow oval pattern through the southerly groundswell. The overcast was fraying and spring sunshine broke through to warm the gray face of the Atlantic.

Skylark's officers heard the garbled transmission. From their perspective, it was impossible to assess the nature of *Thresher*'s "minor difficulty."

At 0917 hours, a garbled voice called from *Thresher*. "Exceeding test depth. . . ."

Then *Skylark*'s hydrophone resounded with a hollow, liquid thud. Two seconds later, the dry thunderclap of a sharper explosion echoed from below.

It was 0918 hours.

Thresher's death came with merciful speed.

As the submarine slid backward into the black maw of pressure, a vulnerable section of hull aft of the engine room finally collapsed.

This implosion produced the first hollow thud heard on *Skylark*.

A crushing slab of seawater slammed into the ruptured pressure hull, tearing watertight bulkhead doors from their hinges like scraps of wet cardboard. The air inside the hull was instantly compressed to 750 pounds per square inch. *Thresher*'s hull became a huge combustion cylinder, the sea a piston. One hundred twenty-nine men were killed within seconds by the invisible blast of superheated air. Diesel fuel and lubricants exploded. The thick curved flanks of the pressure hull were shredded. *Thresher* erupted like a giant depth charge.

This monstrous explosion was heard thousands of miles away through the hydrophones of the navy's SOSUS network underwater surveillance system.

Thresher's hull split into three pieces: the bow section with its sonar dome, the stern section, hanging from the freewheeling propeller, and the thickly shielded reactor compartment, the heaviest single piece of debris.

Angular momentum influenced the plunge of this wreckage. As speed increased, the heaviest debris chunks fell almost vertically.

Clots of oil streamed back toward the surface. The bow and stern sections trailed clouds of rock wool insulation, sheaves of severed electrical cables, tools, charts and blueprints, clothing, and the bodies of the dead. Weak undersea currents wafted this lighter debris into a long spreading trail.

Thresher's heavy debris continued in near-vertical free fall.

The hull sections and the reactor compartment hit the silty sediment of the continental rise at speeds of over 100 knots. They gouged deep circular impact craters. The massive steel dome of the reactor struck with so much momentum that it buried itself under several meters of mud.

For a long time, the plume of smaller objects, tugged by faint currents, drifted down to the west of the main impact craters, like dead leaves on a moonless winter night.

Thresher's bones had come to rest in 8,400 feet of water. The terrain around the wreckage was cut by narrow gullies, bisected by low stony ridges.

Had there been light, the bottom would have looked like the badlands of the Dakotas, covered by a crusty layer of dirty old snow.

July 12, 1984, 1320 Hours

Argo's powerful lights cut the endless night of the continental rise. I sat in the control van, watching the crusted white ocean floor glide silently past on the bank of television monitors.

Half covered in the pale gray sediment, an empty rubber glove slid by. Then a scrap of insulation. A rubber boot appeared a few moments later. We were crossing over *Thresher*'s debris field.

The van was *Argo*'s nerve center, two converted steel shipping containers joined together like a mobile home, crammed with electronics and my team from the new Deep Submergence Laboratory. The windowless van was perched on the stern of the Woods Hole Oceanographic Institution research vessel *Knorr*. A thin coaxial cable ran from a winch on the ship's superstructure, through a starboard derrick, and down into the Atlantic swell. The cable dropped for 8,400 feet to the *Thresher*'s grave.

Argo flew at the end of this cable tether, an improbable kite of white steel tubing the size of a station wagon, mounting a single jaunty tail fin. At Argo's bow, two extremely sensitive Silicon Intensified Target (SIT) video cameras were focused on the bottom, 45 feet beneath the vehicle.

We were in our second day of mapping *Thresher*'s debris field and videotaping the entire site for the U.S. Navy. During the twenty-one years the submarine's wreckage had lain on the bottom, it had been visited by the navy's deep-diving bathyscaphe and the research submersible *Alvin* from Woods Hole. These manned dives had been brief forays that yielded a confusing and incomplete picture of the wreckage.

But on this expedition, my brand-new *Argo,* an unmanned sled mounting one of the world's most sophisticated television camera and sonar systems, had already spent more time flying back and forth across *Thresher*'s wreckage than the manned dives had accomplished in two decades.

With Argo deployed, Captain Richard Bowen, skipper of the *Knorr,* had left the bridge to control the ship from the "driver's" console inside the van. As if playing an elaborate game of Pac-Man, he used twin joysticks with top-mounted thumb balls to keep the vessel moving with slow precision along the track I had laid down on the marine survey sheet on the chart table beside me. To Captain Bowen's left, Earl Young sat at another console. Earl was *Argo*'s "flyer," the member of the team who controlled the vehicle's altitude above the ocean bottom.

These robotic control consoles, the winking digital displays, and the whirring sonar graph printer evoked the bridge of a futuristic submarine. Certainly all of us in the control van felt we were down there with *Argo*, gliding above the rippled gray frosting of the bottom.

This powerful sense of "telepresence" was exactly what I had dreamed of when I conceived of the *Argo* system five years earlier. Our scanning human eyes and restlessly curious brains had been transported to the ocean bottom. The rest of our vulnerable human bodies remained above the crushing depths in the comfortable air-conditioned control van.

We were near the end of this search line. Tom Crook, the navigator, gently tapped out new instructions to the nav computer, erasing the last track and displaying a new survey line for Captain Bowen to follow.

Bowen quickly responded and carefully pulled back on the joysticks controlling *Knorr*'s powerful thrusters.

Knorr continued to hold its head in the wind and sea, but the entire ship began to slide sideways. Then the water around the forward thruster boiled, as if a violent eruption had exploded just beneath the surface.

Earl Young pulled his winch control lever, raising *Argo* clear of any possible obstacles as the vessel slowed for the turn and the camera sled stalled. The bottom was littered with glacial erratic boulders that had been rafted out here by icebergs over the past ten thousand years.

Once on the new search heading, Earl steadied *Argo* at an altitude of 45 feet.

Some people call our sweeping back-and-forth search pattern "mowing the lawn." The alternating furrows of *Argo*'s survey lines also reminded me of the boustrophedon pattern of ancient Greek inscriptions in which the direction of writing shifted from left to right and back to left, "as the ox draws the plow."

I had planned *Argo* to be a vehicle of exploration just as audacious as its namesake in classical Greek mythology. And when the new system matured, *Argo* would have its own heroic sailor, the smaller robot vehicle, Jason, which would sally from his vessel on a fiber-optic tether to be tested, and, hopefully, to endure and conquer. Jason would be equipped with color-television eyes and a manipulator arm with grasping claws.

The *Argo-Jason* system would carry my team to the remote depths of the planet's oceans. There we would no doubt encounter monsters and perils, as had the first ship *Argo* and its captain Jason. And those hazards would have to be vanquished if we were to discover the Golden Fleece of knowledge. But that would have to wait for money and sponsorship, the bane of explorers from time immemorial.

I'd named *Argo* and *Jason* to echo the epic journey of classical myth that is central to the human concept of exploration. Mythical epic journeys in which a single adventurous figure or a bold band of comrades explores the unknown to gain wisdom can be found in all the world's cultures. And most of these epic exploration myths follow the same archetypal form. The hero or explorer becomes possessed of a dream. He journeys forth into new, uncharted territory. There he is tested by danger and overcomes hardships. Finally, he returns with the prize of wisdom.

Although I certainly did not consider myself cast in a heroic mold, exploration of the undersea had always been my dream. And now with *Argo,* I was well launched on my own epic journey of discovery.

"Debris," Earl Young sang out, scanning his television monitor, "thin gauge piping, electrical cable."

My mind returned from the heroic past and the adventurous future to the cold practicalities of the present survey. The navy had requested a complete mapping and video record of the entire *Thresher* debris field. This was motivated by more than sentimental or morbid curiosity.

Although deep submersibles had probed the wreck, this would be the first rigorous survey and documentation of the debris field. The navy still had questions as to the exact cause of *Thresher*'s sinking. It had been convincingly surmised during an exhaustive engineering analysis that one of the narrow silver-brazed seawater pipes had burst at test depth. These brazed pipes had been a cheaper, expedient alternative to stronger welded pipes in that generation of nuclear subs. But the navy learned a lesson: the deep sea judged expediency harshly. *Thresher*'s sister ships were fitted with welded pipe joints.

The destruction pattern of the implosion that ripped apart *Thresher*'s hull had not been completely established. The navy needed this information in order to assess the strength and environmental integrity of the reactor vessels in its aging nuclear submarine fleet. I had been able to convince the Office of Naval Research and the Navy's Deep Submergence Program to help fund Argo as the best system to accomplish this task.

Now *Argo* was passing its first operational test. In two days we had charted almost all the *Thresher* debris field on videotape and had amassed detailed sonar images of the wreckage. Working through our patient ox-plow pattern of line searches, we had videotaped every visible fragment of debris from the submarine in three compass quadrants—north, east, and south. But we had been unable to establish "closure," an end to the debris, to the west.

This puzzled me. *Thresher* was the first shipwreck I had explored on the deep ocean bottom. During years of diving with the Woods Hole submersible, *Alvin,* and on weekend dives with the Boston Sea Rovers scuba club, I had encountered wrecks of fishing boats and small ships in shallower water.

They had all formed the standard circular debris field, with the ship's hull in the center, surrounded by hatch covers, broken rigging, and deck cargo.

I'd assumed that this wreckage pattern would hold no matter the depth of the sunken vessel. As a kid growing up in southern California, I'd been fascinated by navy movies and nautical adventures on television. I always remembered the unmistakable World War II images filmed through the periscope of a German U-boat. The sub's torpedoes streaked through the water trailing bubbles and blasted into the side of a hapless merchant vessel. As the ship's crew jumped for safety and took to the lifeboats, the vessel rose on a steep angle, its stern high, then disappeared beneath the surface with a final blast of steam, leaving survivors and floating wreckage bobbing on the waves.

In my mind, the stricken ship would then fill with water and settle to the bottom. Certainly, during scores of dives in *Alvin* and in the French bathyscaphe *Archimede*, I had macabre visions of the pressurized crew sphere failing and being instantly crushed by the pressure. Such horrible images are an occupational hazard in my profession. But I had never thought about the effects of a violent implosion when a surface ship or submarine plunged past crush depth and was ripped apart by the relentless pressure.

Now I was obliged to carefully consider the entire process of a deepwater sinking.

I gazed at the television monitor above Captain Bowen's console, watching the insulation scraps and shredded copper tubing that seemed scattered randomly on the gray sediment ripples of the bottom.

A Bach concerto played softly on the stereo. Someone had just buttered a fresh batch of popcorn, and the warm aroma filled the control van. Then, as *Thresher*'s light debris moved past *Argo*'s television eye, a clear picture of the sinking process suddenly emerged in my mind.

When the thousands of tons of ambient seawater pressure ripped through the submarine's hull, knocking down thick bulkheads like cardboard boxes, the explosion that shredded the hull would have expelled vast quantities of debris into the water. The heavier pieces would have accelerated into a near-vertical free fall. But just as farmers used to winnow their wheat by throwing the threshed grain into the air and allowing the wind to carry off the lighter chaff, weak underwater currents would separate the heavier wreckage from the lighter debris.

"It's not a circle," I whispered, tapping the survey sheet on the chart table. "It's got to be a trail. No wonder we couldn't get closure to the west."

As this submerged winnowing continued during *Thresher*'s long plunge to the bottom, a perfectly sorted array of material had been formed. The very lightest chaff—paper, plastic, and rock wool insulation—would lie farthest from the heaviest wreckage. The closer to the main debris, the heavier the fragment. This debris trail would form an unmistakable arrow, pointing directly to the heart of the wreck.

Argo passed beyond *Thresher*'s debris. *Knorr* rumbled slowly along the search line. Country music replaced Bach on the stereo. I was now certain that we would find no more wreckage on this track. I understood that *Thresher*'s debris trail led away to the west. It was suddenly all so clear.

Vessels that sink in very deep water are exposed to currents longer than wrecks in the relative shallows close to shore. There was probably a distinctive light-to-heavy debris trail for every ship sunk in deep soundings.

Instead of doubling back north when we finished that search line, I conferred with navigator Tom Crook, and we laid out an easterly search track, beginning at the point where we'd seen the light insulation and rubber glove.

Twenty minutes later, *Argo* followed *Knorr*'s cable tether like an obedient puppy, now heading almost due east.

"Wreckage," Earl called, scanning his TV screen.

Twisted piping gave way to heavier scraps of metal, then to the familiar dark angles of *Thresher*'s rudder protruding from the lip of the impact crater. We were over the central debris. As I had hoped, the trail of lighter material had led like a highway to the shattered remains of the submarine's hull.

I had just found the Rosetta Stone that would decipher the mystery of deep ocean shipwrecks.

September 1, 1985, 0048 Hours

The stereo in the control van played golden oldies. The Beatles followed "I Heard It Through the Grapevine."

Knorr had just turned onto search line number nine, the ninth east-west Argo track of this second phase of the expedition. Somewhere, 12,500 feet below the calm, star-flecked surface of the North Atlantic, the wreckage of R.M.S. *Titanic* had lain unseen for seventy-three years. For the past week, my Argo team from the Deep Submergence Laboratory of the Woods Hole Oceanographic Institution had been plowing these waters, searching for the ill-fated liner's debris trail.

Titanic was, without question, the most famous shipwreck in history, the Golden Fleece of undersea exploration. On April 14, 1912, the world's largest, most luxurious ocean liner struck an iceberg and sank on its maiden voyage, killing over 1,500 passengers and crew.

The expedition to find the ship was the most important single mission of my career as an undersea explorer and scientist. I had staked my reputation on finding *Titanic*. But now it appeared that my gamble would end in failure.

The month before, my partners in this joint French-American expedition had scoured the nearby ocean bottom using their advanced *Sonar Acoustique Remorqué* (SAR). This instrument produced beautifully detailed echographs of the deep ocean floor. But not a sign of *Titanic*. The SAR search had been predicated on the traditional approach: a vessel the size of *Titanic*, almost 900 feet long, displacing 45,000 tons, had to produce a substantive sonar image on the bottom. But my close friend, the veteran marine engineer Jean-Louis Michel, who had designed the SAR system, had come away empty-handed.

He was deeply disappointed but not surprised. *Titanic* had eluded three recent well-organized search expeditions. They, too, had been based on the assumption that *Titanic*'s huge wreckage mass could be located by sonar or magnometer.

Since testing my new *Argo* system on *Thresher* the year before, however, I understood that *Titanic* had to have left a wide, distinctive debris trail at least one mile long. I knew from the historic record that the night of the sinking, the captain of the nearby steamer *Californian*, fearing iceberg collision, had let his ship drift with no power to her screws until dawn. *Californian* had been borne southeast on a heading of 170 degrees at an estimated speed of 0.7 knots. So had *Titanic*'s lifeboats.

Therefore *Titanic*'s debris trail, winnowed by this same current, had to be spread along a north-south axis.

So, instead of repeating the futile sonar searches among the masking hills and gullies of the deep ocean bottom—which could have easily hidden the ship's hull—I was plowing the depths southeast of Jean Louis's unsuccessful SAR search area, running slow, patient east-west *Argo* lines slightly less than 1 mile apart, hoping to intersect *Titanic*'s estimated 1-mile-long debris trail at a right angle.

But seven days of these exhaustive searches had produced nothing but hundreds of hours of gray, almost featureless ocean bottom, crossed by the occasional lifeless track of a deep sea slug or albino crab. And we were running out of time. In four days, I would have to order *Argo* reeled in and stowed for the return trip to Cape Cod. The *Knorr* was an expensive vessel, already booked by my Woods Hole colleagues for other expeditions.

If we didn't find *Titanic* on this trip, the chances of another expensive expedition based on *Argo*'s new but unproven technology and my debris-trail theory were indeed slim.

I left the control van a little after midnight and returned to my small cabin to snatch a few hours' sleep. But lying in my bunk, sleep did not come easily. I tried reading Chuck Yeager's autobiography, willing my mind away from the frustrations of the deep ocean to his exciting adventures on the high frontier of supersonic flight.

In the control van, Jean-Louis Michel steered *Knorr* from the driver's console. Dependable Earl Young was the *Argo* flyer on this watch.

Bill Lang, a bearded young Woods Hole video specialist assigned to the documentation team, turned to *Argo* engineer Stu Harris. "What are we going to do to keep ourselves awake tonight?"

For seven long days, they'd stood their watches in this van, four hours on, eight hours off. All they had seen on *Argo*'s video monitors were miles of featureless gray mud.

But Stu didn't answer. His eyes were fixed on the *Argo* monitor. "There's something," he said softly, pointing to the screen.

Suddenly, all the sleepy members of the watch were upright in their chairs, staring intently at the monitors. Stu Harris reached across the console to switch *Argo*'s video eye from the forward-looking camera to the downward-looking zoom lens.

Irregular debris appeared, only to disappear quickly. Then the mottled gray image of a round man-made object crept onto the screen. Stu scanned the monitor. It was 0105 hours local time. *Argo* flew 14.6 meters above the bottom at a depth of 3,784 meters (12,230 feet).

"Wreckage!" Bill exclaimed.

The circular object crept across the screen. As it came into the full glare of *Argo*'s floodlights, three smaller circular images appeared on the crusted metallic face. This was not an anonymous glacial erratic boulder. The object was an artifact, metal shaped by human beings.

In confirmation, *Argo*'s sonar operator, Navy Lieutenant George Rey, sang out, "I'm getting a hard contact."

The circular object disappeared from the top of the screen as *Argo* flew slowly west.

"Someone should go get Bob," Bill Lang suggested.

The cook, John Bartolomei, tapped on my cabin door and stuck his head inside. "The guys think you should come down to the van," he said casually.

I pulled my jumpsuit over thick flannel pajamas, jammed on my boat shoes, and was down the clanking, brine-slick outside ladder in three bounds.

Inside the van, team members were gazing at the monitor that showed the replay of the wreckage we had just passed over. Jean-Louis Michel had spread open a book containing facsimiles of photographs of *Titanic* under construction in northern Ireland. One 1911 photograph showed the distinctive iron-kettle shape of a boiler with its three unique circular vent orifices. My eyes shot from the book to the TV monitor and back to the book.

"Yes, Bob," Jean-Louis said, with his Maurice Chevalier accent. "It *ees* a boiler."

I stood for a moment, completely still, my mind pulsing with images. We had just passed over the middle of *Titanic*'s debris trail. There could be no question of this. To the south lay the lighter material, to the north, perhaps within a few hundred meters of this track, lay the ship itself.

"God damn," I finally said in a quiet, incredulous voice. "God damn. . . ."

We had found *Titanic*.

Part One

THE DREAM

ONE

I was lost.

The cars and trucks careening around the unfamiliar rotary sprayed our new little VW bug with dirty slush. In California, where I came from, we always kept our cars clean and shiny. But I sure wasn't in California anymore.

"I still can't read the signs," Margie said with a sigh, as we began our third circuit of the traffic circle.

I squinted through the smeared windshield, trying to make sense of the snowy road signs.

"We're in Revere," I finally decided. "North of Boston . . . on the wrong damned side of the river."

Margie frowned, the road map crumpled on her lap, trying her best to navigate in this alien territory. "Well," she agreed, "we sure are lost."

We had arrived at the downtown Boston end of the Massachusetts Turnpike on a snowy afternoon in March 1967. Instead of crossing the Fort Point Channel Bridge into South Boston and on to our destination, First Naval District headquarters, the unyielding rush hour traffic had pushed us north across the Charles River and all the way into the blue-collar neighborhood of Revere.

A bakery truck with rusty fenders cut us off. Seeing our black-and-gold California license plates, the truck driver crowded us further into the inner lane.

"We just missed another turn," Margie said, watching the bewildering pattern of roads leading off the circle.

I nodded, grimly trying to negotiate the traffic and spot

the exit that would lead us back south across the river. But it was hard to see. The damp chill of the northeaster bearing down on New England overpowered the little car's defroster. Suddenly, I could imagine driving around this rotary for hours until we ran out of gas. If I'd been in a better mood, the situation would have seemed comic.

Here we were, a newly married young couple, all our worldly goods packed into suitcases and cartons, crammed into this tiny Keystone Kops car about as far from home in southern California as it was possible to be without leaving the contiguous forty-eight states. And we were caught up in this crazy merry-go-round of a traffic rotary, spinning in blind circles as the snow and slush piled deeper.

In many ways the immediate situation reflected my overall plight. We didn't have rotaries and these warrens of narrow, confusing streets in southern California; we had freeways that looped and twirled with logical precision, linking the entire Los Angeles megalopolis into an accessible grid. And we sure didn't have blinding wet snow and ankle-deep slush. Even the skeletal black winter trees and the drab peaked-roof frame houses seemed foreign and vaguely menacing.

On the next circuit of the rotary, I found a hole in the traffic and took the first exit. The Volkswagen jolted over slush-filled potholes and bounced off tongues of black ice left over from the last blizzard.

"Where're we going?" Margie asked, wiping her foggy window to peer out.

"I don't know," I admitted. "Let's just try to find a motel."

I wanted to stop the car, go into a warm, brightly lit room, and regain the feeling that I had control over my life. The snafu of getting lost in this rush-hour snowstorm had shaken my confidence. My life had been swept into a sudden whirlwind, like Dorothy in that Kansas cyclone. Unfortunately, the swaybacked frame duplexes, laundromats, and liquor stores of working-class Boston did not resemble the enchanted land of Oz.

While searching for a motel we could afford—our bankroll consisted of a one-thousand-dollar cashier's check taped under the dashboard—I thought about the strange events that had led us to snowy Boston.

First and foremost, I never thought I'd become a newly commissioned ensign assigned as the scientific liaison officer for the Office of Naval Research in New England. In fact, I had never planned to serve in the navy at all.

Only a year before, I'd been a graduate student in oceanography at the University of Hawaii in Honolulu. Technically, I was a second lieutenant in the intelligence branch of the U.S. Army, having earned an ROTC commission with my undergraduate degree in physical sciences from the University of California at Santa Barbara, which had no navy ROTC program. But my army active-duty obligation had been deferred until I completed graduate school.

I had enjoyed grad school in Hawaii and had even found an engrossing part-time job as a dolphin trainer at Sea Life Park. Actually, it would have been fairer to describe my work with spotted dolphins and rough-toothed porpoises as those clever animals training *me*.

My first-year course work in Honolulu was not specialized, although I was already leaning toward marine geology. The Hawaiian Islands gave me a good perspective on the vastness of the world's oceans. Almost three quarters of Earth's surface (71%) lies beneath salt water. Seen from space, a gleaming blue ball frosted with clouds of condensed water vapor, it was easy to see why some 1960s marine science boosters had started to call Earth "the Ocean Planet." And I was fascinated by the image of all those undersea geologic features hidden by the planetary cloak of water. I wanted to explore that secret world.

Then unforeseen events intervened, as they so often do, and set in motion the chaotic vortex that had dropped Margie and me in our overloaded VW Beetle onto these icy, potholed streets 6,000 miles from Honolulu.

The war in Vietnam was heating up as large numbers of American combat troops were committed. Hawaii was a favorite R and R destination. One night I ran into two young army intelligence lieutenants with whom I had trained at ROTC summer camp the year before. They were unwinding after six months in Vietnam. Over too many drinks at the Officers' Club on Waikiki Beach, they finally admitted that duty as a combat intel officer in this particular war involved treating Viet Cong suspects in ways I never intended to treat any human being.

I wasn't afraid to go to Vietnam, and I certainly wasn't a pacifist, having been the ROTC's Distinguished Military Graduate at UCSB in 1965. But I vowed I would never throw a VC prisoner out of a Huey helicopter to extract information from his comrades. Also, serving in the navy after graduate school rather than the army made a lot more sense, given my abiding interest, indeed my obsession, with the sea. My normal logical approach to problems, however, did not impress the navy recruiting office in Honolulu.

The petty officer with whom I discussed the idea of switching my commission just smiled and shook his head. "The navy doesn't take army officers," was all he said.

But even as a relative military novice, I knew the armed services had a bureaucratic procedure for every imaginable situation. Pressing the navy personnel offices in Pearl Harbor, I discovered the "Inter-Service Transfer." After completing the forms and interviews, two officers assured me that my navy commission would be forthcoming in due course. But I remained slightly dubious. In any event, I assumed that my active-duty deferment would also be extended until I completed graduate study.

In the summer of 1966, I landed one of the best jobs any aspiring ocean scientist could imagine. North American Aviation's Ocean Systems Group offered me a full-time position. The deal was almost too good to be true. I would work in the group's research program, developing potential missions for their first manned deep submersible, *Beaver Mark IV*, in the Long Beach, California, facility, near my parents' home. Best of all, North American would pay for my doctoral program at the University of Southern California.

In Honolulu, I had been dating Marjorie Hargas—an adventuresome young woman working her way around the world—for several months. And when it came time to return to California, it was clear neither of us could face saying good-bye. We were married soon after arriving in Southern California.

My first assignment in the Ocean Systems Group was as challenging as it was intriguing: helping design a permanent undersea work facility to be serviced by the *Beaver*.

This industrial submersible operated on the lock-in/lock-out principle. That is, there were two personnel spheres in the squat cylindrical superstructure, one for the operating crew of pilot and copilot, one for the divers. The crew's sphere operated at 1 atmosphere; the divers' sphere could be pressurized to the seawater depth, all the way down to 600 feet. This allowed the divers to open the hatch and work outside, connected to the sub by "hooka" breathing hoses. After their work shift, the divers could undergo controlled decompression in their own sphere aboard the sub or in a decompression chamber on the support ship, or they could remain at the ambient work-depth pressure in an undersea habitat.

The concept was to actually build an underwater oil-exploration and production base that was completely independent of the surface, an inner-space station.

These were the heady, optimistic days of big, government-funded science programs, when nothing seemed impossible or inappropriate for America and its aerospace companies. With the country caught up in the adventure of the Apollo moon program, it seemed to many that the ocean would inevitably be the next frontier for America to conquer. All the big aerospace companies were gearing up for the anticipated bonanza of a "wet NASA" by developing deep-sea submersibles and the undersea habitats that we all believed were inevitable.

To me this was a dream come true. The sea had drawn me to it since childhood. As a young kid in the San Diego suburb of Pacific Beach, I'd spent endless summer days exploring the shores of Mission Bay. While most of my friends were fascinated by the destroyers and aircraft carriers steaming in and out of San Diego's busy navy bases, I was obsessed with the world *under* the sea. To me, the surface of the ocean was boring. But I found the skittering hermit crabs, clams, and anemones beneath the bland face of the tidal pools endlessly intriguing. Even as a boy of six or seven, I sensed that there was a whole world hidden beneath the waves.

Submarines fascinated me. After I read Jules Verne's prophetic science-fiction novel, *Twenty Thousand Leagues Under the Sea*, I was gripped by the challenge of actually exploring the hidden ocean depths. One edition of the book had an especially evocative illustration: a team of divers from Captain Nemo's futuristic submarine, *Nautilus*, trudging along the ocean bottom, bearing the casket of one of their dead crewmates to an undersea grave. It seemed possible that humans would one day live and work beneath the sea, and I wanted to be in the vanguard of the wave of exploration that would make this dream reality.

Now, as a young man assigned to North American Aviation's Ocean Systems Group, this utopian dream seemed within my reach.

I was already familiar with North American's program because my father, Chet, was one of the company's most senior missile design engineers and had found me a summer job with the nascent Ocean Systems Group two years earlier. And I was back working under Dr. Andy Rechnitzer, a graduate of the Scripps Institute of Oceanography.

Growing up in Pacific Beach just south of La Jolla, I'd been virtually in the shadow of Scripps. As a high school senior in 1959, I had won a competition and spent an absolutely absorbing summer working as a Scripps trainee. But I'd been turned down for admission to Scripps graduate school, probably because my grades at Santa Barbara were not in the very top few percent as Scripps required. And at this stage of my life I was uncertain of my future. The best bet seemed to be the combination of the North American job and grad school at USC, a course that led almost invariably toward a career as an industrial scientist.

The position at the Ocean Systems Group was a sinecure if there ever was one. Not only would the company fund my graduate study, it would pay me a decent salary to do work I loved. Even at this stage of my intellectual maturation, I was pulled between the abstract world of basic science and the engrossing hands-on challenge of practical technology. Dr. Rechnitzer's group seamlessly melded science and technology. A marine biologist, he had been a member of the team that made the historic 1960 dive in the navy's bathyscaphe *Trieste* to the deepest point in the world's oceans, the 35,800-foot Challenger Deep off the island of Guam.

Now Dr. Rechnitzer led the company's effort to expand their pioneering *Beaver Mark IV* into an entire undersea system. The submersible would be analogous to a space shuttle, transporting aquanauts to submerged stations. I was twenty-four years old, less than two decades removed from that little kid with sun-bleached hair, crouching with his tin cans and bottles at the tidal pools of Mission Bay. But now I was involved with the practicalities of real hardware, testing the properties of exotic new alloys and resins as building materials for submerged habitats, not playing with tin-can replicas of the fictional *Nautilus*.

In three years I'd have my doctorate. I would serve my active-duty military obligation, preferably in experimental submersibles, then continue my exciting profession as a seasoned, mature marine scientist. Driving to work on the sunny freeways each morning, the broad blue expanse of the Pacific seemed like a highway beckoning me toward this limitless future.

Then one night after dinner, there was a knock on the door of our small Long Beach apartment. A young navy lieutenant in a freshly pressed khaki work uniform stood on the landing, an official-looking manila envelope in his hand.

"Robert Ballard?" He thrust the letter toward me. "Ensign Robert Ballard?"

"Ensign? I'm a second lieutenant."

"According to this letter, you're Ensign Ballard now."

The letter from the Bureau of Naval Personnel stated that I was being called up for active duty.

"You report in thirty days," the lieutenant said, handing me a receipt to sign for my orders.

I later discovered that when I left the University of Hawaii and took the job with North American Aviation, the proper navy authorities were not informed that I was still enrolled in graduate school at USC or that I had married. Naval personnel records simply indicated that I was out of school, single, and immediately available for active duty. In fact, my first orders called for me to report to bachelor officer quarters.

This was a harsh blow. My elaborate and carefully laid plans had suddenly been blown away. Like countless thousands of other young men in this turbulent time, I had become just another byte of data in a vast, impersonal equation when orders stamped with my name had come spitting out of the electronic maw.

Well, I thought, trying to put the best face on this calamity, *at least I won't be heading for a foxhole in Vietnam.*

North American even won me a three-month stay of sentence to finish the semester at USC. I also learned that my navy service would be in the Office of Naval Research. Even though I'd been trained as an army intelligence officer, I had six years' course work in hard sciences. So maybe duty with ONR wouldn't be so bad.

After getting lost in the blizzard, we managed to salvage our first night in Boston from complete disaster. My new superior, Commander Aulick, spared us from a dingy motel by putting us up in his home in the quiet town of Cohasset, about a twenty-minute drive from the navy base on Summer Street in South Boston. Early the next morning, I put on my new winter blue uniform for the first time. The trousers were creased, the black low-quarter shoes spit shined. At least I looked like a naval officer.

But when I came down the stairs for breakfast, I found Commander Aulick dressed in blue jeans and a thick sweater.

"Better change clothes," he said, pointing out the front window. "It snowed all night. The driveway's buried, and we've got to shovel out before we can go to work."

First Naval District headquarters was in the Fargo building, a dilapidated old structure that once housed the brig. I made the mistake of snapping off a smart salute to the first navy official I encountered on the steps. But he was a chief petty officer and should have saluted me. The chief glanced at the thin gold stripe on my sleeve designating a brand-new ensign, shook his head, and laughed scornfully. Then, inside the overheated building, I compounded the error by saluting my commanding officer, Captain Terry, with my hat off, common courtesy in the army.

But he reminded me that "sailors don't salute uncovered." This was not an auspicious beginning for my naval career. And the day only got worse. It was immediately apparent that the position of ONR liaison officer was basically a bureaucratic make-work job. My responsibilities included reviewing contracts to make sure the requisite number of carbon copies were attached, initialing forms where required, and keeping the files in my cubbyhole office in order. A high school dropout clerk could have done the job. Looking out the office window at the banks of new snow already turning black, I felt homesick for the blue sky and warmth of southern California. I longed to see a street lined with palms, bright hibiscus hedges separating comfortable ranch houses with red-tiled roofs.

But this emotion was more than just nostalgia for my youth. My service as a navy officer meant delaying graduate school by three years. And I seriously doubted that I'd have the stamina or financial independence to start all over again at age twenty-seven. I was also afraid that the once-in-a-lifetime position with North American was gone forever.

Maybe it was the nasty weather, perhaps it was this dreary old base. But I suddenly felt I had been uprooted and dumped in a terminal backwater, my bright future as a marine scientist in California irrevocably truncated.

Staring out at the dark, greasy water of Boston Harbor, I was seized by a pessimistic insight. *My life is ruined.*

A week later, my plight didn't seem so grim. The sun was out as I drove downhill toward the village harbor of Woods Hole. The only potentially interesting aspect of my navy assignment was liaison to the Woods Hole Oceanographic Institution (WHOI) located on the southwest corner of Cape Cod. And this was my first visit to the Institution.

The village on the wooded peninsula below me was a cluster of weathered clapboard and cedar-shake Victorian homes nestled around two splendid natural harbors and a gleaming circular boat basin called Eel Pond. The redbrick administration and laboratory buildings of WHOI crowded the length of Water Street. I could see two blue research ships, their decks studded with derricks, tied alongside the Institution's docks. The sunlit water of Buzzards Bay and Vineyard Sound looked clean and alive, much more inviting than the gray face of Boston Harbor. And the trees on the hillside above the village were just beginning to bud under the warm influence of the Gulf Stream that bathed the southern shore of Cape Cod.

Maybe, I thought, *this just might be a tolerable place to spend a couple of years.*

That first day, I was introduced to WHOI's director, Dr. Paul Fye. I was ushered into his spacious wood-paneled office and given a seat at the cozy fireplace. He was a confident, precisely spoken man in his late fifties. Fye's doctorate was in physical chemistry, a rigid and demanding discipline. Having previously been a senior administrator in the Naval Ordnance Laboratory, which had briefly run its own nuclear weapons development program parallel to the Manhattan Project, Dr. Fye was familiar with the high-stakes bureaucratic poker game of winning government grants. He was a slight, wiry man with carefully brushed gray hair and a neatly trimmed mustache. His waxy pallor indicated he spent more time in conference rooms than on the bridges of research ships. He had a reputation as an exacting taskmaster who pushed himself just as hard as he did his subordinates.

On Dr. Fye's desk, a small plastic model of the Institution's pride and joy, *Alvin*, the deep-diving research submersible, was prominently mounted. The bill of a swordfish that had attacked *Alvin* on a dive off the Bahamas was mounted with equal prominence above the fireplace mantle. One whole wall was taken up with a floor-to-ceiling bookcase, laden with collected reprints of research papers published by the Institution's scientists. This was a none-too-subtle statement that Woods Hole, like other high-pressure research institutions, lived by the cruel mandate: Publish or Perish.

Once more, I was acutely conscious of the thin gold ensign's rank stripe on the sleeve of my blue wool uniform jacket.

Probably out of nervousness, I blurted out that I'd grown up in southern California very near Scripps.

"Well," Dr. Fye said, a cool undertone to his wry smile, "I'm glad you finally made it to the *best* oceanographic institution in the world."

"Yes, sir," I replied, taken aback.

I was soon to learn that the rivalry for prestigious achievements and competition for government research funding was intense and sometimes bitter between Woods Hole and Scripps. The only other possible competitor was the Lamont-Doherty Geological Observatory, connected to Columbia University in New York. My speaking admiringly of Scripps was analogous to a management trainee at Ford telling his new boss how much he liked General Motors.

My audience with the director was brief. As a very junior scientific liaison officer for the ONR, I was not expected to set policy or negotiate contracts between WHOI and the navy.

The Woods Hole Oceanographic Institution, I learned, was a unique American phenomenon, a tranquil retreat for basic scientific research that was simultaneously engaged in the fierce struggle of the marketplace. WHOI scientists were as much independent entrepreneurs as they were tenured academics. They operated under the prestigious banner of Woods Hole, but they had to beat the government thickets to flush out their own funding. It was this often precarious source of income that paid the salaries of the scientists and their staffs, as well as the substantive operating costs of laboratories both on shore and aboard WHOI research ships. Each of the Institution's tenured scientists in effect ran his own entrepreneurial company, loosely confederated under the small management team led by Dr. Fye. The administration of the Institution took an annual percentage of the incoming revenue—mainly from the Office of Naval Research and other branches of the navy—but otherwise did not interfere with the quasi-independent research teams.

The Institution was chartered in 1930 by a small group of academic oceanographers looking for a quiet place to gather for summer research projects. It grew slowly during the Great Depression, the labs spreading into an ad hoc assemblage of village houses, still overshadowed by the older and well-established Marine Biological Laboratory.

The Institution's research laboratories flourished during World War II, helping develop secret sonar and underwater communications electronics for navy submarines, as well as more effective depth charges, and even long-life antifouling paint for the navy and merchant marine, so that our ships could steam the vast reaches of the tropical Pacific for months without becoming barnacle encrusted. As World War II evolved almost seamlessly into the cold war, the funding for individual WHOI projects continued.

Unlike Scripps and Lamont, which were part of larger universities, Woods Hole was private and independent and received no funding from the State of Massachusetts. When I got there in 1967, 85% of its annual funding came from the navy. Therefore, even as a brand-new ensign, I still represented the Office of Naval Research and I found people treated me with unusual deference.

Paul Twitchell, a meteorologist with the Boston ONR office, gave me the guided tour of Woods Hole. Crossing from one Institution office to another along Water Street on my introduction rounds that first day, my eye was drawn to the center of Eel Pond. The midget research submarine *Alvin* lay on a mooring, its stubby white conning tower "sail" bright against the calm water of the boat basin.

Standing at the rail of the drawbridge, I felt an unusual

attachment to the little vessel, even though this was the first time I'd actually seen it. During my brief summer job at North American's Ocean Systems Group in 1962, the company had bid unsuccessfully to build this manned deep submersible as a research vessel that WHOI would operate for the Office of Naval Research. Eventually, the mechanical equipment division of the big Minnesota conglomerate, General Mills, won the contract. *Alvin* was commissioned at Woods Hole in June 1964.

The midget sub was named for its energetic chief proponent, WHOI geophysicist Allyn Vine, a quintessential eccentric academic genius whose thought processes had been described as supersonic. Al Vine had worked extensively with American submariners during the war, channeling the latest basic discoveries of his discipline directly into the technology and tactics of combat survival. It was Al Vine and his colleagues who had charted the existence and characteristics of the thermoclines, abrupt boundaries separating layers of different temperature of water. The sonar of World War II was easily deflected by thermoclines. Once WHOI scientists made the navy aware of this, American tactics were adapted accordingly. Depth charges were set to detonate below the thermocline when it was suspected a German U-boat might be lurking there. These tactics eventually proved successful and broke the Nazis' stranglehold on the Atlantic convoy routes.

Familiar with the strange ways of submarines, Al Vine was convinced that a small deep-diving research sub was the best way to study the physical and biological properties of the ocean bottom. He launched a one-man crusade to develop such a research sub. Eventually, allied with a cohort of like-minded scientific converts, Vine overcame bureaucratic resistance to see the vessel built.

The finished product riding at its mooring in the Eel Pond was a bulbous Fiberglas pollywog, twenty-two feet from its blunt nose to its swiveling stern propeller, which looked like a misplaced factory ventilator fan. Two smaller directional props sprouted on either side of the sail's base like table fans tacked on as an afterthought. The little sub's white exterior skin hid its innovative heart, a 6-foot-10-inch diameter pressure vessel sphere of ultrastrong HY 100 steel alloy. This was the cramped personnel compartment, meant to accommodate a pilot, copilot, and one researcher. (When I got involved with the *Alvin* program I fought for years to change this crew ratio to one pilot and two scientists. Finally, in the late 1970s, I was successful.)

Alvin was certified to operate safely at a depth of 6,000 feet, where ambient seawater pressure was over a ton per square inch. The remote-control manipulator arm jutting from its specimen-tray chin ended in a powerful pincher for gripping samples.

She was an ingenious compromise design, somewhere between a seagoing vessel and a spaceship.

Only the year before in the spring of 1966, *Alvin* had proved her worth. A midair collision between a U.S. Air Force B-52 and its refueling tanker over southern Spain had resulted in four 10-megaton hydrogen bombs falling from the sky. The weapons' firing systems were unarmed, so there was never a danger of a thermonuclear explosion. Three of the bombs were found on land, but the fourth had fallen into the Mediterranean off the coast of Andalusia. After a two-month search in terrible bottom conditions—a steep slope of cloying mud—*Alvin* successfully located the wayward H-bomb and won the heartfelt admiration of the Pentagon in the process.

William Rainnie, one of the sub's first pilots and a pioneer with deep submersibles, managed *Alvin*'s search for the H-bomb. He was now the full-time project manager for WHOI's Deep Submergence Group, which was fully funded through ONR contracts. I met Bill Rainnie my first day at Woods Hole in his offices on the second floor of the rambling old cedar-shake house at 38 Water Street. Because the ground floor was still occupied by a pharmacy, the *Alvin* project office was known to everyone at the Institution as the Drugstore.

"You'll like it here, Bob," Rainnie told me. "There's plenty of interesting work to keep you busy and some really first-rate minds."

I certainly liked Bill Rainnie at first sight. A lanky ex-navy submarine officer with a smoking Pall Mall stuck perpetually in the corner of his mouth, Rainnie was about as unflappable a science project officer as I could imagine. He spoke in a calm, soft voice only after carefully considering what he had to say. Bill had graduated from the U.S. Naval Academy in 1946, but resigned his commission after eight years of bouncing his young family from one submarine base to another. One of the things that drew me to Bill was his clear engineer's perspective, coupled with an almost childlike awe of scientific discovery.

Old navy man that he was, he quickly set to work getting me "squared away" at WHOI. I had the distinct sense during that first meeting that Bill Rainnie would be one of my lifelong friends.

He consulted the large chart with *Alvin*'s crowded research project schedule hanging on the curved wall of his turret office in this old Victorian house. "We've got some navy dives coming up in the Bahamas this summer," he said, casually watching my reaction to his words. "Maybe we can take you down on a local test dive before we ship out. That is, if you'd be interested."

"You bet I would."

The other person who really impressed me during that first visit to Woods Hole was Dr. Kenneth O. Emery, a renowned marine geologist known throughout the science world as "K.O." There was a certain formality about Dr. Emery, an obvious probing intelligence that radiated from the quick blue eyes behind an old-fashioned pair of gold-rimmed bifocals perched on his aquiline nose. My first impression was of an old-world "Herr Professor." Although he lacked any trace of arrogance, I naturally addressed him in a respectful voice.

K.O. Emery was one of the world's true experts in the history and structure of the sedimentary rocks of North America's continental margins. He had studied under the father of marine geology, the legendary Francis Shephard, at the University of Chicago. Then K.O. Emery had followed Shephard to complete his doctorate at Scripps and later established the graduate program in marine geology at the University of Southern California.

While working at USC, Dr. Emery had published his classic book, *The Sea Off Southern California: A Modern Habitat for Petroleum*. If Shephard had been marine geology's reigning monarch, K.O. Emery was the heir apparent. Emery was one of the handful of senior scientists who understood the complexity of the sedimentary structures lying along continental shelves, which had been laid down over millions of years by countless rivers sculpting and re-shaping the land mass. Keenly aware of the potential for major petroleum and natural gas discoveries in the rich and ancient sediments lying just offshore of the eastern American seaboard, he could have become rich as an exploration geologist working for a major oil company. But he preferred academic research. K.O. Emery was happy to share his survey data with oil companies through the Institution's Ocean Industry Program, however, because he believed strongly that such basic research should benefit society, and locating new petroleum resources was an obvious benefit.

Glancing around K.O. Emery's office, I immediately saw that his interest extended beyond geology. His desk and worktables were piled with obscure ethnology monographs tracing the movements of Indian tribes; he understood that the ancestors of historic tribes had lived on the dry continental margin during the last Ice Age, and it piqued his restless curiosity to speculate about where their settlements had stood. Equally, he realized that the great mammals of the Pleistocene, including shuffling herds of mastodons, had grazed the hills of the Georges Bank, where Bedford cod trawlers now dragged their nets.

But K.O. Emery's mind probed beyond purely academic interests. He published papers on a stunning variety of subjects. One in draft form lay on a worktable. Its subject: the chaotic distribution of soft-drink and beer cans along the shoulders of America's highways. And he carried this questing brilliance into his everyday life. His and his wife Kate's home, a small farm on Oyster Pond, about two miles from WHOI, was surrounded by a carefully tended orchard and beehives. Most of the food on their table came from the garden and orchard, the result of endless hybrid experiments, all meticulously logged in dusty notebooks in his barn. Following his nearly compulsive discipline to document as much as possible about his life, K.O. even wrote a small book on the natural history of Oyster Pond, which lay just below his study window.

Dr. K.O. Emery was the epitome of the polymath.

But his formidable intelligence was mellowed by an obvious human empathy. During our first meeting, he spoke warmly of the University of Southern California and told me how unfortunate he found it that my graduate study had been interrupted by mandatory military service.

"You will, of course, continue on for your doctorate after the navy," he said, fixing me with his lively eyes.

"I'm not sure, sir," I admitted honestly. "I'd like to, of course, but I've also got to make a living."

He nodded. "Yes, I realize that. And it's never easy as a man grows older."

K.O. Emery was in his early fifties when we met. He had received his Ph.D. in 1941 and had done antisubmarine warfare research at Scripps during World War II. Undoubtedly, he had seen many graduate students' careers thwarted by that war.

Even though we had just met and he was a renowned scientist, whereas I was not even enrolled in graduate school, he showed an interest in my future.

"You can keep your hand in here, Bob," he said. "I'd be happy to have you join our research cruises."

That night, driving back to our new apartment in the quiet South Shore town of Cohasset, midway between Cape Cod and Boston, the dark old snowbanks and bare winter oaks did not look so alien. I felt a faint but unmistakable stir of optimism.

Maybe my life wasn't ruined after all.

K.O. Emery was good to his word.

In September 1967, I found myself wedged into a workstation in the science lab aboard the WHOI research ship *Chain*. This three-week cruise was a geologic survey of the continental rise, the deepest and most seaward section of the continental margin, Dr. Emery's favorite haunt. We were surveying a long segment of the rise off the northern Atlantic seaboard. K.O. Emery was the chief scientist, and his assistant, Dr. Elazar "Al" Uchupi, was my informal mentor. Al and I shared the graveyard watch—midnight to four A.M., noon to four P.M.— in the lab, a stuffy narrow steel box jammed with recording instruments, stuck above the bridge.

The steel bulkheads of the lab twanged and the deck beneath my rubber-soled boat shoes jolted, as if lightning had struck nearby, accompanied by an instant thunderclap. But the night sky outside the open porthole was moonlit with a few puffy fair-weather clouds.

"That was a good one," Al Uchupi said, gripping his contraband Cuban cigar in his teeth and exhaling a choking cloud of smoke.

"I guess I'll get used to it," I answered, glancing aft.

This cruise was a seismic profiling survey of the deep

sedimentary rocks of the continental rise, almost 8,000 feet below our keel. To probe those layers of rock, we towed a powerful high-energy sound wave generator, the "sparker": in effect, a man-made lightning-and-thunder device. Banks of diesel electric generators on the stern charged a series of huge capacitators in the sparker with more than 100,000 joules of static electric energy. About every twenty seconds, this tremendous pulse of energy was discharged into the water from the tip of an electrode that served as a giant spark plug.

That discharge produced a flashing explosion, so bright the glare could be seen by orbiting astronauts at night. The shock wave shook the 1,800-ton vessel along her entire 200-foot length. This man-made thunderstorm was repeated endlessly, every twenty seconds, around the clock. My first two days aboard *Chain*, I slept fitfully until exhaustion took over. The high-energy pulses from the sparker blasted down and were reflected off the bottom as a strong acoustic echo. The harder the bottom, the more energy was deflected. But a considerable portion of each pulse passed through the sediments and continued downward, deeper into the rock layers. Finally, when the energy wave encountered increasingly hard layers of rock, it would reflect back to the surface.

Chain also trailed a long seismic array, a thick tube embedded with hundreds of small hydrophones, sensitive to the faint echoes reflected from the deep layers. These and other data were recorded in banks of instruments clamped to workstations in the crowded science lab. The seismic profile recorder spewed out endless reams of paper tracings that displayed a jagged profile as if someone had cut open a slice of the ocean floor and exposed its inner layers. After I'd learned to read the profile tracing, I was reminded of the layer diagrams I'd done as a geology student at UC–Santa Barbara. On our field trips, we'd head to the mountains and find promising road cuts through interesting strata, where the rippling layers of sedimentary rock were well exposed.

But marine geologists, I now realized, were not afforded such luxuries as road cuts. Marine geologists had to slice their own profile through the sedimentary layers using such powerful instruments as the sparker. Marine geology differed from the land science in other important ways as well. On my college field trips, we'd survey all day, then sit around a campfire at night toasting marshmallows before a hard-earned sleep. At sea, surveys did not shut down for the night. The team worked twenty-four hours a day, standing an inflexible watch schedule, usually four hours on, eight hours off.

Al Uchupi, a former graduate student of Dr. Emery at USC, had recently earned his Ph.D. in marine geology. A solitary, thoughtful Basque with an unmistakable Brooklyn accent, Al had a real passion for research. He loved to stand the midnight-to-four graveyard watch, when most of the ship was asleep. I was lucky to have him as a mentor early in this informal scientific training. Although Al's sole indulgence at the time, thick Cuban cigars smuggled back from the Caribbean often made those long night watches uncomfortable, especially when the sea was up and the stuffy lab, perched high on the super-structure, snapped through sickening pitches and rolls.

I had been on two brief summer oceanographic cruises as a Scripps trainee in 1959. Then, too, I had suffered from the ceaseless drudgery of round-the-clock data collection and the discomfort of bad weather on a cramped ship. But now I was a junior member of an actual science party, and Al Uchupi made a point of explaining every aspect of our work so that I would learn what the profession of oceanography entailed.

There were dozens of recording instruments in the lab, which the four members of each watch had to constantly moni-tor. Al and I sat before a rank of precision graphic recorders, which whirred endlessly, disgorging long ribbons of data trac-ings. Other recorders connected to the ship's echo sounders put out a constant stream of depth soundings. Still other instru-ments recorded Earth's magnetic and gravitational fields, important factors in determining the composition of the sediment reflecting the sparker pulse waves.

Our job was to make sure all these recording instruments were properly annotated every five minutes and to carefully log the water depth of the survey line. We also had to continually change the magnetic tapes backing up the paper traces from the hydrophone array for subsequent analysis ashore. Finally, there was a set of instruments for the proton magnetometer also towed astern, which gave us a better understanding of the composition of the sedimentary rock passing almost 2 miles beneath our keel.

There were times during our watches when Al and I went through a seemingly slapstick routine of exchanging more than a dozen logbooks to be annotated, as if we were working on some kind of goofy assembly line. I was reminded of the mythical Sisyphus, but instead of pushing a boulder up a mountain only to have it roll back down, sometimes Al and I would no sooner finish our logbook notations than he would shove me the first book to annotate and grab the second for himself.

During that first week aboard *Chain*, I understood a fundamental truth about modern science that applied in particular to hands-on oceanography. The powerful advanced instruments we brought to bear on a scientific problem produced literally overwhelming amounts of data. Data was collected on a twenty-four-hour basis at sea, but usually reviewed for only eight hours a day ashore. For every day spent at sea gathering data, it took a week or more to analyze it later. Then the scientists had to ponder the essence of this analysis, write up preliminary conclusions, ponder all that once more, and finally produce a final analysis in the form of a written presentation. A three-week cruise like this could keep a team of geologists busy for the rest of the year.

Then there was the whole business of life at sea on a cramped, spartan research vessel. Being the most junior member of the team, I drew a top berth in the crowded foc's'le, my bunk only two feet beneath the steel plates of the main deck. The second morning of the cruise, I was deep asleep, despite the incessant thunder of the sparker. But then Bo'sun Jerry Carter up on deck cut loose with a pneumatic rust chipper on the plates inches above my head. I bolted upright and slammed my forehead into the steel plate, opening a nasty gash. But I stood my next watch, the cut bandaged, and my head throbbing every time the sparker blasted.

To add to my general discomfort, Hurricane Dora rolled up the Gulf Stream on September 17. Although Dora's eye was well out to sea, *Chain* was caught between the hurricane and the shallows of Cape Hatteras. The primitive weather satellites of the day did not give us a clear picture of the storm track. In less than twenty-four hours, the broken overcast and nagging easterly chop on the face of the open groundswells had been transformed into a heavy, rumbling mass of squall clouds and a pounding sea with wave crests approaching 30 feet. Now we had to worry about survival, not data collection.

Chain's skipper steered her into the sea and wind, and kept up enough speed so that the vessel's head would not fall off as the huge seas slammed over the bow. We sealed watertight hatches and battened down portholes. But the sea found its way into the vessel, sloshing through passageways. Everything was wet. People were seasick, but there was no way to ventilate the compartments. The cook secured the galley, and those of us who could eat subsisted on greasy cold cuts and crackers.

For two days, *Chain* fought the sea. But on the third morning, clammy and aching from the battering below decks, I hauled myself back to the lab and set to work at my station beside Al Uchupi.

Even though K.O. Emery could not have predicted that hurricane, I wondered if he had intentionally selected this exhausting cruise to be my initiation into professional oceanography. Too many young people, he understood, had a romantic image of marine research, which they viewed as an effortless amalgam of yachting and sudden scientific breakthrough. But on this vessel, nothing was effortless, and breakthroughs would come only after painstaking months ashore analyzing the mountain of data we were wresting from the ocean bottom.

But the hardship and the drudgery only piqued my interest. After two weeks on *Chain,* I knew that marine geology was indeed an attractive field. Al Uchupi certainly helped in this conversion process. On those rare moments when the hectic pace of our data logging slowed, Al would regale me with stories of expeditions to Baja California and the Caribbean. But each of his sea stories included a nugget of valuable scientific information that had been uncovered on the cruise.

Al also had an encyclopedic knowledge of European history and loved to launch on soft-spoken, elaborate recitations while puffing on his sulfurous Cuban stogies.

Unfortunately, all our colleagues weren't so pleasant. It was on this first *Chain* cruise that I witnessed the ugly side of professional rivalry and the shipboard caste system some academic scientists insist on perpetuating. Another watch leader was a woman geophysicist who carried an almost visible chip perched firmly on her shoulder. She did not have a Ph.D. and was one of the few female scientists at WHOI at the time, which might have explained her penchant to prove that women could be tough taskmasters. In any event, she was both a perfectionist and a hypocrite.

Her favorite trick was to slip unannounced into the lab during our watch and immediately begin changing the settings on all the recorders. "This is awful," she'd hiss. "Your sensitivity levels are way off. Where did you learn to calibrate instruments?"

But then we discovered that less than an hour into her own watch she would inevitably change the calibrations back to the same levels we had used.

"Don't worry about her," Al said. "She's insecure and

feels she just has to throw her weight around to be taken seriously. Real leaders don't have to."

Al was right, of course. And I vowed that should I ever rise to the position of chief scientist on an expedition, I would never allow such a person to poison the morale of my team.

But in the fall of 1967, the chances of ever becoming a chief scientist seemed remote.

Seeing that I had thrived on *Chain*'s rough seismic survey cruise, Al Uchupi called me to his office one brisk October morning. "How would you like to write a scientific paper?" he asked, a twinkle in his eyes.

After almost six months of commuting between Boston and Woods Hole, I was beginning to think of myself as an ocean scientist.

"I would like that very much."

Al explained that there were reams of unanalyzed depth-sounding data collected in the Gulf of Mexico wasting away in the Woods Hole archives. Known as "smooth sheets," these were lines of depth soundings taken over the years by survey ships hunting for shoals and other navigational hazards in the gulf. Each sheet was about 20 feet square and held thousands of individual soundings. He wanted me to analyze hundreds of these smooth sheets to produce accurate contours for a series of topographic charts that would be amalgamated into a single detailed bathymetric chart of the gulf.

This was probably a trial that Al had conceived to test my determination to become an oceanographer. Such donkey work was the bane of novice scientists in those precomputer days. But I recognized the challenge as a kind of initiation. I dutifully loaded up my VW Beetle with piles of the sheets and set up a worktable beneath the cobwebs in the basement of our apartment house in Cohasset.

All winter long, I spent my nights bent over the drafting table, inching forward my meticulous contour lines. When I completed this drudgery, I spent additional months analyzing the data, reading as much material as I could find on the submarine geology of the gulf, then drafted and redrafted the explanatory paper to accompany my graphic work.

"Here you are, Al," I said, handing him the final draft and charts. "I'd appreciate your comments on this."

A day or so later, Al told me he had passed on my draft paper for Dr. Emery to review.

"Well," I badgered, "what did *you* think of it?"

Al's owl face remained blank. "Let's get K.O. Emery's comment first."

The next morning, I found the paper in my pigeonhole. It had a single line of comment written in red pencil across the cover page: "Unfit to read."

Burning with embarrassment, I made my way to Al Uchupi's office and dropped the paper on his desk.

"Hell, Al," I said with real indignation. "That's all he wrote: 'Unfit to read.' How's that supposed to help me?"

Al puffed on his cigar and smiled, his round face warm with amusement. He laid the paper on his blotter. "Bob, you've just committed the cardinal sin of science. You've mixed all your observations with your conclusions."

He opened the paper and tapped a series of paragraphs with his pencil. "This is fact, your observations. They amount to hard data. But this"—his pencil tapped a staccato rhythm—"all this is pure conjecture. For a scientist, never the twain shall meet."

All that morning, Al Uchupi patiently explained the fundamental principles of professional science: "First present the facts carefully, give them your best interpretation. But never go beyond what the facts permit."

I was embarrassed by my amateur effort but deeply appreciative of Al's thoughtful comments.

"If you're going to write for K.O. Emery," Al told me, "you stick to the facts. You base your interpretation on the data. That interpretation may be wrong, but the facts are sacred. Maybe another scientist can use them one day."

That was a lesson I never forgot.

A year later, my rewritten paper was accepted by the *Bulletin of Marine Science*. I sent a reprint to Dr. K.O. Emery with this note: "Thanks for your valuable comments."

TWO

The day *Alvin* sank, October 16, 1968, I was in Ottawa preparing to deliver a lecture that evening to the Canadian Defense Force on the future of the American deep submergence program.

The presentation was the kind of bread-and-butter chore young officers assigned to the Office of Naval Research were expected to perform. Even though the Vietnam War was steadily gobbling up the defense budget, there was enough vestigial wet NASA optimism around for the navy to be proud of its growing manned submersible program.

There were two look-alike *Alvin* submersibles under construction at the Electric Boat Company in Groton, Connecticut. The navy was also building a classified deep-diving miniature nuclear research submarine, the NR-1. And there were two deep submarine rescue submersibles, capable of dives to 5,000 feet, being completed. The navy also still kept the bathyscaphe *Trieste* operational out in San Diego.

At this time, the U.S. Navy was far and away the most active deep submergence organization in the world. Even though I had not yet dived in *Alvin*, Bill Rainnie had promised to get me out on the vessel as soon as possible, probably after WHOI took over operation of the new larger *Alvin*-derivative deep submergence vessel (DSV) his group had unofficially named *Columbus*. When the Institution had these two DSVs in operation, I was confident I'd get my chance, especially because, even as a junior officer, I was the funding conduit between the ONR and Woods Hole.

Preparing for my lecture that warm October evening in Ottawa, I again felt the familiar tug of impatience. I was eager to make my first dive. I've always been a hands-on person, who can best understand a sophisticated piece of equipment such as *Alvin* by actually working with it.

And even then, I recognized the incredible scientific potential of the stubby little white submarine. Geology, including marine geology—which I firmly intended to be my profession—involves visual observation. Geologists are trained to recognize a bewildering variety of rocks and land forms. Geologists are also inveterate sample collectors. When they see something interesting, they reach for their hammer to knock off a chunk to take back to the lab for detailed analysis. Above all, good, experienced geologists have the ability to process what they can see and touch into a scientifically accurate, larger descriptive synthesis.

An experienced geologist can break a fragment of Niagara Escarpment limestone from a cliff and—if he has chosen the proper sample—analyze this fist-size hunk of white stone to trace a couple of million years of Earth's history for 20 miles on either side of his collection site. Geologists observe, all the way from the microscopic crystalline structure of a rock sample to the sequence of exposed strata to overall shape of a valley or ridge.

The key observational factors involved are the scientist's trained mind, his eyes, and the hammer in his hand.

These same principles apply to marine geology. And the nimble little white submarine allowed WHOI's marine geologists the vital element of observational presence on the ocean bottom. They could observe with their eyes, analyze with their trained minds, and use *Alvin*'s mechanical arm to collect crucial samples for laboratory analysis. K.O. Emery had already tested *Alvin*'s potential as an expedition research vehicle during the DSV's second full research season the year before. One day I hoped to do the same.

I was about to step up to the lecture hall podium that evening and address the assembled Canadian military audience when a secretary handed me a pink telephone message slip. Not wanting to delay my talk, I slid the message beneath my notes.

"You'd better read that, Lieutenant," the woman said somberly.

I opened the folded paper. Al Uchupi had just called to tell me that *Alvin* had sunk on the continental slope south of Cape Cod during a routine dive with the WHOI Buoy Group, the engineers who designed the submerged research moorings. Apparently the sling cables hoisting *Alvin*'s launch cradle on the catamaran tender, *Lulu,* had parted during launch. The little sub had pitched forward into the slipway between the pontoons. Seawater had flooded into the sail and through the open hatch. In about sixty seconds, *Alvin* was on its way to the bottom. Paul Stimson, a Buoy Group engineer, pilot trainee Roger Weaver, and experienced *Alvin* pilot Ed Bland had somehow managed to claw their way out of the flooding sphere and the narrow Fiberglas conning tower of the sail as the DSV sank. The vessel was now on the bottom in 5,200 feet of water about 135 miles southeast of Woods Hole.

Gripping the pink message slip, I felt a hot stab of shock. No one had drowned, but the vessel in which I hoped to study the ocean bottom was probably lost forever, another lifeless heap of wreckage, like *Thresher* that lay on the bottom less than 200 miles away near Corsair Canyon.

Approaching the rostrum, I saw that word of the disaster had already swept through the lecture hall. "Well," I said, clearing my dry throat, "this is probably not the best time to talk about the U.S. Navy's deep submergence program because it looks like half that program is deeply submerged in an unplanned manner. . . ."

My heart was not in the joke and no one in the audience managed even a chuckle.

Two days later, I was back at Woods Hole learning details of the accident from Bill Rainnie and the gang in the Drugstore.

"The situation is definitely not good, Bob," Bill Rainnie explained. He looked haggard from lack of sleep, pale beneath his seafarer's tan.

The only positive factor was that *Alvin* sank in a known position at experimental Buoy Alpha anchored in 5,200 feet of water at 39 degrees 52 minutes north and 69 degrees 12 minutes west. But there was no way to verify that *Alvin* had sunk straight to the muddy clay bottom.

Because *Alvin* was a DSV meant to operate at such depths, there was probably no structural damage. Submerged, with the hatch closed, *Alvin* was basically weightless or neutrally buoyant. But with the personnel sphere flooded with seawater, the sub weighed a little over 3,000 pounds.

No one had ever retrieved a nontethered object that heavy from the deep-sea bed. In any event, WHOI ships had to find the sunken sub before any attempt at salvage could be made. And that was not easy. The Institution research vessels *Chain* and *Gosnold* were already out on the site, but their sonars were not sensitive enough to distinguish a target as small as *Alvin* on that vast, featureless slope of mud.

The next week, Hurricane Gladys struck, ripping Buoy Alpha off its anchor mooring. The Institution rented the General Motors Corporation's Deep Ocean Work Boat (DOWB), a crude submersible designed for simple tasks such as cable tending. The DOWB was General Motors' entry in the undersea sweepstakes, but it hadn't proved very effective, probably because it had no true view ports in its pressure sphere, relying instead on two clumsy (albeit inherently safe) optical devices that allowed the two-man crew to peer out the top and bottom of the sphere. The only reason DOWB was used in *Alvin*'s salvage attempt was that the new head of the Woods Hole Department of Ocean Engineering, to which the Alvin Group belonged, was Dr. Scott Daubin, who had just come from

General Motors. He obviously wanted to give DOWB a chance to make headlines through a successful salvage.

But the weather continued bad, with gales almost sinking the DOWB's support vessels. The GM submersible itself was unable to locate *Alvin*.

The fall weather closed in. Cape Cod was battered by a new string of gales. Any hope of locating and salvaging *Alvin* had to be postponed.

Leaning into the stinging, salty wind that winter as I dashed between Institution buildings on the Woods Hole peninsula, my eye was often drawn to the empty Eel Pond. *Alvin*'s mooring buoy tossed on the choppy surface. I doubted I would ever see the jaunty little white sub ride that familiar mooring again.

But the next summer, WHOI and Bill Rainnie's *Alvin* group got lucky. The navy lent Woods Hole its advanced research vessel *Mizar,* which operated a highly sophisticated underwater search system. On June 14, 1969, *Mizar*'s camera snapped a grainy black-and-white picture of *Alvin*, lying upright on the muddy bottom, still trailing the handling lines attached for that ill-fated launch attempt. The picture revealed the critical information that the hatch to *Alvin*'s personnel sphere was still open. The salvagers, who needed a strong lifting point, realized the best method of raising the sub would be to lower a T-shaped toggle bar down inside the steel pressure sphere and lift from that point.

Two months later, the Reynolds Corporation deep-diving *Aluminaut* managed—after a number of frustrating failures— to insert the toggle bar through the open hatch into *Alvin*'s crew sphere. The toggle bar was attached to a mile and a half of stout nylon hawser. Later that day, *Mizar*'s big winches raised the sunken vessel to just below the surface, where scuba divers wrapped a strong cargo net around *Alvin*. With *Alvin* still submerged, *Mizar* towed the sub to the shallow water of a bay off Martha's Vineyard. They placed her on the bottom, where a Woods Hole salvage barge with a crane made the final lift, depositing the battered little sub aboard the barge for the short trip back to Woods Hole.

Among the flotsam from the flooded crew compartment, which included imploded cans of emergency drinking water, the salvagers found a soggy baloney sandwich, part of the crew's lunch the day *Alvin* sank. Engineer Cliff Winget nibbled on a piece of the sausage, which he found salty but still tasting like baloney. The rest of the crew's lunch was equally well preserved by the frigid, salty water of the deep bottom.

Hearing of this bizarre find, we only hoped the submersible itself was equally unscathed.

While *Alvin* was undergoing a complete strip-down and overhaul at the Woods Hole dock, I carried on with my mundane navy assignment and tried to absorb by osmosis as much marine geology and deep submergence engineering as I could from Al Uchupi and Bill Rainnie's Deep Submergence Group.

I had also become active with the Boston Sea Rovers, one of the oldest diving clubs in the country. The Sea Rovers membership was eclectic, to say the least, cutting across social and economic lines to include bank presidents, stevedores, surgeons, auto mechanics, college students, and the heirs to old New England fortunes. The love of the sea and of diving brought us together. So did a thirst for cold beer and lobsters steamed over a roaring campfire.

While the Sea Rovers were principally a fraternity, there were several women members, including marine biologists Eugenie Clark, renowned for her study of sharks at the Cape Haze Marine Laboratory, and Ruth Turner of Harvard, the world expert on wood-boring ocean worms.

The male members ran the spectrum from guys like Andy

Holman to Bunky Hodge. Andy was a quietly religious, extremely muscular former frogman who always dove with old-fashioned twin navy UDT tanks. On diving excursions, he'd be the first in the water and the last out. He never seemed to get cold, and he always brought back the most lobsters. He was absolutely fearless underwater, and a powerful swimmer who could beat any current. Andy always smiled and never spoke a foul word. Bunky Hodge, in contrast, was rail-thin and boisterous. He spoke nonstop, with a smoking cigarette dangling from his lip. He seemed to have invented what we now call the "F word" in polite society. Bunky could drink one can of beer after another all day long and it didn't seem to affect him. Despite being so lanky and thin, he was a fine diver.

Walter Feinberg was the patriarch. We called him the keeper of the flame because he told the best stories of the early years of the club, which dated back to the pre-Aqua-Lung dark ages. Walter was in the paper business and rich by any standard. A contemporary of Walter was Frank Scalli, an executive of U.S. Divers, the world's leading manufacturer of scuba gear, and a close friend of Jacques Cousteau and Melville Bell Grosvenor of *National Geographic*. Frank always managed to convince Jacques Cousteau to come to the annual Boston Sea Rovers clinic, a raucous affair that combined equal parts of advanced diving technology, sea stories of dubious pedigree, and overindulgence. At one of these shindigs, Frank Scalli introduced me to Grosvenor, which was my first contact with *National Geographic*.

The great thing about the Sea Rovers was all the class consciousness and rabid business competition that marked life ashore in New England disappeared when you pulled on your wet suit and climbed aboard the grungy little diving boat skippered by Wally Gaudet, an old sea dog who ran an auto shop in north Boston.

From May through Indian summer, we dove every Saturday. I usually got up around five in the morning in our rented house in Cohasset. Fortunately, our first son, Todd, who was born in July 1968, was a good sleeper. I'd tiptoe out to the car, with Marjorie and the baby still asleep. The club rendezvoused at Wally's boat, tied up on the dilapidated commercial wharf beside the New England Aquarium. The wharf pilings were rotten and crusted with barnacles; the decking was even more precarious. By 8:00 A.M. we'd all be aboard, and Wally was headed to the outer reaches of Boston Bay.

Our favorite diving holes included Graves Light, Harding's Ledge, and Outer Brewster Island. Depending on the weather, we always found a good lee to drop the anchor. Then everyone except Wally was over the side, diving in pairs or groups of four. We normally dove in 30 to 60 feet of water and stayed down at least an hour on the first sortie. Scuba diving was not as popular then as it is now, and the lobsters were plentiful in the outer islands. By lunchtime we always had several gunnysacks full.

The Rovers had a traditional fish-catching game that looked deceptively simple. The idea was to herd flounder and cod into our open lobster bags without spearing them. Flounder rested on the bottom partially covered with sand. Their instinct told them they couldn't be seen that way. We would open the bag in front of them, then tap the fish on the tail. It would invariably scoot into the open maw of the sack. The real pros in the club could accomplish this feat time and again, even as the bag began to fill with lobster and other flounder. It took me a while to master this skill.

After a couple beers and a bowl of clam chowder, it was back in the water for the afternoon dive. By midafternoon, there were usually three big trash cans full of lobsters, surf clams, and several cod and flounder.

Then we'd find a quiet bay on a deserted island, anchor, and swim ashore. Everybody had a chore. We'd build a huge driftwood fire and steam the catch and a big sack of sweet corn in wet seaweed. Everyone except a few teetotalers made the most of the beer and the big wine jugs. We usually kept our wet suits on for warmth and just peeled back the tops. We ate with our hands, ripping apart lobster shells and dunking our food in tin cans of melted butter. After a while everybody was pretty greasy, so we'd just dive back in the water to wash off. Those island feasts were something straight out of a medieval Viking saga.

After all that wine and beer, the sea stories invariably turned to famous shipwrecks as we stood around the flaring cooking fire. Some of the guys had dived on coastal vessels sunk by U-boats during the war, others had found the wrecks of old schooners that had foundered on New England shoals. But there was one famous wreck that we all agreed was the ultimate prize, RMS *Titanic*.

I remember one beautiful late summer afternoon in 1969, soon after they'd managed to salvage *Alvin*. The club was out on a deserted islet near Grave's lighthouse. A cool northeast breeze blew across the treeless and barren island. Most of us had switched from beer to mugs of coffee. A bottle of brandy passed around as we stood by the campfire. Frank Scalli mentioned it was a shame that *Titanic* could not be salvaged as easily as the little Woods Hole sub.

"It's too damn deep," Bunky Hodge stated unequivocally.

"That's a fact," Walter Feinberg added. "She's on the bottom in more than two thousand fathoms. And that's where she'll stay. *Titanic* is beyond the reach of man."

Sipping the hot coffee in the chill sea breeze, I pondered Walter's statement. There were, of course, bathyscaphes that could descend to *Titanic*'s grave in over 12,000 feet of water. But those clumsy vertical ocean "elevators" would be of little use maneuvering around a huge wrecked liner like *Titanic*. In my mind I could picture nimble little *Alvin*, which had just been returned to the dockside workshop at the Woods Hole for overhaul. That was the vessel needed to explore *Titanic*.

Too bad, I thought: 12,000 feet is twice as deep as *Alvin* can dive.

A few weeks later, in September 1969, I was out on the Institution research ship *Gosnold,* working with Al Uchupi and Bob Oldale mapping the geological features that lay beneath the Gulf of Maine. Instead of the cataclysmic sparker, *Gosnold* used a big compressed-air gun to generate powerful echo waves. I was in the main lab, working the instruments with Al, when the bridge called over the squawk box to announce someone wanted to speak to me on the single sideband radio.

I jumped up, alarmed. Margie would only call me in an emergency. Todd had just begun to walk. Like any new father, I was ultrasensitive to my first son's safety. I ran up the clanging metal steps to the bridge and grabbed the radio handset. But I heard a man's voice, not my wife's.

It was Captain Terry, my commanding officer in the Office of Naval Research in Boston. He had just been notified that the navy had initiated sweeping budget cuts brought on by the endless outlay of the Vietnam War. Junior reserve officers on active duty, he explained, were being given the immediate option of joining the regular navy or leaving the service.

"You have the choice, Bob," Captain Terry said. "You can either become a career officer or leave the navy now."

I looked around *Gosnold*'s bridge. We were steaming on a northwest heading through an open southerly groundswell. It was a gorgeous Indian summer day, the sea burnished, the sky a deep blue. There was no land in sight, and I suddenly felt exposed and isolated, completely unprepared to make a decision that would affect the rest of my life.

I punched the transmit button. "Captain, you've got to be kidding. I'm in the middle of a cruise and won't be back until next week. Do I have to make a decision before we return to Woods Hole?"

"That's affirmative," Terry said. He was not a man to use macho military jargon. But he obviously wanted to impress me with the urgency of the situation.

"I'll have to get back to you, sir."

I returned to the main lab and pulled my chair close to Al's to explain what I had just learned. As the saying goes, I was on the horns of a dilemma. Al listened sympathetically, puffing his cigar thoughtfully as I laid out my options.

If I chose to become a regular navy officer, I could go back to graduate school on the navy's nickel. But then I would owe them two years' active-duty service for every year I spent in school. It would probably take me four years to complete a Ph.D. Add eight years of navy duty to that and I'd be just about forty before I could really get on with my scientific career.

"There's no way I can go that route," I told Al.

He nodded. "I agree."

But then I faced the dilemma's other horn. "If I don't opt for the regular navy," I said, "I'll be out on my ear without a job, probably in a couple of weeks. Al, I've got a wife and kid to support. I'll get the GI Bill for a year or two of grad school, but that won't be anywhere near enough money."

Al nodded again, squinting Buddha-like against a cloud of cigar smoke. "I agree."

This was no time for him to be the dispassionate scientist neutrally assessing the data. I needed advice.

I looked around the crowded little shipboard lab with its blinking and clacking instruments. The situation was certainly ironic. This was where I'd always wanted to be, aboard an oceanographic research vessel. But I wasn't a scientist or even a graduate student. I was a lieutenant in the U.S. Navy Reserve. At least for the next few days. The navy had suddenly come into my life in 1966 when that officer in his crisp khakis had knocked on the door of my Long Beach apartment. It was the

navy that had led me to Woods Hole. Now the navy was about
to precipitously disrupt my life again.

When I had left USC and North American Aviation, I'd
been on a military leave of absence. This meant I could pack
up and return to California and probably pick up where I'd
left off almost three years earlier. But I now recognized that
Woods Hole, not southern California, was the perfect place
for a guy of my temperament.

The question was, how could I stay here, earn my Ph.D.,
and somehow support my family?

I called Captain Terry back and promised to give him my
decision the day after *Gosnold* returned to port. He wasn't
happy but cut me at least that much slack.

As soon as *Gosnold* tied up at the Institution dock, I
trotted over to the nearby Bigelow Building to see Dr. K.O.
Emery. He was the dean of graduate studies at Woods Hole
and I sure needed his advice.

After I outlined my problem, Dr. Emery slid off his gold-
rimmed glasses, pinched the bridge of his nose, and closed his
eyes for a moment in reflection. He was focusing his formidable
intelligence on my dilemma.

"I think I've got a solution," he said. "Why not enter the
Woods Hole–MIT joint graduate program using your GI Bill
for tuition? I'm sure one of the labs here has enough research
money to supplement your income with a part-time job until
you complete your degree."

It was, of course, the perfect solution.

The next morning, I told Captain Terry that I was opting
to leave active duty, but requested that I be allowed to retain
my navy reserve commission. Even then, I realized that my
future in marine science would undoubtedly involve close cooperation with the U.S. Navy.

I sought Bill Rainnie's advice about a possible job at the
Institution. The Alvin Group had fallen on hard times. The top

two floors of the Drugstore had been condemned as structurally unsafe. And I found Bill and his hardworking team camped out in a couple of old trailers on the hillside parking lot off Challenger Drive.

Ironically, a month earlier, one of my last duties for the ONR before I went aboard the *Gosnold* with Al Uchupi had been to bring Bill Rainnie still more bad news. I had accompanied a group of officers from ONR's Code 466 who visited Rainnie's group to discuss future projects. The budget "shortfalls" caused by the Vietnam War had reached the point where the ONR had to cancel its plans to fund two submersibles at Woods Hole. Originally, the navy had planned to operate both *Alvin* and its larger variant, *Columbus,* out of the Institution. But in the summer of 1969, the navy was forced by budget constraints to cut one submersible from the program.

Woods Hole had a choice, ONR officers explained. The Institution could either accept the new submersible—already christened *Sea Cliff* by the navy—or keep *Alvin*, which had just been located on the bottom but not yet salvaged. In either case, these officers explained, ONR Code 466 funding for the Woods Hole submersible program was going to drop from 100% to zero over the next three fiscal years. The Institution therefore would have only one, not two, deep submersibles, and all navy funding for the Alvin Group would end in thirty-six months.

This was not the kind of news that Bill Rainnie's beleaguered team welcomed.

The ONR believed that *Sea Cliff*, then in the final stages of construction at the Electric Boat Company in Groton, was better equipped to meet the navy's particular needs; the submersible had heavy manipulator arms for handling ordnance and retrieving bulky sunken material. But this so-called *Alvin* look-alike had in fact grown like Topsy and now weighed more than 24 tons. *Sea Cliff,* unlike *Alvin,* had been built to stringent traditional navy specifications. Its small pressure sphere was crammed with redundant safety equipment. While *Alvin*'s pilots devised ingenious ways of removing unnecessary equipment every season to make the submersible easier to operate and to free up space and payload for scientific equipment, *Sea Cliff* represented a trend in the other direction. Therefore the new vessel was much less suited for the type of scientific research Bill Rainnie's group conducted. And *Sea Cliff* would be much more expensive to maintain and operate than *Alvin*.

Rainnie's team made a difficult and courageous decision. They opted to continue with *Alvin*, even though the submersible had not yet been salvaged from the continental slope bottom and no one knew her condition.

When I went to see Bill in his trailer-office exile that September, *Alvin* had been salvaged and was in its initial stripdown before complete overhaul. It was now clear that the submersible would dive again. But what was not at all clear was who was going to pay the Alvin Group's annual $750,000 operating budget once navy funding evaporated.

"Well," Bill joked when I came in the trailer, "it's the White Tornado."

I'd earned that nickname for my apparent hyperactivity, rushing about the Woods Hole campus in my white navy uniform over the past couple of years, trying to find time for both my official ONR business and my personal scientific interests.

I related my conversation with Dr. Emery and told Bill of my plans to complete my doctorate there at Woods Hole.

"I'm going to need a job, Bill."

"That's interesting," Bill said. "I've been thinking about putting your talents to use."

Given my seemingly boundless energy and unlimited optimism, Bill explained, he and his colleagues thought that I'd be the ideal salesman to go out and drum up paying customers for *Alvin*.

"Are you serious?"

"You bet I am," Bill replied. "Somebody's got to bring some money in here and we figure that since you're such a cheerleader for *Alvin*, you're the best man for the job."

A position like that was too good to be true. Bill Rainnie knew that I'd had a summer job at North American Aviation's Ocean Systems Group dreaming up projects for the company's submersible *Beaver Mark IV*. Bill's team had never dealt with such crass commercial realities as salesmanship. They'd existed in a warm cocoon of apparently limitless government funding. Given all that, I was probably the best guy at Woods Hole for the assignment.

Even though I had not yet dived on *Alvin*, I was firmly convinced that the agile and hardy little submersible was the perfect tool for virtually hundreds of marine scientists and oceanographers. Someone just had to convince them of this obvious fact.

Since the navy broke the bad news on future funding, I'd been urging Bill that *Alvin* needed a long-term, multidisciplinary project such as exploring the entire eastern continental shelf of North America.

Bill had countered that what *Alvin* really needed was another lucrative hunt for a lost H-bomb in order to build up a reserve in the budget coffers for the lean days ahead. But I saw such one-shot projects as counterproductive because they maintained the dependence on military funding. We needed to convince scientists—and their sponsoring government agencies—that their careers would benefit by using *Alvin*.

I certainly wasn't opposed to well-publicized heroic ventures for the submersible; the greater the publicity, the more scientists and their patrons learned of *Alvin*'s potential.

"What we really need, Bill," I said, "is for *Alvin* to go out and find *Titanic*. With that kind of publicity the funding would just come rolling in."

Bill smiled ruefully. "Yeah," he muttered, "wouldn't that

be great. Meanwhile, Bob, we've got the real world to deal with."

I went to work for Bill even while my employment application was being processed in the WHOI personnel office. The immediate challenge, as I saw it, was to begin plugging in budget gaps with a patchwork quilt of small grants and user fees. The days of blanket navy funding were gone forever.

"Wet NASA" was a pipe dream that never blossomed. Even the real NASA was in trouble. The Apollo moon-landing program had been truncated to feed the bottomless maw of the Vietnam War. Any funding system I devised for *Alvin*'s future was going to be permanent.

The glory days of the Pentagon's deep pockets, I correctly guessed, had definitely ended. But I'd learned there were smaller, less obvious sources of government funding than the Office of Naval Research. One, the new Defense Advanced Research Projects Agency (DARPA), looked promising. So did the recently established National Oceanographic and Atmospheric Administration (NOAA). Then there was the National Science Foundation. Finally, there were any number of universities and marine science institutes that would probably pay for a short series of *Alvin* dives to meet their special interests and requirements if they were approached in the proper manner.

While many scientists and engineers at Woods Hole would have probably found the hustling and uncertainties inherent in this job repugnant, I thrived on the challenge. Throughout history, I realized, explorers have always been faced with the challenge of patronage. And if Christopher Columbus was not too proud to cajole Queen Isabella into hocking her jewels to fund his little flotilla, I certainly didn't consider the twentieth-century equivalent beneath my dignity. After all, the vast unexplored sea floor was certainly a new world.

Even as my career as a scientific research salesman was getting under way, the plans to complete my doctorate in geology at Woods Hole suddenly foundered. The Institution provost, Dr. Arthur Maxwell, reviewed my application to the joint WHOI-MIT graduate studies program. Because I was now signed on as an employee of the *Alvin* group, he decided, I would not be eligible to study for my doctorate at Woods Hole.

"It's a bad idea for the Institution to award Ph.D.s to its own employees," Maxwell told K.O. Emery.

Maxwell was the provost and had the final voice in this matter. Ironically, he himself had done exactly what I had planned. As a full-time employee of the Scripps Oceanographic Institute, he had earned his doctorate from that same institution. But apparently what was good for Maxwell's goose was not good for Ballard's gander.

Once more my future looked uncertain at best. I still hoped there was time for me to retreat to southern California and salvage the job and graduate school program at North American Aviation.

But K.O. Emery and Bill Rainnie intervened to keep me at Woods Hole. After I'd explained my alternative plan to Dr. Emery, he again thought for several moments, then picked up the phone to call his friend, Dr. Robert McMaster, at the nearby University of Rhode Island.

Bob McMaster was an established marine geologist with a warm and flexible nature. Unlike many academic scientists caught up in their own achievements, Dr. McMaster took a real interest in his students' future.

K.O. Emery explained my new dilemma and asked if I could possibly be enrolled as a doctoral student at the Rhode Island graduate program while actually doing my research at Woods Hole.

"Why not?" Dr. McMaster replied. "Send Ballard over and we'll work this thing out."

By the end of the next day, the deal had been struck. I would remain an employee of Bill Rainnie's *Alvin* group, and

Bob McMaster would take me on as a graduate student for a doctorate in marine geology. K.O. Emery and Al Uchupi would both be on my thesis committee. I would take my course work at the University of Rhode Island but do my thesis research at Woods Hole. Since I already had some sixty graduate units from the Universities of Hawaii and Southern California, I'd only be required to take a couple of formal courses to establish residence in Rhode Island. McMaster thought that I'd be ready for my candidacy exams and be able to move on to my thesis in about a year.

In the world of academic science, a doctorate was an absolute necessity, a hurdle everyone had to cross in order to be taken seriously. Without that degree, a person—no matter how brilliant or insightful—was considered merely a technician, not a true scientist.

In December 1969, with *Alvin* ripped apart for its postsalvage overhaul in the Woods Hole workshops, I finally got my first chance to dive in a submersible.

Grumman Aircraft was eager to show off their new submersible, *Ben Franklin,* and had contacted K.O. Emery to see if he was interested. With *Alvin* out of commission, this was an excellent opportunity to do some research off the east coast of the United States.

"Think that might be of interest to you, Bob?" K.O. asked one chilly fall afternoon, peering mischievously over his gold-rimmed glasses. He knew I'd give almost anything for a dive.

"You bet, sir," I replied immediately.

I contacted Bill Rand, head of the Grumman program, and before I knew it, K.O., Al, and I were planning our dive series off the coast of Florida.

The research submersible *Ben Franklin* was Grumman's entry in the Wet NASA sweepstakes. Compared to other miniature deep-diving research subs, *Ben Franklin* was a luxury liner. It had been designed by Auguste Piccard's son, Jacques, as a "mesoscaphe," a large, long-duration submersible meant to drift in the world's great ocean currents, such as the Gulf Stream, at moderate depths, anywhere from the surface to 2,000 feet.

K.O. Emery, Al Uchupi, and Roland L. Wigley of the U.S. Bureau of Commercial Fisheries biological lab at Woods Hole now scheduled two brief research dives to conduct a biological and geological survey of the narrow continental shelf and steep slope just offshore the sub's homeport in West Palm Beach, Florida.

But any vision I might have had of a sunny winter boondoggle in southern Florida disappeared when Dr. Emery, Wigley and I drove to Logan Airport. Instead of strolling around, trying on sunglasses at the tourist shop, or sipping a Bloody Mary in the lounge, I found myself jammed into an uncomfortable waiting-room seat, my lap piled with data books and yellow pads.

K.O. Emery and I were drafting a paper on the use of research submersibles in oceanography to be submitted to *Marine Technology*. As he considered any time not spent in purposeful activity to be squandered, we worked while waiting for the Eastern Airlines jet to begin loading. We worked all the way down to Miami. We even worked in our West Palm Beach hotel. It was a beautiful clear Florida winter day: the late afternoon sun, warm, the Atlantic, pale blue and sparkling. But I was stuck in the hotel room, my back to the bay window, reading a series of science articles about deep-diving submersibles and trying to produce accurate summaries of those reports for K.O. to incorporate into our research paper.

That night, instead of sipping margaritas and eating grilled grouper around the pool, we ate room-service cheeseburgers and drank coffee while we carried on the drudge work. An expedition with K.O. Emery was anything but wasted time.

The next day, we met our hosts from Grumman and were given our briefing on the *Ben Franklin* by her captain, Don Kazimir. Sitting in its launch cradle on the concrete dock of the commercial harbor in West Palm Beach, *Ben Franklin* looked bulbous and ungainly, an illustration for a turn-of-the-century science fiction novel. The long gray steel pressure hull was of typical cylindrical design. But the symmetry was broken by a long, squat rectangular understructure reminiscent of a railroad gondola car. This was the huge compartment containing the massive batteries that gave the sub its long submerged endurance.

Compared to *Alvin*, this sub was a monster, almost 50 feet long. The year before, *Ben Franklin* had drifted submerged for a month, riding the Gulf Stream all the way from West Palm Beach to the southern cape of Nova Scotia. When we climbed on board, I was surprised to find the sub's interior even roomier than the compartments I'd seen in films of World War II subs. And *Ben Franklin* had plenty of amenities. Each of the eight long, comfortable bunks had its own small porthole. The nose of the crew compartment was an actual observation lounge with a cluster of circular windows facing different directions. There was a galley with an electric stove to heat frozen meals, and even a shower.

But this was not a tourist trip. Bill Rainnie of the Alvin Group had lent Grumman his vessel's manipulator arm so that *Ben Franklin* could collect biological and geological samples. And I knew with K.O. Emery on board as chief scientist we wouldn't have much time for rubbernecking.

We dove the next morning. The sub's support ship, R/V *Privateer*, towed *Ben Franklin* from the harbor to the edge of the continental shelf about two miles east of the port. With the sub on the surface and the sun beating on the steel hull, the interior was stuffy. But then Don Kazimir and his assistant pilot closed and sealed both hatches and the submerged ventilation system kicked in. The air was recycled through chemical scrubbers, which gave a faint but unmistakable odor of laboratory disinfectant.

Don and his assistant went through the classic submariners' predive exchange.

"Hatches sealed."

"Pressure in the boat."

The hull was sealed to the sea and pressurized at one atmosphere, as signified by the row of green lights on the diving panel.

Don Kazimir spoke with *Privateer* on the squawking sonar phone and our tow line was cast off. There was a powerful flushing sound as the ballast tanks flooded and we began to dive. The almost transparent greenish tropical seawater darkened slowly as we descended. But there was still plenty of light to see when we neared the bottom at a depth of 34 meters (111 feet).

I kept my face close to the forward windows as we descended. The water color was now a friendly, warm aquamarine. We skimmed above the ripply sand surface of an ancient coral reef that had marked sea level on this coast 15,000 years before, when so much of Earth's water was bound up in the massive ice sheets of the last glaciation.

K.O. Emery relented slightly and gave me some rather non-taxing data-recording duties on this first traverse, knowing how excited I was to be finally diving in a submersible. I was able to log depth and heading information from the repeater instruments up in the observation lounge and still keep a fascinated eye focused out the window. The dive was scheduled to last twenty-one hours and make observations at six bottom stations located between 3.0 and 7.6 kilometers east of the harbor. Our depth ranged from 32 down to 165 meters.

As *Ben Franklin*'s electric motors whirred quietly, churning the sub's fanlike propellers, we sailed along the gradually sloping bottom to our first station. Judging by the rippling sinews on the bottom sand and gravel, the north-flowing Gulf Stream was still powerful down to a depth of 50 meters. But as we moved east down the steeply sloping shelf, the visual evidence of the current became less pronounced.

The rich blue water of the Gulf Stream darkened and grew cooler as we descended. But once free of the silty conditions close inshore, our observation distance increased to almost 25 meters on both sides of the sub. At our first station in 38 meters of water, the bottom was crowded with marine life, filter-feeding coral, sponges, and a bewildering variety of other semifixed invertebrates. There were large schools of amberjacks, butterfly fishes, and trigger fishes swarming past the portholes. From where I sat, these warm tropical shallows did indeed seem reminiscent of the benign ocean matrix in which Captain Nemo lived and worked aboard his fictional *Nautilus*.

But by the time we reached Station V at a depth of 157 meters (511 feet) near midnight, all hint of warmth had vanished. The purpose of this station was to observe a bait barrel filled with chum and fish parts that *Privateer* had dumped for us the day before. Here the dead coral lumps and fine coral sand of the shallower soundings had given way to a drab gray surface of silty mud. For the first time, I saw this typical ocean bottom, which stretches from these relative shallows of the continental shelf all the way down to and across the great abyssal plains. This bottom was composed of a fine sediment of organic matter and the microscopic calcified remains of tiny organisms living in the upper ocean layers that had drifted down like snow from above.

The schools of brightly colored tropical fish were gone. There were a few cylindrical sea cucumbers undulating slowly in the weak bottom current. A lonely formation of four hake sailed by my porthole, seemingly not interested in the bait barrel. But the ghostly white Jonah crabs, most 8 or 10 inches across the carapace, definitely were attracted by the bait. Hundreds of crabs trudged soundlessly across the bottom in clumps and columns, leaving faint pockmarks in the silt as they moved inexorably toward the barrel starkly illuminated by *Ben Franklin*'s floodlights.

K.O. Emery and Roland had finished their observations for the night, having retrieved several excellent samples of fossil coral with the mechanical arm. They were now sleeping in their bunks. I was the only one in the forward observation dome. Tired as I was from the trip and the excitement of my first dive, I was unable to sleep. I lay there for hours, my face near the chill Plexiglas circular window, watching those silent white crabs. The water temperature had dropped to only 13 degrees Celsius. At this depth, the pressure of seawater was equal to 15 atmospheres, 227 pounds per square inch.

But it wasn't the cold, the pressure, or the sheer weirdness of lying there gazing out at a section of the planet's surface never before observed by humans that struck me most. It was the slow, relentless march of those dead-white crabs. They were the inevitable scavengers of the ocean bottom, a mindless cleanup crew that filled a particular evolutionary niche. When a fish, shark, turtle, or porpoise died and fell to the bottom, the crabs were waiting.

My warm and comfy Captain Nemo image of the friendly ocean depths had disappeared. I certainly no longer harbored any romantic notion of the nobility of being buried at sea. I could still picture my childhood image of those *Nautilus* pallbearers in the armored diving suits, bearing the casket of their comrade to his ocean-bottom resting place. But now I understood what happened when the humans left. The crabs came. They devoured every scrap of flesh.

The only reason the crabs had not eaten the baloney sandwiches and apples left behind when *Alvin* sank was probably because there'd been faint electromagnetic discharges from the sub's batteries that kept the relentless crabs at bay.

Watching the silent procession of these bone-white crea-

tures across the gray silt, I made a mental note to tell Marjorie
and my colleagues that I definitely did not ever want to be
buried at sea.

At *Ben Franklin*'s final bottom station later that night, I
was again the only observer who stayed awake. Once more
the Jonah crabs creeping silently across the silt were the only
animal life on the bottom. But large schools of blue runners
swept through the floodlit area around the sub like sudden
flocks of barn swallows. Two small sand sharks prowled past
my window, staring in with flat, lifeless eyes.

Then as I stifled a yawn and was just about to doze off,
a metallic shimmer flashed across the observation port. A sleek
blue-gray swordfish plunged past my window and buried his
long bill deep in the silt. He thrashed wildly, kicking up clouds
of sediment, then disappeared in a shimmering streak as quickly
as he had appeared. It was as if he were demonstrating to this
huge intruder what would happen if it continued to trespass
on his domain.

Alvin had been attacked by a swordfish in nearby waters
during a dive in July 1967. The fish had embedded its sword
deep into the little sub's Fiberglas skin—fortunately missing
any vital plumbing or electrical cable—just as *Alvin* reached
the bottom at a depth of 1,985 feet. Pilot Marvin McCamis
brought the submersible back to the surface as fast as possible,
the thrashing seven-foot swordfish still attached to the belly.
The fish died from the sudden pressure change and snapped
off its impaled sword in its death throes. But the recovery
scuba divers waiting on the surface snagged the dying fish
before it sank. That night the crew of *Lulu* had fresh swordfish
steaks for dinner.

I watched the swirling gray cloud where this swordfish
had struck the bottom near *Ben Franklin*'s nose. When the
sediment had settled, all I saw was the slow march of the Jonah
crabs.

I realized that I would be drawn back to the deep ocean

often in the future, once *Alvin* was returned to service. But after my solitary vigil in *Ben Franklin*'s observation dome, any adolescent Jules Verne illusion I had harbored about living in the benign embrace of the ocean mother was shattered. The deep ocean was an unforgiving environment, as indifferent to human life as the vacuum of outer space.

For those who forgot that lesson, I now understood, the crabs were always waiting.

Part Two

GOING FORTH

THREE

Strange as it now sounds, the chance to conduct research on deep-diving submersibles was actually not the most exciting part of my Ph.D. program.

I had begun studying for my doctorate in marine geology just when the entire field of Earth sciences was being ripped apart by a revolution every bit as fundamental as Darwin's theory of evolution had been to the biological sciences or the Big Bang theory to astronomy. In effect, I found myself plunged into the scientific equivalent of a civil war.

For me, this intellectual conflict began one winter night in 1968 when I attended a lecture by Professor Patrick M. Hurley at the Massachusetts Institute of Technology. Hurley was a well-known geologist who led a group at MIT that had been recalculating the dates of certain sedimentary rock formations found in the North American Appalachians, the Channel Islands near the French coast, the northern British Isles, and Scandinavia.

As I sat in the big MIT amphitheater surrounded by bearded graduate students staring intently at Hurley's slides, I was overcome by a sense of excitement and uncertainty. Hurley's dry, methodical presentation built layer by layer— just as ponderously as the sedimentary strata he studied— toward an unmistakable conclusion: the rocks that had formed the Taconic and Acadian episodes in the North American Appalachian formation were the same as those of the Caledonian episodes of mountain-building of northwestern Europe.

What he was proving with his slow exposition of data

and slides was literally earthshaking. The northeastern corner of the North American continent and the northwestern corner of Europe had once been joined together, just as some Siamese twins share an attachment point at sternum or hip.

Hurley and his team had also discovered indisputable evidence of another continental connection, this one across the present-day South Atlantic. Careful comparison of the continental rock of the bulging east coast of Brazil and the West African bulge of the Ivory Coast produced the same type of relationship. There was clear evidence that the continents of Africa and South America had once been joined, the protruding lobe of Brazil nestling neatly into the West African Bight.

Professor Hurley was offering the first concrete geologic evidence that I had encountered to prove the long-posited, but generally discredited, theory of continental drift, (which acquired the more scientifically acceptable nomenclature of plate tectonics a few years later).

When I left the lecture hall that night, I walked across the snowy MIT campus toward the Charles River, my brain swirling with conflict. Hurley's data were persuasive. His fieldwork slides had shown an unmistakable section of sedimentary strata ending on a low escarpment in northeast Brazil—then reappearing on a jungle-clad bluff in the Ivory Coast, separated by 2,400 miles of ocean. These rocks were positively matched through radiometric dating. They weren't similar structures; they were the *same* formation on two different continents, as if they were pieces of a jigsaw puzzle cut from a unique piece of plywood, then spread apart on a coffee table.

"This is crazy," I muttered, marching along the icy sidewalk.

Hurley's data presented an inescapable but bizarre inference: the present-day coasts of South America and West Africa—and mountain ranges in North America and western Europe—had been in close contact at some time in the past. But now these continents had separated, leading to the formation of the North and South Atlantic oceans.

For years as a student, I'd heard disdainful references to various theories of continental drift. Every geology professor I'd studied under had dismissed such speculation as crackpot pseudoscience. It was absurd to think that the unimaginably massive continents floated around planet Earth like lily pads on a pond. But now an established MIT professor had joined the ranks of other respectable geologists who no longer found the theory of continental drift the domain of charlatans.

Like many undergraduate geology students, of course, I'd been intrigued by the apparent jigsaw-puzzle fit of the North and South American coastlines with the long western coast of Africa. But my professors, when they'd deigned to answer questions on the subject, had dismissed this symmetry as a "coincidence."

Continents did not move. End of discussion.

I had been schooled in classic geology at UC–Santa Barbara and the graduate schools of the University of Hawaii and USC. This classical approach can best be summed up by Marshall Kay's "geosynclinal cycle." Kay, one of the giants of land geology, taught at Columbia University. He built on the work of a nineteenth-century American geologist, James Hall. According to Kay's model, the motion affecting the endless buildup and erosion of continents was vertical not horizontal. Continents rose and fell more or less in place on Earth's crust. They did not move across its surface.

Over the billions of years of Earth's history, the model stated, continental rock was eroded by water to flow as sediment into ocean basins where thick strata of sedimentary rock were formed on the continental shelves and slopes. As this sedimentary rock slowly sank under the immense load, long subsidence troughs in Earth's crust—the "geosynclines"— were formed, leaving room for more sediment to accumulate.

These massive deposits would eventually sink into Earth's hot interior and trigger a mountain-building episode, leading to the uplift of adjacent sedimentary rock formations into great mountain ranges like the Rockies, the Alps, or the Appalachians.

The classicists believed that continents could grow on their edges in this mountain-building sequence, but the continents themselves certainly did not move.

Marshall Kay was still one of the dominant forces in academic geology when I began graduate school.

But when I arrived in New England, I was confronted with the first serious discussions of continental drift and soon heard Professor Hurley's solid evidence defending the theory.

And I learned that the theory of continental drift wasn't new, after all, but was rather an old idea gaining new support. First advanced in the 1920s by a German arctic meteorologist named Alfred Wegener, the theory was initially based solely on data collected on land, bolstered by the hypothetical map-image fit of today's continents into an ancient supercontinent, Pangaea.

Wegener's concept had been around almost fifty years, but it was only after the technical advances of World War II that science had the proper tools to test it. Up until the late 1940s and 1950s, geophysicists—the abstract purists of the Earth scientists—had successfully challenged the theory of floating continents. How, prominent geophysicists like Harold Jeffreys asked, could solid stone continents plow their way through the equally solid stone ocean floor? This hypothesis defied all known laws of physics.

But after the invention of echo-sounding sonar and the perfection of ocean seismic profiling, survey ships discovered that the layers of sedimentary rock on the ocean bottom were not anywhere nearly as deep as they should have been if the geosynclinal cycle model was accurate. In other words, the ocean floor appeared to be geologically much younger than the continents.

And in the 1950s, research ships using new sounding techniques also expanded earlier hydrographic surveys that had found mountainous shallower terrain in the middle of the Atlantic. Combined data from new oceanographic centers now showed that a single monstrous mountain range 74,000 kilometers (42,000 nautical miles) long snaked through all the seven seas. This incredible chain, the world's largest geologic feature, was named the Mid-Ocean Ridge.

And it was through the study of this submerged mountain system that the theory of continental drift achieved its first validity in contemporary science.

It had long been understood that Earth's magnetic field had reversed itself periodically over the ages. Today's north had been south a few million years ago, and so on, back through the epochs. When the molten magma of iron-rich basaltic rock cooled and solidified, the tiny suspended iron particles "froze" to reflect Earth's then prevailing magnetic polarity. These fossil compasses left unique signatures, which had been well documented. Using sensitive ship-towed magnetometers developed in World War II to detect submarines, oceanographers surveying the geophysical properties of the Mid-Ocean Ridge in the 1950s discovered bands of magnetic anomalies lying in intriguing zebra-stripe patterns on the sea floor on either side of these ridges. Long parallel strips of normal and reversed magnetic polarity rock alternated in symmetrical patterns on each side of the axis of the Mid-Ocean Ridge.

These magnetic zebra stripes had the same width and sequence on both sides of the midsea mountains. The inference was obvious: the magnetized basalt of the sea floor had extruded as one molten mass along the axis of the ridge, then split to spread horizontally in parallel bands on both sides as new basalt rose at the heart of the midsea mountains.

Here was proof that the supposedly solid rock sea floor was in fact a moving plastic conveyer belt.

But what incredible energy system fueled this gigantic conveyer belt?

The first answers to the riddle came from seismologists using ultrasensitive new instruments to monitor distant underground nuclear explosions for compliance to the 1963 Nuclear Test Ban Treaty. These seismographs gave scientists a view of earthquakes and volcanic eruptions that showed crustal rock descending into the molten mantle along the curved ocean trenches that paralleled the "Ring of Fire" encircling the vast Pacific basin.

This research led to the conclusion that the plates of generally lighter granitic rock on which the continents, as well as the oceanic crusts stood, did indeed float on a spherical pond of semi-molten magma. The discredited early theory of continental drift gave way to the proven phenomenon of ocean-floor spreading, then to the unifying revolutionary theory of plate tectonics. Tekton was the name of the carpenter in the *Iliad*, and tectonic meant construction in geological theory.

Wegener's flawed speculation that the continents plowed through solid rock was supplanted by the concept that crustal plates—from 50 to 150 kilometers thick—ride on a deeper layer of high-temperature rock. Beneath these crustal plates, which collectively make up the lithosphere, a much deeper layer called the asthenosphere is the source of molten magma that flows upward to fuel the volcanoes belching out lava onto the ocean floor. If Earth were the size of a hen's egg, the lithosphere would be as thick as the egg's shell. The fluidity of the deeper layer, maintained because of the tremendous pressure to which it is subject, makes possible the movement of the rigid plates of crust.

The upwelling molten rock spills forth through a rift in a midocean ridge spreading out on either side to form new sea floor. As the parallel zebra stripes of the solidified basalt fossil compasses showed, this spreading continues until the ocean floor eventually abuts a crustal plate traveling in the opposite direction. When this occurs, the old and heavier ocean floor descends back to the molten interior under a deep ocean trench to be remelted.

In this new theory, the crustal plates are separate and distinct. So it's at their junctures that we stand to learn the most about their motion and the nature of the molten rock of the asthenosphere below. The plates of the lithosphere are always in a state of collision or separation, or are grinding alongside each other, as in the case of California's famous San Andreas Fault. If two plates are separating, as it was theorized in the case of the North American and European crustal plates, new crust forms as molten volcanic magma that extrudes upward along the expanding seam of the Mid-Atlantic Ridge. In places where plates collide, the buckling action can create mountain ranges such as the Andes and Himalayas.

Alfred Wegener's speculation that the continents could be reassembled like a jigsaw puzzle gave way in 1965 to a much more accurate shape reassembly conducted by Cambridge University geologist Sir Edward Bullard. Bullard and his colleagues used newly available computer analysis to show that the best fit among North and South America, Africa, and Europe came at a depth of 1,000 meters along their continental shelves. It was obvious that these submerged shelves—extending from only a few miles seaward along some coastlines out to several hundred miles off the coasts of North America and northwestern Europe—represented the true shape of the continental tectonic plates. Just as Hurley's comparative geological surveys had shown the same rock formations on the coasts of Brazil and West Africa, there had to be a geologic match between the submerged bedrock of the continental shelves of North America and Africa, and North America and Europe—*if* their plates had once been in contact.

For a graduate student in geology like me, the new theory

of plate tectonics was astounding in its implications. The theory literally knocked geology sideways, erasing in one bold stroke the vertical tectonics that had been the foundation of the science for over a century.

When I went to the University of Rhode Island to complete my doctorate, plate tectonics had thrown the Earth science community into a civil war. On the one side were the land geologists who defended the old classic model of vertical tectonics, based on Kay's geosynclinal cycle. On the other side were oceanographers, mostly marine geophysicists, who staunchly defended the new plate tectonics paradigm.

No sooner had I started my course work, than I found myself right in the middle of this increasingly acrimonious debate. I wanted to do research that would help prove or refute plate tectonics. On the urging of Al Uchupi, the focus of my thesis was to be the geology of the continental shelf in the Gulf of Maine north of Cape Cod.

I was particularly interested in the Mesozoic era, which extended from 225 to 65 million years ago. Plate tectonics held that during the early part of this era the continents of North America and Africa had separated to create the Atlantic Ocean.

I believed that a geologic formation in the Appalachian Mountains called the Newark Group—a system of soft red sedimentary rock and basaltic lava flows extending offshore onto the continental shelf under the Gulf of Maine—would show evidence of this plate separation.

Land geologists had studied this system in the Appalachian range. There, rivers like the Connecticut had cut V-shaped valleys through the soft red sediments, which were later transformed into a characteristic U shape by the Pleistocene glaciers of the last Ice Age. But most of the Newark Group lay offshore, partially buried in the deep basins of the Gulf of Maine. If I could only map this great system, I should then be able to reveal the geologic history of the early Mesozoic or late Triassic period just before the continental plates decoupled from one another. There also should have been evidence out there from the early Jurassic, when the floor of the Atlantic Ocean had begun to form.

But classical land geologists believed the Newark Group had been formed during the early Mesozoic by geosynclinal action.

Both these theories could not be right. One had to be wrong, and a geological survey of the Newark Group could help prove the validity of plate tectonics or serve to discredit it.

It was hard to maintain neutrality. Half the professors on my thesis committee believed in plate tectonics. The other half were classicists who did not. And I really didn't know where Dr. Emery stood. He was a classic land geologist, but at Woods Hole he was surrounded by young marine geophysicists who were pioneering the theory of plate tectonics. Good scientist that he was, K.O. Emery was withholding judgment until he saw irrefutable data.

The burden of providing that data would fall to young doctoral candidates such as myself. Any geology graduate student worth his salt in those days wanted to make a contribution to this scientific revolution. In general, adherents to the classic theory were land geologists who stayed on land. The strongest proponents of plate tectonics concentrated on the geophysics of the sea floor near the Mid-Ocean Ridge. Everyone seemed to avoid the ground in between, the continental margin. Unfortunately for me, the Gulf of Maine represented the far reaches of the continental plate, just as it drops off into the abyss.

The practical offshoot of this was that my thesis committee was made up of men who probably knew less about the area I was studying than I did.

To further complicate my life, I had to prepare for the ordeal of eventually defending my thesis. I had to fully immerse myself in countless volumes of scientific papers on the Appalachian Mountain system by the traditional heavyweights of the field who classic geologists still worshiped. My recurrent nightmare was being asked by a classical man if I had read this or that obscure paper by Rogers on the tectonics of the Appalachians or some long-forgotten published lecture by Belt on the post-Acadian rifts of eastern Canada. So, for the next four years, I spent all my spare time reading mountains of these classical papers. How could I challenge the pantheon of classical geology at Yale, Harvard, and Princeton if I wasn't fully versed in their ultimately flawed theories?

My position was akin to that of a young biologist at the time of Darwin obliged to read the classic literature that held that all creation stemmed from the Garden of Eden in 6000 B.C.

Working on my doctorate was in many ways one long exercise in problem solving. I knew, for example, that American oil companies had conducted extensive seismic surveys of parts of the Gulf of Maine, especially the deep sedimentary formations under Georges Bank. But oil companies were not about to give these expensive seismic maps to an obscure graduate student to use in his thesis research. The information was too sensitive, representing billions in potential earnings if government oil and gas drilling leases for this offshore area were offered up to bid.

When I approached the oil companies requesting access to their seismic maps of the bedrock, their answer was not only no but hell no.

This problem, however, was solved by the deep respect petroleum geologists had for my mentor, K.O. Emery. Oil company representatives often sought his advice and funded an annual program through which they had access to our research data years before it was published in scientific journals. It was at one of these annual meetings that I met oil company geologists who had conducted offshore seismic surveys on the Georges Bank. K.O. Emery made it clear that I was his protégé. I soon had confidential access to those base maps that revealed the most seaward segment of the Newark Group, the very underpinning of the continental shelf that was created as the continents began to separate 180 million years ago.

But the next problem wasn't so easy to solve.

How could I conduct a thorough geologic mapping survey of the Gulf of Maine with *Alvin* out of action, still undergoing her postsalvage overhaul?

Bill Rainnie provided the answer. He was looking for ways to use *Alvin*'s support ship, *Lulu*.

"Bill," I suggested one afternoon over a beer at the Captain Kidd, a local Woods Hole bar. "*Alvin* is a great submersible, but it really hasn't been used yet as an effective scientific tool."

"What do you mean by that?" Bill asked coolly.

Bad-mouthing *Alvin* was not a good idea around Bill Rainnie. I explained that up to then the sub had been working on its own as an exploratory vehicle for biologists and geologists. That was why so many dives came up with no usable data.

"The best way to use *Alvin*," I suggested, "is as a means to follow up on previous reconnaissance studies. She's a surgical tool. We shouldn't use it unless we know exactly where to go and what to do with it."

Bill sipped his beer and glanced at me with a mixture of interest and suspicion. He knew I was negotiating for something.

I laid out my case. Why not, I suggested, let me use the idle *Lulu* as my reconnaissance survey vessel for the Gulf of Maine. Towing seismic arrays and a proton magnetometer, I would try to pinpoint where the bedrock outcrops were located. This would take a year or so of cruises.

"Then when *Alvin*'s back in operation," I said optimistically, "I can dive with her right on the outcrops where I need to take my samples."

Bill considered my audacious proposition. I was suggesting monopolizing his surface ship for an indefinite period, then tying up *Alvin* for the better part of a couple more seasons.

"Can you get someone to pay for all this?" Bill asked.

"I'm sure going to try."

By the summer of 1970, I had somehow cobbled together a financial support package that allowed me to use *Lulu* as an unlikely seismic research vessel for my mapping project in the Gulf of Maine. My main sponsor was the Pentagon's Advanced Research Project Agency (ARPA), which was always interested in projects that might eventually provide technological spin-offs beneficial to one of the armed services. Working with scientists from the Department of Marine Geology and Geophysics, as well as with engineers from the Alvin Group, we managed to write an ARPA funding proposal to equip *Alvin* with a precision navigation system, a towed magnetometer, a portable gravimeter, and a hard-rock drill. It was a shot in the dark. But for some reason ARPA liked the project. The agency would not only fund the development of this critical equipment, ARPA would also fund the field tests—my thesis research—as well.

In retrospect, it was probably the prospect of developing a precision navigation system for tracking *Alvin,* using three-dimensional triangulation from a surface vessel and a network of submerged acoustic transponders, that convinced ARPA to ante up the support money.

A year before *Alvin* was ready to dive again, I was out on the Gulf of Maine aboard *Lulu* towing my own custom-designed seismic array from the clumsy little vessel.

If my funding arrangements for *Alvin* were a strange compromise, *Lulu* itself was the mother of all compromises. The

Office of Naval Research hadn't been able to provide WHOI with enough money to build a proper mother ship for *Alvin*. Instead, Dan Clark, a marine construction man who often did projects for the institution, had salvaged a couple mothballed navy minesweeping pontoons, each 96 feet long, and welded them together with steel connecting arches to form an ungainly seagoing catamaran. The port pontoon held the engine room and galley. The starboard pontoon was known as the "tube of doom." An ill-ventilated and spartan crew dormitory, guaranteed to drive even the oldest sea dog to retching queasiness in bad weather, occupied this pontoon's lower level. Above it were a small lab, a tiny laundry, and equipment lockers. *Lulu* didn't have enough power for long ocean passages and was usually towed by a larger vessel.

But on my Gulf of Maine surveys, *Lulu* chugged along on her own power. The captain, Dale Butler, was not overjoyed with his new assignment. During dive operations, he and his crew only worked in daylight hours launching and recovering *Alvin*. Sunset to sunrise was off-time. Now I was working his ship twenty-four hours a day, trailing a long seismic array with an airgun that went off like a 500-pound bomb every twenty seconds. The shock waves pounded the tube of doom where the weary off-watch crew was trying to sleep.

Late one night in September 1970, while I was in the narrow little lab on the starboard pontoon, a big, sullen crewman pushed his way into the lab and told me to "shut down that goddamn airgun."

The guy looked like he'd been hitting the bottle, red-eyed and swaying. *Lulu*'s chief bo'sun, George "Brody" Broderson, a tough and savvy old-timer and an absolute wizard with anything mechanical, heard the disturbance and intervened to send the sailor back to his bunk.

"That airgun takes some getting used to," I told Brody.

He squinted at me, a sour look on his weather-beaten face. "That it does," was all he'd admit.

Brody loved the old *Lulu* and *Alvin*. He certainly enjoyed the far-flung global dive expeditions. He did not appreciate this mission, but he was much too professional a sailor to complain.

I was back hunched over my data table twenty minutes later when I heard the hatch squeak open and felt a cool puff of damp night air. For some reason, I looked up just in time to see the disgruntled sailor, obviously driven nuts by sleep deprivation, lunging at me with a long-bladed rigger's knife in his hand.

Then in a blur of speed, Brody sprang from the open hatch, knocked the man down, and disarmed him.

After the inevitable bout of loud and frantic confusion, I learned that Brody had kept watch outside the lab door. A good bo'sun knew his crew, and Brody knew the man was in bad shape.

"I think we'll shut down for the night," I told Brody.

He stroked the white fringe of his beard. "Not a bad idea," he allowed.

By the spring of 1971, *Alvin* had been completely overhauled and recertified for deep submergence. Its first postsalvage trip was up to the New England Aquarium in Boston, where the Boston Sea Rovers were having their annual convention, and I'd arranged to have *Alvin* placed on display at the aquarium. The club members got a special tour on Saturday morning, and almost 5,000 people came to see the submersible during the rest of the weekend. This generated a lot of publicity, as I'd hoped, and served as a kind of unofficial coming-out-party-cum-resurrection for the little sub.

But *Alvin*'s real mission was science, not public relations. As soon as all her modifications were thoroughly checked out in shallow dives in Woods Hole harbor, she went back to sea.

Bill Rainnie and his engineers had used the overhaul to

modify the Fiberglas sail and hull cowlings, upgrade the ballast system, and generally tweak *Alvin* into a higher performance research vehicle. Because commercial replacement parts were too expensive, Rainnie's team became masters of improvisation. For example, Cliff Winget, one of Bill's lead engineers, replaced the three Fiberglas spheres that held the vessel's trim liquid—a devil's brew of mercury and oil—with four surplus stainless steel balls that had served as hydraulic reservoirs on P-47 fighters in World War II.

This was a pattern that would be repeated over the coming years until the sub resembled the proverbial New England farmers' "family ax" that had been given five new heads and seven new handles as it came down through the generations.

I'd completed my surface surveys in *Lulu* in September 1970. By mid-July 1971, I was ready to dive in *Alvin*, testing the sub as the surgical research tool I had described to Bill Rainnie. But I had to find equipment and sponsors in order to finish all the research that I had planned in the Gulf of Maine. Because Dr. Fye required that the WHOI ship R/V *Gosnold* escort *Lulu* when using *Alvin*, I was able to turn the *Gosnold* into an improvised seismic survey ship to work the general area where *Alvin* was diving.

This impromptu use of a free vessel was the type of informal patronage that I would use repeatedly in the future. Al Uchupi and I wrote a proposal for the National Science Foundation to fund the seismic work on *Gosnold*. Their research grant was my first as a coprincipal investigator. I was very proud of receiving this grant, which marked the true beginning of my scientific fund-raising career. I was learning a lesson that few history books ever taught about exploration: a grand vision meant little unless you could obtain the practical wherewithal to mount an expedition.

The seismic surveys aboard *Lulu* the year before had shown us the general location of a number of hard-rock outcroppings that were probably remnants of the older granitic highlands on which the soft red sediments of the Newark Group had been laid down. The problem with mapping the submerged geologic formations of the Gulf of Maine was that the retreating glaciers had dumped deep layers of sand and gravel that completely buried the lower Newark Group in the submerged valley floors.

In July 1971, I was the chief scientist on a week-long cruise to dive on the outcroppings. This was the first real test of my concept of using *Alvin* for precision sample-retrieval work rather than as an exploration vessel.

I was nervous on the windy, overcast morning of July 18, 1971, when I joined veteran *Alvin* pilots Val Wilson and Ed Bland on *Lulu*'s rough plank main deck. Val and Ed had over 200 dives each. For them this quick dip down to a mere 140 meters (455 feet) should have been a relatively routine assignment. But this was my first dive on *Alvin,* and only the submersible's twentieth open-sea dive since it was sunk during launch on the continental slope in October 1968.

So everyone was tense.

The old launch procedure had inherent risks. The crew used to climb aboard *Alvin* as it sat in its cradle, chocked to *Lulu*'s deck. Then the derrick would lift the little sub down into the open slipway between the pontoons. The pilot would stand in the sail, using a remote control box connected by a cable through the crew sphere's open hatch to operate *Alvin*'s big stern propeller. It was this open hatch that had caused the flooding that sank the vessel when the cradle cable snapped and pitched *Alvin*'s nose into the surging sea.

After the sub was lost, Rainnie's team had decided to install a permanent junction box in the sail, which was hard-wired down through pressure-proof penetrators in the personnel sphere, eliminating the cable through the open hatch. In the new launch procedure, the pilot could control *Alvin* as it lay, still suspended in its cradle, awash in *Lulu*'s slipway, with the hatch closed beneath his feet.

The only problem with this system was that *Alvin* was now lowered down into the slipway with the hatch closed to prevent accidental flooding. This meant that Ed Bland, the copilot, and I had to scramble aboard the sub while it lay awash in its cradle.

There was a sloppy cross-sea rolling in the gulf this morning, and *Lulu*'s pontoons were surging in the swell. The trick was to scurry across the narrow gangplank to the little sub without soaking your feet. Wet socks and sneakers made for a miserable dive when the sub reached the cold water of the bottom.

"After you, Bob," Ed Bland said, gesturing grandly.

The rolling pontoon beneath my feet was greasy and wet. *Alvin*'s superstructure rose and fell sharply in the slipway, even though Brody's crew were steadying the sub as best they could with the launch lines.

I made it across the gangway in one lunge and climbed up *Alvin*'s swaying Fiberglas sail smartly enough, placing my feet where I'd been trained to. As Ed unsealed the hatch, I dropped into the cramped personnel sphere. The 80-inch diameter pressure sphere was certainly comfortable enough for one person, but the multiple racks of instruments crowding the curved interior did not leave much room for a crew of three. At this busy and confusing stage of the dive, I had to stay out of the way. I jammed myself beneath the port instrument racks on the custom-made cushions on the floor of the sphere. Ed Bland dropped lithely down beside me and reached back up to reseal the heavy hatch. A moment later I heard Val clamber into the narrow Fiberglas sail to take up the pilot's launch position.

This was always a very tense moment. With a sea running between the pontoons, *Alvin* could come adrift in the narrow slipway and smash against one of the pontoons. Brody, a professional actor when on the beach, always managed to make launches especially dramatic, as he alternately cajoled and excoriated the men on the lines. They loved it. Like Brody, the crew sported faded red berets, proud souvenirs of the exhausting and dangerous but ultimately successful dives to retrieve the lost H-bomb off the Spanish coast.

While Val worked in the sail with the launch crew to finish lowering *Alvin* into the water before backing out, Ed was frantically checking out *Alvin*'s electrical systems. Most of the sub was now awash. If we were going to have a problem with our circuits, this was a good time to spot it, so we could still come back aboard for repairs.

My job was to disappear, but since that was impossible, I scrunched yogalike under the instrument rack, the knees of my jeans against my chin, and tried not to touch any switches.

The final phase of the launch operation took less than five minutes, but it seemed like an eternity. Slowly, the big propeller on *Lulu*'s starboard pontoon slid past my view port. The VHF radio inside the sphere crackled with static.

Next, divers jumped into the surging water of the slipway. I could see them fighting the swell, frantically swimming around *Alvin*'s flanks to detach the six handling lines.

As soon as that was completed, *Lulu*'s stern props kicked into action, sending up a milky froth, and she disappeared into the blue-green surface waters of the Gulf of Maine. I felt balanced between two worlds, as if in suspended animation, a silent, immobile observer.

My dreamlike state was broken as Ed popped the hatch and Val came tumbling down into the sphere, bringing with him a chill curtain of seawater from a wave breaking over the sail. The hatch clanked down and Ed resealed it as fast as possible. Val now picked up the sound-powered phone to speak with the divers standing on the partially submerged hull of *Alvin*.

"How're my lift props doing?"

"Both are turning," came the response.

"Can you see my tracking beacon?"

"Roger that."

"Great!" Val replied, reading from his checklist.

"Has John taken the safety line off the sample tray? Fine!"

"Stand by, I'm going to call *Lulu.*"

He took the VHF radio mike.

"*Lulu,* this is *Alvin.* My hatch is shut, my blowers on, leaks and grounds are normal. Request permission to dive."

"*Alvin,* this is *Lulu,*" the voice of Jack Donnell, the third pilot, sounded in the speaker. "Is your tracking beacon on?"

"Roger that."

"You have permission to dive," Jack called. "Your depth is 450 feet. Have a nice dive."

"Bill, can you hear me?" Val dropped the mike and grabbed the phone to talk to the support diver standing astride *Alvin*'s superstructure.

"I'm venting the ballast tanks. I'm starting down."

As Val opened the ballast tanks, the cold waters of the Gulf of Maine came rushing inside. *Alvin* was now heavier than seawater. She silently slipped beneath the waves, a final swell crashing over her sail. The last thing to disappear beneath the surface was the circular yellow current meter that was spinning like a top in the strong wind.

I was now glued to the portside view port of *Alvin,* which was assigned to the chief scientist of the dive. My window looked down and off to the left side. A rack of instruments was just inches above my head, and I tore off patches of my already thinning hair each time I brushed the sharp-edged rack.

Ed was seated on the opposite side of the sphere, but he was too busy with his long checklists to notice the water outside his starboard view port slowly turning from light blue to indigo to black.

Val was perched on a small stool no higher than a salad bowl in front of Ed and me, looking out of the forward view port. Ironically, Val had a much better view of the scenery than the chief scientist did. It was clear throughout this dive that I was a passenger who was to be tolerated. It was normal procedure for the pilot to do what he wanted first and then ask the scientist what he had in mind for the dive.

Val was a tough nut, a chief petty officer and a World War II diesel combat submariner. More importantly, he had been a COB—Chief of the Boat—the man who really ran the submarine but who tactfully allowed the officers to think they were in charge.

When I first came bouncing into Val's life, he knew all about young navy ensigns in their spotless white uniforms with tiny little gold bars on the shoulders. He had seen ensigns come and go in wartime. They were cannon fodder, the first to die and the least missed, since they knew so little and only got in the way.

Although I was no longer in the navy, I was on my first dive and was obviously, as far as Val was concerned, an "ensign in science," someone who had yet to prove his worth.

This was a long "short" dive. But from those first hours aboard *Alvin*, Val and I would develop a strong mutual respect. Of all the pilots I would dive with over the next twenty-five years, Val was the best.

During the first minutes of the dive, Val's face ran with sweat, the tension of the dangerous launch phase showing in his eyes.

Submariners hated the surface. They wanted depth as fast as possible.

Ironically, a shallow dive was more of a headache than a deep one. The short transit time up and down presented a problem: the pilots needed every bit of that descent time to verify that all the systems were working properly. And we all needed time to relax and settle in.

A deep dive, perhaps down to 6,000 feet, took about an hour to reach bottom, while my first dive would take less than ten minutes to reach bottom. And at such a shallow depth, the tidal current could be strong and visibility would be poor, much worse than the clear deep Atlantic bottom water. Further, instead of landing on a soft sediment bottom and skiing along an alpine slope of soft mud, we could easily land on the hard granite outcrop we were looking for. And we would definitely encounter a landscape of giant glacial boulders.

Val and Ed knew the dive was not going to be a cakewalk. And they wanted to make sure I knew it also. From the tense, staccato exchanges between the two pilots, I quickly realized this was deadly serious business. I was impressed by their skill at operating *Alvin*. They were clearly pros at their job. They had to be.

Hitting a sharp-edged boulder at the terminal descent speed of 100 feet per minute could smash one of the recessed windows. At 14 atmospheres seawater pressure on the bottom, the sphere would flood and we would die in seconds.

Unlike *Ben Franklin*, *Alvin* was a highly maneuverable diving machine. *Alvin*'s weight—mainly its heavy banks of lead acid batteries and its instrument-filled steel sphere—was almost exactly compensated for by nine hollow aluminum spheres encased in a dense epoxy foam in which millions of microscopic glass spheres were suspended. This "syntactic" foam could withstand the pressure of the ocean down to *Alvin*'s test depth limit plus a 50% safety factor. The foam was found throughout the entire length of the submarine, wherever it could be stuffed or shaped into the contours of the Fiberglas hull.

With *Alvin*'s buoyancy and weight thus almost balanced, there was no need for large negative-positive ballast tanks. And as the *Thresher* disaster proved, such a ballast system can't function at the tremendous outside pressure of great depths. Instead, the little sub used an ingenious pumped-oil system to increase and decrease displacement. With the 600 pounds of viscous oil filling exterior rubber membrane compartments, the sub's buoyancy was positive. But this variable ballast system, as it was called, had a limited capability and was only needed on the bottom. It was the surface air tanks that kept *Alvin* afloat. Now that they had been flooded, *Alvin* was on her way down at a terminal velocity.

There were redundant safety features built into this simple system. On the bottom, positive ascent buoyancy could be immediately achieved by dropping cast-iron ingots. In a real emergency, the submersible's mechanical arm could also be dropped, particularly if it was entangled with the bottom. Next, we could drop the science tray if a large rock fell into it. Under normal conditions, the variable ballast pump was used to compensate for any samples you collected by pumping oil out of a rubber bladder and into one of the holding tanks. This way our weight stayed the same, but our displacement increased, compensating for the rock that was just picked up and placed in the tray.

Compensating for the sample's weight was one problem solved. But placing that weight in the forward tray and pumping ballast also shifted the center of gravity of the sub, causing a nose-down trim. To overcome this forward shift, the pilot could turn on a pump that sent mercury from a storage reservoir in the bow to a similar reservoir in the stern, thereby trimming up the sub.

In the old days, this mercury could also be pumped out of the submersible to attain positive buoyancy and thus escape the bottom, but environmental laws now forbid such dumping of a toxic metal.

If after all the "normal" emergency procedures, we were still stranded on the bottom, we could take more desperate measures. In the next step, we could drop *Alvin*'s two heavy battery banks like blockbusters from a bomb bay, which would instantly provide thousands of pounds of buoyancy. And in a final and irreversible procedure, the pilot could mechanically unscrew the forward portion of the submersible—including the pressure and sail—and rocket to the surface, leaving more than half the sub behind.

The only problem with this final, desperate action, was that it had never been tested. Val and Ed feared the sphere would tumble violently on its way up, turning its occupants into a fine sauce as they were pounded into putty by all the instruments broken loose from their racks.

As we neared the bottom, Ed turned on our exterior lights, flooding the water with a turbid, chalky glare.

The swishing echo of the sonar now sounded with a solid ping.

Val dumped two descent weights. Our descent velocity fell to near zero. Now Val tripped the switches of the variable ballast system. I heard a pump whirr, and oil struggled with the ambient pressure. A moment later, *Alvin* had neutral buoyancy.

There would be no crash landings on boulders today.

"*Lulu*," Val called on the acoustic phone, "we have neutral trim and are driving down."

Alvin's designers had seen the sub as a cross between a submersible and a NASA-type manned spacecraft. The large swiveling fan propeller on the stern combined the functions of horizontal propulsion and steering. The two smaller swiveling lift propellers on the top of the superstructure were like a spacecraft's maneuvering thrusters. On this first dive I marveled at the sub's dexterity and ease of operation.

Using the vertical props, Val took us down the last 50 feet to the bottom.

Alvin's landing skid touched down on a mixed surface of pebbles and silt among a few half-buried glacial erratic boulders. The entire Gulf of Maine had been scoured by the glaciers of the last Ice Age, which had dumped a load of massive boulders and a fine flour that now filled the water with a fog as we tried to move forward toward our first sample site on a granitic outcrop a few hundred yards away.

Val maneuvered *Alvin* in a slow arc, scanning ahead with our short-range sonar. After a few minutes, he got a solid echo bearing 50 degrees True. We were on the outcrop of gray crystalline rock only thirty minutes after reaching the bottom.

Now we went to work with the new diamond bit coring device that ARPA had funded. This high-powered miniature mining drill was affixed to *Alvin*'s remote manipulator arm. As Val deftly maneuvered the sub only inches above the smooth, curved surface of the outcrop, Ed Bland leaned over his shoulder to peer ahead, searching for an appropriate fissure where he could anchor the bit to start drilling for a core sample.

But this did not prove an easy task. Because *Alvin*'s ballast was so carefully balanced, when the diamond bit dug into the hard crystalline bedrock, the torque was transmitted back up the manipulator arm causing *Alvin* to pendulum. The greater the swinging motion, the more frequently the drill bit jammed and we'd have to stop.

As Ed worked the controls, the passenger sphere bobbing and swaying, I thought of the space-walking astronauts who had also grappled with the problems of torque management in a near-weightless environment. In fact, NASA used a huge water pool in Houston for the astronauts to perfect the techniques of tool manipulation in space.

At Woods Hole, the sea was our training tank. It took us almost five hours to retrieve two usable core samples. But we did accomplish our mission. It would have taken a geologist on land much less time to retrieve similar samples, of course. But *Alvin* was one of a few research submersibles that could carry a marine geologist down to this outcrop to drill for specimens.

As we rose to the surface, cold and cramped from hours in the sphere, I was satisfied that *Alvin* was every bit as much the surgical research tool that I had envisioned.

Over the next fifteen months, I conducted seven more cruises to the Gulf of Maine, diving in *Alvin* dozens of times to retrieve research samples for my geological survey of the submerged Newark Group and the harder basement rock surrounding it. We managed to retrieve usable samples on almost every dive. This success compared to a 100% failure record for a simultaneous conventional dredging operation we were conducting from *Gosnold* for comparative purposes.

When *Alvin* found its target, it brought back the bacon.

On top of this busy cruise schedule, I had to continue my study marathon in preparation for the series of daylong written general exams administered by the members of my thesis committee. As I'd feared, the classical model diehards made sure I was well versed in the still-sacred dogma of geosynclines. But my friend and mentor Al Uchupi was a little more flexible. When it came time for him to give me his general, the question sheet on the desk of the WHOI office bore a single question: "Describe the history of the earth beneath your feet." Unfortunately, 200 meters beneath the glacial moraine debris underlying Woods Hole lay pre-Cambrian granite dating back 580 million years. It was a long day writing in Al's office.

By early 1972, I was well into writing my doctoral dissertation, "The Behavior of the Gulf of Maine and Adjacent Region During Continental Collision and Subsequent Separation." I was firmly convinced from my research that the complex geological formation of the Newark Group had been created during the 100-million-year-period spanning the late Triassic and early Jurassic when the North American, European, and African crustal plates began to separate, giving birth to the Atlantic Ocean.

My evidence lay in the detailed geologic mapping effort I had conducted in the Gulf of Maine. I'd discovered previously unknown linear rift systems hidden beneath the continental shelf by using traditional seismic profiling techniques. But I was also able to carefully sample selected bedrock outcrops using *Alvin*.

From this extensive database, I was able to create a detailed sequence of events that resulted in the ultimate separation of the continents and the creation of the Atlantic Ocean. In essence, I reconciled classic land geology and its submerged seaward extensions of land formations with the revolutionary new concept of plate tectonics.

Reaching such a conclusion based on analysis of expedition data was one thing. Producing a defensible thesis that incorporated this conclusion was quite another. I now discovered just how "hard" a science geology actually was.

My life at this time was certainly not a *Leave It to Beaver* model of harmony. Todd and our second son, Douglas, born in October 1970, didn't see much of their dad during those exhausting graduate-student years. Neither did Marjorie. I was either at sea, in the Woods Hole library, holed up in my office drafting one laborious paragraph after another in a frustrating attempt to distill field data into comprehensible prose, or earning my keep, drumming up paying customers for Bill Rainnie's Alvin Group.

But as I staggered through this seemingly endless drudgery, I learned that the champions of plate tectonics among the world's pioneering oceanographers also had plans to use deep submersibles as scientific research tools.

In late 1971, K.O. Emery received a letter from Dr. Xavier Le Pichon, a well-regarded French marine geophysicist who had recently graduated from Columbia University's Lamont Geological Laboratory. Le Pichon was a pioneer in plate tectonic theory. Although he was a late convert to deep submersibles, recent dives in the French bathyscaphe *Archimede* had convinced him that a human presence in a submersible on the bottom was a potentially important contribution to the Earth sciences.

Moreover, Le Pichon was now one of the leaders of the French government's *Centre National pour L'Exploitation des Oceans* (CNEXO), the gallic wet NASA. CNEXO was a consolidation of France's various marine research programs. Unlike most American oceanographic institutions, CNEXO's leadership rested in the hands of engineers, not scientists. CNEXO's goal was to exploit as well as to explore the oceans. And improving manned submersible technology was definitely on their agenda.

But the project Xavier Le Pichon described in his letter did not involve mundane upgrades to technology. It was a combination of basic science and adventurous exploration: the submerged geologic survey and mapping of a typical section of the North Atlantic's Mid-Ocean Ridge and its central rift valley.

Le Pichon was asking K.O. Emery if he believed research submersibles could conduct this field-mapping program better than conventional towed-surface seismic and sonar arrays.

"Here, Bob," K.O. Emery said, handing me Le Pichon's letter one afternoon in the winter of 1971. "You're our new expert on mapping with submersibles. You draft the reply."

I dropped everything else and took Le Pichon's expedition prospectus to my small office. Although the English was a little creaky in places, the CNEXO outline was audacious and fascinating. They proposed that the central rift valley of the Mid-Atlantic Ridge was the ideal place to conduct on-site field research into the still theoretical separation of crustal plates through the dynamic process of ocean-floor spreading, which was one of the pillars of plate tectonics.

French geophysicists had already surveyed the Atlantic Mid-Ocean Ridge from the surface. Now CNEXO was proposing that the next round of research on the ridge would be in the realm of field marine geologists. Le Pichon believed that this research should be an international program involving an American deep submersible. At that time, the only well-tested practical research submersible that would be capable of diving on the Mid-Atlantic Ridge was *Alvin*.

However, *Alvin*'s ability to dive to the nearly 9,000-foot depths of the Mid-Atlantic Ridge's central rift valley was not yet proven. In fact, the little sub was still restricted to a 6,000-foot test depth.

But that would soon change.

Over the previous couple of years, a conspiracy among the engineers of the Alvin Group was brewing to make the sub a truly deep submersible. These plans involved replacing *Alvin*'s HY 100 steel pressure sphere with a sphere made of titanium. This metal was just as strong as steel, but 40% lighter. So a slightly thicker titanium pressure sphere that could withstand the pressure of greater depths would not weigh more than *Alvin*'s original steel sphere.

Even before I left the navy, Bill Rainnie's team were maneuvering to acquire a new titanium pressure sphere. But neither Bill's team nor the entire Institution could afford such a sphere. Titanium was relatively rare outside the Soviet Union—where plans were afoot to build a new class of attack sub with a huge titanium pressure hull. But we discovered that the Naval Applied Science Laboratory at the Brooklyn Navy Yard had an ongoing test program for titanium pressure vessels.

They planned to build two titanium pressure spheres similar to *Alvin*'s steel sphere and test them all the way past crush depth in huge hydrostatic chambers. This so-far unapproved plan, tentatively called Project Titanes, would be well funded. To Bill Rainnie's chronically impoverished engineers, destroying two perfectly good titanium spheres in the name of research engineering was a sacrilege.

Bill finally managed to convince both the Woods Hole administration and John Freund in the Naval Ship System Command to set aside one of the spheres for a "long-duration" test aboard *Alvin*. This was bureaucratic legerdemain. Once installed on *Alvin*, the titanium pressure sphere would be anything but a theoretical test object; the sphere would literally become the heart of *Alvin*'s new deep-diving capability, which we all longed for.

Most of the sea bottom—about three quarters of Earth's surface—lay at an average depth of some 12,000 feet. That's where we wanted to go. And we needed a titanium pressure sphere to get there.

One beautiful spring morning in 1968, I was meeting with the Alvin Group's engineers in the shabby trailers that had replaced the team's quaint offices in the Drugstore on Water Street, when we got the news that the navy had approved Project Titanes.

Bill Rainnie consulted a loose-leaf data binder on his cluttered desk. "When the new sphere checks out," he said, "we should get certified down to a test depth of 12,000 feet."

My eye went to the large blue global ocean chart hanging on the trailer wall. It might be several years, I realized, and there were many uncertainties involved in eventually certifying the new sphere, but one day *Alvin* would dive to the deep ocean bottom.

I studied the canyons cutting the continental margin abyssal of the North Atlantic. My gaze rested south of the continental slope below the Grand Banks southeast of Newfoundland. Somewhere in that dark unknown lay the grave of *Titanic*.

In the fall of 1971, the new titanium sphere was still undergoing engineering tests. But most of us in the Alvin Group were confident that the submersible would be ready to dive on the Mid-Atlantic Ridge when and if an international geological expedition actually came about.

It soon became clear to me, however, that K.O. Emery was still preoccupied with his lifelong work on continental shelves and had little interest in the CNEXO project. Then Dr. Jim Heirtzler, the ambitious new chairman of the Institution's Department of Marine Geology and Geophysics, quickly moved in to fill this vacuum. Jim had gone to graduate school with Xavier Le Pichon, and as one of the true believers in plate tectonics, could clearly see the splendid opportunity the French proposal offered.

One morning in December 1971, Jim Heirtzler told me to "find the time" to prepare for a high-level workshop to be organized by the ocean science committee of the National Academy of Sciences, which would be held at Princeton to evaluate the American participation in the international Mid-Atlantic Ridge expedition.

"Okay," I said. "That's great. When is the workshop?"

"On January 24," Jim Heirtzler said. He was lean, with sharp, angular features and looked like a hawk as he glanced up from his desk calendar. "Think you'll be ready?"

"You bet," I replied a little too readily.

That night I dug into my *Alvin* dive logs from the Gulf of Maine, searching for hard data to prove the effectiveness of a manned submersible in such an ambitious expedition.

Suddenly I set down my logbook and swallowed hard. I had one month to prepare a presentation to a dauntingly prestigious gathering of my scientific peers.

And I would be the only one at that Princeton workshop without a Ph.D.

FOUR

I stood in the pit of the Princeton amphitheater, gazing up at the steeply angled banks of seats from where the Gods of Oceanography glared down at me. This was a classic university lecture hall, reminiscent of Oxford or Cambridge. To me the room evoked that Victorian painting by Eakins in which somber medical students fill a surgical amphitheater to observe the famous Dr. D. Hayes Agnew perform an operation.

The difference here, however, was that I felt like the naked patient about to be sliced open, not the surgeon.

It was the second day of the Mid-Atlantic Ridge workshop sponsored by the Ocean Science Committee of the National Academy of Sciences. I had used every bit of the four weeks since Jim Heirtzler had announced the workshop to prepare for my presentation on the role of submersibles in the proposed scientific expedition. But looking into the faces of giants in marine geophysics, such as Maurice Ewing of Lamont, Anton Hales of the University of Texas, and Frank Press of MIT, gave me a bad case of nerves. My mouth was dry and my lips were trembling as I opened my notes and began to read what I hoped was a well-reasoned, persuasive presentation.

As Al Uchupi and K.O. Emery had coached me, I spoke slowly and tried to enunciate clearly, pausing frequently to make eye contact with my audience.

But that was a daunting experience. When I looked into the face of "Doc" Ewing, he scowled back at me, a huge rigid scarecrow of a man, his head sheathed in a mane of white hair. Maurice Ewing was no friend of submersibles. As the powerful, and reportedly ruthless, head of the Lamont-Doherty Geological Observatory at Columbia University, he had already made known his feelings that any research on the Mid-Atlantic Ridge should be controlled by marine geophysicists using proven research technology aboard surface ships, not by ill-disciplined upstarts and daredevils in midget submarines. And when Doc Ewing made his feelings known, the Earth science community worldwide sat up and listened.

As if to bolster this dominant position, Ewing was seated beside an equally renowned geophysicist, Dr. Frank Press of MIT. Press had also laid the groundwork for the invisible intramural struggle that was the true purpose of such symposia by firmly aligning himself in the camp of the traditional geophysicists and against us parvenus from Woods Hole with our jaunty little toy, *Alvin*.

Such renowned geophysicists were interested in Earth's internal structure and depended on measurements of seismic waves, magnetism, and gravity, not on direct observation from submersibles. To them, geologists were lowly technicians, dispatched to retrieve specimens that would verify the literally profound hypotheses the geophysicists constructed.

And here I was, not even a geologist with a Ph.D., deigning to lecture these assembled titans on the scientific need for deep-diving submersibles in the planned multiyear, multimillion-dollar international expedition to the Mid-Atlantic Ridge. This was going to be the one of most expensive and prestigious expeditions of the National Science Foundation's proposed International Decade of Ocean Exploration. And the big-league oceanographers perched above me like rows of vultures naturally assumed they would plan the scope and direction of the expedition's research, and definitely keep a close grip on the budget.

Money, of course, was the key to their opposition to submersibles. Geophysicists had always controlled the funding pipeline on oceanographic expeditions by default: until submersibles such as *Alvin* had appeared, geologists couldn't reach the deep ocean bottom, which had been the domain of the geophysicists' remote sensors. Now I was proposing a new paradigm that might usurp their magnetometers and seismographs. And if manned exploration did become the paradigm for deep ocean research, men like Ewing would have to share their lucrative government grants with mere geologists.

But there was another, more subtle aspect to their opposition. The Mid-Atlantic Ridge expedition would probably provide concrete validation of plate tectonics. Field research might finally prove that the central rift valley in the ocean bottom mountain range cradles the principal fissure from which the North American and African crustal plates diverged and through which new volcanic rock rose from the mantle to weld onto the spreading sea floor. Whoever produced this validating detailed data would be forever associated with a major scientific revolution. Heavyweights such as Ewing were naturally concerned that money spent on *Alvin* would mean projects they considered more important might have to be abandoned.

I worked through a concise description of my geologic field mapping survey of the Gulf of Maine, in which I had proven *Alvin* could be used as a productive research vehicle, provided it followed rigorous surface surveys using the traditional methods of marine geology and geophysics. Although I was the youngest person in this amphitheater, I had more experience field mapping with a submersible than anyone.

"And so," I concluded, "my colleagues and I at Woods Hole are convinced that deep submersibles, when used in conjunction with traditional field research techniques, can make a definite contribution to any international expedition to the Mid-Atlantic Ridge."

No sooner had I closed my notes than the clear, unemotional voice of Dr. Frank Press sounded in the amphitheater.

"Mr. Ballard," he began, taking the opportunity to underline that I lacked a doctorate, "could you please name *one* significant scientific paper in which a submersible has made a contribution?"

I froze, my mouth even drier than before, if that was possible. Everyone in the room knew the answer to Press's question. Several minor biology and geology papers had been published after *Alvin* dives. But my thesis on mapping the submerged Newark Group was still in draft form. There was no other significant scientific literature based on research done in submersibles. Yet the Governing Board of the National Research Council, which had the responsibility to review the recommendations of this symposium, had already stated that only research proposals addressing issues of "national significance" would be considered. Dr. Frank Press had checkmated me on my very first question.

My eyes flashed around the encircling bank of seats. Forty skeptical faces glowered back. "Well, sir . . ." My cheeks burned with embarrassment. If there had been a trap door under the lectern, I'd have bailed out right there.

"Dr. Press," a young animated voice echoed through the amphitheater, "I don't believe that's a fair question for Mr. Ballard."

Bruce Luyendyk, a handsome young geophysicist who had just signed on to the staff of Woods Hole after winning his doctorate at Scripps, stood to face Frank Press. Bruce had done his Ph.D. research using Scripps' Deep-Tow System, a cross between a geophysics and geology unmanned submersible platform that combined magnetometers and side-scan sonar with still and single-frame video photography. He had a respect for both disciplines and unlike many of his colleagues, had a real desire to dive to the sea floor in a submersible himself.

"It's certainly not the fault of the submersibles that they've produced no significant research," Bruce continued, undaunted by the cold glare of his more senior peers. "It's the fault of the scientific community for not being flexible enough to exploit their potential."

I could hear murmurs of assent above the grumbling of the titans.

The next question was an honest inquiry, not a political javelin. Thanks to Bruce's intervention, I managed to survive the question period. His challenge to Frank Press took real courage. This was still the early 1970s, when young scientists of Bruce's and my generation had not yet won tenure at their institutions and high-ranking chairmen and institute directors such as Press and Ewing virtually held the power to make or destroy our careers. But this was also a period of roiling ferment in which brilliant young minds like Bruce's, which were not burdened by the baggage of flawed traditional thinking, were about to make solid contributions to the plate tectonics revolution.

During the catered dinner that night at the university, I found myself seated at the same table as Maurice Ewing.

Ewing was generous with the wine bottle, which followed an equally generous round of cocktails. He and the old-timers had been jovial, ostensibly interested in my work with *Alvin*. But I remained wary and was careful how much I drank. My fears were well founded. Over cups of coffee, Ewing began to zero in for the kill, badgering me to produce a "realistic" estimate of how much a deep submersible expedition to the Mid-Atlantic Ridge would actually cost compared to the "proven methods" he and his colleagues favored.

"Aren't those little subs actually expensive toys?" he asked, a harsh edge to his voice. "What can you possibly do in a submersible that can't be done from the surface or with deep-towed unmanned vehicles?"

Before I could answer, Dr. Fred Spiess from Scripps piled on. "I agree," he said. "They're just too expensive and unproven."

Xavier Le Pichon, representing the French CNEXO group at the symposium, had listened to this onslaught intently. His field research contributions to plate tectonic theory had already elevated him to a position of prestige near that of the older scientists at our table. Xavier had a round youthful face and a slender build that gave him an almost adolescent appearance. But his eyes burned with a fierce intellectual intensity.

Although he was not yet a committed member of the deep submersible camp, Xavier kept an open mind on this subject. He also recognized that the participation of Woods Hole in the proposed expedition might be the element that made the project possible.

"Excuse me, gentlemen," he began with typical formality. "May I make a few points on this matter?" Xavier's English was fluent and lightly accented, and it was his habit to enter every conversation determined to win the rhetorical point.

Now Chuck Drake, a brilliant geophysicist from Dartmouth in his thirties, spoke up for submersibles. As a Lamont graduate, he demanded respect from both Doc Ewing and Frank Press. But Chuck Drake, having dived in the French bathyscaphe *Archimede* in the Puerto Rican Trench, was a convert to deep submersibles. He now told Ewing that deep-diving vehicles were bound to play a critical role in what would probably be known as "the second phase of plate tectonic theory," its actual field verification. Later, I discovered it was Chuck Drake who had convinced Xavier Le Pichon to write K.O. Emery about the potential use of *Alvin*.

I sat back in my chair, sipped my wine, and watched the giants parry and thrust as if I had a good seat at the center court at Wimbledon.

From where I sat, the prosubmersible Young Turks of geophysics won the match.

But old Doc Ewing couldn't resist a parting shot at me. "Ballard, you may get a chance to try with your little submarine," he said gruffly, wagging a thick finger in my face. "But if you fail, we'll melt that submersible down into titanium paper clips."

Despite such threats, the symposium's final report, "Understanding the Mid-Atlantic Ridge: A Comprehensive Program," released later that year, recommended rigorous geological and geophysical surveys be followed up by more detailed investigations "using the capabilities of deep-towed vehicles and submersibles."

With the support of men like Bruce Luyendyk and Xavier Le Pichon, and the powerful patronage of Jim Heirtzler, an influential WHOI department chairman, *Alvin* and I were given the chance to participate in one of the most important scientific expeditions of the century.

On July 4, 1972, the United States and France jointly announced that the French-American Mid-Ocean Undersea Study (FAMOUS) would begin its expedition to the Mid-Atlantic Ridge in 1973. The first season would be mainly traditional surface survey work and photo reconnaissance using deep-towed vehicles. The French navy's bathyscaphe *Archimede* would also make a few reconnaissance dives in 1973. But the bulk of the submersible diving would come in the 1974 season, with *Archimede* supplemented by the small French deep submersible *Cyana* and *Alvin*.

The principal expedition site would be the central rift valley in the Mid-Atlantic Ridge, an area about 60 miles square straddling the 36th parallel north, about 400 miles southwest of the Azores island of São Miguel.

French and American expedition planners chose this site because of its unmistakable conformation as a typical volcanic rift structure, theoretically marking the separation points of the North American and the African crustal plates. Samples of basaltic rock, which earlier surveys had recovered, were thought to be extrusions of magma that were continuing to form the spreading sea floor. Press accounts of the pending expedition spoke grandly of the site as "the edge of creation."

The average depth of the Mid-Atlantic Ridge rift valley

at this site was 9,000 feet, deeper than either *Alvin* or *Cyana* had ever worked.

Now that it was official that Woods Hole would participate in the upcoming FAMOUS expedition, the power struggle to control the program at the institution shifted into high gear. Bill Bryan, a geologist, and Joe Phillips, a geophysicist, were accomplished researchers who had spent years investigating the Mid-Atlantic Ridge to verify plate tectonic theory. They were also skilled at grantsmanship, having already brought substantial NSF funding to Woods Hole. They were the logical choices to lead the Institution's participation.

But bureaucratic politics aren't logical. And Jim Heirtzler, the new chairman of the Department of Geophysics and Geology, was definitely a political animal. Even though he had never dived in a submersible and had little field experience, he recognized the importance of directing a segment of a large, complex project like FAMOUS.

An intramural conflict with Bryan and Phillips on one side and Heirtzler on the other soon erupted. I was still a member of the Alvin Group in the Ocean Engineering Department, a grad student, not a scientist. So I had little voice in supporting Bill and Joe. Heirtzler took his case to the provost, Art Maxwell, another geophysicist, arguing that the multidisciplinary project had to be "overseen" by a department chairman. Maxwell agreed. Within a few weeks, Heirtzler's oversight became strict day-to-day management. This was bureaucratic trench fighting at its worst. As I would see so often in my career, such struggles for authority are a hidden aspect of scientific exploration that the public never witnesses.

When confronted with this power grab, both Bill Bryan and Joe Phillips backed off. They were up for tenure and had families to support. Neither man could afford a knock-down-drag-out battle with Heirtzler. But the struggle did leave bad blood. Bill later got tenure, and Joe did not. Luckily, I was able to watch from the sidelines without jeopardizing my nascent career.

After the smoke cleared, I was still firmly involved in the project. This meant I had to quickly learn a lot about vulcanism and basaltic rock, the key geological elements of the Mid-Atlantic Ridge. So far most of my research had involved the geology of continental shelves, where rocks were white, not black. Once more I had to carry on a massive juggling act, trying to budget time to prepare for Project FAMOUS, earn my keep in the Alvin Group, pass my general exams, and chip away at my thesis. It was a good thing I was twenty-nine years old and had plenty of energy.

Despite this work load, I eagerly accepted the opportunity to join the Woods Hole planning team that went to CNEXO's scientific research facility in the old Breton port of Brest. My previous foreign travel had been limited to Canada and Mexico. Going to France so early in the project was an unexpected bonus.

Even in the rainy gales of late autumn, Brest was a beautiful old port city with crenellated sixteenth-century battlements guarding the ancient harbor. The city had been tastefully rebuilt from the ruins of World War II. Xavier Le Pichon ran a tight little CNEXO empire of scientists and engineers, a sheltered enclave on the European state-sponsored science model, which had no real analogue in the States. The French government met their every need, and there was none of the entrepreneurial hustle that marked life at Woods Hole.

I was immediately impressed by the extreme formality with which Xavier and his colleagues organized their planning sessions. To Americans used to brainstorming and bull sessions over pitchers of beer, with new concepts sketched out on soggy paper napkins, these CNEXO meetings seemed more like UN peace conferences.

Claude Riffaud, the senior CNEXO official, set the tone.

Like many Frenchmen, he was short and wiry with sharply chiseled features. Prematurely bald, he usually had a smoking Gauloises set firmly in the corner of his mouth. There was a tempered resilience to his manner, probably stemming from his years in the French Underground during the war, when matters of life and death were his daily business. Claude was a postwar colleague of Jacques Cousteau and had been involved in the French navy's diving program after the war.

Claude ran his meetings from a tight, fixed agenda, which, while allowing ample exchange of ideas, discouraged casual banter. He always insisted on producing formal minutes and precisely worded reports containing recommendations that we all had formally agreed upon. For some reason, he gave me the job of drafting these meeting reports. I had to work in longhand, but the task was made easier by Jean Francheteau, a CNEXO geophysicist who wrote the French version.

Jean, who would later become one of my closest friends, was an ideal man to work with. He had attended graduate school at Scripps in California, where he had met his American wife, Marta. A handsome bear of a man with a huge head and bushy mustache, he had an easy sense of humor and a habitual smile. But beneath that jovial exterior, he was the most well-rounded scientist on the joint American-French team. I soon discovered he was an excellent field geologist and equally well versed in the arcane details of marine engineering. In fact, Jean had so many subdisciplines that he could carry on in-depth discussions with any member of the expedition.

Given my dual background in deep-submergence technology and Earth sciences, Jean and I worked well together writing the final report of these preliminary planning meetings.

But if the formal daytime meetings were businesslike and dry, the evening social life was decidedly wet. Claude Riffaud loved hosting grand French dinners, which always began with "*les* cocktails" and which included multiple courses accompanied by vintage wine. The desserts were always topped off with strong coffee and Cuban cigars. The French considered America's economic embargo of Castro's Cuba an incomprehensible form of national masochism.

It was Claude who introduced me to Armagnac, the fiery-smooth brandy from Gascony in southwest France. I was so taken by the drink that when I was in Paris after the meetings in Brest I decided to buy a bottle to take back to Cape Cod. Since I was staying in a small hotel on the Left Bank near the Sorbonne, I went into a small wine store on the Boulevard St. Germain.

I was immediately accosted by a severely dressed, rather haughty saleswoman who addressed me in rapid, condescending, and barely comprehensible French.

"*Pourais-je vous offrir quelque chose, Monsieur?*"

I knew she was asking what I wanted. But I was too embarrassed to blurt out anything in that offensive tongue in the exalted presence of this *Parisienne.* I desperately searched the shelves, then spotted the distinctive flat circular shape of the Armagnac bottle.

Pointing, I said, "Armagnac, Madame."

She nodded her approval, took down the bottle, and wrapped it in brown paper. I thrust forth a handful of unfamiliar French francs and she selected one of the larger notes, then gave me a few coins as change.

"*Merci, Monsieur.*"

Walking back to the hotel along the lovely cobbled sidewalks, I went through a quick mental exercise in currency conversion. I froze in my tracks beneath a chestnut tree. *My God, I just spent a hundred and fifty dollars!* Pulling back the neat paper wrapping, I discovered I was the proud owner of a bottle of 1929 Armagnac. No wonder that arrogant sales clerk had deigned to offer her approval of my choice. I was a lowly graduate student scrimping to raise a family on a meager paycheck. A luxury like this was out of the question. But I didn't have it in me to go back to that store and admit my mistake.

When I returned to my new home in the old farming community of Hatchville near Falmouth on Cape Cod, I hid the bottle in a closet and didn't say a word about it to Marjorie.

The next spring, it was Woods Hole's turn to entertain our CNEXO colleagues. I convinced the tightfisted Heirtzler to ante up for a real New England lobster bake. The party was a great success with the French, and I invited all the guests over to my house for after-dinner drinks. When I placed the bottle of vintage Armagnac on the dining room table, the Frenchmen fell silent. Every one of them locked his sonar on that bottle and sidled over to the table to pour a glass. A few minutes later, one of the American wives came into the room.

"I hear you've got some fancy new liqueur."

"Help yourself," I told her, trying not to sound too enthusiastic.

She took a large tumbler, clunked it full of ice cubes, and nearly emptied the bottle. Then she took a tiny sip, grimaced theatrically, and dumped the rest down the sink. "This is awful," was all she said.

A collective gasp cut through the Frenchmen. The woman would have evoked less outrage if she had burned the tricolor before their eyes. To men like Claude Riffaud and his colleagues, certain things were sacred. Vintage Armagnac was one.

For the next several years, every time someone from CNEXO visited Woods Hole, he brought an excellent bottle of Armagnac. I'm still drinking them to this day, although I haven't received a new bottle in years.

In April 1973, I flew to Toulon in the south of France to meet the French navy dive team who would operate the bathyscaphe

Archimede. The bathyscaphe's support ship was a large and comfortable former seaplane tender named the *Marcel le Bihan*, named in honor of a French pilot who had intentionally crashed his plane into a German ship during World War II, "the first kamikaze," according to Claude Riffaud.

The *Archimede* was the biggest deep-diving submersible in the world, displacing over 200 tons. Its personnel sphere was made of 6-inch-thick steel alloy and was meant to operate down to depths of 36,000 feet, the deepest spot in the ocean. But it was a clumsy old submersible, more an elevator than a nimble research vessel like *Alvin* or *Cyana*. And the bathyscaphe was far too heavy to lift, even with the ship's huge seaplane crane, which dominated the superstructure. This meant the *Marcel le Bihan* had to tow *Archimede* to its dive site, a requirement that restricted operations to good weather.

I sailed aboard the *Marcel le Bihan* for two days to familiarize myself with the bathyscaphe in preparation for my planned dive on the Mid-Atlantic Ridge in July. It was my first experience aboard a French ship. Once more the cultural differences were obvious. This was decidedly not a baloney-and-Budweiser ambiance like *Lulu*. When we arrived at the dive site off Toulon, it was a beautiful spring Mediterranean morning. But since it was nearing noon, the ship's captain steamed in a lazy circle while lunch was served, rather than getting down to work.

I joined the officers in the wardroom for a very formal affair with three courses and two kinds of wine. When the captain wanted plates cleared, he pushed a buzzer on the side of the table and silent enlisted crew members entered. A meal like that would have cost a lot ashore in France. And you simply would not have found a meal like that in most American restaurants.

Even though all the officers were very polite and I got along well with the chief bathyscaphe pilot, Lieutenant Commander Gerard de Froberville, I sensed a definite coolness from some of the men who clearly harbored an anti-American prejudice. The Vietnam War had just ended for the United States after ten years of bloody stalemate. During that period, France and America had become estranged, and Charles de Gaulle had withdrawn French forces from the NATO alliance.

But fortunately, after several somewhat tense meals in the wardroom, one of the decidedly cool officers asked me with rigid politesse where I was from. On a hunch, I replied Wichita, Kansas, which I had left for California as a little kid.

"Wichita?" the man asked, obviously fascinated. "The home city of Sheriff Wyatt Earp?"

Wyatt Earp was better known in Dodge City, but I didn't correct him. "Yes," I replied. "In fact, my grandfather was also a sheriff. He was killed in a gunfight."

This was the truth. But my dad's father had hardly been a gunslinger facing desperadoes at the OK Corral. The reality of turn-of-the-century Kansas was a lot less romantic than the cowboy movies.

But you couldn't convince these French navy officers of that. Every evening thereafter they assembled with their coffee cups around me in the wardroom, firing off questions about towns and events in "*le* Far West" that were completely unfamiliar to me. It seemed they had all been raised on a French cowboy hero named Lucky Luke whose exploits had made Kansas famous to every schoolboy in France.

After the revelation of Bob Ballard's cowboy pedigree, my stock in the French navy rose considerably.

On the hot morning of August 5, 1973, I stood on the aft deck of the *Marcel le Bihan*, staring down at the rust-flecked, lemon-yellow superstructure of *Archimede*. It was a cloudless, calm morning on the dive site, 410 miles southwest of the Azores. French navy technicians in swimming trunks and T-shirts worked on the bathyscaphe's narrow deck, preparing for the dive.

I swallowed painfully, my throat almost sealed with a strep infection I'd been fighting for several days. Sometime before dawn, I had woken in my stuffy berth, the sheets soaked with sweat. I'd lain there until morning, shaking with a fever, but I had resisted the temptation to report to sick bay. Doing so would have ruined my chance to be the second scientist and the first American in history to dive on the Mid-Atlantic Ridge.

The day before, Xavier Le Pichon had made the first dive in *Archimede*, piloted by Lieutenant Commander Gerard de Froberville, and accompanied by CNEXO's Jean-Louis Michel, a person who would later play such a critical role during our joint discovery of *Titanic*. Xavier had graciously insisted that I be the second scientist to dive, as befitted the spirit of international cooperation of Project FAMOUS.

But it was hard for me to muster any enthusiasm for this historic occasion. The sun pounded on my head and sliced back from the dazzling face of the slight groundswell surging between the bathyscaphe and the tall topsides of the mother ship. I had to keep reminding myself that the dive would be over by the end of the day and then I could turn myself in to the ship's doctor.

This dive site was well clear of the Azores "hot spot" on the Mid-Atlantic Ridge, an area geologically similar to Iceland and the Hawaiian Islands. Hot spots are a phenomenon of the earth's crust, characterized by plumes of molten magma welling up through "pipes," resulting in excessive volcanism and island building. Some geologists had likened them to blisters in the lithosphere. At that point in plate tectonic theory, no one was sure if those volcanic extrusions were due to weak spots in the crust or intense localized pressure in the mantle.

But the FAMOUS dive sites were far enough away from the Azores hot spot to explore a segment of the Mid-Atlantic

Ridge more characteristic of the total system: a snaking parallel double ridge formation separated by a central rift valley almost as deep and steep as the Grand Canyon. The entire sea floor in this area was fractured by smaller rifts and seismically very active, evidence that the process of crustal plate separation and sea floor spreading was active.

The *Marcel le Bihan* was one of several vessels in the area of the dive site on this hot August morning. The U.S. Navy's research vessel *Mizar*, was somewhere over the southern horizon, with a deep-tow photography apparatus called the Light Behind Camera System (LIBEC). The cooperation of the U.S. Navy in Project FAMOUS was vital. Working for ONR, I had been privy to a series of detailed bathymetric, or undersea topographic, maps based on surveys conducted by the navy using the top-secret SASS Sonar System. The quality of these maps was so good that they often looked like precision land topographic maps based on aerial photography. When I'd first approached the navy to obtain SASS Sonar maps, I was told, "No way, José." That system was part of the navy's burgeoning submarine ballistic missile program and not available for civilian use.

But Joe Phillips from the Woods Hole team had been cultivating a collaborative relationship with a scientist at the Naval Research Laboratory in Washington. Hank Fleming understood the importance of precise bathymetric maps to the overall effort. After several months of secret meetings involving Joe, Hank, and the various naval powers-that-be, the navy agreed to join Project FAMOUS and map the site with its two classified survey ships, the *Bowditch* and *Dutton*. Those vessels had been working the ridge the year before and earlier that summer, and we now had the first "sanitized" but amazingly detailed SASS maps with a promise of more to come.

This was a wonderful break for which Joe Phillips deserved all the credit. It was sad and ironic that the man who made such an important contribution to the success of Project FA-

The French submersible *Cyana* undergoing a series of final repairs aboard its support ship *Le Suroit* before leaving the Azorean port of Ponta Delgado for Project FAMOUS. *Emory Kristof © National Geographic Society*

Artistic rendering of the Mid-Atlantic Ridge rift valley, where Project FAMOUS dives took place. The French submersible *Cyana* can be seen in the foreground exploring Mount Venus, while the bathyscaphe *Archimede* can be seen in the background. *Davis Meltzer*

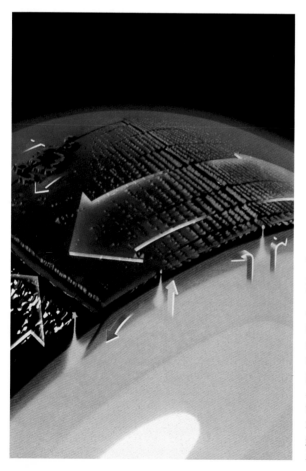

The Mid-Ocean Ridge is formed along the boundary of separating crustal plates, while the major mountain ranges on the Earth's surface are created where plates collide. The San Andreas Fault is the third example of plate motion where plates grind past each other. *Rob Wood*

The French tri-colors flap in the breeze as the *Marcel Le Bihan* sets sail from the Azorean port of Ponta Delgado with *Archimede* under tow.
Robert Ballard

Dr. Xavier Le Pichon peers out of *Archimede*'s sail after completing his historic first dive into the Great Rift Valley. *Robert Ballard*

Jean Francheteau (foreground, right) and other members of the 1973 *Archimede* dive team work on data in the science lab aboard the *Marcel Le Bihan*. *Robert Ballard*

The author climbs aboard *Alvin* as it rests on *Lulu*'s launch cradle while fellow Project FAMOUS divers and pilots look on. *Emory Kristof © National Geographic Society*

A diver inspects *Alvin*'s ascent and descent weights before the submersible floods its ballast tanks and begins to fall toward the Mid-Atlantic Ridge rift valley. *Emory Kristof © National Geographic Society*

A support diver attempts to follow *Alvin* as it begins its free fall toward the ocean floor 8,500 feet below. *Emory Kristof © National Geographic Society*

Alvin's pilot peers through the forward viewport while the author uses the submersible's mechanical arm to recover a rock sample from Mount Pluto during Project FAMOUS.
Robert Ballard

The most common rock found on the surface of the Earth, a "pillow lava," forms when molten lava comes into contact with the freezing bottom waters of the Mid-Atlantic Ridge.
Robert Ballard

Tjeerd H. "Jerry" van Andel and the author share navigator duties aboard *Lulu* during the *Alvin* dive.
Emory Kristof © National Geographic Society

When *Alvin* pilot Jack Donnelly entered a fissure in search of warm spring water, the tiny sub became trapped for more than four hours. *Davis Meltzer*

Size comparison of the three manned vehicles that participated in Project FAMOUS. From top: *Archimede, Alvin, Cyana. Davis Meltzer*

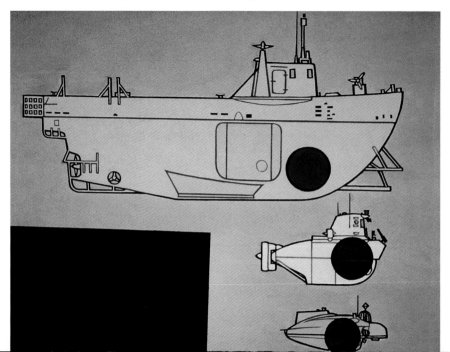

Bill Bryan, Dr. Jim Moore, and the author carefully inspect fresh lava samples collected by *Alvin* on a dive to the rift valley of the Mid-Atlantic Ridge during Project FAMOUS. *Emory Kristof © National Geographic Society*

Self-portrait of *Alvin* resting at 12,000 feet on a small break in slope on the wall of the Cayman Trough. *Emory Kristof © National Geographic Society*

The author's mentor, Dr. K. O. Emery, and chief pilot Larry Shumaker complete pre-dive checks before flooding *Alvin*'s ballast tanks during Cayman Trough dive series in 1976. *Robert Ballard*

A diver inspects the *Angus* camera sled to ensure it is operating properly before lowering it 22,000 feet to the floor of the Cayman Trough, where it will photograph some of the deepest volcanoes in the world. *Emory Kristof © National Geographic Society*

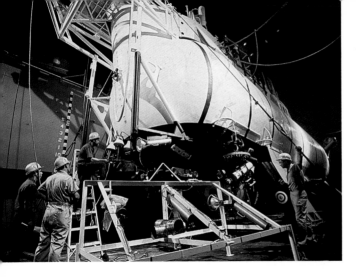

The bathyscaphe *Trieste II* resting inside the drained well of its support ship, the U.S.S. *Point Loma*, prior to its dive series in the Cayman Trough. *Emory Kristof © National Geographic Society*

Trieste II pilot Kurt Newell and co-pilot George Ellis check the bathyscaphe's vital sub-systems after crashing into the side of an undersea volcano 20,000 feet down inside the Cayman Trough. *Robert Ballard*

The author grabs a quick cup of hot chocolate inside *Alvin* during the Cayman Trough dive series. *Robert Ballard*

Dr. K.O. Emery (second from left) in front of the submersible *Alvin* discussing the results of that day's dive in the Cayman Trough with other members of the scientific team. *Emory Kristof* © *National Geographic Society*

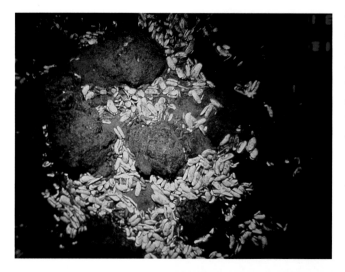

The *Angus*-towed camera sled glides above the first hydrothermal vent discovered in the Galapagos Rift in 1977. *Woods Hole Oceanographic Institution*

Alvin rests on *Lulu*'s launch cradle while scientists prepare the sub for a dive to the Galapagos Rift the next morning. *Emory Kristof* © *National Geographic Society*

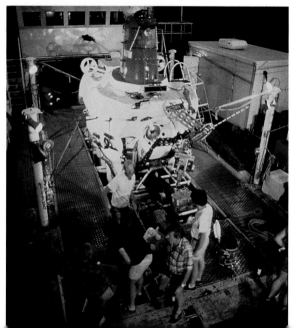

The author talks to the surface during Galapagos Rift dive while pilot Dudley Foster checks instrument panel. *Emory Kristof © National Geographic Society*

A field of giant clams rests on fresh lava flows on the East Pacific Rise at 21 degrees North. *Woods Hole Oceanographic Institution*

Giant clams taken from both the Galapagos Rift and East Pacific Rise at 21 degrees North. *Emory Kristof © National Geographic Society*

Large hydrothermal vents of clams, tube worms, and other exotic creatures, discovered by *Angus* and explored by *Alvin* on the East Pacific Rise. *Woods Hole Oceanographic Institution*

A small purple octopus looking for food moves among shells of mostly dead giant clams in a Galapagos Rift hydrothermal vent. *Robert Ballard*

A cluster of large red-headed tube worms living around the opening of a hydrothermal vent in the Galapagos Rift. *Woods Hole Oceanographic Institution*

The wall of a drained lava lake in the Galapagos Rift reveals numerous "bath-tube" rings, formed as it emptied its molten contents. *Robert Ballard*

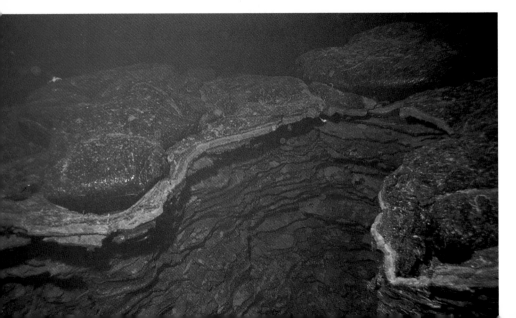

Alvin photographs a lava pillar inside a drained lava lake. *Woods Hole Oceanographic Institution*

The French submersible *Cyana* being hoisted aboard the *Le Suroit* after recovering mineral deposits from the East Pacific Rise in 1978. *Robert Ballard*

An artist's rendering of a "black smoker" being investigated by *Alvin* while *Angus* explores a low temperature vent in the background. *Robert Hynes*

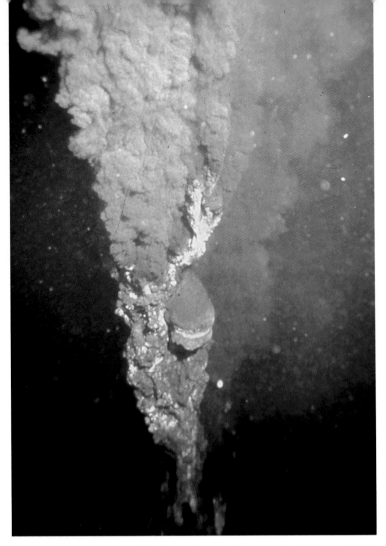

A high-temperature "black smoker" photographed from *Alvin*'s viewport during a dive on the East Pacific Rise. *Robert Ballard*

The author holds a sample of a "black smoker" chimney, revealing its interior crystalline mineral composition. *Emory Kristof © National Geographic Society*

MOUS was denied tenure at Woods Hole. But I learned a great deal from watching Joe's tenure battle unfold. I saw that a person not only had to be highly intelligent, which Joe certainly was, but I was also coming to realize that scientific contributions sometimes did not mean as much in the career of a "scientist" as did skill in bureaucratic trench fighting.

Beyond the navy's contribution, a Scripps research team was out on the ridge with its Deep-Tow System, equipped with a side-scan sonar, temperature sensor, and magnetometer. Other French vessels were working to the north with a narrow-beam sonar system, charting the steep contours of the rift valley. And there was the British research ship *Discovery* farther south, charting small rift systems with a powerful new towed side-scan sonar that went by the acronym GLORIA. Every couple of days, research aircraft passed overhead in long, slow, box patterns conducting aerial magnetic surveys.

This was a major international expedition, and I was right at the heart of it, even though I had not yet won the coveted Ph.D. that officially proclaimed me a professional geologist.

But it was clear that the French were deeply impressed by the scope and quality of the American technology being brought to bear on this scientific undertaking. In fact, Project FAMOUS eventually amounted to what could only be called a massive technology transfer from the United States to France. Although CNEXO had more than its share of brilliant scientists and engineers, France simply did not have an advanced technology military-industrial base comparable to America's.

One vital piece of technology that Woods Hole contributed to the expedition was the acoustic navigation transponder system that the Alvin Group had developed with the ARPA funding we'd finagled soon after I'd joined the team. Skip Marquet, our group's wizard of an engineer, was the mastermind behind this revolutionary navigation system, which I'd help debug diving with *Alvin* in the Gulf of Maine.

Just as land geologists determined the position for specimen sampling using fixed reference points called benchmarks, underwater geologists in submersibles needed similar reliable landmarks. But in the icy black depths of the abyss, we couldn't use a surveyor's transit to take bearings off prominent ridges or the summits of undersea volcanoes. Light was the medium of the atmosphere. Communication undersea depended on sound waves.

The system developed by the Alvin Group was elegantly simple. Acoustic transponders—battery-powered sonar pingers set to precise different frequencies—were deployed in a triangular network several miles wide, floating on anchors 300 meters above the sea bottom. The transponders could both receive and send sonic pulses. The exact timing of these pulses in fractions of milliseconds, when coordinated with signals from a submerged vehicle and a surface ship, enabled us to navigate with precision in the black abyss almost 2 miles below the surface.

In effect, we had developed a system of transportable "lighthouses" that supported the proven traditional navigational technique of triangular bearings.

But there were several problems with this system. First, steep topography such as the near-vertical walls of the rift valley of the Mid-Atlantic Ridge could mask or distort the sonic bearings with false echoes. Then there were our little friends the dolphins, who lived in an eternal world of sound. For them, the transponders were fascinating visitors with whom they attempted to conduct a dialogue. The mockingbirds of the sea, the dolphins were quickly able to reproduce the sonic frequencies of the interrogation pulses. This would have been fun, except the constant response pinging from the transponders often wore down their batteries.

Unfortunately, my raw strep throat and spiking fever did not allow me to enjoy the spectacle of this impressive scientific panoply. All I wanted was to get through the dive and check in to sick bay. I sucked on a bitter lozenge one of the French sailors had given me and watched the launch crew finish the preparations of *Archimede*, which wallowed in the slight swell, 100 meters to starboard. Now it was my turn to jump into the inflatable Zodiac and head over to the bathyscaphe.

Lieutenant Gilbert Harismendy, a cheerful Basque French navy submariner, would be the pilot on today's dive. His CNEXO support engineer, a wiry little guy named Semac, was already down inside the thick-walled personnel sphere, protruding beneath *Archimede*'s bulky metal float filled with aviation gasoline.

"We are almost ready, Bob," Harismendy said, pointing to the the rung ladder inside the bathyscaphe's yellow sail, which led down through the float to the sphere some 20 feet below. His English was thickly accented, difficult to understand with this nagging fever.

I climbed down the narrow access tube, grateful to be out of the sun. As I settled in the cramped personnel sphere, which actually was more confined than the smaller *Alvin*'s, I was again impressed by how cumbersome these hulking bathyscaphes actually were. *Archimede* was, in effect, an undersea balloon, a steel-hulled dirigible that used aviation gasoline rather than helium for buoyancy. Designed by August Picard, the Swiss balloonist, *Archimede* and her sister bathyscaphes had been a practical compromise design that permitted deep-sea exploration before the advent of new materials such as syntactic foam and welded titanium alloy. But I couldn't get over the sense of boarding a steam locomotive after tooling around in a sportscar like *Alvin*.

The personnel compartment was stuffy and quite dark. There was only one small observation port in the 6-inch-thick steel sphere. The crew and observers had to look out through individual binocular eyepieces linked by optics to this tiny single viewport. It was not a very satisfactory system for a geologist who depended on sight to identify features on the sea floor.

Lieutenant Harismendy backed away from our mother ship, then clambered down the long tube to the personnel sphere. He and Semac locked and carefully verified the seal of the hatch. As in *Alvin*, I sat at the aft end of the sphere, trying to stay out of the way. The two crewmen tripped a series of switches, reading from a printed checklist. There was a faint flushing sound aft, and the unpleasant rolling of the surface swell diminished. Harismendy had flooded the main ballast tank. We were on our way to the bottom.

Unlike *Alvin* and other modern submersibles, *Archimede* had a very crude system for controlling its weight-to-buoyancy ratio. To submerge the bathyscaphe, you vented buoyant aviation gasoline, making the vessel heavier than seawater. To rise, or compensate for picking up a rock specimen, the bathyscaphe carried tons of disposable ballast: steel shot stored in three magnetized silos aft of the personnel sphere. On a normal dive, the pilot interrupted the electromagnets to dump ballast upon nearing the bottom. For the ascent, he dumped most of the remaining steel-shot ballast, which permitted the thousands of gallons of aviation gasoline in the bulbous hull to reexert its positive buoyancy. This was a crude but reliable system, which, unfortunately, did not make the huge bathyscaphe very maneuverable in the horizontal plane.

Archimede's second dive was meant to reach a scarp or cliff that the new bathymetric maps had revealed near the center of the rift valley. Xavier, Jean Francheteau, and I had theorized that the steep linear cliffs in this area of the rift valley might be one of the fracture zones marking the area of separation fissures between the African and North American crustal plates. We understood that there was no single, easily discernible split in the sea floor indicating this tectonic feature. Rather, we then believed, the entire rift valley—four miles wide in some places—was a zone of multiple cracks and fissures through which volcanic rock squeezed up in a fascinating variety of shapes to "accrete" or add on to the spreading sea floor.

My job today was to conduct a careful visual observation of these new lava flows, retrieve samples, and document how the sea floor was being rifted apart and transported in opposing directions toward the North American and African crustal plates.

Once below the surface swell, the descent was uneventful, the silence interrupted only by the occasional chirp of an instrument and brief monotone exchanges in incomprehensible French over the acoustic phone linking us to the *Marcel le Bihan*. I sat curled against the cold aft wall of the sphere, keeping my throat swaddled in a turtleneck sweater.

After a ninety-minute descent, our depth sounder pinged loudly as it acquired the rocky bottom. Lieutenant Harismendy braked our descent by revving the downthrusting propeller and dumping a bit of steel ballast. We bumped hard, the sphere twanging dully. Looking out into the floodlit sea through my eyepiece, I saw a swirl of milky sediment. As the murk cleared, I saw we had landed against the side of a long, straight scarp, one of a series that rose steplike along the eastern wall of the central rift.

"On the bottom, Bob," Harismendy announced, more to practice his halting English than to convey obvious information.

Working patiently, he maneuvered the hulking bathyscaphe down the next steplike scarp and brought us to another bouncing stop near a promising pile of glistening black lava extrusions. I was only the second earth scientist to ever see these strange forms, which Xavier had described as "lobate and semicircular" in his preliminary notes from his previous dive. Eventually, the bizarre lava flows of the Mid-Atlantic Ridge's central rift would acquire a variety of exotic names: "toothpaste lava," "haystack lava," and "pillow lava," to cite only a few.

The shape of these extrusions was a function of both invariable and variable factors. The immutable factors were obvious. Lava was hot, 2,200 degrees Fahrenheit. Seawater was cold, just above freezing. And the ambient pressure down here at 9,200 feet equaled almost 300 atmospheres, more than 2 tons per square inch. When the molten lava extruded, its surface instantly solidified into black, obsidianlike glass. In some cases, a hollow elongated pipe was formed that allowed lava to flow in a long hose along the sea floor. Sometimes, pillows the size of a living-room hassock were formed. Under the right conditions these pillows could swell to the size of a barnyard haystack.

All this fascinating new geology was yet to be thoroughly analyzed, however, as I crouched at my binocular view port, trying to pick out a sample of fresh-looking toothpaste lava for *Archimede*'s clumsy mechanical claw. The problem was not simply the crudeness of the tool. The bathyscaphe had so much surface area and mass that inertia kept it pitching and rolling after Harismendy's careful maneuvers with the thrusting propeller. Every time he stabbed at the nearby lava tube with the claw, the big old submersible tilted away.

And our language problems made coordination between me and the crew next to impossible.

In my frustration, I found my fist clenching, as if I could somehow thrust my hand through the thick-walled sphere, out into the devastating pressure, and seize the chunk of black rock with my fingers. Finally, we managed to snag a likely looking chunk. Harismendy worked his controls, the propeller sending up blinding gray clouds of sediment, and we crept toward the next unseen scarp wall.

Then we had a problem.

"*Ah, merde,*" Semac swore softly, pointing to an amp meter on the panel between him and Harismendy.

I saw the sudden unmistakable needle dip. We'd just suffered a serious power outage somewhere in the bathyscaphe's complex electrical system.

Before I could ask what was wrong, I was thrown forward

into Harismendy's back as *Archimede* pitched sharply nose down.

Regaining my position at the rear of the sphere, I saw the blinking ruby digits on the master depth sounder flashing in a wild blur. We were ascending at maximum velocity.

Although I couldn't follow my crewmates' terse exchanges in French, it was obvious the power problem had tripped the electromagnets in the ballast silos and we had just jettisoned several tons of steel shot. The silos were aft of the crew sphere, so we had a serious nose-down trim problem. That wasn't catastrophic, but it made the long climb to the surface uncomfortable. I dug the rubber soles of my boat shoes into nearby instrument racks and hung on.

"Going up, Bob," Harismendy said sheepishly.

The mishap came toward the end of the scheduled dive in any event, so I wasn't really disappointed. Lieutenant Harismendy was about to uncork the half-empty bottle of Beaujolais that we'd sampled with bread and cheese on the descent, when Semac grabbed his arm and muttered something in tense, staccato French. I heard the word *incendie,* fire. Then I smelled the smoke.

Acrid fumes with the unmistakable stench of burning electrical insulation wafted toward me from the instrument racks. Harismendy and Semac lunged toward the control panels, flipping switches to cut unnecessary power from the bathyscaphe's huge batteries. But even as they worked, the stinging smoke billowed around us from an unseen fire.

With my throat already half swollen shut from the strep infection, I hacked and coughed painfully, my eyes dripping.

Jesus, I thought, *this is a hell of a place to burn to death.* We were still a mile beneath the surface in the black, cold grip of the deep-sea pressure. There was nothing we could do to speed up the ascent.

Harismendy gripped the handset of the acoustic phone and spoke in clipped, strained tones to the *Marcel le Bihan.*

Semac killed still more switches, but the choking smoke grew denser. For the moment a flash fire did not seem probable because there wasn't enough oxygen in the sphere to support open flames.

Now Harismendy grabbed his emergency oxygen mask stowed beneath his low pilot's seat. I grabbed mine and, squinting against the blinding fumes, struggled to remember the emergency drill I had practiced only two days before. The emergency breathing system consisted of a full face mask with a tube to the sphere's main oxygen manifold and a chemical scrubber to remove carbon dioxide from the exhaled breath.

I pulled on the mask as I'd been instructed, snugged down the straps, and tried to breathe. I choked again, my throat burning, my eyes almost swollen shut with fumes. Fighting panic, I tried to reason with myself. The first few breaths were bound to be smoky with residual air from the sphere. But when I breathed deeply again, my lungs went into a sudden fiery spasm. I was getting no air, only bitter smoke.

I clawed at the straps, pulling the mask from my face. But Harismendy leaned over, dragging it back down over my nose and mouth. He thought I was panicking. I could feel the blood pooling in my swollen throat, my cheeks hot and taut. I was on the verge of suffocation. Gripping Harismendy's strong hand, I managed to force the mask from the corner of my chin and sucked a mouthful of smoky air. Then Semac joined his partner to reseat the mask firmly on my face.

The dim emergency light grew dimmer. A cold chill ran through my chest, followed by a sudden pulse of heat.

"No," I shouted, shrugging away from both of them to pull the mask off my head. The two Frenchmen gazed at me wide-eyed. My face must have been a deep clotted red. Before they could push my mask back down, I dragged my finger across my throat, the universal symbol that I was not getting air.

Harismendy looked confused, then nodded with brusque understanding. *"Pardon,* Bob," he said, reaching past my shoulder to twist open a small white valve on the oxygen manifold. For several minutes, I had been trying to breathe a mixture of smoke and my own spent breath. No wonder I was red in the face.

"Okay, Bob," Harismendy said, gesturing to my mask. "Now it ees all okay."

Gingerly, my eyes half-closed against the smoke, I slid the mask back across my face and took a shallow breath. I had oxygen. As my mind cleared, I realized that we had missed a vital step in the emergency drill. Harismendy was responsible for opening all our valves on the oxygen manifold, but in the confusion, he had forgotten mine and I had failed to double-check.

The clumsy old bathyscaphe rose inexorably toward the world of sunlight and air. I vowed silently to make damn good and sure that every briefing the French navy gave me in the future would be translated into English.

The sea remained black outside my viewer for a long time. I breathed evenly, savoring the sweet dry oxygen, my throat cooling slowly. Five years earlier, at Cape Canaveral, three Apollo astronauts in training had died horribly when fire swept their spacecraft. Thankfully, submersibles did not use a similar pure oxygen atmosphere. But the bubble of air inside this sphere was just as fragile as that carried by those little diving stream spiders that trespass beneath the surface in search of prey. If their bubble was burst by a twig or pebble in the churning current, they died.

Were we really that much different?

In some ways, Project FAMOUS was almost as audacious as the Apollo program. The Apollo 13 astronauts stranded in their crippled spacecraft en route to the moon had been farther from safety than any submersible crews would ever be. But the threat of the deep undersea only inches from the vulnerable bubbles of surface environment within our pressure spheres was just as deadly and unforgiving as the deadly vacuum of space.

Maybe, I thought ruefully, this near tragedy was simply the

ocean's way of reminding us that we were trespassing in a world humans could never master. But we were determined to try.

The ancient Greeks had a name for such arrogance: hubris.

The winter, spring, and summer of 1974 were the busiest months of my life. At the end of January, I went to the Bahamas with several of my American FAMOUS colleagues to participate in training dives in the mile-deep Atlantic canyon known as the Tongue of the Ocean. This had been one of *Alvin*'s early deep test sites and presented enough geological variety that Bill Bryan and I were able to help coach Drs. Jim Moore of the U.S. Geological Survey and Tjeerd H. "Jerry" van Andel of Oregon State University on the techniques we would use collecting samples and running observational surveys in the central rift valley of the Mid-Atlantic Ridge that summer.

Jim Moore was a volcanologist who had done pioneering fieldwork scuba diving off the big island of Hawaii to observe the interaction of molten lava and shallow seawater. It was he who discovered the formation process of pillow lavas, which initial deep-sea photography had revealed in abundance in the Mid-Atlantic Ridge. Jim was a tall, lanky guy with folksy manners who reminded me of Will Rogers. It was almost comical to see Jim fold himself up like a carpenter's ruler to squeeze into *Alvin*'s pressure sphere.

After my rough initiation into diving on the Mid-Atlantic Ridge aboard *Archimede* the previous year, the Bahama training dives were a piece of cake.

But the rest of the spring and summer was hardly relaxed.

Besides the painstaking drudgery of preparation for that summer's ambitious diving expedition on the ridge, I faced the most challenging hurdle of my academic career: defending my thesis. This ordeal took place in late June, just days before I was scheduled to fly to Lisbon and on to São Miguel in the Azores to join the *Alvin* team.

My thesis defense was held in the same paneled, claustro-phobic room off the library at the University of Rhode Island's lower Narragansett campus, where I had already passed some of my worst hours as a graduate student suffering through my general exams. In the generals, one member of the faculty was notorious for giving students a hard time. Professor Jean-Guy Schilling was a perfectionist and not only demanded profes-sional excellence of himself but also of everyone that he worked with, particularly graduate students. His questions were never easy, and I can remember to this day the one he asked me: "Mr. Ballard, explain the various forms of energy on the planet and their interrelationship, if any." I could have written for a solid month on that subject and still not satisfied him.

I saw Professor Schilling the same way Jason viewed the crashing rocks of the Bosporus: a gauntlet you had to pass through without getting killed.

On the day of my defense, Al Uchupi insisted on taking me to lunch in the White Horse Tavern, one of the oldest taverns in the United States. And he made sure I had exactly two drinks, no more, no less.

"I want you loose in there, Bob," Al said. "And remember, this isn't the generals. Today, you're the expert. You know more about the marine extension of the Newark Group than anybody in that room. Don't forget that."

As always, Al's advice was right on the money.

But I still fought back a silent shudder as I entered that stuffy little conference room and saw Professor Schilling sitting in the back, patiently waiting for his opportunity to test my mettle.

Dr. Froelich, the physicist who was the chairman of my thesis committee, moved the proceedings along at a good pace. Al Uchupi was right. I was the real expert here on the tectonics of the Gulf of Maine.

After a couple of hours of rigorous but reasonable ques-tions, I happened to note that the dip angle of some of the red sedimentary Newark strata never exceeded 15 degrees. Even as I spoke, I realized I had made a mistake. I recalled Al's warning: "In your thesis defense, Bob, never raise data you can't explain." And I couldn't have made the blunder at a more inopportune moment. All the members of my thesis committee had completed their questioning of me; the chairman now turned the questioning over to the other faculty in the examining room. I had just broken that cardinal principle. Professor Schilling now had an opening.

"Mister Ballard," Schilling began in a precisely worded manner, "please use the laws of physics to explain your observation of the dip angle in those sedimentary strata."

My cheeks flushed. A chill gripped my stomach. I did not have a clue. Rather than face Schilling's questioning stare, I spun on my heel and looked at the blackboard, begging for an answer to emerge on the smeared slate. All I could think of was Snell's Law, which states that the angle of incident is equal to the angle of reflection of seismic sounding waves. Seizing the stub of chalk like a life preserver, I wrote a plausible formula.

"The length of my hydrophone array was . . ." My voice sounded tinny in my ears. I had no idea where I was going with my gibberish.

Out of the corner of my eye, I saw the plain, typewritten sheet that held the names of my six thesis committee members. When this defense ended, they would have to sign to endorse the award of my doctorate. Now I was making a complete fool of myself. I pictured breaking the news to Marjorie. Six years of graduate study, of Hamburger Helper and clothes from the Sears catalog were meaningless sacrifice. I was not going to receive the doctorate I had chased for so long.

But as my hand worked through the long equation, the solution—15 degrees—suddenly appeared as if by magic. I spun back to face my examiners, trying to mask my surprise.

Professor Froelich, the examining chairman and a specialist in acoustics, immediately responded. "Perfectly correct. Next question."

I had dodged Schilling's first silver bullet, but I knew there would be time for one last try. It came a few minutes later. Although I don't remember the exact nature of the question, Professor Schilling didn't like the answer and expressed his frustration with my response.

"I don't follow your logic," Schilling snapped. "Let's go back to your supposition."

But Jelle De Boer, a structural geologist on my committee and a specialist on the Newark system and its tectonic history, intervened. "There's nothing wrong with his answer, Dr. Schilling," Dr. De Boer fired back. "His response to your question was from a structural geologist's perspective. I had no problem understanding it."

With that exchange, Professor Froelich declared the examination over and I and all non-thesis-committee-members were asked to leave the room.

Once outside, most of the people who had watched or participated in the proceedings gave me a nod and a smile, then quickly rushed back to their laboratories to get on with their research.

Surprisingly, Professor Schilling remained behind. "Bob, I want to be the first to congratulate you on your defense." He shook my hand and walked away.

I must say, I didn't know how to react. I was angry for all the mental stress he had caused me over the years but knew that I was not the only graduate student in the program to suffer his slings and arrows. Clearly, however, he held no ill feelings toward me. From his perspective, he was simply doing his job. And in many ways he was.

Passing the final tests to attain a doctorate in science is meant to be a difficult challenge. Yet, for the person suffering through those examinations, it is easy to view those penetrating questions as personal. They threaten your very existence; they endanger the dreams you want to reach. Either you pass this test or you don't, and people like Jean-Guy Schilling are there to test you as no friend could possibly do. After I had successfully defended my thesis, I understood why the doctorate qualified you as a professional. Science at the level I wanted to practice demanded true excellence, just as Professor Schilling always insisted. It *was* a profession, not a hobby.

Later, I would learn that passing examinations to become a freshly minted Ph.D. did not end the academic challenges I would have to meet during my long scientific career. They were only the beginning. Winning tenure would prove an even more challenging test. Today was just a warm-up for the future if I ever hoped to reach my final goals.

Before these revelations actually sunk in, the door of the examination room opened and Dr. Froelich ambled out, grinning widely, his hand extended.

I was now Robert D. Ballard, Ph.D., but there was no time to sit back and savor this victory; *Alvin* was leaving for the Mid-Atlantic Ridge.

On the dazzling Monday morning of July 1, 1974—the day after my thirtieth birthday—I clambered across the narrow gangplank over *Lulu*'s slipway, then mounted *Alvin*'s sail to begin our second dive on the Mid-Atlantic Ridge. Volcanologist Jim Moore of the U.S. Geological Survey was right behind me. Our pilot, Jack Donnelly, slipped lithely into the sail, then dropped down beside me. I helped him ease down the pressure hatch and seal it. Chief pilot Val Wilson, dressed in swimming trunks, took his station in the sail to back *Alvin* out of *Lulu*'s slipway.

I felt a rush of eagerness, mellowed by satisfaction. The hectic spring and the ordeal of the thesis defense were behind me. It seemed fitting that I just turned thirty, the official farewell to youth, according to long-haired Aquarians. And the fact that the ratio of scientist to pilot aboard *Alvin* was now two-to-one in favor of science marked a change I'd been urging for years. Like me, the little submersible had come of age as a mature research vehicle.

We were at our principal dive site, a spot on the blue summer North Atlantic near latitude 37 north and the 33rd meridian of west longitude. About 2,800 meters beneath us lay a serpentine mountain range bisected by a wide central rift valley of chaotically jumbled geologic features. Had the almost 9,000 feet of black ocean suddenly become transparent, the fractured volcanic wasteland of the ridge would have looked nearly identical to that part of the Great Rift Valley in Djibouti on the eastern Horn of Africa.

On our first dive the day before, Val Wilson had taken fellow pilot Larry Shumaker and me down to the bottom on a reconnaissance dive. *Alvin* had performed perfectly in the rough terrain of the rift valley. But today would be a long science dive on some of the most fascinating geological features in the world.

Here the sea floor terrain was a classic example of the Mid-Atlantic Ridge. A near-vertical west wall with a sheer thousand-foot drop formed the rampart of the North American crustal plate. West of this snaking cliff face, the expanding sea floor was a jumble of volcanic domes, fracture gullies, and smaller escarpments. To the east of the west wall, the central rift valley was shattered by linear fissures and minor escarpments along a generally northeast-southwest axis. Two conical volcanic prominences, surrounded by lesser volcanic hills, dominated this section of the rift, Mount Venus to the north, and Mount Pluto close-by our dive site. The elevations marking the eastern edge of the rift valley were less sheer in their vertical rise, evidence, some of my colleagues thought, that the African crustal plate was moving away from the plate-margin rift zone at a relatively faster rate than the North American plate.

Photographs from LIBEC, Scripps' Deep-Tow, and from the new Woods Hole's ANGUS (Acoustically Navigated Geological Undersea Surveyor) revealed that the floor of the rift valley was thick with recent lava extrusions. This was strong evidence that the huge crustal plates were in fact moving away from each other and that fresh molten lava from magma chambers in the mantle below was rising to fill the void.

But I found it truly amazing how narrow the zone of fresh volcanic intrusion turned out to be. Here were two giant plates, thousands of miles across, slowly drifting apart, yet the actual zone into which the fresh lava flowed, creating the earth's outer skin, was only a mile or so wide. It was fortunate for the *Alvin* team that the boundary between the North American and African plates was so narrow. On one dive, *Alvin* could drive from one plate to the other, passing across the narrow zone of injection along the central axis of the rift valley. Had the boundary been wider, manned submersibles would not have been the ideal exploratory tool they turned out to be.

"Oxygen on, blower running," Jack Donnelly announced formally to Jim and me. He double-checked the hatch seal, speaking softly as he touched each key component of the stainless steel locking mechanism.

I took position on Jack's left at the portside window. From here I looked up through the warm, blue surface water at the barnacles and rust patches on *Lulu*'s port pontoon.

"*Lulu,*" Jack called on the VHF, "my hatch is closed, leaks and grounds are normal, my tracking pinger and underwater phone are on." He glanced at his instrument panel and punched the radio mike again. "No joy on the bottom sounder."

This burst of jargon assured our surface controller, Dudley Foster, on *Lulu*'s bridge, that we were ready to submerge. Our most powerful sonar echo sounder detected no bottom, which meant there were no submerged obstacles beneath us. The reference to "normal" leaks didn't mean that we had any leaks inside the pressure sphere. That item on Jack's checklist referred to *Alvin*'s battery banks. Like much of *Alvin*'s electrical system, the heavy lead-acid batteries were stored inside large bathtublike Fiberglas containers full of oil. By replacing the air in the containers with oil, the entire system was pressure compensated and was unaffected by hydrostatic pressure as the sub dived to great depths.

Later, when I wrote of this dive in *National Geographic*, Woods Hole director Paul Fye insisted that I change the words to read, "no leaks or grounds." So much for scientific accuracy. But Fye's concern for perceived safety was valid. The previous summer, when I'd almost been suffocated aboard *Archimede*, two other research submersibles had sunk, fortunately with no loss of life.

Fye also had the nagging sphere-penetrator to consider. When we'd installed *Alvin*'s new titanium pressure sphere, the engineers added a number of tapered, threaded penetrators that pierced the pressure hull carrying conduits of electrical wires. Although built on the same safe conical design as those in *Alvin*'s original steel sphere, no one really understood the friction principles that held the titanium penetrators seated and leak-free at great depths. In fact, there had been some "weeping" around the new penetrators in test dives. It was Fye's recurring nightmare that one of these theoretically weak spots in *Alvin*'s new titanium sphere would blow at depth, instantly slicing the occupants into hamburger.

I certainly didn't like to think of this possibility, but you had to trust the engineers. And Skip Marquet assured me that the penetrators were grossly overdesigned. Looking out at *Lulu*'s pontoons disappearing from view as Jack prepared for this dive to the Mid-Atlantic Ridge, I certainly hoped Skip was right.

"Request permission to dive," Jack called.

"Roger, *Alvin*," Dudley replied. "You are clear to dive. Present water depth is eighty-seven hundred feet. Good luck."

Jack flooded the surface ballast tanks, adjusted our trim, and we sank beneath the glistening aquamarine chop. Out of habit, I scrutinized the instrument panels, automatically following Jack's preliminary descent checklist. He was a solid, unflappable pilot who never took safety for granted. At the end of every predive briefing, Jack always concluded, "Should all else fail, here's how you jettison the entire sphere." He would tap the emergency release screw and look us each in the eye. "But please, let's always try to get her home some other way." Emergency jettisoning of the pressure sphere and sail would be the end of *Alvin*.

We were falling at terminal velocity of 100 feet a minute. Quickly the warm blue surface water faded into the familiar indigo. Below 1,000 feet, the last glow of sunlight disappeared. To save power, we didn't run any exterior lights on the descent. As I gazed out the port at the black void, sudden twinkling bursts appeared. We were descending through groups of deep-swimming shrimp and fish possessing bioluminescence. The pressure wave of our passage frightened the creatures, and they rippled with muted neon green-and-yellow sparkles.

"Six thousand feet," Jack announced calmly. We were more than two-thirds of the way to the bottom.

The pressure on the sphere was almost 200 atmospheres, more than a ton per square inch. This would be a good time for a penetrator to fail if it was so inclined.

"*Alvin*, this is *Lulu*," the echoing voice of Dudley Foster sounded in the acoustic phone speaker. "Your present position is X equals five five point six, Y equals one zero zero point four. We suggest you drive a course of one hundred eighty degrees at fifty amps for twenty minutes to close your bottom target. Over."

"This is *Alvin*," Jack replied. "Understand."

Our surface navigator had plotted our position by taking *Alvin*'s pinger and triangulating it within the transponder network floating from anchors on the bottom. Jack swung his joy-stick to turn our stern swivel propeller, bringing us onto a heading due south. He increased prop revolutions to a power setting of 50 amps and noted the time on his clipboard. Jim and I gripped the detailed bathymetric map between us and used a grease pencil on the plastic surface to plot our course. Instead of falling inertly like a clumsy bathyscaphe undersea elevator, we were on a glide slope now, diving like a fighter-bomber on its distant target.

Twenty minutes later, our instrument panel tweaked and chirped with multiple sonar soundings. We were nearing the bottom at a depth of 8,500 feet and the forward short-range sonar had acquired a solid contact. The tiny oscilloscope showed us we were right on the money, approaching the tall, steep west wall of the rift valley, 500 yards ahead.

Jack dropped two descent weights and the sub rose slightly. Jack neutralized buoyancy with the variable ballast system and informed *Lulu* that we had neutral trim and were "driving down."

Five minutes later, our floodlights produce chalky back-scatter of glow from the bottom. The high-frequency echo-sounding altimeter pings with regular contact.

"I have visual," I called from my portside window. The bottom is somber curves and angles of black and gray, lava cliffs, and flows.

Jack eased his descent rate, peering around my shoulder out the port window. "Current less than a quarter knot."

That meant we faced no danger of being banged hard into rough terrain features as I had the year before in *Archimede*.

At 10 feet, Jack got a good view through the clear icy water. "The bottom seems to be a lava flow, sloping steeply to the west," he radioed *Lulu*.

After we received a position fix from our surface navigator, Jack rested *Alvin*'s bottom skid neatly against the steep flow, and Jim and I set to work taking lava samples. Here in the center of the rift, the lava was so recently extruded that it was not coated with the ubiquitous gray manganese deposits that marked bottom rocks farther east and west on the edges of the Ridge. This was firm evidence that tectonic process sea-floor building was still in progress.

Here the lava showed all the typical features we'd seen in the reconnaissance photos: toothpaste cylinders, which were foot-thick twisting black tubes as the name implied; pillow lava, looking like sooty hassocks. "Haystack" formations, 12 feet tall and 30 feet wide, rose like termite hills on the African Veld all the way from the foot of the western cliff to Mount Pluto. And glassy sheets flowed like black toffee where the slope dipped steeply.

Jim was like a kid in a candy store, dictating a nonstop stream of observations into his tape recorder as we worked the remote manipulator arm to snare samples.

We moved to our next planned dive station at the base of the towering west wall. There were talus piles here, mounds of fractured basaltic rock, just as there were at the base of continental mountain cliffs.

It was then that I realized that we were much more like geologists conducting a mountain field survey at night in a helicopter than traditional deep-sea divers. Here, almost 9,000 feet below the surface, the colorful term "the mountains of the sea," which we'd used talking to the press about the ridge, took on reality.

At another station, Jim found collapsed feeder tubes that allowed us to peer down 20 feet into the magma pipe that eventually connected these bottom features to the mantle below.

After a lunch of pepper steak sandwiches that filled the cramped sphere with the pungent aroma of onions and fried green peppers, we proceeded to our next station. Jim and I talked nonstop into our recorders. We used the exterior black-and-white video camera to tape notable features, and the twin-camera stereoscopic system strobed off a picture every ten seconds to produce a near-continuous photographic record of our survey track. This was pretty damned sophisticated geology, a mile-and-a-half under the surface of the Atlantic.

Our first encounter with a dramatically obvious tectonic feature came toward the end of the dive. Crossing the steep scarp that marked the center of the rift valley, Jim and I spotted a fresh narrow fracture running toward the south.

"Look at that fault line," Jim said. "It's clearly linear."

"Roger that," I replied.

The fracture line headed like a plumb cord, straight across the glassy lava flow, splitting individual rock features as if with an invisible cleaver. Such linear surface fissures on this small scale were also seen along California's notorious San Andreas Fault and the fractured lava sheets of the Horn of Africa. The narrow faults outside *Alvin*'s windows were undoubtedly a microcosm of the immeasurably larger tectonic process that was driving the two sections of the Atlantic's basaltic sea floor apart.

As Jack deftly maneuvered the submersible, Jim and I took dozens of pictures of the fault line and dictated rapid field observations into our recorders.

If there was ever any question of *Alvin*'s worth as a precision tool of scientific research, our work today would help settle the issue.

Our team dove with *Alvin* every day we were on the site, only returning to Ponta Delgado for fresh water and supplies. During our second full week on the ridge, I was surface navigator in the control van aboard *Lulu* when Jack Donnelly took my fellow geologists Bill Bryan and Jim Moore down to the bottom of the rift valley to thoroughly investigate a system of linear fissures. They were hoping to find a fracture deep enough to show evidence of hot seawater. The French teams diving to the north had noticed intriguing polychrome mineral deposits on some of the lava formations, possible evidence that water percolated down through fissures to be heated by the magma, then superheated, flowed back up through vents where dissolved minerals were precipitated.

I was grateful for the cramped van's air conditioner on this stifling, calm afternoon out on the Azores high. Keeping close track of the dive plot, my busiest time came when *Alvin* was in transit from one planned survey station to the next. The rough terrain of the ridge played havoc with our acoustic transponder system, sometimes giving us false echoes that produced bad fixes on the plot. As *Alvin* moved, I had to constantly decide which fixes were good and which to reject.

When the submersible stopped at a survey site, I could relax and take a short break, even chat with people around me in the van.

A couple of hours into the dive, I was relaxing during one of these routine sampling stops. Then I noticed that as time passed, the plotting pen marking *Alvin*'s position continued to chatter up and down on the same spot. Slowly a large blob of ink began to grow on the sheet. *Alvin* had been stationary for quite a while. These dives were carefully orchestrated, designed for the scientists to optimize bottom time. Remaining too long in one spot was a waste of resources.

"*Alvin,* this is *Lulu*," I called, trying to nudge Jack Donnelly along. "Are you still at station four? Better get under way. Mission time is running out."

I heard my own ghostly Donald Duck echo reflect from the bottom so far below.

Then Jack Donnelly's voice sounded in the speakers. "We're trying," he said, his voice tight. "We don't seem to be able to rise."

Jack, his voice still edgy, explained that the two geologists had spotted a deep fissure, wide enough for *Alvin* to enter. The submersible had ventured down inside, hoping to find evidence of seawater heating at the bottom. In the icy blackness, the submersible had crept ahead, slightly nose down, the temperature sensor probing the water like a retriever searching for a downed bird. As the two geologists marveled out loud at the size of the tectonic fracture, Jack concentrated on the view straight ahead. No one realized that the upper walls of the fissure, like the inward curling lip of a split tin can, were closing above them.

Then Jack called: "Can you get Val? I need to talk to him."

He was asking for Val Wilson, *Alvin*'s senior pilot. Something was very wrong down there. Jack's voice was flat and calm, consciously purged of emotion. It was the voice you heard from an airline pilot with a crippled plane. I imagined it was the tone *Thresher*'s skipper had used to describe the "minor difficulties" he was experiencing at test depth. But *Alvin* was now almost eight times deeper.

It grew very quiet in the van. Val was beside me at the navigation plot speaking in that same clipped monotone. For the next ninety minutes, Val issued specific instructions, telling Jack to rotate the twin lift props first in one direction, then in another, while simultaneously applying brief forward and astern power to the big swivel prop.

While Val worked with Jack, I called the *Marcel le Bihan* to learn the exact position of the French submersibles that were diving on the rift valley around Mount Venus to the north. During the planning phase of Project FAMOUS, both the French and American diving teams had discussed emergency procedures involving our three submersibles. Our first concern had been to avoid collision with the three subs operating in a relatively small area of extremely rugged terrain. But we had also discussed the remote possibility that one of the submersibles might have to come to the aid of another.

Now it seemed this remote possibility was a lot more probable.

I gripped the radio mike and frowned with frustration, aware that *New York Times* science writer Walter Sullivan was aboard the nearby *Knorr*. Like any good reporter, he monitored the expedition radio net to determine where the interesting action was on any particular day. I had to find some way to alert the French of the emergency without inadvertently leaking the news to Sullivan. If word of *Alvin* stranded on the sea floor almost 2 miles below the surface reached the States, we would be deluged by radio calls from our sponsoring institutions—not to mention frantic media queries—right in the middle of a bona fide life-and-death emergency.

"*Marcel le Bihan,* this is *Lulu.* May I speak to Commander de Froberville," I asked.

After a long pause, Gerard came on the phone. "*Bonjour,* Bob. What can I do for you?"

"How did your dive go, and when do you think you will be ready for your next dive?"

Gerard paused for a long time, and then he realized what I was up to. "We ended the dive early this morning. And it just so happens we will be ready for our next dive very soon. In fact, we were thinking of moving over toward your present location and diving close to your site."

"Great. Stay in touch and I'll call you back shortly with our status."

Gerard now knew we were in trouble and he accelerated his dive preparation just in case we needed him. As soon as he could, he would begin towing *Archimede* over to our position.

Luckily, we didn't need French support that afternoon.

For a long time, Jack Donnelly's voice echoed back from the depths, announcing no progress. In the van, we licked our dry lips, watching the dive clock grind relentlessly ahead. *Alvin* carried life support for three crew members for three days. But if she were truly jammed down in that fissure, there was little we could do, even with the other expedition submersibles, in three days. And the nature of the emergency was such that *Alvin*'s doomsday bailout feature, jettisoning the crew sphere, was in fact the single most disastrous option. Without directional control, the sphere with its attached sail and superstructure might have remained jammed forever in that overhanging fissure.

The only solution was for Jack Donnelly to power his

way out in increments, just as he had powered his way into this trap.

Despite the air conditioning, we were all glistening with rancid sweat, as Val patiently coached his fellow pilot more than 2,000 meters beneath us.

Finally, after more than two hours, Jack Donnelly's voice rose strongly from *Alvin*. "We're clear and under way again and proceeding to our next station." His tone was easy, almost relaxed, as if nothing had happened.

Good to his word, Jack stubbornly completed the main assignments on the remainder of the dive. When *Alvin* arrived back on the surface in the rosy dusk of the Atlantic sunset, Jack Donnelly piloted the little sub skillfully into *Lulu*'s arched slipway, climbed from the sail, and gave a jaunty "A O.K." with his hand to his anxious colleagues on the deck above. *Alvin* was scratched and some of the prominent exterior equipment was dented. On later inspection, we found smashed crumbs of black lava in the cracks between the submersible's superstructure sections, proof of the grim struggle that had unfolded 8,000 feet below.

"That was like backing a Cadillac out of a VW parking space," was all Jack said.

None of us talked about what would have happened if *Alvin* had remained stuck in that narrow parking space on the ocean floor.

Alvin's marathon dive schedule on the Mid-Atlantic Ridge— seventeen dives in twenty-three days out on the site—ended on August 16, 1974. The French finished their dives on the northern zone about the same time. For a week or so longer, the surface vessels continued their work, then rendezvoused back in the crowded little harbor of Ponta Delgado.

The accomplishments of this international expedition to

verify plate tectonic theory were unprecedented. The French had completed twenty-seven dives in both *Archimede* and *Cyana*, thoroughly exploring the great transverse fracture zone north of our site around Mount Pluto. The expedition had taken more than a ton and a half of geologic samples from all the major features. More than 100,000 photographs were waiting to be analyzed. While the submersibles dove, other data rolled relentlessly into the expedition instruments. It would take years, if not a decade, to complete the analysis. This was, after all, the relative Dark Ages before the advent of the powerful personal computer.

But even before this rigorous analysis began, we already had a much more thorough understanding of plate tectonics in action at this "crucible of creation," as the press now called the Mid-Atlantic Ridge. The central rift valley was a seam torn open in the planet's outer skin. The extruding magma formed a long welt—the vast Mid-Ocean Ridge—that snaked around Earth's surface, outlining the seaward edges of the major crustal plates.

Later it would be determined that the African side of the Atlantic sea floor was moving away from the North American plate at a rate of about 1 inch per year. This infinitesimal fraction of the proverbial snail's pace did not seem sufficient at first to account for the gargantuan ballet of continental drift. Then, of course, Earth scientists applied simple multiplication: 260 million inches approximated the present width of the North Atlantic Ocean.

From my perspective, *Alvin*'s brilliant success as a precision research tool on a truly revolutionary scientific expedition was our proudest achievement.

I joined Dudley Foster and the expedition leader, Jim Heirtzler, on *Alvin*'s last dive to the haunting black terrain of the Ridge.

Rising through the dark abyss toward the warmth and light at the end of the dive, our sample tray filled with lava specimens, I knew that old Doc Ewing would definitely never have the satisfaction of running his thick fingers through a pile of shining titanium paper clips.

Part Three

BEING TESTED

FIVE

"*Lulu*, this is *Alvin*," I called, holding the mike of the acoustic phone close to my lips so that my words weren't drowned out by the pinging sonar and chirping instruments that made the submersible's new titanium pressure sphere resound like the inside of a Swiss watch.

"Roger, go ahead," Larry Shumaker's voice echoed back from our tender on the distant sunlit surface of the Caribbean.

I glanced at the depth gauge above Dudley Foster's knit watchcap and punched the mike button again. "We've reached the base of the fault scarp at 3,660 meters. We are now at Sampling Station One."

Leaning closer to the circular portside window, I peered at the somber black outcrop of gabbro 6 feet away. The angle of the rock was too steep to hold the crusty gray-white sediment we knew lay higher on the monstrous terraced scarp staircase. *Alvin* was now at its officially approved test depth, 3,660 meters (12,000 feet), my deepest dive up to this time.

Although we knew *Alvin* was about to be certified by the navy for a safe operational depth of 4,000 meters (13,124 feet), the director of Woods Hole, Paul Fye, had made it quite clear to me that 12,000 feet was our maximum dive limit on this expedition, not one foot deeper.

And it was unlikely I would ever go deeper in *Alvin*, at least not while Fye was in charge of the Institution. Following the near loss of the submersible and its crew in that fissure on the Mid-Atlantic Ridge, Fye had issued strict orders forbidding *Alvin*'s pilots from engaging in such "risky maneuvers." Fye had also insisted that we install a small, aft-facing TV camera on the sail to assist maneuvering in tight places. But we had already begun to face the camera forward because its tiny monitor in the sphere gave us much better definition for scientific work than our regular TV system.

It was January 28, 1976, our first dive on the Cayman Trough, one of the deepest and most spectacular submerged terrains on the planet.

Alvin hung like a gnat on the side of the steeply terraced quarry wall. We were at maximum depth, but only halfway to the bottom of the east wall of this vast submarine trench. The Cayman Trough stretched 1,500 kilometers across the Caribbean from Central America well out into the Atlantic. At its deepest, the trench plunged more than 7 kilometers— 23,000 feet—almost straight down from the hump of Grand Cayman Island to the north of our position. This massive gash in the planet's surface was longer and four times deeper than the Grand Canyon.

The trough was also one of the most dramatic and intriguing examples of plate tectonics on Earth. Geologists believed that it was an unusual type of boundary between two crustal plates—called a "leaky" transform fault—where the plates ground inexorably past each other.

To the north of the trench, the American plate, which carried the continental United States, was moving inexorably west at about 1 centimeter a year. The southern side of the Cayman Trough was formed from the Caribbean plate, which was grinding toward the east. In most such plate boundaries— notably the San Andreas Fault—the fissure is tightly closed. But in the Cayman Trough, there was an unusual zigzag dogleg running perpendicular to the general east-west fault line. This opened a deep chasm between the two plates, which allowed molten lava to "leak" up from magma chambers below and form a steep-sided miniature rift valley in the spreading gap.

The Cayman Trough was a unique window into the earth's

interior. Because crustal plates extended tens of kilometers deep into the lithosphere, this gash in the earth presented the type of gargantuan "road cut" that no geologist could resist exploring. The scarps on either side of the trough were like the sides of layer cakes, which we hoped would reveal the structure and composition of plates all the way down to the upper mantle.

My preliminary research indicated this great tear in Earth's skin might allow us to map and sample an entire profile of crustal plates, research impossible anywhere else on Earth.

I was excited to be finally diving on the trough. And this was my first major expedition as chief scientist, the formal recognition that I had—at thirty years old—virtually come of age professionally.

Jelle De Boer, an energetic and insightful structural geologist from Wesleyan University, was my scientific crewmate today. Jelle had served on my thesis committee, and I wanted to thank him for his strong support over the years by inviting him on this expedition. He was crouched at the starboard porthole staring intently as Dudley maneuvered closer to the gabbroic outcrop to grab a sample with the mechanical arm. You simply did not find this deep-lying gabbro on land, except in rare upthrust areas, where the dark igneous rock was sometimes found in isolated patches.

Dudley craned his neck, trying to peer up the cliff face as high as he could. When climbing such a vertical scarp a pilot's constant fear was a brittle, unseen overhang that might break loose on impact and lodge in the sub's superstructure. If this happened, we would have no way of dumping the additional weight, and even if we jettisoned all our ballast, we might not be able to return to the surface.

"Looks just as sheer as the structures above," Jelle said, his voice ringing with excitement.

He had good reason for emotion. In his first dive in the deep ocean, *Alvin* had taken him down to 12,000 feet and was about to bring him face-to-face with a cross section of a crustal plate scientists had never seen before.

And our network of pinging sonar transponders deployed on the steep slopes of the trough gave us an exact navigational fix. If we eventually recovered samples of so-called Plutonic mantle rock from the trough's west or east scarps, we would have a precise location for the specimens. This was pretty sophisticated science.

I was proud that I had helped set the pattern that worked so well during FAMOUS, in which *Alvin* dove with two scientists and only one pilot. That expedition had helped shift the submersible's original role as an engineering-cum-research vehicle to that of a critical scientific tool. As I had argued at the Princeton seminar, *Alvin* would permit scientists to conduct research in areas previously thought inaccessible to humans. And it was my intention to demonstrate the submersible as this new paradigm during my first assignment as chief scientist on a major expedition.

Alvin's new role as a sophisticated scientific research vehicle was notable in the interior of the pressure sphere: racks of certain redundant engineering instruments and controls had given way to scientific sensors. Avoiding accidents was still a preoccupation, indeed almost an obsession, of Dr. Paul Fye and WHOI's new safety officer, Jim Mavor. Jim was the engineer and marine architect who had earlier made a name for himself as an amateur marine geologist who had equated the legendary Atlantis with the Greek Aegean island of Thera. Mavor had been Fye's field marshal in the Battle of the Penetrators, which many in the Drugstore believed had unreasonably restricted *Alvin*'s depth limit only a few months earlier.

I glanced at Jelle. He was absorbed in Dudley's delicate approach to the rock face and not concerned by the omnipresent danger. We were enveloped by a crushing matrix of black, near-freezing water. Ambient pressure at this depth was 2.5 metric tons—5,500 pounds—per square inch. If one of *Alvin*'s recessed portholes was cracked by an unseen, jagged finger of hard rock, the catastrophic flood would extinguish our lives faster than ants crushed beneath a car tire. If one of the many new penetrators through the pressure hull suddenly failed, a sword of high-pressure seawater would slice us in half. Sometimes on a deep dive, staring at the ring of shining hexagonal nuts felt like gazing into the maw of a loaded cannon.

This danger was not abstract hyperbole. Indeed, the unyielding, mindless danger of the deep marine environment was certainly the strangest aspect of my chosen profession. I was a scientist, but I had also become an explorer and had to accept all the risks and rewards of voyaging into unknown territory. On this expedition, I knew we would make important discoveries about the fundamental nature of crustal plates, maybe obtaining in a few weeks more samples and data than earlier researchers had gathered in years using traditional techniques. But to accomplish this, we had to take terrifying, catastrophic risks every time we dove to these great depths in such rugged terrain.

Yet no one, no matter how dedicated, can function well in a state of abject terror. So, in order to conduct the mundane tasks of science—endlessly logging time and position and calibrating instruments—we had to learn to virtually swallow our fear, to trust in all the stolid, unglamorous legwork of the engineers who had designed and built the submersible, just as astronauts perched on the pinnacle of a Saturn V booster filled with 2,000 tons of explosive fuel, about to blast off for the moon, had to ignore their naked vulnerability and concentrate on the mission at hand.

A battered coffee thermos and nested styrofoam cups were wedged beneath a data drum near my knee. The scraps of our lunch sandwiches were wrapped in a brown paper bag beside the thermos. A Beatles tape sat atop the cassette player, ready for the slow ascent to the world of sunlight. My workplace was decidedly mundane, not heroic.

Then I scanned the ring of shining hexagonal heads of the penetrators' high-pressure sealing nuts around my view port for any hint of moisture.

In *Alvin*'s early days, former taxi mechanic George Broderson had tightened penetrator nuts by slamming his socket wrench handle with an 8-pound sledge hammer. He had then bluffed navy inspectors into believing the nuts had been meticulously torqued to precisely 125 foot-pounds. Who was right— Brodie, with his instinctive, grease-pit mechanic's instinct, or those BuShips bureaucrats filling in all the forms in quadruplicate?

Brodie was *Alvin*'s mother hen; he loved that little sub and the people who dove in her. But the type of demanding navy bureaucrats who would have been outraged at Brodie's deception had also signed off on *Thresher*'s silver-brazed pipe joints.

Trust is a very human emotion. I trusted men like Brodie, Dudley Foster, and my other comrades on the *Alvin* team. In many ways, we were more like crewmates exploring uncharted seas in an ancient wooden vessel than we were professional colleagues, in the modern sense of the term.

We were startled by a sudden flare of warm color in the stark black-and-white view outside the portholes. A pastel pink octopod more than a meter long glided silently past *Alvin*'s nose. The creature was compressed into a torpedolike cylinder, its eight legs gripped into a streamline sheath.

"He flies with his ears!" Dudley exclaimed, pointing at the octopod's bizarre elongated body.

Indeed, the animal had two translucent pinkish fins, looking almost identical to the ears of a farmyard pig, which it used for propulsion.

None of us had ever seen anything like this creature. I fired off a burst of strobe-flash color photographs. In the glare, the octopod spun and suddenly extended its arms.

"Wow," Dudley said. "When he opens up, he looks like a big umbrella."

Jelle De Boer was gazing at this rare specimen like a kid on his first visit to the zoo.

In fact, when we sent the photographs of this pink-"eared" octopod to Smithsonian biologist Clyde Roper, he wrote back: "Fantastic! Phenomenal photos of the deep-sea octopod!"

He told us that it was a cirrate octopod and that our specimen was the largest ever photographed alive.

"Let's catch one!" he urged.

I promised him I'd keep my eye out for this strange creature in the future.

Dudley now completed his infinitely cautious approach to the outcrop and had skillfully trimmed *Alvin* so that we remained stock still, only inches from the gleaming blue-black hump of manganese-encrusted igneous rock.

Jelle constantly scanned the instrument panel, then gazed back out the view port. He was checking the sub's gyrocompass, trying to determine the direction of "strike" of the multiple fault planes cutting through the massive outcrop in front of us. From this pattern of fault planes, he could determine the overall stress field affecting the entire region, in much the same way as a forensic pathologist can determine the type of blow by the fracture lines in a victim's skull. Jelle was a great field geologist, and I was really pleased to see that after only a few hours in the sub he was feeling perfectly at home on *Alvin*.

"Gotcha," Dudley whispered. Using the insect claw of the mechanical arm, he finally managed to pry a piece of black rock out of a small joint running along the face of the fault scarp.

"*Lulu*, this is *Alvin*," I called again. "Moving up the scarp to Station Two."

As we ascended 2,000 feet to our next specimen collection

site higher up the east wall, Jelle poured himself some steaming coffee to ease the chill. He balanced the foam cup while dictating terse field notes into his minicassette recorder.

"This is kind of a neat way to do science," Jelle said, grinning broadly.

Jelle's comment was very satisfying. I had invited a broad range of scientists, both veterans and newcomers, to participate in the Cayman Trough project. The old-timers included Al Uchupi, K.O. Emery, and Jerry van Andel. Besides Jelle De Boer, the newcomers were Jeff Fox of the State University of New York at Albany, Ray Wright, a Jamaican geologist, and Jack Corliss of Oregon State University.

I'd met Jack only seven weeks earlier at the American Geophysical Union's annual meeting in San Francisco where the Woods Hole team was presenting papers on FAMOUS. He was one of the Young Turks of plate tectonics and seemed fascinated with the possible use of *Alvin* to investigate the rapidly spreading sea floor in the Galapagos Rift of the South Pacific. Jack Corliss was the type of scientist who marches to his own band, not just a different drummer. He buttonholed me on the way to the podium at the San Francisco hotel and jawboned for five minutes about the need for *Alvin* in the Pacific. The fact that there was a roomful of other scientists waiting to hear the paper I was about to deliver seemed lost on Jack. He kept talking even as I wedged past him to place my notes on the podium. To me, his obvious passion for knowledge—when compared to some academic bureaucrats—was refreshing. Before the day was out, I'd invited him to dive with me on the Cayman Trough.

Assembling this eclectic research team was my way of paying homage to my mentors while encouraging open-minded younger Earth scientists to take advantage of *Alvin*'s expanding potential as a research vehicle.

When we finally surfaced at the end of our first day's long dive on the Cayman Trough east wall, I saw in Jelle De Boer's rapturous expression that my first leadership test was starting well.

Four days later, I dove with Jerry van Andel, with Jack Donnelly as our pilot. This was our last traverse of the trough's east wall before we shifted attention across the rift valley to the western scarp. Our first four dives at *Alvin*'s new test depth of 3,660 meters had been uneventful. We had gotten over our initial nervousness at working on such steep terrain so deep beneath the surface.

As we set to work collecting samples, it occurred to me that we'd become accustomed to this spectacular terrain in record time. I suppressed the thought that we might actually have become slightly complacent, a dangerous lapse in the deep ocean.

Working this section of the scarp was like climbing a giant staircase. The steps themselves were shallow slopes of whitish brown sediment pouring down the immense wall. And the risers were near-vertical outcrops of black rock, so colored by the sediment-free encrustations of manganese.

At our second specimen station, Jack Donnelly moved us smartly into the base of a large partially fractured igneous rock hoping to retrieve a sample of manageable size.

"Easier said than done," Jack said, a comment he often made on a geology traverse.

We had a crowbar gripped in the claw of the mechanical arm. Jack had jammed it into a crack and was using all his considerable dexterity to maneuver *Alvin*'s mass back and forth, prying the crowbar against the unyielding igneous rock.

For the next fifty-five minutes, we wrestled to retrieve the specimen. Three times the crowbar shifted abruptly as Jack applied maximum amps to the whirring maneuver propellers, slamming the little sub against the rock face with a resounding crunch of Fiberglas and the terrifying twang of metal on hard crystalline stone. Of course Jack knew the scarp around us was free of sharp protrusions. But the force of the collisions made my mouth go dry each time we crunched.

Finally, Jack dropped a football-sized chunk of gray-black stone into specimen bin number three.

"Let's head up for the next one," he said, tweaking his maneuvering joystick.

For all the excitement in his voice, Jack could have been a miner loading coal.

But as we climbed up the rock outcrop, our floodlights spreading a cone of dazzling glare, my throat went tight, and the flesh on my neck tingled.

With my face pressed to the cold Plexiglas view port, I realized the "solid" outcrop we had been working on was not part of the cliff face.

"Take a look at that," I said, my voice sounding tinny in my ears.

"Yeah," was all the emotion Jack Donnelly acknowledged. "I see what you mean."

We had been wrestling with the base of a giant blackish gray boulder. From this new perspective, we could see immense skid marks gouged through the sediment above this massive slab.

As I peered closer, I saw dull white crabs feeding in the skid marks like birds searching for worms in a freshly tilled field. The boulder, hundreds of times *Alvin*'s weight and mass, was precariously balanced on the edge of a ledge, as if just waiting to fall. What would have happened to our fragile little machine and its crew if the boulder had slipped loose and careened downslope while we were picking at its base like a blind, hapless mole sniffing at the bait of a crude but effective Iroquois deadfall trap?

My earlier transient apprehension about the dangers of complacency while working in the deep ocean returned with a rush. We completed the rest of that traverse by the book and by the numbers.

From the beginning, I realized that the Cayman Trough expedition would be much more of a hybrid of purely scientific research, "exploration" (in the popular sense of the word), and technology demonstration than my previous projects. This was due to the chronic problem of patronage, the need to patch together funding and technical support from an eclectic variety of sources.

And on this, my first major assignment as an expedition leader, I had managed to assemble an unusual mix of sponsors.

Because the data from this expedition would be carefully scrutinized, I was determined to produce both high quality and large volume, knowing full well that many of the Earth science establishment still viewed the use of submersibles as a gimmick, despite the success of Project FAMOUS.

Detailed bathymetric maps were the key to bringing back precise geologic data and rock samples from the huge dark canyon of the Cayman Trough. The navy's SASS sonar system had been an invaluable tool on the Mid-Atlantic Ridge. But the sonar was still classified "Secret," and access to naval research ships equipped with the sonar was next to impossible. Fortunately, I'd made friends in the shadowy world of advanced naval research and was able to convince the navy to survey the Cayman Trough with their ship *Bowditch*.

Bill Rainnie had always accused me of being a used car salesman manqué, and I guess he would have appreciated my success with the *Bowditch*. Not only was I able to join the survey expedition—the navy even provided a film crew to document how well this ultraclassified vessel and its sonar system performed.

I'd planned the Cayman Trough research based on three

principal geologic research tools—beyond the splendid wind-fall of the navy's precise bathymetric maps. In this first phase, *Alvin* would document and sample the exposed layers of the fault scarp walls down to its new maximum depth of 12,000 feet. Simultaneously, I'd use the greatly improved deep-towed camera system ANGUS to explore and photograph the floor of the rift valley. Finally, during the summer of 1977, we'd use the navy's bathyscaphe *Trieste II* to dive down to a section of the rift floor that lay 20,000 feet deep and retrieve samples of fresh volcanic flows that had been reconnoitered and photo-graphed by ANGUS.

In order to fund this ambitious project beyond the rela-tively basic grant from the National Science Foundation, I solicited support from *National Geographic*. After an appar-ently convincing dog-and-pony show, the magazine's editors agreed to do an article on the expedition and also shoulder the expense of providing a miniature color film laboratory installed aboard *Knorr*, in which we would process the still pictures taken by ANGUS.

This was the popular exploration aspect of the expedition. Such "entertainment" might have raised some collective gray eyebrows among the titans of academic marine geology. But I had to face a different world than they'd known as young scientists. By the mid-1970s, science had indeed acquired attri-butes of mass entertainment: the Apollo program, if nothing else, guaranteed that cultural phenomenon. And I saw no irrec-oncilable conflict between good science and a popular article in *National Geographic*.

Finally, I reserved a spot on the diving team for Walter Sullivan, the *New York Times* science reporter who had written so well about FAMOUS but had been unable to dive on the Mid-Atlantic Ridge. I knew he was aching to dive in *Alvin*, and I also realized having a friend on the *Times* was a tactically astute move. Like any institution head, Paul Fye liked good publicity.

*   *   *

As the first weeks of the expedition unfolded, a productive but exhausting work pattern developed. *Alvin* dove during the day and was hauled aboard *Lulu* each night for battery charge and maintenance. While *Alvin* rested aboard her tender, I rode a Zodiac over to *Knorr*, where work continued around the clock, alternating between dredging for bottom samples and camera runs with ANGUS. We towed the unmanned camera sled on long traverses back and forth across the rugged Cayman Trough each night, taking hundreds of color photographs of the terrain below.

ANGUS had evolved in complexity and potential since the camera sled's present incarnation had been welded together by an Azorean mechanic on the dock at Ponta Delgado during FAMOUS. And operating ANGUS at its full potential in this deep trench required a whole new set of skills.

Unfortunately, our first photo traverses with ANGUS took place before the *Bowditch* was able to map the trough and construct our finely detailed base maps. So we had only a rough idea where the central axis of the rift lay where we would find fresh lava flows.

We controlled ANGUS from *Knorr*'s spacious main lab at the stern of the ship. The scene in the lab during those early sweeps was often tense. None of us had ever towed a delicate remote sensor such as ANGUS so deep, among such rough, uncharted submarine terrain before. Even with the ship moving at less than 2 knots across the surface, the delay in response due to the 20,000-foot winch cable connecting ANGUS and *Knorr* meant that the camera sled could be hung up on an unseen outcrop and ripped away before we could respond.

I remember one late-night watch when it seemed we were about to lose ANGUS with its expensive new cameras in what would have been a financially devastating blow. Cathy Offinger was at the navigator's console, a reassuring female presence on this cruise, who diffused the inherent male rivalry of the team, making our group feel more like a family than a football team on which everyone was competing for a varsity letter. With a degree in English literature from Skidmore, she brought a wider, more humanistic perspective to our team of overly specialized scientists and nuts-and-bolts technicians. Cathy's thick mane of rich red hair bent patiently over the scroll of the navigation-track log made me confident that we knew *Knorr*'s exact position. My confidence was also bolstered by Earl Young, seated quietly at the ANGUS flyer's console. Calm to the point of unflappability, Earl gazed at his altimeter readings, his eyes seemingly unblinking behind wire-framed glasses, for hours while the sled was deployed. He was like a brain surgeon employing delicate probes, cold and precise.

The first sign of trouble that night was the dull shudder sounding through the hull as we shifted from one sweep track to the next. I was handling the controls connected directly to *Knorr*'s side thrusters, which allowed me to maneuver the big vessel independently of the bridge and engine room. But with each new traverse, the ship seemed to wallow longer before settling on track.

Knorr's captain, Emerson Hiller, entered the main lab, and I gratefully relinquished thruster control to him.

"She's blowing," he muttered, wiping salt spray from his face.

Indeed, in the next half hour, the wind peaked past 25 knots and kicked up a short, nasty sea. We were flying ANGUS only 4.5 meters from the bottom in order to keep the big color still cameras in focus. As the ship began to pitch on our next southerly track, Al Uchupi approached me in the lab. "With this wind and the seas building," he whispered confidentially, "we could lose the vehicle down there."

He was right, of course. But I didn't think we had yet reached a critical point. If I called a halt now and this weather proved to be a brief dry squall, typical of the winter Caribbean, we'd waste hours winching ANGUS back to the surface and lowering her again. Time on an expedition site was our most precious commodity. Every day, every hour at sea cost more than months and days of mundane research ashore.

"Let's keep on this track for a while," I ordered.

The ship began to roll and snap through the mounting sea, the bow and stern rising 3, even 4 meters with each passing wave crest. You didn't have to be a wizard in geometry to understand this motion was transmitted down the long cable.

Earl Young fought the roller coaster as best he could with quick, precise movements of the winch handle.

Suddenly, Captain Hiller broke his silence. "We've got a problem."

I followed his gaze to the cable-tension gauge above Earl's station. The tension on the 4 miles of thick steel cable was soaring toward 15,000 pounds. Maximum work load was 20,000; catastrophic break could occur anytime above that load.

"She's hung up!" Hiller shouted.

"Back her down," I yelled to Earl. "Dump cable fast."

The tension gauge climbed inexorably toward 20,000 pounds.

Now I've done it, I thought. On my first expedition, I made a bad judgment call and lost some of our most valuable instruments. Without ANGUS providing reconnaissance below *Alvin*'s diving limit, this phase of the project could have been rightfully categorized as more adventure than science by potential critics.

Captain Hiller worked on the directional thrusters expertly, stalling the ship, then slowly moving it backward. ANGUS was most likely hung up on a vertical scarp wall, and Captain Hiller hoped to pop it loose as Earl slowly took in cable.

The cable tension gauge peaked dangerously high; then the needle dropped.

"She's free," Earl Young said, his voice still calm.

I sighed, as much from apprehension as relief. "Let's bring her up," I said wearily, "and see how much damage we've done."

An hour later, the ANGUS's dripping white tubular framework was lashed to the stern. In the floodlights, the dents and gouges were all too evident. But the rugged welded steel cage had protected the delicate cameras and instruments.

Then my colleague, Bill Bryan, leaned forward to extract a fractured hunk of basaltic rock from the tubular framework. ANGUS had not only survived her collision in the Cayman Trough rift valley, it had brought us back a beautiful specimen of recently extruded lava. Bill handled the chunk with respect. "Watch out," he warned, as others reached for more chunks. "These fresh glass surfaces are razor sharp."

The next day, someone in the ANGUS crew scrawled this graffito on the side of the rugged camera sled: "Takes a licking but keeps on clicking."

The difficulty of balancing the scientific and exploration–public relations aspects of the expedition came to a head when we tried to get a good color photograph of *Alvin* working at its maximum diving depth of 12,000 feet. Emory Kristof of *National Geographic*—one of our key patrons—was determined to photograph the submersible at test depth.

The idea was to carry a camera and strobe in *Alvin*'s forward science tray, land the sub on a ledge of the steep scarp, offload the camera and strobe, then trigger the camera with a flash of our own strobe. That sounded simple. We waited until some of our last dives on the western scarp, then I took Emory down with me, Dudley Foster once again the pilot.

The descent was uneventful. But when the fault scarp came into view, we saw we were approaching a very nasty, near-vertical slope of black basalt that offered only one small ledge. Dudley worked with all his considerable skill, pumping ballast and fluttering the small thruster props to edge *Alvin* onto the ledge. But there wasn't room for the entire sub, so we rested *Alvin*'s chin on the narrow bench and set to work with the mechanical arm to offload the heavy battery-operated camera in its pressure-compensated Fiberglas box.

No sooner had Dudley gently positioned the camera and released the mechanical claw than the sub began to rise. Dudley was torn between pumping ballast to stop our slight up-angle and working fast to position the big strobe next to the camera. Even working fast, however, *Alvin* began to drift off the scarp face before Dudley could complete his task.

"Watch it, Dud," I warned.

Dudley swore under his breath and flipped the thruster joystick, trying to nose us back down. But the cable between the camera and strobe went taut, pulled the strobe off the tray, and both strobe and camera tumbled off the ledge and out of sight down the vertical cliff.

Dudley struggled to regain trim, then used our floodlights to scan the slope below. We could just make out the dull gleam of the camera equipment lying on another tiny ledge a hundred or so feet beneath us.

"Well," I said, "we'll have to go down and set it up again."

Dudley looked troubled, then pointed to the depth gauge. We were at exactly 3,660 meters. "I'm sorry," Dudley said. "The camera is below our maximum depth limit."

I saw his predicament. Dr. Fye and Jim Mavor were certain to carefully review our dive logs, especially since I was on my first expedition as chief scientist. But would an extra 100 feet— all in the good cause of such favorable publicity—make that much difference?

"Let's just get the damn thing," I urged Dudley.

He was in charge of the sub, not me. "Okay," he finally relented.

Half an hour later we had our picture, the first photograph

of a submersible working in the deep-sea environment. That ghostly color image of *Alvin,* swathed in the chalky glare of disturbed sediments, its projecting mechanical arms and thrusters like the limbs of a robotic insect, eventually became one of *National Geographic*'s most recognized photographs.

On my last dive on the steep west scarp, I worked with Jeff Fox, the marine geologist from Albany. Larry Shumaker, *Alvin*'s new chief pilot, took the sub right up to a sheer dark wall, again at our maximum depth of 12,000 feet. He probed the black surface with the mechanical claw.

"These rocks are softer than the others," Larry said. "Their outer surface seems flaky."

We watched for a telltale chalky underlayer that would signify manganese-coated sediment. But the dark color of this softer rock remained consistent.

"What is it, Jeff?" I asked.

Jeff Fox's face was right up to the starboard viewport, gazing with unusual intensity. "I don't know," he answered after a long while. "We'll have to wait until we get a sample back on the surface."

Even before Brodie and his recovery crew had *Alvin* lashed down to *Lulu*'s rough plank deck, Jeff Fox had recovered our samples from the specimen tray and was examining the mysterious soft-surfaced rock with an eyepiece.

"Tremendous!" he exclaimed, holding up the chunk of dark stone. "That's altered peridotite and dunite."

Jeff's voice was ringing with excitement. The deeply tanned deck crew, wrestling with *Alvin*'s tie-down lines, looked quizzical but didn't understand the significance of our find.

But I did. Descending the scarp wall to 3,600 meters, *Alvin* had passed right through the surface layers of the crustal plate and had actually entered the upper mantle, as proven by Jeff's sample of distinctive igneous rock.

I stood in the fading Caribbean sunlight, watching frigate birds soar and wheel above the coppery surface of the sea. In just a few weeks, our team had helped advance the verification of plate tectonics—the mysterious thermodynamic engine that continues to shape our planet—a major step. Our original hypothesis that the rugged topography of the Cayman Trough opened a unique window on Earth's interior had proven correct. For a young scientist stretching his professional legs for the first time, this was a victory worth savoring.

My second encounter with the Cayman Trough in June 1977 was much different from the first, near-flawless dive series in *Alvin.*

As planned, the navy provided its hulking, unwieldy bathyscaphe *Trieste II,* together with her big escort ship, the USS Point Loma. I flew down from Boston to Panama City at the Pacific end of the canal to join the *Point Loma* at the U.S. naval base at Rodman, just across the Bridge of the Americas. The events of that trip should have served to warn me that this last phase of the Cayman Trough expedition was probably ill-fated.

After almost fourteen hours in the air, I climbed wearily off the jetliner at the international airport east of Panama City and staggered through the steamy tropical night to find a taxi for the long ride to Rodman.

As I was handing my duffel bags up the *Point Loma*'s gangway, I was suddenly stricken by a terrible realization. I had left the highly detailed—and extremely sensitive—SASS sonar bathymetric maps, still in their thick cardboard tubes, in the overhead storage bins of the Eastern Airlines Boeing.

While the chief of the watch on the ship stared dumbstruck, I dumped my bags, whistled for the Panamanian taxi driver who was backing his big old Chevy off the dock, and sped back 21 miles to the airport. It was after midnight and I risked an international incident by bullying my way past the Panamanian National Guard sentries armed with M-14s to sneak back onto the parked airliner. My maps were still there. An hour later, I was drinking Coke in the *Point Loma* wardroom, wishing the U.S. Navy didn't run dry ships.

The first two dives in *Trieste II* were interesting but reasonably uneventful, once you got used to the idea of dropping to 20,000-foot depths in the unwieldy massive bathyscaphe. *Trieste II*, obsolete as she was, did fulfill our minimum requirements. Using detailed ANGUS photography and the precise SASS maps, we were able to retrieve samples of freshly extruded lava from the trough's central rift.

But on the last dive, the jinx that had almost snuffed out my life aboard *Archimede* came back with a vengeance.

This final *Trieste II* dive began with a wet Zodiac ride out to the wallowing bathyscaphe from Point Loma. My crewmates were Lieutenant Commander Kurt Newell and his copilot, Chief Petty Officer George Ellis. Although both Commander Newell and Chief Ellis had spent much of their professional life in nuclear submarines, they had made only a few dives in the *Trieste II*. Moreover, they had never taken their bulbous "elevator" into such rugged and dangerous countryside. And today's dive would test their skills to the limit.

We climbed down the long, echoing tower tube to the pressure sphere and prepared to submerge. It was a hot Caribbean morning, and I took a last glimpse at the sunlit sky, as if hoarding a cache of bright warmth against the sixteen hours of cold dark that lay ahead.

After Kurt Newell received formal permission to dive, he twisted a small valve wheel, venting 50 gallons of aviation gasoline from the bathyscaphe's bloated steel flotation hull. We were on our way to the bottom of the Cayman Trough, 20,000 feet below. The gentle rocking of the bathyscaphe in the rolling Caribbean swells gave way to the familiar motionless silence. Like *Archimede*, this bathyscaphe had only one tiny view port. The crewmen monitored the sea around them by video camera.

On the long fall to the bottom, I managed to curl up and sleep for at least two hours, having already seen the spectacle of descent from the sunlit surface to the black abyss dozens of times before.

I awoke three hours and forty minutes into the descent, chatted with Kurt and George, and lent a hand calibrating a few instruments. After a sandwich lunch, we set to work preparing for bottom contact, allowing us ample time for any instrument or equipment glitches. I knew that our allotted two hours on the bottom would go quickly, and I hoped we'd be able to photograph the fresh lava flows that ANGUS had discovered the year before.

Five hours and ten minutes into the descent, the first faint trace of a bottom contour began to appear on our echo sounder. As George Ellis read out the depth—"altitude"—I slipped down between him and Kurt and craned my neck to peer through the tiny oval view port. Kurt had all the floodlights lit now, and all I could see in the glare was slowly falling organic sediment, the ubiquitous marine snow, that drifted down from the distant surface, appearing for all the world like thick flakes in the headlights of a car during a winter storm.

After several minutes, I was almost mesmerized by these tiny particles and the drone of George's altitude readouts.

"Five hundred feet," he intoned like a priest in some arcane ritual. "Four hundred feet . . . three hundred . . . coming down, plenty of room. . . ."

For all its massive bulk, the bathyscaphe was most vulnerable as it plunged toward the bottom at terminal velocity of 100 feet per minute. Kurt Newell had to time his ballast release maneuver precisely so that we slowed in time to prevent hard impact, which might damage our thin-sided gasoline buoyancy tanks. But if he lightened our load too quickly, we'd have to waste our limited battery power on the props, thrusting down to the bottom, instead of driving horizontally across the lava surface.

Staring out the view port, I strained for any trace of solid substance.

"Two hundred feet," George called.

Suddenly, I saw the unmistakable dark angle of a steeply sloped and rocky contour.

"Bottom!" I shouted. "I see bottom. It's coming up fast."

"That's impossible," Kurt yelled back. "The echo sounder reads one hundred and fifty feet."

"I don't care what it says," I said, my voice strained as I twisted my neck to make sure my words were understood. "I see the bottom."

To his credit, Kurt Newell did not argue. Instead, he lunged for the ballast-release timers and gave all three a vicious twist, dumping several tons of steel shot in a mini-avalanche. This would slow our descent, but the massive bathyscaphe had tons of built-up momentum.

Seconds later, the rounded bow of the vessel crashed into the steep rock face I had glimpsed from the view port. We were careening down the side of a steep volcanic cone. Now I understood our predicament: since the bathyscaphe hull was over 70 feet long, the echo sounder mounted on our stern had detected the side of the volcanic slope much farther down. Now our bow was crashing into the cone's steep upper contour.

I sucked in my breath involuntarily as I watched the gray steel snout of the ballast hull gouging through the chunky lava flow, sending up sooty billows of pulverized basalt. It looked like a locomotive's cowcatcher grinding inexorably through a concrete wall. The crash was more stately than violent. But I watched horror-stricken as a thick steel girder in the bow bent like a paper clip.

Suddenly I saw a shimmering curtain of tiny rainbow bubbles rise past my view port. "I see gasoline in the water," I called out, trying to overcome my runaway emotions.

Gasoline meant the flotation tanks had ruptured with the violent collision. The lifeblood of the bathyscaphe was pouring out in a possibly near-fatal hemorrhage. If we lost our flotation, we would never reach the surface. Never again. Without flotation we were dead. No rescue vessel on Earth could reach us.

Kurt and George scurried to dump the remaining ballast, an emergency jettison maneuver they had never before needed to perform.

No one spoke a word. There was nothing to be said. We each stared at the blinking, dull ruby digits of the metric ascent-rate display. This had become the monitor of our ultimate fate. If the bathyscaphe had enough positive buoyancy remaining in its leaking gasoline flotation tanks, the vessel would continue to rise toward the surface at a rate of about 100 feet, or 30 meters, per minute.

And in the first heart-thudding, timeless period after our emergency ballast release, the blinking red digits did seem reassuringly consistent: 30, 30, 30, 29, 29, 30. . . .

But the instrument wasn't perfectly calibrated, and it sometimes took as long as half an hour to register a decrease in ascent rate of a few meters, which could well have been a fatal trend signaling an irreversible loss of buoyancy.

At some point in that interminable silent limbo, the digital display began to flutter chaotically: 31, 29, 30, 28, 27, 31 . . . 30.

It was hardly reassuring. I closed my eyes and breathed in the slightly medicinal, chemically scrubbed air, then gazed again at the winking red heartbeat of the ascent gauge: 29, 29, 28 . . . 31, 30. . . .

This was the old glass half-full, glass half-empty dilemma. With a vengeance.

Kurt and George were stoic submariners. They knew the ultimate fate that awaited us if the ascent slowed, then reversed to the final plunge. Unlike *Thresher*'s brave crew, whose lives were mercifully extinguished in that final blast of black heat as the sub imploded, we would die the slow sleep of carbon dioxide poisoning, once our spent breaths overpowered the life-support system.

Hours later, punchy from too much adrenaline, I felt the familiar rocking surge as the bathyscaphe's conning tower broke the surface and the old steel hull responded to the thrust of cresting waves.

We were back from the bottom. I clenched my jaw with wild impatience, waiting for the access tube to be pumped so that we could unseal the hatch.

Finally, I clambered up the dripping ladder and stood at the top of the conning tower, sucking deep lungfuls of cool sea air.

Never, I vowed, gripping the chill, rust-flecked edge of the tower, will I *ever* dive in a bathyscaphe again. The *Archimede* had nearly killed me on the Mid-Atlantic Ridge, and today *Trieste II* had almost succeeded where the French submersible failed. There simply had to be a better way for humans to explore the deep ocean than in these clumsy old dinosaurs.

The sun was below the western horizon, and Venus rode in the lavender sky like an airplane's landing light, casting an eerie shimmer across the dark swell.

The simple act of breathing had never been so luxurious.

SIX

Knorr cut slowly through the calm night, her wake a curl of sparkling phosphorescence. Overhead, the equatorial sky was thick with stars.

It was February 15, 1977, our first night on the Galapagos Rift. Nine thousand feet below, the camera sled ANGUS glided through the icy darkness, just 4 meters above the lifeless terrain of recently extruded lava that dominated this boundary between two great, diverging crustal plates. Every ten seconds, the strobes flashed and the sled's camera snapped another picture. At the end of this twelve-hour run, we would have three thousand overlapping images, a detailed record of the bottom.

We were 650 miles southwest of Panama, about 200 miles north of the Galapagos Islands, where Charles Darwin had experienced his pivotal insights on the nature of evolution over a century before.

The Galapagos Rift was a much faster-spreading center than the Mid-Atlantic Ridge, where we conducted Project FAMOUS. To the north of the rift, the Cocos Plate was pulling away from the Nazca Plate at a speed of 6 centimeters a year, more than twice as fast as the North American and African plates on the Atlantic sea floor. As the plates dragged apart, molten magma rose to fill the rapidly widening gap, creating a jumbled terrain of pillow lava and volcanic mounds, cut by angular stress fissures.

Towing ANGUS, we held *Knorr*'s speed below 2 knots. With no breeze, the deck was sweltering. But the spacious main lab was pleasantly cool, thanks to the ship's powerful central air-conditioning system. I was grateful for the comfortable conditions because flying the camera sled on these long watches was hard enough without having to also contend with equatorial heat and humidity.

A Bach fugue had replaced Hank Williams on the stereo. I glanced around the lab, making sure everything was under control before stretching my legs on deck. Earl Young had just relieved Al Driscoll on the flyer's station, and Cathy Offinger was holding down the navigator's position, where she could monitor both *Knorr*'s and ANGUS's coordinates, which appeared as neon green dots on the screen of the new HP-2116 computer, the most advanced piece of technology on this cruise. Captain Hiller was in my chair, controlling the vessel's track with the cycloidal thrusters.

Just as I reached for the heavy steel hatch leading to the fantail, Scripps graduate student Kathy Crane pointed to the paper scroll on which the relatively crude telemetry from ANGUS was registered in parallel ink traces.

"Looks like a temperature anomaly," Kathy said. She tapped the scroll with a pencil eraser, noting that the bottom line of the acoustically transmitted data from the sensitive thermistor mounted on ANGUS was showing a sudden jump in temperature from the prevailing 2.5 degrees Celsius typical of these depths. Kathy's thesis was on the Galapagos Rift, and her experience on the previous year's Deep-Tow expedition out here was proving invaluable.

I turned from the hatch and approached the stacked instrument displays. The scroll transient that Kathy had noted was lasting unusually long. We were used to such glitches, given the relatively primitive telemetry system, which relied on often garbled acoustic signals, rather than a more dependable hardwire connection. But that was one of the redeeming features of ANGUS, which my team had begun calling "the dope on the rope." Our camera sled was a rugged cage of welded steel tubes protecting a simple instrument package consisting of an echo-sounder altimeter, navigational pinger, the camera and strobes, and a basic electronic control system not much more complicated than a quartz watch. The addition of the thermistor for this expedition represented a quantum jump in complexity for ANGUS. Indeed, the camera sled was crude compared to some of the overly sophisticated and equally vulnerable instrument-laden towed vehicles, such as Deep Tow, used by geophysicists of the Scripps Institution of Oceanography.

But the unusual temperature data registering on the telemetry scroll was lasting much too long for a simple telemetry garble.

"Son of a gun," I muttered. "I think we actually *are* getting a temperature anomaly on our first ANGUS run."

I could see Kathy Crane thought so, too, but she was wary of saying so out loud for fear of jinxing our apparent good luck.

"Let's make sure to log all this, gang," Cathy Offinger reminded us. At times of excitement, she was always a cool head.

Kathy Crane leaned over the scroll. "Anomaly begins at exactly nineteen-oh-nine," she said, ticking the edge of the moving paper with a felt pen.

At that moment, Dr. Richard von Herzen of Woods Hole and Jack Corliss of Oregon State came into the main lab from the forward hatch. More than any other scientists out here, Dick, Jack, and Jerry van Andel were the moving forces behind the Galapagos Hydrothermal Expedition.

This ambitious endeavor had begun when I returned to Woods Hole from Project FAMOUS and gave a presentation on the expedition to my colleagues at the Department of Geology and Geophysics. Dick von Herzen had expressed special interest in the photographs we'd taken of the open fissures cutting across the floor of the rift valley in the Mid-Atlantic Ridge. These distinctive gaping cracks or "gjars" were found across the newly extruded lava of the valley floor but disappeared a short distance away from the central axis as they were slowly filled with sediment.

Dick von Herzen was a specialist in heat flow who spent his professional life sailing the world's oceans, dropping heat probes to the bottom to measure the amount of thermal energy flowing up from deep inside the earth. Over the years, he had evolved a systematic model of heat flow from the molten core up through the mantle, through the crustal plates and sedimentary rocks of the ocean floor.

He was especially intrigued by the midocean ridges, which, we now understood, were sculpted by heat. Unlike mountain ranges on land that were thrust up by pressure, the MidOcean Ridge that spanned the planet marking the separation zones of crustal plates was a geologic feature literally swollen by heat energy. Its underlying rock was newly formed from molten magma and retained its heat for a considerable period.

The eventual heat loss, we were coming to realize, took place while the oceanic crust moved away from the central axis of the ridge in both directions. The ridge itself was a thermal welt—like a raised burn scar—on Earth's face, which eventually subsided to form the lower, outer flanks of the ridge system, and finally came to rest at the abyssal depths of the ocean basin floor. What intrigued Dick von Herzen was that the shape of this topography seemed to beautifully fit the theoretical cooling curve of the ocean crust.

Xavier Le Pichon and Jean Francheteau from Project FAMOUS had coauthored professional articles that predicted heat-flow measurements on the flanks of midocean ridges around the world would agree with the theoretical predictions from their computer-generated cooling curves.

Then we messed up this theory with our Project FAMOUS data. The predicted cooling curves did fit the flanks of the Mid-Atlantic Ridge system quite nicely, but they were skewed all over the place along the axis of the central rift valley itself.

The temperature measurements on the zone of newly extruded lava sea floor turned out to be much lower than anyone had predicted. This aberration perplexed heat-flow specialists like von Herzen, as well as earlier researchers such as Clive Lister of the University of Washington.

"Some process," von Herzen told us, "is stealing heat from the bottom of the ocean. The question is, what type of process can this be?"

Like all good scientists, Dick von Herzen, Jerry van Andel and their colleagues tried to think of every possible way to explain this incongruity, a process called multiple hypotheses. As soon as you propose one explanation, you try to refute it by data in hopes of zeroing in on the truth. Then you conceive a series of experiments to test the validity of the surviving hypotheses before undertaking actual field research.

The hypothesis they most favored was that some form of hydrothermal circulation was taking place along the axis of the rift valley. This circulation carried cold seawater down inside the fissured crust, where it became superheated around the magma chambers underlying the axis of the rift valley, and then rose back to the surface of the sea floor in the form of hot springs similar to geysers found on land. Like any heat-exchange system, thermal energy was lost or "stolen" in the process.

The fissures we had mapped out in the valley of the Mid-Atlantic Ridge clearly provided a direct channel for seawater to penetrate deep into this newly formed volcanic terrain. But we had not encountered any hot springs while diving on the ridge.

But the Mid-Atlantic Ridge's rift valley was classified as a slow-spreading axis. The North American and African plates were separating at only about 2.5 centimeters, or 1 inch, a year. In the Pacific, especially along the Galapagos Rift and the East Pacific Rise, the plates were separating much faster— between 6 and 18 centimeters a year. This meant considerably more heat was rising to the surface with the greater volume of molten rock, which in turn meant that the magma chambers were replenished more frequently with molten material. All things considered, there was a much greater chance of finding the theoretical hydrothermal circulation on a central axis of the midocean ridge system of the Pacific Ocean than in the slower-spreading segments of the Atlantic and Indian Oceans.

But as we academic scientists all understood, arriving at such an interesting hypothesis was one thing, finding the funding and technical support for a major expedition to prove the hypothesis was another matter altogether.

To their great credit, von Herzen, van Andel, and later Jack Corliss, fought a long and difficult struggle to bring the Galapagos Hydrothermal Expedition to reality. They formed key alliances with John Edmond at MIT and brought Scripps into the program.

After a hard-fought battle, the Woods Hole–Oregon State–Scripps–MIT alliance received funding from the National Science Foundation as part of the ongoing International Decade of Ocean Exploration. What finally convinced our sponsors—or at least what they published in a precruise news release—was the implied promise of discovering the geological mechanisms that might be responsible for rich concentrations of valuable minerals on the ocean floor. It was known, for example, that hydrothermal activity on land often resulted in deposits of precious ore. So, with that questionable El Dorado in mind, the National Science Foundation told the world's press that one purpose of this expedition was to "understand the formation of metal-rich deep-sea sediments" as well as the transfer of heat through Earth's crust.

Von Herzen, Corliss, and van Andel couldn't have given less of a damn about speculative deep-sea silver mines, but if the camouflage of such public relations gimmicks was necessary to help pay for the cruise, so be it.

None of us, however, could have ever guessed that the Galapagos Hydrothermal Expedition, which began as a quest for relatively obscure data by marine geologists and geophysicists, would produce monumental discoveries in biology, just as revolutionary as the Big Bang had been to astronomy and plate tectonics was to Earth sciences.

This historic research began inauspiciously enough. The year before, a team from Scripps had been out here on the Galapagos Rift in their research vessel, *Melville,* the sister ship of *Knorr.* They had surveyed the area with their Deep Tow geophysical vehicle but had unfortunately found only a few elusive temperature anomalies. Deep Tow sonar images and some grainy black-and-white photographs showed "mounds" of what might have been precipitated metal oxides from the hypothetical hydrothermal vents, but overall, the Scripps people recovered only inconclusive evidence of hydrothermal circulation in this moderate-spreading tectonic axis.

Among the sometimes confusing data from the Deep Tow cruise was a photograph of some ghostly white clamshells— and a brown beer bottle—lying near the central axis of the Galapagos Rift. The Scripps team had assumed that this was a garbage midden thrown over by a passing ship and had accordingly named the site "Clambake."

The clams and beer bottles were the farthest things from our minds as we watched the thermistor telemetry scroll on the first night of our ANGUS runs on the rift. After three minutes, the parallel lines on the scroll rejoined, indicating that ANGUS had passed out of the area of the temperature anomaly. Since we were using color film instead of real-time television, we had no way of immediately knowing what the bottom might look like in the area of the temperature anomaly. Instead we had to finish the twelve-hour run, then winch ANGUS back on board to develop the 400-foot roll of film in order to match the photographs with the three-minute temperature spike that began at 7:09 P.M.

Our hope was that we'd see some kind of a fissure or maybe even a conical vent in the generally featureless sea floor of pillow and flow lava that marked the central axis of the low rift valley.

I slept soundly for several hours while the camera sled was hauled back on board and allowed to warm to surface temperature to prevent condensation damage. But I woke in time to be in the photo lab for the final processing of the night's film. After breakfast, Jack Corliss, Dick von Herzen, and my ANGUS team clustered around the lab table as Pete Petrone, our photo technician on loan from *National Geographic,* put the roll of film on our scanning projector and we zeroed in on the twenty frames of color images spanning the three-minute temperature anomaly.

"Clams!" Jack exclaimed.

We gazed at the unmistakable image of large, chalk white clam shells jumbled together in profusion, almost hiding the black mounds of pillow lava on which they had taken hold.

"Hundreds of clams," I added, counting as fast as I could. "And look at the color of the water."

Instead of the limpid clarity normally found on a new deep- ocean lava flow completely devoid of accumulated sediment, the water around these clams was turbid with milky white smears.

This was no garbage dump from a fishing trawler banquet. Those clams were alive, healthy and robust, somehow flourishing in a black, near-freezing desert, as if the stark floor of the Galapagos Rift were no more hostile than a sunny tidal mud flat on Cape Cod.

On scores of dives to abyssal depths, I'd seen the occasional tubelike holothurian, brittle star, and scavenging white crab. But I knew these creatures survived on a fragile predation food chain that ultimately depended on nutrients found in the accumulations of ancient sediment, built up from the ceaseless "snow" of organic matter falling from the sunlit surface layers. Neither I nor any other experienced marine scientist in this lab had ever heard of a thriving colony of bivalves like these clams—relatively complex creatures with demanding metabolisms—existing in the chill, near-sterile depths of these sediment-free volcanic sea-floor rifts. Yet, without question, the hundreds of clams in our pictures formed a robust, living colony, and were not simply several bushels of clamshells dumped off the stern of a passing ship.

"What's going on down there?" Jack Corliss asked, voicing the question we all were thinking.

Luckily, we didn't have to wait long for an answer.

Lulu with *Alvin* on board was steaming toward us from Panama as fast as the little catamaran's engine would push her. Our original research plan called for Jack Corliss, the expedition coordinator, to conduct an ambitious series of dives in *Alvin* aimed at investigating the geology, geophysics, and chemistry of the rift. My role as the expedition's co-chief-scientist with Dick von Herzen, was to guide the diving program with ANGUS reconnaissance and to make sure all our disparate talent and resources were productively used during our precious seven weeks on the rift.

Now, a sudden and unexpected event had completely upset our meticulous schedule.

I went to the radio room and called Jerry van Andel aboard *Lulu* to announce our find.

"Amazing!" Jerry replied over the single sideband channel. Having worked closely with our team on Project FAMOUS, Jerry knew ANGUS and *Alvin* would be sharing the same transponder network, so *Alvin* could be vectored to anything ANGUS had found. "Get us some good coordinates. We'll be at your position by tomorrow afternoon."

Fortunately, we had already laid down precisely positioned transponder nets, so we knew exactly where the mysterious clam bed lay along the rift's central axis. Using the transponders Earl Young had playfully named Sleepy, Dopey, and Bashful, we radioed the coordinates to *Lulu* so that Larry Shumaker and his pilots could begin planning their unscheduled first dive. Once again, we had benefited from an earlier navy SASS sonar survey of this area and were now equipped with detailed bathymetric maps.

At 4:10 on the afternoon of February 16, *Lulu's* captain cut power to her forward propulsion unit as the vessel arrived on station off *Knorr's* port bow. Within minutes, *Lulu's* Boston Whaler was launched and bouncing over the waves toward *Knorr,* where Corliss, his Oregon State colleague Jack Dymond, and John Edmond were eagerly waiting to transfer to the rusty little catamaran tender.

Dive 713, scheduled for the next morning, would be anything but unlucky.

Alvin dove on the mysterious clam bed at 10:00 A.M. Jack Donnelly was pilot, with Jack Corliss and Jerry van Andel as scientists on board.

At the terminal descent rate of 30 meters per minute, it took *Alvin* an hour and a half to reach bottom in 2,550 meters of water. Jack Donnelly displayed his typical skill by arriving on the ripply field of glassy black "pahoe-hoe" lava flows only 270 meters from the calculated coordinates of the clam colony. He drove *Alvin* carefully across the bottom while Corliss closely monitored the digital temperature sensor in the pressure sphere, which was connected to the thin white plastic wand of the sensitive heat probe. This thermistor was calibrated to beep at every thousandth of a degree Celsius increase in temperature.

For fifteen minutes, as the little submersible inched along on a northwest heading, the temperature probe remained silent. The rippled lava field gave way to distinctive humped pillows, all of them glassy and new, devoid of sediment. But then *Alvin* encountered the first small cracks and fissures in the lava sea floor. Simultaneously, the temperature probe's monitor inside the pressure sphere began to beep, and the flashing red digits indicated a relative increase in the ambient water temperature.

"There are the clams," Jerry van Andel called on the acoustic phone.

Alvin had entered a strange 20-meter-wide oasis of life, completely isolated from the surrounding desolation of the lava fields. The white clams were piled in overlapping ranks, their shells ajar, as they drew in and expelled the seawater. As *Alvin* crept onto the mound of the clam colony, Jack Donnelly cautiously probed obvious fissures with the heat sensor. The temperature probe's monitor jumped to a relatively balmy 16 degrees Celsius (or 61 degrees Fahrenheit). In *Alvin*'s powerful floodlights, the milky smears of the strobe-lit ANGUS photographs became shimmering clouds of sky blue, indicative of suspended minerals, notably manganese.

"We're sampling a hydrothermal vent," Jack Corliss announced over the acoustic telephone.

Debra Stakes, an Oregon State graduate student, manned the underwater phone in *Lulu*'s van. The expedition had come out to the Galapagos Rift to find proof of hydrothermal activity, and they'd struck pay dirt. She congratulated her professor on this success on the very first dive.

But Jack Corliss was as much bemused as he was pleased by this discovery. "Debra," he asked, "isn't the deep ocean supposed to be like a desert?"

"Yes," she replied tentatively. Like all the rest of us on this cruise, marine biology was not her forte.

Jack stared out the view port at the living creatures around him on the wrinkled black basaltic mounds of the clam colony. Beside the obvious overlapping ranks of huge white clams— some the size and shape of old-fashioned oval china dinner plates at the corner diner—he saw skittering white crabs, chunky albino lobsters as big as a boxer's fist, and clusters of bizarre flowerlike creatures looking for all the world like overgrown orangish dandelions about to burst with seed. As *Alvin* paused, white crabs clambered onto the sub's specimen tray. This was anything but a lifeless desert.

"Well," Jack Corliss finally called *Lulu,* his voice almost trembling, "there's all these *animals* down here."

The first *Alvin* dive on the rift discovered not one but two hydrothermal vents along the linear mound of the central axis. When *Alvin* returned to the surface, the specimen tray contained five live mussels with chocolate-colored shells, a clam, and several chunks of lava encased with mats of living matter that could have been either colonial microorganisms or coral. Unfortunately, the normally reliable seawater sampler had malfunctioned, and they retrieved only half a liter.

On the next day's dive, Jerry van Andel and his Oregon State colleague, Jack Dymond, were not so lucky. Dudley Foster took them to a likely looking mound near the first clam colonies. But they found no hydrothermal vents or any unusual signs of life. They did discover some bizarre pillarlike structures of basalt streaked with bright smears of purple, green, and yellow, but the ambient sea temperature never rose above 3 degrees Celsius.

On the third dive in as many days, Corliss and MIT chemist John Edmond returned to the first clam colony. The milky blue shimmering clouds were in much greater evidence than they had been earlier. Scores of white crabs clambered over the clam shells, scavenging morsels among the occasional dead bivalve. Today, pilot Jack Donnelly managed to retrieve a full 12 liters of water samples before returning to the surface.

It was after dark by the time the Boston Whaler returned from *Lulu* with the water samples, and most of us were at dinner when John Edmond depressurized the sample flasks to begin his chemical assays. But the overpowering, unmistakable rotten-egg stench of hydrogen sulfide was quickly spread throughout the ship by *Knorr*'s efficient air conditioning. We rushed to the lab but didn't stay long. Even John, used to playing with sulfur-rich volcanic minerals, was having a hard time breathing.

That night we discovered that the water collected around the clam colony contained an incredible amount of dissolved hydrogen sulfide, enough to poison most land creatures.

But obviously Clambake I, as we now called this site, was rich with life. We sat around the dayroom, sipping beers like so many sophomores in over their intellectual heads, speculating on the nature of this discovery. If only there was a qualified biologist among the fifteen-odd Earth scientists out here on the rift.

But as geologists, we recognized that the chemistry of this hydrothermal system had to be complex. Seawater seeping down through fissures in the lava floor toward the magma chambers was heated to the point where its chemical composition was altered drastically. At high temperatures and pressures, the seawater must have lost some of its suspended minerals to the surrounding rock while drawing other mineral compounds. On percolating back toward the sea floor, these sulfates were probably converted to hydrogen sulfide, which precipitated out as the heated water rapidly cooled, and produced the shimmering milky clouds the dive teams had observed and photographed.

"Hydrogen sulfide," Edmond told us, "can be metabolized by certain anaerobic bacteria."

That made sense. Most of us had smelled the unforgettable bad-egg stench of the mud in swamps and bogs. And we all had a vague, high-school biology recollection of paleo-microorganisms that had evolved in the early epochs before the planet's atmosphere contained free molecular oxygen. But was such a primitive food chain somehow functioning around those warm water vents on the floor of the Galapagos Rift?

For answers we turned to the nearest cooperative biologists we could find, Holger Jannasch and Fred Grassle at Woods Hole. I arranged the single-sideband radio equivalent of a conference call the next morning. After Corliss, van Andel, and Jack Edmond carefully described the variety of the creatures and the details of their habitat, we asked Holger and Fred for advice on how to proceed, in effect, trying to compress four years of undergraduate biology fieldwork into one scratchy radio-telephone call.

"First off," Holger advised, "take core samples in a careful grid pattern every couple of meters."

"We'll need to carefully analyze the organic qualities of the mud," Fred added.

The four of us grouped around the big radio console in the *Knorr*'s communications room exchanged quizzical glances.

"There's no mud, Fred," I explained, looking at the color prints from the latest dive.

Jack Corliss took the microphone. "It's all bare lava, I'm afraid, just naked stone."

The speaker hissed with static, then Holger's voice returned. "I don't see how that's possible. There must be some mistake."

But there was no mistake.

Over the next five weeks, we completed twenty-one successful dives on the rift. In the process, we discovered and thoroughly explored four more unique colonies of living creatures in the near-sterile desolation of the deep-sea bottom.

At one site, Clambake II, we found a virtual graveyard: hundreds of empty clamshells, picked clean by scavenging crabs. Significantly, there were no warm-water vents at this once-thriving colony. Some obscure change in the substrata plumbing had shut down the life-giving hydrothermal vent, breaking the unique food chain and dooming the immobile clams to extinction.

As we explored farther down the axis of the rift, we discovered a distinctive feature of these oases. Some were dominated by clams. Another—like the mistakenly named "Oyster Bed"—was the domain of brown-shelled mussels, while the most prevalent large organism at the Dandelion Patch was the hitherto unknown stalklike creature with the bulbous multipetaled head. The colony around the teeming Garden of Eden vent was made up of distinctive rings of dominant animals: first the dandelion creatures, then white crabs, then a ring of white-stalked, red-fleshed worms with shimmering crimson crowns.

Because we had no way of transmitting pictures to biologists ashore, it was up to Earth scientists to venture away from their own field to speculate about the underlying causes of this dominant species pattern.

Tanya Atwater, a geophysicist from MIT, came up with as likely an explanation as any other. "Maybe," she told us one night, as *Knorr* cruised slowly beneath the glittering dome of equatorial stars, "all these animals started out life as free-swimming larvae. Then," she twirled her fingers to mimic falling marine snow, "they drifted down and down until they became lost on the dark ocean bottom. Then they discovered the plumes of hot water, grew up, and reproduced to start the colonies."

Jack Corliss added a variation to this hypothesis, which he called the "Founder Principle." Under this theory, the dominant species at any given hydrothermal vent oasis was the first to drift there in larval form, be it clams, mussels, worms, or the strange orangish pink dandelions, which the biologists had been unable to classify by radio conference.

The more we considered these hypotheses, the more logical they became. Obviously, complex creatures such as clams and mussels did not spontaneously generate from inanimate lava, as in some medieval pseudoscience. And the newly formed sea floor along the rift's central axis had equally obviously never been a coastal shallow that had sunk to these depths by geological subsidence. Still, the complex metabolic linkage we call the food chain operating down there without the benefit of photosynthesis remained mysterious for much of the expedition.

The only common feature to all these vents was the prevalence of rich hydrogen sulfide solution in the water.

This unusual evidence, coupled with our impromptu self-tutorials in biology and a good deal of radio-telephone coaching from Woods Hole biologists, led us toward a startling conclusion: there *was* a hydrogen sulfide–based food chain operating almost 2 miles beneath the surface along the central axis of the Galapagos Rift.

In this "chemosynthesis," which was completely independent of the sunlight-fueled photosynthesis food chain that prevailed elsewhere on the planet, primitive bacteria metabolized the sulfides and were, in turn, eaten by an ascending order of microorganisms that, in their own turn, supported even higher life forms all the way up to the clams and crabs.

Halfway into the cruise, we realized that we had stumbled onto a major scientific discovery. I saw normally staid colleagues actually skipping with pleasure down the ship's corridors to and from the lab. All of us relished the joy of discovery, even of nature's more mundane secrets. But the implications of the bizarre and fragile chemosynthesis oases clustered around those warm-water vents on the Galapagos Rift was anything but mundane.

The fact that this chain of life existed in the black cold of the deep ocean and was utterly independent of sunlight—previously thought to be the font of *all* Earth's life—had startling ramifications. If life could flourish, nurtured by a complex chemical process based on geothermal heat, then life could exist under similar conditions on planets far removed from the nurturing light of our parent star, the Sun.

I could picture conditions similar to those of the Galapagos Rift in sea-floor lava tubes hidden beneath the frozen surface of the Jovian moons.

In effect, we had discovered what amounted to an entire separate branch of evolution down in those dark lava mounds, a virtual new planet for biologists to explore.

One night, drinking a cold beer on the fantail as ANGUS slalomed unseen below, back and forth across the rift, searching for more vents, John Edmond summed up what we all felt.

"You know, Bob," he said, "this is what it must have been like sailing with Columbus."

Taking turns with my colleagues, I was able to dive in *Alvin* to explore these unique chemosynthesis ecosystems twice during this expedition to the Galapagos Rift. Larry Shumaker and Brodie had been working almost around the clock to keep the submersible on line, and we did manage to dive every day for weeks on end, a record *Alvin* never achieved before.

My most vivid memory was the dive with Jack Corliss and Jack Donnelly on March 10, 1977. By now, the pilots knew the terrain of the central rift axis very well. The parallel ridges marking the expanding sea floor were relatively low compared to the awesome terrain of the Mid-Atlantic Ridge or the Cayman Trough. Our thermal vents with their oases of life were strung like beads along the lumpy central spine of alternating pillow and ripply pahoe-hoe lava that marked the extrusion tubes to the magma chamber below. Jack Donnelly, receiving last-minute navigation instructions from *Lulu,* glided us to a landing almost on top of our objective, Clambake I.

"Go one hundred yards farther," Larry Shumaker called on the acoustic phone from *Lulu,* 9,000 feet above, "then hang a right."

"Roger," Jack Donnelly replied, as if he were a taxi driver casually acknowledging orders from his dispatcher.

With our floodlights gleaming on the low mounds of new, sediment-free lava, we drove ahead, only a few feet above the bottom. Then the temperature probe pinged like the impatient timer on a microwave oven, signaling the warmer waters of the Clambake I oasis.

"Here we go," Jack Corliss said, shifting his huge bulk within the confines of the pressure sphere to lean toward the starboard view port. Jack was a very big guy, well over 6 feet tall and weighing close to 240 pounds. Because of his long, sun-bleached hair and Grizzly Adams beard, as well as his penchant for hippie sandals, some of the crewmen had taken to calling him Jesus Christ. Jack was clearly a product of the 1960s, a flower child who would sooner make love than war. Despite his size, Jack was so enthusiastic about diving that he never showed any sign of claustrophobia in *Alvin*'s cramped pressure sphere.

My face was pressed to the portside view port, but I was conscious of the pinging temperature probe monitor. Suddenly, our floodlights revealed a swaying field of orangish pink dandelions, their puffy heads pulsing with fine webs of filaments in response to *Alvin*'s pressure wave. The lumped mounds of pillow lava were thick with jutting chalk white clam shells, some of them a foot in length. In a few isolated clusters, cocoa brown mussels had formed subcolonies. (When we opened the clams on the surface, to our amazement, the flesh inside the shells proved to be a rich, meaty red, like the face of a freshly cut steak.)

Passing over the center of the colony, we saw shimmering clouds of warm water rising from the vents between the pillow mounds.

"It's like being in the middle of fountains," Jack Corliss whispered. He had been down among these vents more than any other scientist on the cruise, but he was still awestruck.

I saw that the shimmer of the rising warm-water plumes was due to more than just suspended minerals. There were roiling clouds of particulate matter rising upward and spiraling down, only to be caught by the rising current and wafted up again.

"Let's get a sample of that flaky stuff," I suggested to Jack Donnelly.

He accommodated my request with deft maneuvers of the vacuum specimen collector mounted on the mechanical arm.

As we rested here in the center of the oasis, I had a close-up view of the irregular margins of the vents themselves. Here the obvious organic material clung in the same thick mats that earlier dives had recovered. In the back of my mind there was a picture of fossilized remnants of such matlike microbial colonies on dry seabed formations in the Australian desert. If I was not mistaken, those calcified bacteria mats were among the earliest fossils in the geologic record. Yet here we were, three billion years later, down on another sea floor, observing thick carpets of what appeared to be the same life form feeding on the caustic chemical soup rich in hydrogen sulfide that wafted up through these vents.

A notion that Jack Corliss had planted in my mind during the descent that morning now returned with the clarity of a revelation. For several years, paleobiologists and planetary scientists such as Carl Sagan had speculated that life on Earth had evolved in warm, shallow seas from complex organic compounds rich in carbon and sulfur, under the catalytic stimulus of intense solar radiation and lightning. Certainly, it was obvious that some form of relentless disruptive energy input was necessary in any hypothetical model in which organic compounds were eventually stimulated through myriad chemical reactions to evolve into self-replicating cellular life.

I gazed at the shimmering, milky billows of dissolved minerals and cascading fragments of microbial colonies that fountained up around our submersible. Was it possible, as

Jack Corliss had boldly suggested, that life might not have been sparked into existence under the relentless sun and lightning bolts of the early planet's surface, but rather had arisen from the endless percolations of superheated seawater carrying rich loads of minerals down through fissures in the deep-sea bottom and back up through hydrothermal vents just like these?

When Jack Corliss first suggested this revolutionary idea, I never would have believed that such an unorthodox concept would eventually gain credence, as it has over subsequent years.

But even while we were still out on the rift, some of the geochemists began making preliminary calculations that supported Jack's leap of imagination.

John Edmond, the unusually loquacious red-bearded Scot from MIT, was intrigued by the sheer volume of hydrothermal circulation that we now believed prevailed all along the 40,000-mile Mid-Ocean Ridge marking the boundaries among the planet's tectonic plates. "Just look at the flow of heated water we're seeing in these vents," John said in his thick brogue. "Why, vents like these must be pushing the entire ocean through them every four or five million years." He went on to speculate in the increasingly arcane jargon of his profession about the chemical transformation that this hitherto unknown mechanism had to have produced over the millions of centuries of geologic time. "Maybe," he said, tugging on his red beard, "if we study the chemistry of this system hard enough, it may finally tell us why the sea is salty."

We laughed at the time, and then realized John was serious; the phenomenon of the sea's salinity was one of those basic unanswered questions that science, out of self-protection, often ignored.

Within a couple of years, Edmond and other scientists had indeed concluded that *all* the water in the planet's oceans circulated through sea-bottom hydrothermal vents on a cycle of approximately ten million years. This complex process would come to account for the amazingly uniform chemistry of seawater worldwide.

By the end of that long dive with Jack Corliss and Jack Donnelly, we had retrieved a generous selection of all the life forms: free-swimming microbes, colonial bacteria mats, clams and mussels, and even a visiting shrimp and rattail fish. The clams we took on this dive were unlike any species we'd seen before (and, in fact, did prove to be a unique species of mollusk). They were huge in comparison to their shallow-water relatives. Their red flesh proved to be unusually rich in hemoglobin, which was probably a survival adaptation for periods of low oxygen content in the water when clouds of dissolved minerals were most abundant.

This bounty was added to the specimens already recovered at the other vent sites. The term "embarrassment of riches" certainly applied to our burgeoning specimen collection. Because this was basically an Earth science and chemistry expedition, we had brought along only one small jar of formaldehyde, almost as an afterthought. We had no preservative solution for these rare creatures, some of them, such as the half-meter long tube worms, very difficult to store. But *Knorr* had laid in a good supply of duty-free liquor passing through the Panama Canal so, much to the chagrin of the cocktail crowd, we sacrificed several cases of good Russian vodka to science. We also ransacked the collection of Tupperware containers meant to preserve delicate crystal and lava samples. Finally, we were reduced to wrapping specimens in Saran Wrap and even raiding the galley for roasting pans and soup tureens.

By the time we got all these unusual creatures home where they could be properly preserved, there was a certain amount of attrition. But we had taken so many specimens that the biologists had a virtual field day.

Among their discoveries was that the gaudy dandelion was actually a new species of siphonophore related to the Portuguese man-of-war jellyfish. But unlike that creature,

which sails the tradewind currents of the world's oceans floating with a gaudy purple gas bag, the dandelion remained seden-
tary, anchored to the bottom by gossamer tendrils, its flower
head an inflated bladder of oily fluid.

We had come to the Galapagos Rift in search of unusual
land forms and complex heat exchanges between the cold sea
and the hot, recently extruded lava. Instead, we discovered
unexpected oases of life—indeed, a unique ecosystem—the
biological equivalent of a new continent.

These discoveries were so important—and our feeble
attempts as Earth scientists at biological field research so inadequate—that the National Science Foundation almost immediately funded a follow-up marine biology expedition to the
Galapagos Rift. In January and February 1979, I joined my
Woods Hole colleague Dr. J. Frederick Grassle, the National
Geographic Society, and a big team of marine biologists from
leading American institutions. The professional biologists went
far beyond our earlier limited quasi-amateur research. My
principal duties on this cruise were to support *Alvin* dives
through extensive ANGUS reconnaissance along the rift.

The biologists discovered that the amount of suspended
nutrient around the vents in the typically 10-to-20-meter radius
oases was three hundred to five hundred times greater than
the level just outside the vent area. They confirmed that the
bright red pigment of the more complex creatures' flesh on the
vents was due to unusually high concentrations of hemoglobin
found in almost no other creatures on the planet. Our amazement at the dinner-plate size of the white clams was justified:
the biology team discovered that gigantism was a prevailing
trait among vent creatures, due primarily to the high concentrations of available nutrient, which was a direct result of the
hydrogen sulfide metabolizing bacteria at the base of this
unique chemosynthesis food chain.

This tendency toward gigantism was revealed in a dramatic flourish when we spotted truly monster variants of the

18-inch white tube worms in a vent field we discovered on our 1979 return trip to the Galapagos Rift that we named the Rose Garden.

When I first saw the tangled thicket of white tube worms with their distinctive ruby snouts protruding in the nutrient-rich water, I literally blinked, confused by the perspective. The worms appeared much too big. Then I realized there was nothing wrong with the perspective. The worms were giants, some of them 12 feet tall, their tubular red crowns at least as long as the entire body of the smaller species we had collected along the rift two years earlier.

When we brought samples of these giants to the surface, the biologists were enthralled. Finding these tube worms was like winning the lottery for the expedition scientists. I was amazed to learn that the creatures had no close relatives and actually represented an entirely new phylum, which lacked eyes, mouth, even a digestive tract, as the term is normally used. The worms absorbed food and oxygen from the water through hundreds of thousands of near-microscopic tentacles lining the flaps on their crimson flanges, which we had mistaken for more advanced gills. Yet these worms were sexually differentiated and broadcast eggs and sperm into the water, an adaptation which meant that they had probably evolved over millions of years to match the conditions of hydrothermal vents on the world's midocean ridges.

Several juveniles had cemented themselves to the plastic-like tubes of the monster adults. And close examination revealed an entire new species of filter-feeding limpet that had also taken hold on the huge tube worm's shell. To a geologist like me, the finding of this limpet was hardly monumental, but to Fred Grassle, Holger Jannasch, and their cohorts, this seemingly insignificant little creature was a major find, a living representative of some of the most ancient fossils from the Paleozoic era.

Here was more proof that the system of thermal vents

supporting chemosynthesis food chains was an archaic, indeed atavistic, branch of evolution, which had proceeded for billions of years undetected on the deep-sea bottom as tectonic forces shaped Earth, until ANGUS and *Alvin* stumbled on the first vent.

Just as significant to the life scientists but certainly less visually spectacular, the microbiologists on this second cruise discovered two hundred different strains of bacteria living within the warm recesses of the vents, metabolizing the rich chemical broth of hydrogen sulfide, carbon dioxide, and—for a few strains—molecular oxygen. Some of these bacteria did indeed grow in the thick mats and clumps in the subsurface spaces of the pillow lava, flourishing in rich beds until the upwelling water peeled them off and carried them to the waiting higher organisms above.

But unlike my Earth science colleagues, the biologists were too professionally cautious to speculate that we had discovered the possible genesis mechanism of life on Earth down in those shimmering warm undersea fountains.

In the 1840s, Charles Darwin had documented unusual diversity among birds and reptiles in the nearby Galapagos Islands, volcanic extensions of the tectonic forces churning beneath the rift. One hundred thirty-some years later, American scientists had made discoveries every bit as important, almost 2 miles beneath these calm equatorial waters. I was proud to have been part of these momentous expeditions.

Between the two Galapagos Rift expeditions, I had the chance to again work with my French colleagues from CNEXO. Jean Francheteau was very keen on exploring a faster-spreading segment of the Mid-Ocean Ridge to compare it to the slower spreading FAMOUS site. The study area lay in the well-known East Pacific Rise zone at 21 degrees north latitude about 100 miles south of Cabo San Lucas, the tip of Mexico's Baja California. The attraction of this area of rifts was the moderate speed of separation between the Cocos and Pacific crustal plates. Jean was particularly interested in a region bounded by two transform faults named Rivera and Tamayo. With the French penchant for acronyms, the expedition that went to 21 degrees north in February 1978 was named RITA (for Rivera and Tamayo).

I joined the French team aboard their comfortable and modern research vessel *Le Suroit*, which was also the tender for the submersible *Cyana*.

With my old friend Jean Francheteau in charge of the effort, it was only logical that he picked a section of the East Pacific Rise where Scripps, the school where he'd received his doctorate, had already carried out considerable field research.

The French had missed out on the exciting discoveries of the Galapagos Rift, which had captured the attention not only of plate tectonic specialists among the Earth sciences but also of the larger ocean science community.

I was eager to work with Jean again, and to enjoy the haute cuisine that prevailed on all French research ships.

Unfortunately, the French did not have their own ANGUS system to help guide their submersible dives. Their analogous RAI vehicle was still in development and unavailable for this cruise.

A second technical handicap was that the French had not yet permitted a second scientist in the three-person *Cyana*— as we had in *Alvin*—and required that two pilots be aboard. The absence of a veteran scientist such as Jean or me on every dive meant the success of the mission sometimes rested in the hands of a novice scientist making his first dive. Later I discovered that this restraint had unforeseen ramifications.

Because we were operating within Mexico's 200-mile Exclusive Economic Zone, the team included several Mexican scientists from the Mexican national university. On a traverse of some of the older volcanic terrain midway through the cruise, an inexperienced Mexican scientist diving in *Cyana* for the first time encountered some unusual polychrome chimneylike structures among the lava fields. He had no idea these structures were uncommon and simply collected a chunk of the glistening granular material without fully documenting the location of the sample. Due to language problems and the fact that *Cyana*'s chief pilot, R. Kientzy, and his copilot were also unfamiliar with this terrain, the Mexican scientist did not adequately explain what he had seen.

The sample of the chimney rock was stored away as a minor curiosity and eventually got lost among the hundreds of other lava and basalt samples stored at the CNEXO lab in Brest. It wasn't until James Bischoff of the U.S. Geological Survey visited the French lab months later and spotted the unusual sample that the French realized the potential importance of their discovery. Bischoff analyzed the glassy granular sample and found it to be almost pure sphalerite, a sulfide of zinc never before found on a volcanic sea floor. The French quickly recovered from their initial oversight and published an article in *Nature* detailing the find.

But even then, no one understood the significance of the chimneylike structure from which the Mexican scientist had removed the sample.

In fact, on our 1977 Galapagos Rift cruise, ANGUS had photographed a series of strange tubular deposits on the southern side of the rift valley. I can clearly remember diving on them a few days later and trying to take a sample with *Alvin*'s mechanical arm. As we attempted to grip the rock, it crumbled into a thousand pieces that sparkled like polychrome sequins in our floodlights. In retrospect, I'm sure they were sulfide chimneys. Had we recovered a sample, scientific history would have been different. But those were the breaks you faced in field research, and I have no complaints.

And the 1978 expedition to 21 degrees north would bring even more frustration to me and my French friends.

Because of all the excitement about our discovery of the Galapagos Rift hydrothermal vents the year before, I hadn't completed the geological field notes of our extensive ANGUS surveys when I came aboard *Le Suroit*. Prior to these Pacific expeditions, my diving experience had focused on the slow-spreading axis of the FAMOUS site, where we had become experts on rift valley lava formations, particularly on pillow lava. Jim Moore, a volcanologist from the U.S. Geological Survey who had dived on the Mid-Atlantic Ridge, and I had just published our detailed *Photographic Atlas of the Mid-Atlantic Ridge Rift Valley* in which we had carefully documented all the various forms of pillow lava we'd seen.

But mapping the faster-spreading Galapagos Rift, we discovered strange lava "lakes." To our astonishment, at a depth of 9,000 feet ANGUS revealed that vast amounts of molten lava had spread across the sea floor. While still molten despite the icy cold and pressure, these lakes had drained back into the tubes of the substrata or onto lower surrounding terrain. And we also saw tall lava pillars standing like tree trunks in these lava lakes, a phenomenon that seemed to defy explanation.

On the way to join the French, I'd stopped off at Stanford, where Jerry van Andel was now teaching, to discuss these findings with him and Robin Holcomb, another USGS volcanologist and an expert on the lava lakes found on land.

We arrived at a possible explanation for the strange pillars: when lava flowed through a forest, then drained away, it was common to find "tree molds" that took the shape of the trunk that had been incinerated. This process was similar to the "lost wax" technique used by bronze sculptors. But because there were no forests on the ocean floor, we realized some cold structure other than wood had formed the core of the Galapagos lava pillar molds. And we surmised that this must have been the relatively colder seawater rising from fissures that had been capped by the lava flow. The water squirting through the hot plastic lava had cooled it to form these distinctive cylinders.

When I left Stanford, Jerry, Robin, and I agreed that I would write the first draft of the paper on what we'd discovered on the Galapagos Rift. I never imagined that the French and I would discover the same unusual features at 21 degrees north.

But that was exactly what happened. *Cyana* encountered these unmistakable lava pillars standing like tree trunks in old, partially drained flow lakes.

I was now caught in a dilemma, my loyalties split exactly in half. I wanted to treat both teams of scientists fairly. Clearly, our initial insights had come from the extensive 1977 dives of the Galapagos Rift. But the 1978 *Cyana* dives gave me a better opportunity to examine these pillars and to even recover one as a sample. It was hollow inside, definitely formed by a column of rising vent water, just as we had hypothesized at Stanford.

It was impossible for me not to share my enthusiasm at this emerging discovery with my French colleagues. They quickly focused their fieldwork on the pillars, better documenting the features than we had on the Galapagos Rift.

After the 1978 cruise, two competing manuscripts—one French, one American—each claiming credit for the discovery, were circulated for peer review. A rather acrimonious exchange of messages across the Atlantic quickly escalated the tension between Jean and Jerry. For a while I feared that my long and happy relationship with my French friends was in jeopardy.

This type of conflict is all too common among academic scientists (and even worse among their industrial counterparts), who must prove accomplishments in order to compete for limited funding. The prestige of discovery often brought tangible reward, and on a more human level, we all wanted recognition for the hard work we put in on expeditions.

I tried to smooth things over, writing Jean that we were all "honest scientists trying to do the right thing." I assured him that our expeditions to the Pacific in 1979 "will provide us with a new set of data that we can all enjoy working on together." Finally, the lava settled with the publication of both papers.

Immediately following the successful 1979 biology expedition to the Galapagos Rift, the Woods Hole team moved up to the East Pacific Rise at 21 degrees north to begin the second phase of Project RITA aboard the Scripps research vessel *Melville*. I was excited about the expedition because it gave me the chance to show Jean our improved ANGUS in action and also to put the bitterness of the lava pillar controversy behind us.

It was clear from the beginning that this was a Scripps cruise. Fred Spiess had been a submarine commander during World War II and ran all his expeditions with quasi-military discipline. When I reported on board *Melville* with ANGUS and its small, informal operating team, it was apparent that our low-key approach to a science cruise was out of step with Fred Spiess's operating style. Moreover, Spiess and his Scripps assistant, Ken Macdonald, were geophysicists who firmly intended that this expedition would focus on geophysical investigations using their Deep Tow vehicle, not on the Woods Hole type of geology-oriented field research in which ANGUS reconnoitered the sea floor for *Alvin*.

And that's the way the expedition unfolded for the first week or so. Spiess almost monopolized *Melville*'s single large power winch with Deep Tow, and ANGUS and her team had to wait its turn. But then Deep Tow ran into problems. Because the sophisticated vehicle was laden with delicate geophysical sensors to measure gravity and geomagnetism as well as fluctuations in seawater temperature, Deep Tow was not able to withstand the inevitable crashes with the rough bottom terrain. So, while Spiess's prized instrument sled was undergoing extensive repairs, I prevailed on him to let us slalom ANGUS across the rough and narrow rift 2,600 meters down.

As I expected, ANGUS did indeed take a licking by slamming repeatedly into the unseen low scarps and lava mounds. But her cameras also kept on clicking, just as the crew had advertised. And her temperature sensor worked just fine. On our first couple of runs through the central axis, we encountered unmistakable evidence of hydrothermal vents and even photographed the distinctive congregations of chalky white clams that marked warm-water oases.

By this time, *Lulu* and *Alvin* had been on station for a week. Bruce Luyendyk, my Woods Hole colleague who had earned his spurs at Scripps, joined Jean Francheteau for the first dives, which concentrated on geophysical measurements. But then Bruce and Jean encountered a field of distinctive pillarlike columns and retrieved samples from them.

The next day, Bill Normark, an American geologist, joined French volcanologist Thierry Juteau on what was scheduled to be a rather mundane gravimetric dive. Instead, their pilot, Dudley Foster, drove *Alvin* into a bizarre terrain of gnarled cylindrical chimneys. As *Alvin*'s floodlights illuminated the area, Dudley shook his head in disbelief. A chimney, fully 6 feet tall, was belching dense black billows of what looked for all the world like coal smoke.

"We've got a locomotive blasting out this stuff," Dudley reported with unusual emotion.

We all knew, of course, that smoke did not exist in a liquid. What Dudley was reporting had to be some unknown type of ultrarich mineral suspension, much denser in concentration than the milky blue fountains we'd seen on the Galapagos Rift.

But that was not the only unusual feature of this smoking black chimney. When Dudley inserted *Alvin*'s temperature probe, he got a reading a little over 32 degrees Celsius (91 degrees Fahrenheit).

Our instrument specialist on the surface was sure the transistorized probe was out of calibration; we'd never seen water that warm down on the Galapagos Rift.

But when *Alvin* was hauled back aboard *Lulu* for the night, we were all taken aback by what we found: the tip of the temperature probe was melted away and the white plastic wand was charred ripply black, as if the probe had been imprudently thrust into the maw of a blast furnace.

I dove with Jean Francheteau the next day. Our pilot, Ralph Hollis, had made sure the replacement temperature probe was built to withstand the type of heat we now believed had melted the first probe.

My first view of the billowing smokestack sent a shiver of amazement down my back. Here, almost 9,000 feet down at the bottom of the Pacific, were structures that looked for all the world like the awkward mud-and-wattle chimneys of ancient kilns or smelters.

Jean spoke my exact thought: "They seem connected to hell itself."

As we inched our way up to the first of the belching chimney vents, Ralph was unusually nervous.

"Let's just get a reading before we go much closer," he said.

His caution was certainly appropriate. The temperature of the billowing black geyser read an incredible 350 degrees Celsius (662 degrees Fahrenheit). This was more than hot enough to melt lead. But more important to us, this searing blast of superheated, mineral-laden water would have shattered *Alvin*'s Plexiglas ports in a fraction of a second. We were less than 10 feet away from death and destruction. And our colleagues on the surface would have probably never learned what killed us.

Over the next twelve days, *Alvin* dove repeatedly on these strange superhot chimney vents. We found two basic types, which we named from their appearance: "black smokers" and "white smokers." Some of these bizarre constructions were almost 30 feet tall. Chemical analysis revealed, as we suspected, that the cylindrical structure of the chimneys was almost pure crystalline zinc sulfide, the mineral sphalerite that Bischoff had identified in the French lab sample.

Unlike the much cooler hydrothermal vents on the Galapagos Rift, these white and black smokers were pouring out a phenomenally greater volume of sulfide-rich minerals. Accordingly, the surrounding hydrothermal oases hosted their own unique chemosynthesis ecosystem. Here giant clams and tube worms existed, as well as weird evolutionary side shunts of more common fish and mollusks.

By the time our month on the East Pacific Rise ended, *Alvin* and ANGUS had documented an entire new system of hydrothermal vents and related animal colonies, discoveries that completely eclipsed the geophysical research that had been the expedition's official purpose.

As with the Galapagos dives, the discovery of the smoker chimneys at 21 degrees north became the subject of a very popular *National Geographic* article, to the chagrin of some of my scientific colleagues and competitors. Fred Spiess was naturally upset that Deep Tow had not made the initial discoveries of the smokers, but he seemed sincere in his congratulations of the ANGUS-*Alvin* team.

Once more, circumstances had combined to place me at the very center of a major scientific discovery. Data from this expedition would be analyzed for years to come. And when our findings were eventually published, marine science was obliged to completely reconsider its previous conclusions about the fundamental nature of the planet's oceans, including the origin of their chemical composition and their role as a matrix of life.

For me, the 1970s had been an almost uninterrupted period of research, study, and participation in historic expeditions, and now was time for me to come ashore and take stock of all that had happened over this hectic decade. This hiatus marked a major turning point in my career. I had been at Woods Hole as a naval officer and as a civilian since 1967. During most of those twelve momentous years, I had worked to promote submersibles as a reliable research tool and helped perfect the technology and supporting infrastructure, including the evolving ANGUS system that had proved *Alvin* such an undisputed success during the 1970s. I now planned to summarize this work in a series of research papers and to decide where my future lay.

I was also scheduled for tenure review, so the decision about my future was not entirely my own. Tenure is the single most important event in a scientist's career. It is the ultimate test grade he or she will ever receive. The formal tenure process usually takes about a year to complete, and involves not only the senior staff from one's own institution but staff members from peer institutions worldwide. As crucial as this process is, however, the scientist being reviewed for tenure doesn't have much to contribute to the decision. My worth was to be judged by what accomplishments I had already made. So I was obliged to sit on the sidelines and watch.

In a villagelike community such as Woods Hole, the tenure decision can be very brutal, especially to the family of the scientist involved. If a person is denied tenure, he has little recourse but to leave, because his social position as a Woods Hole scientist—which placed him in the upper middle class of this part of Cape Cod society—would have suddenly evaporated. Denial of tenure was a mark of failure, which the family also bore.

Given the long history of scientists every bit as qualified as me being denied tenure at the Institution, I knew there was a strong possibility I wouldn't make the grade. I had already planned to take my family back to California, where I had grown up, if I was denied tenure, and to try to find an academic position there, preferably at Stanford, where Jerry van Andel had said there might be an opening in the geology department.

Using all the salesmanship I had learned over the years, I managed to convince my old patron, the Office of Naval Research, to fund a sabbatical year at Stanford during which I could write and publish papers on all my intense basic research during the decade.

In 1980, Marjorie, our two sons, and I drove across the country to Palo Alto. That sunny, tranquil Stanford campus was the ideal place to write my papers on plate tectonics, volcanism, and the complex hydrothermal process at work on the planet's Mid-Ocean Ridge. This rigorous scientific writing kept my mind away from the tenure review unfolding inexorably on Cape Cod.

In optimistic periods, I had to consider what I would do if in fact I did receive tenure at Woods Hole. Would I just pick up where I'd left off? I was already scheduled to participate in a major sea-floor mapping project with Jean Francheteau, and the National Science Foundation was considering my proposal for another ANGUS-*Alvin* expedition to the East Pacific Rise in search of more smokers.

If I arrived in early middle age as just another successful academic scientist, I was destined to conduct such research for the remaining twenty-five or thirty years of my career. But I had been going to sea on one expedition or another for over a decade, making dive after dive to the floor of the Mid-Ocean Ridge. I'd seen millions of pillow lavas, thousands of fissures, endless fault scarps. The walls of my Stanford study were stacked high with boxes containing tens of thousands of color slides. Yet despite all this research, I had actually traveled only 40 miles across the virgin volcanic terrain, mapping a mountain range 40,000 miles long that spanned the planet.

As I wrote my papers at Stanford, I slowly became convinced that manned submersibles, as splendid a scientific tool as they had proved to be, actually had a questionable future.

After using ANGUS to help map critical segments of the Mid-Ocean Ridge, I realized that a more advanced and sophisticated form of remotely operated unmanned vehicle could ultimately become a much more important scientific and exploratory tool than *Alvin* ever could be.

Palo Alto, of course, lay on the edge of Silicon Valley, the heart of America's high-technology frontier. It was here that I learned of startling new advances being made in fiber optics. It was only a matter of time, I saw, before this innovation would revolutionize oceanography. What I envisioned was an evolutionary quantum jump beyond ANGUS, a deep-towed vehicle carrying sensitive new video cameras, connected to the surface by fiber-optic cable through which broadcast-quality color television images as well as remote operation commands could be transmitted.

In my mind, this super-ANGUS would far surpass *Alvin*'s capabilities. It would remain on the sea floor for weeks on end with complete safety and at far less expense than any manned submersible.

During those peaceful days on the Stanford campus, I began to design this new vehicle. I saw the basic towed sled as a remotely operated mother ship, which in turn would launch a smaller exploration vehicle, also connected to the towed sled by fiber-optic cable.

I planned to call my new vehicle the *Argo-Jason* system in honor of the first bold explorer of Western civilization. Armed with nothing more than my overactive imagination and a decade's hands-on experience exploring the world's sea floors, I convinced my friend Sam Matthews of *National Geographic* to publish an illustration of this hypothetical system in a major article he wrote on the future of oceanography. Sam even agreed to describe *Argo* and *Jason*—which existed on paper only—as being in the "design and prototype stage." This was bread on the water; maybe I'd win development funding for the system with this ploy.

As if in concert with this optimism, my phone rang one morning while the *Argo-Jason* sketches still littered my desk. It was John Steele, the new director of Woods Hole.

"Congratulations, Bob," he said. "You have been awarded tenure at the Institution."

Part Four
OVERCOMING

SEVEN

I leaned tiredly against *Knorr*'s bow rail, gazing into the dark Atlantic. Away to the west, the last bronze afterglow of sunset drained from the sky. Ragged clouds, the first weather of an approaching storm front, churned by, low overhead. Engine vibrations rumbled up through the soles of my boat shoes as *Knorr* breasted the mounting swell.

My shoulders sagged and I felt the salty spray on the rail soak into my sweater sleeves. Fatigue mixed with the first cold weight of despair.

Tonight, Saturday, August 31, 1985, marked the fifth week of our joint French-American expedition's quest to find *Titanic*. In only five days the ship would have to depart the search site, 300 miles southeast of Newfoundland. The ambitious expedition seemed certain to end in failure.

I walked aft, instinctively avoiding the derricks and winches that cluttered the shadowy main deck of the research vessel. On the deserted fantail, I saw the familiar tubular white framework of ANGUS, lashed in its deck cradle. The tough old camera sled had been repainted yet again, its cameras and strobes carefully inspected, ready for immediate use. But we would not launch the ANGUS until *Argo*, her more advanced sister, discovered the wreck of the Royal Mail Ship *Titanic*, which lay somewhere nearby on the bottom, more than 12,000 feet below these cold Atlantic waves.

In the patchy light of the deck lamps, I could just distinguish the arm of *Knorr*'s main crane jutting over the starboard side of the ship. There was still enough light to see the large take-up drum slowly feeding cable to the traction unit welded to the main deck. From there the taut cable snaked up toward a large sheave held by the main crane, then made a sudden right angle and disappeared into the dark water.

This was the long umbilical cord connecting *Argo* to the ship. As *Knorr* crept across the surface at less than 2 knots, the cable dropped almost straight down. *Argo* glided just above the sea floor, its sensitive video eyes completing yet another long search track.

For days, *Argo*'s unblinking cameras and sonars had scanned the lifeless bottom of mud flats, sand ridges, and smooth-bottomed gullies, finding only the occasional glacial erratic boulder dropped by a passing iceberg. The powerful floodlights revealed only the rare track of a scavenging crab or the solitary chunk of a sea slug in the chill desert below.

I turned from the stern rail and looked forward to *Argo*'s squat blue rectangular control van, the nerve center of the mission. If I pulled open the heavy metal hatch of the control van, I could end this solitary vigil. The van was an oasis of light, warmth, and comradeship. I knew soft music was playing on the stereo. *Argo*'s crew would be seated at their stations, breaking the monotony of the long watch with the day's light-hearted shipboard gossip. But now, I also knew, there would be a sour undertone. Our morale was at its lowest ebb tonight, and some of my team members had begun to question our search strategy. If I entered the van now, my glum mood would only make matters worse.

I returned to the fantail and stared down at the slowly curling wake. How the hell was it, I thought for perhaps the hundredth time in the past few days, that a ship the size of *Titanic* had managed to elude this combined expedition's impressive technology and human skill for over five weeks? Again the cold knot of despair clotted in my chest. At times like this, the enormity of the mission became all too obvious. Despite *Titanic*'s legendary size—her hull almost 900 feet long, her displacement over 45,000 tons—finding the wreck amid the sand ridges and gullies 2.5 miles beneath the surface was far more difficult than searching for the proverbial needle in a haystack.

Yet I had often boasted that finding *Titanic* should be a relatively easy task, provided I obtained the proper technology and assembled the ideal team of experts. I clenched my fists, then tried to relax. Those boasts now haunted me. My French coleader, Jean-Louis Michel, and I had assembled the most advanced underwater search technology in the world. Our expedition members were the most skilled and experienced experts to be found anywhere. But *Titanic* had eluded us, just as it had the three other expeditions that had ended in failure in recent years.

After a decade of phenomenally successful scientific expeditions, I was not used to failure. Moreover, I had staked my personal and professional reputation—and by extension, the prestige of Woods Hole—on the success of this expedition. And my competitive nature did not easily accept failure. But as the last tepid warmth of sunset vanished on the western horizon, the prospect of failure seemed inevitable.

This expedition had been widely and favorably publicized by the news media on both sides of the Atlantic. Had this publicity—which neither I nor Jean-Louis had managed to control—actually jinxed the expedition to defeat? I shook my head. That type of speculation was stupid, anathema to an experienced scientist. Still, at times like this, the suspicion continued to nag that *Titanic*'s tragic legacy somehow extended beyond the death of that great ship seventy-three years before to thwart anyone audacious enough to search for her grave on the Atlantic floor.

Audacity was, of course, one of the hallmarks of the *Titanic* legend. On the night of April 14, 1912, the boldness of *Titanic*'s captain, Edward J. Smith—who, ironically, was scheduled to retire from a long career with the White Star Line after completing the liner's maiden voyage—was seen by most of the world as the principal cause of the tragedy. Captain Smith, as both legend and the historical record revealed, had disregarded radio reports from other ships that a drifting field of icebergs straddled *Titanic*'s route between the British isles and New York. Instead of shutting down the ship's engines and drifting for the night as the captains of other nearby liners chose to do, Captain Edward J. Smith disdained even slowing the huge liner and steamed ahead at 22 knots.

And when *Titanic*, her flooded hull mortally slashed by the rapier edge of the iceberg, tilted near vertical and rumbled beneath the calm, star-flecked Atlantic at 2:20 on that cold morning, no doubt Smith himself tasted bitter hubris, the essential element of tragedy since the days of the classic Greek dramatists.

Hubris has been defined as "overweening presumption" that implies a pompous disregard of the limits governing human powers. Certainly Captain Smith's arrogant indifference to the menace of the ice field could qualify as hubris. But as others who had become obsessed by the legend of that great ship believed, *Titanic*'s very existence was hubristic. In 1912, the liner was the largest, most luxurious vessel ever built. Her double-bottomed hull was divided into sixteen water-tight compartments, each of which could be sealed by automatic bulkheads in the event of flooding. For this reason, the press had heralded *Titanic*'s maiden voyage as the first ocean crossing by an "unsinkable" liner. Perhaps mindful of that haughty boast, the White Star Line did not insist that the ship carry enough lifeboats for all the twenty-two hundred passengers and crew on board.

Certainly, the fact that this voyage had attracted the very cream of the British aristocracy and their American peers, including celebrities such as the Astors, the Strauses, and the Guggenheims, inflamed emotions worldwide. It wasn't simply that almost fifteen hundred adults and children died that night in the cold Atlantic. Rather, the fact that so many of the richest and most powerful figures of the glittering Edwardian age perished aboard the most optimistic and technically advanced artifact of that era lent classical dimensions to the tragedy.

In many ways *Titanic* was the steel-plated epitome of optimistic Edwardian civilization, whose ethos had become the limitless power of technology. But only four years after the ship sank, that optimistic civilization was murdering itself in the blood-soaked mud of the Somme. After *Titanic*, the shipyards of Europe built U-boats and destroyers, not luxury liners.

When the huge liner disappeared beneath the surface, leaving behind only a handful of lifeboats and flotsam, the unquenchable element of mystery was added to the human tragedy.

And I had become infected, indeed obsessed, by this mystery years before. As a teenager, I had read and reread *A Night to Remember*. I'd stayed up late to watch the TV reruns of the *Titanic* movies. Years later, I'd drunk beer around bonfires with the Boston Sea Rovers, weaving crazy plans for dives to the cold depths of *Titanic*'s grave.

From those old dreams, I had slowly built toward the reality of this night, with *Knorr*'s deck plates thumping beneath my feet as the ship towed *Argo* above the rolling sand hills of the deep-sea floor south of the continental slope. Over all those years, I had nurtured the secret confidence—as improbable as it seemed—that one day it would be me who found the *Titanic*. I'd even been so bold as to name my sophisticated new deep-tethered search vehicle *Argo*. By any stretch of the imagination, that audacious optimism qualified as hubris.

I felt *Knorr*'s slow progress to the west shudder as the ship's driver in the van stalled the big Mixmaster cycloidal thrusting propellers, preparing to shift north at the end of this search track, only to turn back east in a mile and commence the next leg. Over 12,000 feet below, *Argo*, our complex and obedient drone, would also slow, its ultrasensitive video cameras no doubt gazing at a dead terrain of gray mud and ripply sand.

Five more days. That's all the time I had left to find *Titanic*.

I gripped the wet rail, watching the wake curve as *Knorr*'s helm and engines obeyed instructions from the control van. Searching for a giant ocean liner sunk almost three-quarters of a century before in a deep stretch of the Atlantic hardly seemed a proper task for a serious scientist. Suddenly, the audacity of this presumptuous undertaking became all too apparent. How had I, a person who believed firmly in the logical precision of the scientific method, come to this time and place?

My quest for *Titanic* began to pass beyond the phase of vague dreams after I returned to Woods Hole from my sabbatical year at Stanford.

In the late 1970s, *Alvin* was steadily upgraded, and the little sub now dove to its new certified depth of 4,000 meters. So I knew that, if *Titanic* was ever located, *Alvin* was definitely capable of reaching the 12,000-foot depths where the wreck probably lay.

But finding *Titanic* was obviously not going to be easy. During my sabbatical, I wrote several long professional papers on my research to the mid-ocean ridges during the 1970s. But with tenure at the Institution, I increasingly turned my attention to improving marine exploration technology, in particular refining my plans for the *Argo-Jason* system. Some of my older colleagues grumbled that these activities were "unscientific and inappropriate" for a tenured geologist working at an institution focused primarily on basic scientific research. This was the same type of complaint I'd heard about the use of manned deep submersibles for field research. Now respected marine geologists, biologists, and geophysicists were virtually lined up worldwide, waiting their turn to dive in *Alvin*.

R.M.S. *Titanic* on its maiden voyage from Europe to New York City.
Ken Marschall

Artist's rendering of *Argo*/Jason system being deployed from R/V *Knorr* while broadcasting a live expedition video back to Woods Hole. *Robert Ballard*

The *Titanic*'s bow section lying upright on the bottom in 12,500 feet of water. *Ken Marschall*

The *Argo* glides over a field of debris that later proves to be from the *Titanic*. *Woods Hole Oceanographic Institution*

We knew we'd found the *Titanic*'s debris field when *Argo* passed over one of the ship's famous boilers, that broke free of the ship when it was torn in half at the surface. *Woods Hole Oceanographic Institution*

Photograph of *Titanic*'s upright bow section, filmed by *Angus* during final day of discovery trip in 1985. *Woods Hole Oceanographic Institution*

The author and Jean-Louis Michel, aboard *Le Suroit*, share their disappointment at failing to find *Titanic* during the French phase of the search effort. *Emory Kristof © National Geographic Society*

The *Argo*, being lowered over the side of *Knorr* during the first few days of the search effort in *Titanic* Canyon. *Emory Kristof © National Geographic Society*

Jean Jarry, Jean-Louis Michel, and the author discuss *Titanic* search strategy in *Argo*'s control van aboard the *Knorr. Emory Kristof © National Geographic Society*

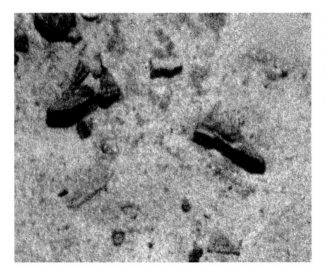

All that remains of a drowned *Titanic* crewmember's body: a pair of shoes, which bottom animals do not eat. *Woods Hole Oceanographic Institution*

Celebrating *Titanic*'s discovery with sparkling wine in paper cups in *Argo*'s control van. *Emory Kristof © National Geographic Society*

Captain Richard Bowen (lower left) controls *Knorr*'s powerful thrusters while the author (center, bottom) watches *Argo*'s video monitors. *Emory Kristof © National Geographic Society*

Alvin's divers communicate with support ship *A-II* before the sub begins a dive on *Titanic*.
Perry Thorsuik

Alvin surface control gives the final OK to launch the sub and Jason Junior during second *Titanic* expedition.
Perry Thorsuik

Martin Bowen operates Jason Junior from inside *Alvin* as we make our first descent of *Titanic*'s grand staircase.
Robert Ballard

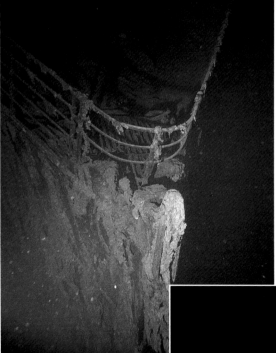

When I first saw the massive hull of *Titanic* it was staring back at me as our submersible lights bounced off the ship's intact glass portholes.
Robert Ballard

A crystal light fixture photographed by Jason Junior as it hangs inside a first-class compartment off the grand staircase.
Woods Hole Oceanographic Institution

Jason Junior peers inside the window of a crewmember's stateroom on *Titanic*'s starboard boat deck.
Robert Ballard

Although the fragile bridge of *Titanic* did not survive its 12,000-foot plunge to the ocean floor, its telemotor, which was once used to steer the ship, is perfectly preserved.
Robert Ballard

All manner of debris can be found around *Titanic*'s stern section, including hundreds of wine bottles that have had their corks pushed inside the bottle by the ambient sea pressure. *Robert Ballard*

The second plaque I was given by the Titanic Historical Society, in memory of those who died during the sinking as well as of Bill Tantum, was placed on the stern's poop deck.
Robert Ballard

I placed the bronze plaque given to me by the Explorers Club on one of *Titanic*'s massive capstans located on the starboard bow. *Robert Ballard*

Bow of *Titanic* festooned with "rusticles." *Robert Ballard*

Artist's rendering of *Argo* illuminating the giant swastika on the bow of the German battleship *Bismarck*. *Ken Marschall*

The moment of discovering *Bismarck* as *Argo* flies over the top of the ship. *Joseph H. Bailey © National Geographic Society*

Argo's control van aboard the *Starella* during unsuccessful 1989 search for *Bismarck. George Mobley © National Geographic Society*

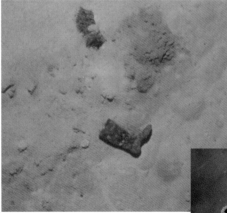

A single boot resting on the bottom is a mute reminder that *Bismarck* carried many young men to their untimely deaths. *Woods Hole Oceanographic Institution*

Argo glides over one of *Bismarck*'s anti-aircraft guns with a flower-like sea anemone decorating its barrel. *Quest Group*

The author removes a portion of *Bismarck*'s superstructure from a model of the ship as he explores the sunken ship in 16,000 feet of water. *Joseph H. Bailey © National Geographic Society*

The author and his son Todd share a moment together in *Argo*'s control van as they explore *Bismarck* resting on the bottom of the ocean. *Joseph H. Bailey © National Geographic Society*

The author standing with his son Todd following the press conference at National Geographic Headquarters in Washington, D.C., announcing their discovery of the *Bismarck*. *Joseph H. Bailey © National Geographic Society*

The crew aboard the *Star Hercules* following the wreath-laying ceremony. *Joseph H. Bailey © National Geographic Society*

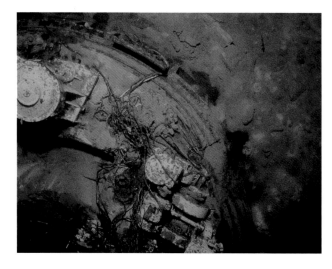

One of *Bismarck*'s main gun turrets lying upside-down in the avalanche caused by the ship's collision with the bottom. *Quest Group*

Argo being launched from *Starella* during the 1989 search effort for the *Bismarck*. George Mobley © National Geographic Society

Artist's rendering of Roman trading ship *Isis*, caught in a storm near Skerki Bank. *Ken Marschall*

Electronic image of the galley portion of the *Isis* wreck. *JASON Project*

Electronic image taken by *Argo* of ancient amphora lying in 2,500 feet of water near the site where the *Isis* wreck was later discovered. *Quest Group*

Moment of discovering the Isis after 1,600 years on the bottom of the Mediterranean Sea. *George Mobley © National Geographic Society*

My professional interest in *Titanic* actually predated my receiving tenure by several years. In 1977, I was contacted by a commercial promotion firm called Big Events, which specialized in making profit from sensational publicity gimmicks. One of their successes had been the purchase of old cables from the Golden Gate Bridge. These were sliced up into little trinket-size pieces and sold as souvenirs. To my chagrin, I discovered their interest in the *Titanic* was to cut up certified authentic pieces of debris that they hoped to sell as very expensive paper-weights. Our discussions didn't go very far.

But I did meet Bill Tantum through Big Events. William H. Tantum IV was widely known as "Mr. Titanic." A big, loquacious man with a walrus mustache, Bill Tantum was the head of the *Titanic* Historical Society. He had studied the tragedy literally since childhood when he had been involved in a ship collision while cruising on a Canadian Pacific steamer.

Bill Tantum probably knew more about *Titanic* than any other single person in the world. He could recite from memory intimate details of the ship's construction and her ill-fated maiden voyage. His collection of books and memorabilia was unrivaled. Above all, he loved to talk about *Titanic*. Bill lived modestly on a military disability pension and devoted his life to the great ship.

It was from Bill Tantum that I acquired my sense of personal mission that led to my quest to discover *Titanic*. Bill virtually made the tragic ship, its passengers, and crew come alive in my imagination. After countless evenings in Bill's book-lined study, I could view the ship's last hours through my mind's eye as if I were watching a videotape. More than any other person, Bill encouraged me to fight the odds, to perfect my technology, to somehow find support for a serious scientific expedition to locate the great ship and document its final resting place on the bottom of the Atlantic.

Bolstered by his support in 1977, I began to negotiate with Alcoa Aluminum to charter their advanced salvage vessel, the Alcoa *Seaprobe*. I saw the ship as an interim compromise tool in the hunt for *Titanic*. The *Seaprobe* was essentially an ocean-going deep-drilling rig, designed to salvage old wrecks. Using linked sections of conventional drill pipe assembled beneath a tall, cross-beamed derrick, looking for all the world like a floating Texas oil rig, *Seaprobe* could also suspend a sophisticated sensor pod containing sidescan sonar, video, and still cameras. The ship had the ability to position itself directly above a chosen spot on the deep ocean bottom and hold station using dynamic positioning while its crew of roughnecks slowly lowered or raised the column of pipe—or the sensor pod— by adding or subtracting one 60-foot section of pipe at a time.

What I really needed, of course, was an unlimited budget to develop the type of deep-tethered video sled that eventually became *Argo*. But in 1977, I had no institutional sponsors or funding for such fanciful technology. I did, however, manage to convince WHOI's Dr. Paul Fye to support a charter of *Seaprobe* for ocean trials, ostensibly to "evaluate" the vessel as a potential scientific tool for the Institution. I also managed to borrow a sophisticated sonar from Westinghouse, a deep-towed magnetometer and the LIBEC Large Area Imaging System from the Naval Research Lab, and an array of underwater cameras from private companies and *National Geographic*. All told, this equipment was worth more than $600,000.

My basic plan was simple: if our sea trials were successful and I demonstrated that the sensor pod on the end of *Seaprobe*'s long pipe could locate and photograph large metal objects on the bottom, I might find backers to take the vessel out next year to the edge of the continental slope south of Newfoundland where *Titanic* had sunk and locate the wreck.

That was my plan. In retrospect, it was the height of naïveté.

As on any cruise, there were problems. Ours began at the Woods Hole dock when the drilling superintendent stormed off the job in a huff over a pay dispute. So we went to sea without him.

My station was in an air-conditioned control room overlooking the cavernous interior of *Seaprobe*'s hull, which we called the "moon pool," the opening to the sea below through which the long pipe was lowered. This was the area directly beneath the derrick through which the roughnecks lowered the assembled sections of pipe, 60 feet at a time, the metallic counterpart to Jack's beanstalk, this time growing in reverse. It was a clunker of a system --technology seemingly dating from the 1920s—but *Seaprobe*'s immensely long pipe was, in fact, a practical way of raising heavy objects from the bottom, and for me, a means of placing expensive equipment near the deep ocean floor.

On this first sea trial, we carried my instrument pod 3,000 feet below the ship, held there by fifty lengths of pipe, one screwed to the next all the way back up through the rectangular opening in the hull and the moon pool to the derrick above on the superstructure.

On the second night of the cruise. I was working in the control room just after two A.M., helping the skeleton crew fine-tune the sonar before our first camera tests the next day. I was almost lulled to sleep by the monotonous pinging of the sonar and the soft whirr of the data recorders. Suddenly, there was a thunderous clang right over our heads, as if the ship had taken a direct hit from a naval gun. Dashing into the moon pool compartment, we encountered utter disaster. The drill pipe had broken, and the huge counterweight suspended high overhead on the derrick had plummeted to the deck like a bomb. The severed communications power cable from the derrick whipped back and forth like a crippled snake flashing sparks on the wet deck. Fifty linked sections of pipe weighing over 30 tons had plunged straight to the ocean floor, taking our precious instrument pod on the fatal dive.

It was only on our somber return to Woods Hole that we discovered our error: when steaming with a long column of pipe dangling below, a specially reinforced pipe section had to be wedged in place in the derrick to take the strain. Woods Hole never should have sailed without the experienced superintendent, but as an academic institution, they refused to pay the same wages as ALCOA, a private firm.

For several tense days it appeared I would be held personally responsible for the cost of the lost equipment. If so, I would be personally and professionally ruined. Then Alcoa found they had actually insured the pod. So I was off the hook. At least financially. But my professional reputation suffered from the accident. Woods Hole began to distance itself from my *Titanic* schemes. After *Seaprobe,* I had to suspend any grandiose plans about Woods Hole helping me to lash together some kind of Rube Goldberg search technology and scoring the exploration coup of the century.

I did temporarily interest the entertainment mogul Roy Disney in the idea. But even Disney was gun shy of anteing up the estimated $1.5 million I knew I'd need to build the type of *Argo-Jason* search technology that I remained confident would one day find *Titanic.* Despite my scientific commitments, I began working with Emory Kristof of *National Geographic* on advanced underwater imaging systems in the hope that we would eventually find funding. The company Emory, Bill Tantum, and I formed, Seaonics International, continued to seek funding and sponsors for a *Titanic* expedition.

Just before I finished my sabbatical at Stanford we were approached by a multimillionaire Texan named Jack Grimm. Grimm—known as "Cadillac Jack" due to his collection of vintage cars—seemed eager to back a *Titanic* expedition. But after Grimm's initial negotiations with Emory, it became clear that we couldn't do business with him. Neither Emory nor I liked Grimm's style. He was all publicity and very little substance. An oilman from Abilene, Grimm often relied on hollow bluster to overcome obstacles. We both felt Grimm viewed the expedition as much more a publicity stunt than the type of serious endeavor we envisioned.

In fact, Grimm was a strange amalgam of sharp business sense and naive romanticism. His personality was what has been charitably called "mercurial" by some and "quixotic" by others. In the past, Jack Grimm had put down good money to back some truly harebrained enterprises: searching for a "hole" in the North Pole, for Noah's Ark on a mountainside in Turkey, for the Loch Ness monster, and even for Yeti, the abominable snowman, in the Himalayas. He knew little of *Titanic*'s true history, and neither Emory nor I trusted Grimm to keep his word when he promised he would not use his fortune to pillage the wreck if we did discover *Titanic*.

I'd forgotten about Grimm while I was off at Stanford working on my sabbatical papers. Then I got the news that Jack Grimm had formed an alliance with none other than Dr. Fred Spiess of Scripps and Dr. Bill Ryan of Lamont-Doherty—Woods Hole's two greatest competitors—who would lead a *Titanic* expedition for the Texas millionaire in the summer of 1980.

As much as I doubted Grimm's competence, I had unlimited faith in both Spiess and Ryan; they were hard-nosed scientists and between them, veterans of more than fifty complex seagoing expeditions.

I was deeply worried that my chances of ever discovering *Titanic* had been shattered.

As if to exacerbate this pessimism, I received word in June 1980—just before Grimm's *Titanic* expedition set sail from Florida—that Bill Tantum had died of a sudden stroke. Less than a month before, he had been in Canada, still trying to promote my search for the *Titanic*. He'd had faith right up to his death that I would find the ship. But it was impossible for me to share his loyal optimism.

*   *   *

Jack Grimm's first *Titanic* expedition steamed out of Port Everglades, Florida, aboard HJW *Fay* on July 14, 1980. I was half a world away, in the South Pacific aboard *Le Suroit,* working with my French colleagues on another East Pacific Rise geology expedition. My remote locale seemed fitting. We were near Pitcairn Island, where Fletcher Christian and his fellow *Bounty* mutineers had sought isolated refuge. If Fred Spiess and Bill Ryan did indeed discover *Titanic* for that rich Texan publicity hound, I wanted to be as far away from the inevitable media circus as possible.

Although Grimm was certainly as quixotic as he'd been described, he was no fool. In selecting Spiess and Ryan, he'd picked among the best-qualified scientists available. But unfortunately for them, Scripps's proven Deep Tow sonar vehicle was already committed for that summer. So Bill Ryan convinced Grimm to fund development of Ryan's own pet project, *Sea MARC I,* an intermediate-range mapping sonar Ryan had designed to explore large geological features like submarine canyons.

Although the optimum definition of this sonar was certainly precise enough to discriminate *Titanic*'s hull, almost the length of three football fields, among the gullies and sand ridges at the base of the continental slope south of the Grand Banks, the *Sea MARC I* did not function perfectly on this first cruise.

Even with the greatest sonar in the world, however, the total search area was large. Bill Tantum and I had spent a great deal of time going over all the known data of the sinking, trying to calculate where the ship might lie. After a lot of work, we concluded that *Titanic* had to be somewhere within a box that covered 100 square nautical miles of sometimes chaotic sea-bottom terrain.

We'd reached that conclusion based on historical facts. *Titanic*'s official final position was established from her CQD radio distress call: 41° 46′ N, 50° 14′ W. This position had been worked out by the ship's fourth officer, Joseph G. Boxhall, who was known as a careful navigator. But Bill and I found evidence suggesting Boxhall was wrong. The liner *Carpathia*, steaming at flank speed from the southeast in response to *Titanic*'s distress message, reached the ship's lifeboats earlier than anticipated, suggesting *Titanic* had actually sunk southeast of the last radioed position.

Because Boxhall had calculated his position from dead reckoning, which in turn was based on a possibly erroneous celestial navigation fix at sunset on the fourteenth, it was certainly possible that *Titanic* could have been 10 or more miles farther east or south than the official sinking position.

And Bill and I were certainly confident that *Titanic* could not have been west of that position. So we tentatively drew our optimum search box to include all the sea bottom covered by a tilted rectangle that was basically east and south of *Titanic*'s last known position but which also included a northern triangular wedge straddling the ship's reported dead-reckoning track from the British Isles.

Bill Ryan had only about three months to complete his design and actually build his *Sea MARC* system before Grimm's first expedition sailed. It was no surprise that Bill was frantically working out last-minute glitches even as the *Fay* steamed out of Port Everglades. But Bill Ryan's desperate efforts were overshadowed by the predictable publicity carnival that Grimm scheduled for the departure. He actually had trained a monkey to point to a spot on an ocean chart where Grimm was certain *Titanic* lay. Grimm was stubbornly convinced that this tawdry gimmick would add substance to the movie he was making on the expeditions. But respectable scientists like Fred Spiess and Bill Ryan rebelled at this bizarre exhibitionism and insisted that the monkey stay ashore. Grimm's reaction fit his character: "Fire the scientists." However, in the end, someone convinced Grimm to keep his scientists and leave the monkey ashore.

Because Grimm himself had been responsible for the historical research, the 1980 expedition went to sea with only one working hypothesis: *Titanic* had sunk east of the line of icebergs that had stopped other liners on that fateful night. But east was only one coordinate vector; the expedition needed reasonable north and south boundaries as well. As they had none, they began their search at *Titanic's* distress call position. If this location was barren, they would work their way across a search box not much different than that Bill and I had planned.

The North Atlantic weather lived up to its terrible reputation. The high, confused seas resulting from northeasterly storm winds running afoul of the east-flowing Gulf Stream made accurate *Sea MARC* runs almost impossible. Then they lost the vehicle's Fiberglas tailfin, and more importantly, its magnetometer. In effect, the sonar vehicle might locate interesting objects but be unable to verify they were made of steel.

Grimm did not help matters by making bombastic media announcements on shore, actually claiming the expedition had found *Titanic*. When the *Fay* returned empty-handed, Grimm pressured Spiess and Ryan to announce one of the fourteen sonar targets they had identified was actually *Titanic,* but the scientists rebelled at this chicanery.

Nevertheless, Grimm managed to keep his team together. And on June 28, 1981, his new expedition ship R/V *Gyre* sailed out of Woods Hole for the next *Titanic* search. This wasn't a deliberate taunt, as the vessel had just finished a charter for the Institution. But to me, the gesture felt like a body blow to my professional reputation. On the second expedition, Grimm sailed with the scientists, and Spiess brought his Deep Tow sonar sled. Bill Ryan also had a new search tool, the Deep Sea Color Video System, another of his pet projects that he had convinced Grimm to fund.

Because of Grimm's poor historical research, the scientific team made their own analysis of the sinking and concluded that *Titanic* had sunk much farther east than originally thought. This was where they concentrated the efforts of the second expedition. They also were obliged to carefully investigate the major sonar targets identified the year before. And they had formed another tentative conclusion, based on a shaky hypothesis—that *Titanic* had remained intact and was lying on the bottom, her sonar image masked by surrounding terrain features such as gullies or ridges.

Grimm's 1981 expedition was not the type of steady, coordinated effort one would have expected of Spiess and Bill Ryan—maybe because the erratic Grimm was aboard the search vessel. Instead of following their historical data and searching new territory east of 50 degrees west, they revisited the tantalizing sonar targets from the year before, one of which Grimm seemed convinced was *Titanic*. Despite a new bout of bad weather, Spiess managed to probe each of the sonar targets with Deep Tow to the degree that each was eliminated as a natural geological feature. After more equipment problems, they switched to Ryan's video system, which hadn't been designed as a search vehicle.

Using this questionable expedient, they eventually did retrieve an intriguing image of a possible nautical artifact. This object Jack Grimm immediately identified as one of *Titanic*'s huge bronze propellers. Ryan and Spiess were less positive. The picture of the "propeller" was not at all distinct, and there was no magnetometer reading to positively identify the steel shaft.

But Grimm was convinced, and the world media were compliant enough to echo his questionable optimism. Careful analysis of the image, however, showed that it was most likely not a propeller or any other debris from the wreck. Undaunted, Jack Grimm did manage to raise enough money for a final expedition two years later. This time Fred Spiess was already committed to other projects. Bill Ryan was the chief scientist who joined Grimm aboard the R/V *Robert D. Conrad* in July

1983. But when they reached the "propeller" site, a long North Atlantic gale made an accurate search nearly impossible. Grimm's tantalizing "propeller" remained an elusive target. Magnetometer readings identified no metal object of *Titanic's* proportions anywhere near the search coordinates. This third expedition was further confounded by Grimm's insistence on overriding Bill Ryan's carefully planned search patterns. Despite Ryan's objections, Grimm wasted precious time repeating *Sea MARC* sweeps across the propeller site.

Defeated as much by his stubborn obsession as by the rotten weather, Jack Grimm's last expedition ended in failure.

Watching, frustrated, from the sidelines, I could see several basic problems with Grimm's approach. To begin with, he lacked faith in his scientists. And he had not conducted the type of rigorous historical analysis needed to create a logical search area. Then he refused to conduct the type of plodding, monotonous sweep pattern necessary to completely blanket the search area once it had been selected. Finally, he hadn't funded any of the expeditions to remain on the site long enough to expand the search area once the original zone proved barren.

Even though those three Grimm expeditions were frustrating and nerve-racking from my point of view, I did learn a great deal from their mistakes.

As so often happened in my career, the process that was to eventually lead me out to *Knorr's* deserted deck on the night of August 31, 1985, began inauspiciously enough one morning in the summer of 1982, when I got a telephone call from my old friend and tennis partner, Dr. Robert Morse. Bob had been Assistant Secretary of the Navy for Research and Development before coming to Woods Hole. The Chief of Naval Operations, Admiral Thomas Hayward, had just called him looking for someone to give a talk to the navy.

"The CNO wanted to know if you would go down to the

War College later this summer and give a speech at the Navy's Seapower Symposium," Bob said.

I was happy to help out an old friend, so I replied, "Sure, Bob, I'll give you a good dog-and-pony show. Just send the details to my secretary."

I didn't give the symposium much thought until a few days before I was scheduled to drive down to the War College in Newport, Rhode Island. Then I asked my secretary, Terri Nielsen, to call the navy for details. I was taken aback when she announced that they wanted me to stay at the symposium for the full three days and that there would be only two other speakers, one the Chief of Naval Operations himself, and the other, Secretary of the Navy John Lehman.

"What's going on?" I asked. "Why are these VIPs talking about marine propulsion?"

"Bob," Terri said, exasperated, "they said the symposium is about sea*power*, not power plants. You know, global strategy, the cold war, that type of thing."

Holy cow, I thought, on the edge of panic. I'd planned to throw some slides of past expeditions into a tray and talk off the cuff. Now what? I had all of two days to prepare for this high-level conference. What the hell could I talk about?

Then I realized that I'd seen more of the sea bottom and knew more about the actual terrain of the ocean floor than practically anybody in the U.S. Navy. And for years I'd thought about undersea warfare that took advantage of sea-bottom terrain features just as land warfare did.

I decided to bid for my long suit, geology. I'd talk about mountain ranges far more impressive than the Himalayas or Rockies and chasms four times deeper than the Grand Canyon. And I'd tell the symposium that this rugged sea-floor landscape could be used by the navies of the world to their tactical and strategic advantage.

My conception of naval "terrain warfare" went back to the days of my unexpected conversion from a young, highly trained army intelligence officer to an unlikely navy ensign. In the ensuing years I'd always been amazed at the apathy of our nuclear submarine officers toward the ocean floors. They always told me the sea bottom was "something to stay the hell clear of" at all costs, not a natural feature to exploit.

Whereas I saw subs as tanks hiding behind submerged ridges and deep inside submarine canyons, U.S. Navy submariners saw their boats as jet fighters soaring through the undersea *sky*. But I knew those subs were more like lumbering blimps and were sitting ducks for modern high-speed homing torpedoes. In a word, the navy had never given the idea a thought.

Maybe I'd make a fool of myself preaching this gospel to the navy brass, but it was a concept I believed in.

The auditorium at the War College was an impressive sight, filled with flag rank officers of all the free world's navies. There was more gold braid out there than I'd ever seen before. The front row was taken up by Secretary Lehman, Admiral Hayward, and a glittering assembly of four-star admirals.

I focused my presentation on the most obvious strategic and tactical terrain features of the world's sea floors, using a beautiful set of color slides developed at Woods Hole.

"Choke points," I said, aiming my light pointer at the screen to highlight the canyons of the Greenland-Iceland-Norway gap in the North Atlantic, the Strait of Gibraltar, and the shallow entrances to the Sea of Japan.

Small combat subs that loved the bottom terrain, I explained, well hidden in the side gullies of these submarine canyons, could deny access to the strategic waterways to any hostile naval force, surface or submerged. This was not popular doctrine at the time the Reagan administration was striving for a six-hundred-ship navy, built around the centerpiece of fifteen aircraft-carrier battle groups.

My detailed presentation was greeted with polite applause, and I spent the rest of the next two days getting to know the officers and civilian officials attending the symposium. Navy Secretary John Lehman seemed quite interested in my concept, especially when I told him, "My colleagues and I are developing new imaging systems that will allow us to see farther underwater than ever before."

After the conference, I got on with work at Woods Hole, thinking nothing more would come of my talk. I had harbored vague hopes that maybe my presentation might help my ongoing but so far futile attempt to convince the Office of Naval Research to fund my *Argo-Jason* project. But deep down I was sure that detailed proposal was lying in some in-box in Washington, slowly gathering dust.

But a week or so later, my phone rang. It was the CNO himself, Admiral Hayward.

"Sure liked your talk, Bob," the admiral said. "In fact, I never thought about that concept. Can you come down to the Pentagon and make your presentation to my OpNav Staff?"

"You bet, Admiral," I said, not understanding that Hayward was referring to the top admirals in the Navy.

Ten days after that I was being led through the rubber-tile maze of the Pentagon toward the E-Ring. As luck would have it, Admiral Hayward had been called away to testify to Congress at the last moment, so my senior host would be Vice Admiral Robert Tom Foley, Jr., Deputy Chief of Naval Operations for Plans and Policies.

I had had an opportunity light years before to dive in the Navy's miniature deep-diving nuclear submarine NR-1. It was in fact nimble enough and had the depth capability to serve as an engineering model for my terrain warfare "tank." The NR-1 even had a set of wheels, which allowed it to roll along the bottom.

Beyond all these weapons concepts, of course, I realized that implementing my submarine terrain warfare concepts would definitely require developing extremely sensitive imaging systems for "terrain-involved" submarines. And I just happened to have plans for what the navy needed in my *Argo-Jason* design package.

Shortly after arriving, I was told that Vice Admiral Ron Thunman, who was Deputy CNO for Submarine Warfare, wanted to see me before my presentation. Still thinking optimistically about navy funding for *Argo,* I was ushered into Admiral Thunman's inner sanctum through an electronic security door with a portholelike window. Thunman dropped the classified document emblazoned with red labels and stood stiffly before a desktop model of the new Los Angeles–class fast attack submarine. The walls of his office were covered with heroic photographs of submarines bursting from the water like breaching whales.

The admiral scowled. "What the hell are you doing, telling the Secretary of the Navy that the oceans of the world are becoming transparent?"

That was just the opening volley of his salvo. He kept up his accusations in the same vein, but I was too stunned for the words to register. I was getting my ass chewed out by a professional.

After my initial shock, hot anger rose in my throat. This was a load of crap. I hadn't volunteered to come here; the navy had asked me. Besides, the Office of Naval Research seemed to be ignoring all my recent requests for funds.

I searched for some way to fight back, then spotted the huge map of the world on the admiral's wall. It was a travesty; the entire ocean was one faceless blue field with only the faintest hint of the great Mid-Ocean Ridge and the other main terrain features hidden beneath the surface.

The commander of all U.S. submarine forces should have had a better map than that. I told him so.

"Do you realize that tremendous mountain ranges lie beneath the sea?" I shot back, jabbing my finger at his silly map. "And do you also realize that great canyons cutting through the continental shelves of the world's oceans could hide your entire submarine force? Or the Soviets'?"

I was still mad as hell. But suddenly Admiral Thunman's weathered face broke with a smile. He held out his hand for me to shake. "Sit down, Dr. Ballard," he said warmly. "Let's talk."

Later that day, I learned I had just passed the "Rickover test," the harsh means of separating men from boys devised by Admiral Hyman Rickover, the father of nuclear submarines.

The offshoot of this meeting was completely unexpected. Just one week later, Admiral Hayward asked if I would return to the Pentagon to discuss the impact that my concept of terrain warfare might have on the navy of the future. This time Rear Admiral Bruce Kollmorgan, who commanded the Office of Naval Research, was invited to the meeting. It was on Admiral Kollmorgan's desk that my *Argo-Jason* proposal had been gathering dust.

During the course of the discussion, Admiral Hayward asked me what was the status of my *Argo-Jason* proposal. Before I could utter a word, Admiral Kollmorgan assured Admiral Hayward that it was "already funded," to the tune of $500,000 a year for four years. This was fantastic news. But I realized I would need fully twice that much. Luckily, I had conferences scheduled later with Captains John Howlan and John Verd, directors of Op-23, the navy's deep submergence program. I'd helped them out over the past few years and now proposed that the *Argo-Jason* system might be just what they needed to help on future emergency searches of the ocean floor.

What convinced them was my suggestion that, unlike *Alvin*, which the navy sometimes had trouble breaking free from its research schedule in an emergency, they could actually reserve a month of *Argo-Jason*'s time each year and use those days whenever they wanted.

"If you own a month," I told them, "you'll always have access."

"That sounds good to me," Captain Howlan said with enthusiasm.

"Quite promising, Bob," Verd agreed.

The wheels of navy bureaucracy spun with amazing speed. By the end of 1982, I had an additional two-million-dollar-plus budget allocated over a four-year period for the development and testing of the *Argo-Jason* system.

Once the funding was in place and we began the development of the *Argo-Jason* system, we also discussed the proper field testing of the equipment. Under my agreement with the navy, their funding insured that *Argo-Jason* technology would be available to them should they need it for a national emergency. In the absence of an emergency, Admiral Thunman's Submarine Warfare branch of the navy would approve each year's projects. So it was only natural that we'd field test the new system searching for sunken submarines.

The submarine community is very close knit, and for them the most sacred objects on the bottom of the ocean are the twisted remains of the lost nuclear subs *Thresher* and *Scorpion*.

Among American submariners, these two vessels were discussed in tones of respect, almost veneration. Older officers in this small fraternity all had had friends on *Thresher* or *Scorpion*. The loss of *Thresher* due east of Woods Hole in April 1963 had shocked submariners around the world, highlighting as it did the hidden vulnerability of their seemingly invincible technology. And in 1968, when *Scorpion* was sunk in the mid-Atlantic—possibly by one of its own homing torpedoes gone awry—the hazardous nature of submarine duty was again emphasized.

But the navy was interested in the two sunken submarines for much more than sentimental reasons. Despite the fact that *Thresher*'s wreck had been visited by both the bathyscaphe *Trieste* and *Alvin*, the navy did not have a detailed visual record of the debris field and the principal hull sections. In particular, they needed to know if *Thresher*'s nuclear reactor and containment vessel were leaking radiation into the surrounding deep-sea environment.

This concern also applied to *Scorpion* but with an added dimension of urgency: that wreck also contained two nuclear torpedoes with plutonium-core warheads. Finally, the navy needed to know, if humanly possible, the actual cause of *Scorpion*'s sinking.

Argo's sensitive low-light video cameras would produce a detailed video map of both wrecks. The sophisticated camera sled could loiter on the scene for days if necessary, until we had completely documented every aspect of the sunken vessels.

With this intriguing navy assignment and the added $600,000 a year budget that came with it, I was able to inaugurate the Woods Hole Deep Submergence Laboratory (DSL) in 1982. The first order of business was the development of *Argo*, the simplest but the key component in the system. Later, the smaller tethered robot vehicle *Jason* would be designed and built.

Argo would be our primary survey vehicle for the *Thresher* and *Scorpion* sites. All along, of course, it was an open secret that the relatively sophisticated video sled capable of mapping the submarines' wreck sites would also be an ideal search tool for finding *Titanic*.

With this multiyear navy funding, we could also build and launch the first version of *Argo* using conventional coaxial cable while we were still working on the more sophisticated fiber-optic tether that would eventually transmit real-time detailed colored television images. Our first version of the sled would rely on low-light black-and-white video, which was perfectly adequate for finding wrecks the size of the submarines and *Titanic*.

In developing the more complex *Jason* technology, we also planned preliminary and intermediary stages. The navy wanted me to put small robots directly inside *Scorpion* to hunt for radiation leaks—and to make sure the warheads of the sub's deadly torpedoes were intact. This interim robot would be called *Jason Jr.* or simply JJ.

By tethering JJ to *Alvin,* we could temporarily avoid the need for a long fiber-optic cable. JJ's images would be recorded in *Alvin* and brought back for viewing and detailed analysis to the surface.

As we completed our plans for *Argo,* the vehicle evolved into a fairly robust but more sophisticated sibling of ANGUS, the tough old "dope-on-a-rope" that had served us so well on earlier scientific expeditions. I planned *Argo* to be integrated with a powerful ship-borne multibeam sonar that would virtually pave the way along the search track. *Argo* itself would have two shorter range but more sensitive sonar systems. One would be forward-looking to detect any obstacles in the vehicle's path. The second, side-looking sonar would investigate bottom features to the left and right.

Argo would have a total of three video cameras, giving the operators, working comfortably in the control van of the research vessel, a panoramic view of the ocean floor. Eventually, when the smaller tethered robot *Jason* was integrated into the system, *Argo* would hover stationary above the bottom while the little robot, equipped with powerful lights, stereo cameras, and mechanical arms, would use its own propulsion system to investigate areas too difficult or dangerous for the larger sled to penetrate. I could see *Jason* (and for the interim, little JJ) probing the twisted hull sections of the sunken submarines, deep inside lava fissures like the one that almost trapped *Alvin* on the Mid-Atlantic Ridge—and, of course, roaming through *Titanic*'s flooded ballrooms and corridors.

DSL concentrated on perfecting deep-sea versions of Silicon Intensified Target (SIT) video cameras. The SIT technology was originally developed for night-vision devices during the Vietnam War. The electronic lenses magnified available natural light ten thousand times, channeling each incoming photon into sensors for digital processing. With SIT technology, we would be able to penetrate the eternal darkness of the ocean floor, maximizing the effectiveness of floodlights and strobes.

With the navy prodding us along, we were able to augment our small informal staff at the DSL, which was basically a group of ANGUS team members strong on intuition and enthusiasm but lacking the supersophisticated skills needed to make *Argo* a reality. One of the key people we hired for DSL was Stu Harris, who became *Argo*'s chief designer. Stu had an advanced degree in electrical engineering and was a world-class expert in electronic visual imaging. The first person Stu hired was Bob Squires, a software engineer, and another video-imaging expert. Later, Tom Dettweiler, a resourceful marine engineer with long experience in deep-towed vehicle technology, came aboard to help build the prototype.

These professionals were the true brains of the DSL. But the hard-working "techies" were its soul. They were veterans of the ANGUS team who had literally pioneered the new science of deep-sea-bottom searches. Earl Young, a crusty old New England seaman, was invaluable. There was probably nothing in *Argo* or its shipboard support equipment—short of complex computer chip boards—that Earl and his teammates Emile Bergeron and Tom Crook couldn't fix, often using hammers and hacksaws out on a rolling, freezing deck at the height of an Atlantic gale.

By the time Jack Grimm came home empty-handed from his final *Titanic* expedition in the summer of 1983, the DSL was at full strength and *Argo* was becoming a reality. I planned to field test the system on the nearby *Thresher* wreck site, then to go out to the mid-Atlantic the next year to investigate *Scorpion*'s wreckage. It now seemed perfectly logical to extend the *Scorpion* cruise to the *Titanic* site. This would be a perfect test of the system: a very deep wreck that no one had yet located or photographed.

On a cold winter morning in early 1984, with snow blowing horizontally across the docks and the Eel Pond, I got a call from Captain George Verd at the Pentagon.

They had agreed to fund our at-sea testing of the new *Argo* vehicle in two separate phases. In the summer of 1984, we would use *Argo* to completely map the wreck site of the *Thresher* in 5,800 feet of water south of Georges Bank.

Then, in the summer of 1985, the navy would support a three-week test of *Argo* at the *Scorpion* site. Our mission there was to carefully map the entire field of wreckage and precisely locate the forward section of the submarine, including its torpedo room and the after section of the submarine that contained the nuclear reactor compartment. Once this job was completed, and only after it was completed, were we free to use the remaining time as we chose.

Hurrah! The navy had just given me a green light to search for *Titanic,* an opportunity I had long awaited. I might not find *Titanic,* but at least my chance to make the attempt had finally come.

I put down the phone and stared out at the bleak snow-covered hillsides of the Institution. Then my eyes turned to the warm blue of the huge ocean map on my office wall. I studied the wrinkled contours at the base of the continental slope. Somewhere in that rolling, muddy terrain, 12,000 feet beneath the surface, the wreckage of RMS *Titanic* had lain undisturbed for over seventy years.

I dashed from my office and ran down the stairs in the Blake building to the workshop where Stu Harris and his team were completing the final assembly of *Argo*.

"Gentlemen," I announced, "our time has come. The door to *Titanic*'s tomb has just swung open."

EIGHT

While *Argo* was being assembled at Woods Hole, I felt obligated to take the concept of terrain warfare one step further. Since the influence of Admiral Hayward and the OpNav Staff had landed my funding for *Argo-Jason*, I wanted to demonstrate to the navy brass that my ideas on submarine warfare tactics actually had merit.

My contact with the Pentagon was now through Admiral Thunman and the submarine forces. This was fortunate because I was convinced the small nuclear research submarine NR-1 was the ideal vessel to demonstrate the potential of terrain warfare.

I planned to ask Admiral Thunman's permission to take the NR-1 into the complex undersea volcanic terrain of the Reykjanes Ridge south of Iceland. The strategic importance of the chokepoints between Iceland and Greenland to the west and Iceland and the British Isles to the east was well known to the navy. Throughout the cold war, the navy had positioned nuclear attack submarines in these choke points to intercept Soviet subs entering the Atlantic.

But these subs cruised at relatively shallow depths and were increasingly vulnerable to improving Soviet weapons and detection technology. I wanted to demonstrate that "terrain-involved" nuclear submarines in the future could hide in the volcanic gullies and behind ridges in these corridors and present a far greater challenge to the Soviets.

But before I made my presentation to Admiral Thunman, I had to do more homework than I had for the War College presentation. The first step was to discover if the navy had anything near the type of battle maps the Pentagon had developed for our land armored forces. Ironically, I found out from a friend that the navy did indeed have detailed bathymetric maps of the sea bottom—including the Reykjanes Ridge—stored in a vault in Mississippi. But most senior officers in the Pentagon were unaware of their existence.

I flew to New Orleans, rented a car, and drove to the Naval Oceanographic Office in Bay Saint Louis, Mississippi. Flourishing my new Pentagon clearance papers, I entered the storage facility and began searching for the maps I needed.

I'm sure the petty officers and civilian cartographers thought I was crazy when I laid the big bathymetric map sheets out on the floor side by side until I had covered my hypothetical battlefield. These maps were still marked "Top Secret" because they had been developed from SASS sonar surveys. So I took a red pencil and carefully outlined the exact area I wanted the oceanographic office to reproduce at a larger scale on their cartographic computer.

"Oh yeah," I added as an afterthought, "when you print out the new sheets, please mark them 'Unclassified.'"

Several weeks passed before the maps arrived. Then I turned them over to a model maker with detailed instructions on the type of multicolored three-dimensional topographic mock-up of my future battlefield that I wanted him to make. He produced a beauty, something worthy of a Smithsonian diorama, which encompassed all the steep volcanic scarps, twisting gullies, and sawtooth side ridges of this section of the Mid-Atlantic Ridge. When the model had been crated up and shipped off to be stored in Captain Verd's Pentagon office, I picked up the phone and called Admiral Thunman to request an appointment.

Captain Verd lent me two young lieutenants to help lug the strange multicolored model of the Reykjanes Ridge down the Pentagon's prestigious E-Ring corridor to Thunman's inner sanctum.

"What's this?" Thunman asked, as the lieutenants laid the model on his conference table. "It looks like some kind of a crazy wedding cake."

"That's your battlefield of the future, Admiral," I said confidently. "I want to take the NR-1 into this terrain and prove a nuclear submarine with a regular crew can work there. Admiral, when we're through, that skipper and his crew will have fallen in love with those cliffs and ridges."

Admiral Thunman shook his head as he walked around the table scowling at the sculpted curves of the model sea bottom.

"I don't have time for this, Ballard," he said. "This is just too far out in the future. Congress is trying to shut me down every chance they get. This"—he swept his big hand across the brown-and-gray flanks of the model—"this is twenty years off, maybe more."

I nodded without speaking.

Thunman stared at me with a strange expression. "The future . . . hell, that's my job, too. All right, Ballard, I'll give you the NR-1."

I had devised an elaborate Rickover test of my own, and Admiral Thunman had just passed with flying colors.

My dive aboard the NR-1 that summer on the Reykjanes Ridge was everything I expected. We covered 120 miles, actually traveling across the bottom at depths below 2,000 feet. We crept up the sides of seventeen different active volcanoes and poked the NR-1's snout deep inside a giant lava tube. NR-1 slipped nimbly along these steeply terraced volcanic scarps, maneuvering close to sheer basalt cliffs and pinnacles. For days on end, we explored vertical rock faces and deep inside gullies without losing a single flake of paint from the submarine's black hull.

It became obvious that our nuclear submarine force had crews capable of operating on this future undersea battlefield, just as I had envisioned, if only the Pentagon and Congress would build them a new class of submarines to exploit the terrain of these choke points.

As pleased as I was with the results of this twenty-day trial cruise, I was eager to return to my real mission: completing the *Argo-Jason* system and searching for *Titanic*.

On July 12, 1984, I sat in the control van aboard *Knorr*, watching the video monitors as *Argo* glided silently above the ocean floor of the continental slope, 8,400 feet below. This was the second day of mapping *Thresher*'s debris field. We were also compiling a complete high-quality videotape record of the entire site for the navy. As we had hoped, and worked so hard to bring about, *Argo*'s sonar and imaging systems were working almost perfectly.

On all those ANGUS expeditions, I'd felt the intense frustration of kiting that camera sled sightlessly across the bottom with only the feeble telemetry signal of its crude sonar altimeter tapping like a blind person's white cane, often too late to prevent a collision with a volcanic outcrop or boulder. But *Argo* had "real-time" eyes, to use the programmers' jargon. And those eyes were sharp. The SIT cameras missed very little detail.

And because the sea bottom here was basically crusted grayish white sediment, littered with *Thresher*'s dark metallic debris, the sharp black-and-white video images transmitted up that long tether created the definite illusion that this control van perched on *Knorr*'s stern was, in effect, the bridge of a deep-diving submersible. The screens seemed more like portholes than television monitors. Everyone in the *Argo* control van, from Captain Richard Bowen, *Knorr*'s skipper, to Stu Harris at his station carefully monitoring *Argo*'s systems, to rock-solid Earl Young manning his winch controls at the flyer's station, had admitted they'd been swayed by this powerful visual illusion. We didn't feel that the control room was connected to the sea floor by thousands of feet of cable. Instead, we felt as if we were actually down there.

This "telepresence" was the goal I had long hoped to achieve. For all intents and purposes, our eyes and minds had been transported to a vantage point only a few meters above the sea bed. But our vulnerable bodies remained safely in the air-conditioned comfort of the control van on the surface.

And by alternating among *Argo*'s forward-looking, telephoto, and down-looking wide-angle cameras—and by switching from visual to sonar imagery—the team in the control van was given a more sophisticated and detailed picture of the sea floor than anyone had ever enjoyed before.

I watched *Argo*'s powerful floodlights illuminate the ripply banks of gray sediment, as if we were gliding above dirty old snow drifts after a December Nor'easter on Cape Cod. Once again, we crossed over a stream of *Thresher* debris. An empty rubber boot twisted up from the mud, then came a foil-backed streamer of insulation. A rubber glove, the fingers clenched into a fist, lay nearby. This light debris had probably come from the submarine's engine room, as the boot and glove were standard protective equipment for the reactor crew.

I glanced at the navigation plot where Tom Crook studied our pulsing green survey line on the computer screen. We were heading south, patiently towing *Argo* 10 meters above the bottom, trying to find closure—the last bits of light material— that would mark the end of *Thresher*'s debris field. Our inability to find the outer edge of the debris, which we believed had been deposited in a circular pattern—just as in shipwrecks close to shore—was puzzling.

But as the intricate counterpoint of a Bach concerto echoed softly from the stereo, the significance of what we were observing suddenly registered in my consciousness.

When *Thresher*'s hull imploded beneath the crushing pressure, the stout bulkheads collapsed like wet cardboard. Clouds of debris were expelled from the shredded hull. The big chunks of plating and machinery dropped in a near-vertical free fall. But faint deep-sea currents separated this heavier wreckage from the lighter debris. I pictured pioneer farmers winnowing their harvest by pitching the threshed grain into the air so the breeze carried off the lighter chaff. If the submarine had struck the bottom in shallow soundings, the light material would have fallen among the heavier debris.

But *Thresher* had sunk in 8,400 feet of water.

"Earl," I said, tapping the chart, "the debris field isn't a circle. It's got to be a trail. No wonder we couldn't get closure to the west."

During *Thresher*'s last plunge, the winnowing continued all the way to the bottom. A logically sorted trail of debris—not a circle—had been laid down. The paper, plastic, and rock wool insulation—the chaff—had to lie farthest from the big, heavy hull sections. The closer to the central wreckage, the heavier the fragment. This debris trail would form an arrow, pointing directly to the heart of the wreck.

I now realized that *Thresher*'s debris field trailed off to the west. Suddenly much more than just the mystery of *Thresher*'s wreck became clear.

All ships that sank in the deep ocean were exposed to currents for a longer time than wrecks sinking in shallow coastal waters. There had to be a telltale light-to-heavy debris trail of wreckage on the deep-sea floor.

And because *Titanic* had sunk in 12,400 feet of water, she had to have laid down a similar debris trail.

I spoke with Tom Crook, the navigator. On the next search track we shifted our survey line to the east, beginning with the scraps of light insulation and the rubber glove.

Argo trailed 8,400 feet below *Knorr*, its video eyes searching the muddy bottom.

"Wreckage," Earl called, scanning his TV screen.

Chunks of warped hull plate lay among twisted piping. Then the unmistakable rusted planes of *Thresher*'s rudder jutted up from the circular impact crater. We were over the main debris. As I had hoped, the chaff trail of light debris had led like a road to the twisted wreckage of the submarine's hull.

We had discovered the Rosetta Stone that would lead us to *Titanic*.

Unraveling the mystery of *Titanic*'s debris field was a major accomplishment. But actually assembling an expedition to successfully exploit this knowledge was another matter altogether.

I was convinced that Jack Grimm had not given his expeditions enough time at sea to conduct rigorous searches and to carefully follow up on promising leads. And I was determined to avoid this mistake. The navy was committed to funding three weeks at sea in the summer of 1985, and I hoped to spend at least two of those weeks on the *Titanic* search after mapping the *Scorpion* wreck with *Argo*. But I obviously needed other resources to conduct a preliminary sonar search.

I turned to my oldest and most reliable allies in deep-sea exploration, the French. Soon after receiving the go-ahead from the navy, I flew to Paris to meet with colleagues from the *Institut Français de Recherches pour l'Exploitation des Mers* (IFREMER), successor to the French government's CNEXO that had backed Project FAMOUS. Over a typically sumptuous dinner in Claude Riffaud's apartment, I managed to convince IFREMER director Yves Sillard that finding *Titanic* would be the maritime equivalent of a successful moon landing. The fact that participation in an international *Titanic* expedition would probably result in the same kind of high-technology transfer to France as had occurred during Project FAMOUS apparently convinced Sillard. IFREMER quickly backed the project and committed two of its most competent people, Jean Jarry, as leader of the French team, and Jean-Louis Michel, who would be my coleader, once the expedition was at sea. I'd worked closely with them during FAMOUS and knew they would bring a high level of skill and dedication to the *Titanic* project.

The division of responsibilities on which we quickly settled exploited both teams' resources. The French under Jean-Louis Michel would initiate the search from their research vessel *Le Suroit*. They would use their remarkably sensitive new side-scanning *Sonar Acoustique Remorqué* (SAR). Jean-Louis was one of the most competent maritime field engineers in the world and he had concentrated on perfecting the SAR system over the previous several years. This deep-towed sonar, which looked like a bulbous red torpedo, used the latest in signal-processing technology. The shadow graphs SAR produced were the most sensitive in the world and actually looked like black-and-white photographs of the sea floor. But for SAR to work well, the big Fiberglas cylinder had to be towed with absolute precision back and forth at an exact height above the ocean floor so that the overlapping swathes of sonar beams could be computer enhanced correctly.

I was confident that the French team under Jean-Louis Michel could accomplish this daunting task, provided the weather cooperated and there were no major equipment failures—two big ifs in any expedition. But I knew that the French stood more than an even chance of finding *Titanic* in the first phase of our expedition. If that happened, *Argo* would become just an ancillary tool used to videotape and film the actual wreck. The discovery itself would be a French accomplishment.

But if Jean-Louis and *Le Suroit* were to have any chance at all of succeeding where Jack Grimm's three expeditions had failed, we needed to agree on a manageable, logically determined search area before the French sailed. That winter we worked long and hard at narrowing down the boundaries of our eventual box-shaped search area.

Since IFREMER's participation in the *Titanic* search effort was now officially endorsed by the French government, while my U.S. Navy sponsorship was unofficial, Jean-Louis could spend money out of his budget to thoroughly research the sinking history of the *Titanic*, while I could not. Ironically, after the French completed their analysis, the results were identical to those Bill Tantum and I had worked out together years before. Using the same limited data, we established a search strategy that focused on the same box.

The choice of this area was based on such variables as the ship's reported position at the time she struck the iceberg, the reports on the ice field from other vessels, and the position at which the liner *Carpathia* discovered the survivors in life-boats the next morning.

Because we knew it was more likely *Titanic's* longitude would be in error than her latitude—given the inherent weak-ness of celestial navigation—our east-west coordinates were more critical than the north-south dimensions of the search box. So we opted for a larger initial search area than Grimm's expeditions had, in order to be sure the wreck lay somewhere within it. The final box was canted toward the northwest, covered some 100 square nautical miles of ocean floor, and was centered on Titanic Canyon, a well-known bottom feature. *Titanic's* reported sinking position was near the box's upper left corner, and the lifeboat recovery position lay at the south-ern base. We located our primary search box here because the French and I agreed that, given the 1-knot current that had apparently flowed toward the southeast on the night of April 14, 1912, the wreck of *Titanic* could not lay farther south and east than the recovery spot of the lifeboats, which had drifted on the surface while the huge liner plunged inexorably to the bottom.

But even narrowing the search box to these reasonably constrained dimensions, Jean-Louis would have an exacting challenge to conduct a SAR survey of the entire area in the four weeks *Le Suroit* was scheduled to spend on the *Titanic* site. He would have to patiently, painstakingly "mow the lawn" with SAR, towing the sonar cylinder at a precise height across the bottom so that the computer aboard *Le Suroit* could construct its intricate, overlapping shadow-graph map.

Le Suroit sailed from Brest on June 24, 1985. After a brief stop in the Azores, they steamed west to the *Titanic* site and set to work. For two weeks, they plowed doggedly back and forth, alternating their northwest heading with southeasterly tracks as the SAR delivered billions of bits of digital sonar data. But instead of the reasonably calm weather predicted for midsummer, *Le Suroit* had to face a continual series of storm fronts that created fierce and conflicting currents. After two weeks of the search, the sonar had mapped only barren sea bottom, finding no shadow-graph target even remotely similar to *Titanic* wreckage.

The ship put into the French island of Saint Pierre in Canada's Gulf of Saint Lawrence for provisions. There I joined Jean-Louis and his team for the second leg of the French search.

I studied Jean-Louis's SAR plots on the way back out to the site. Despite the bad weather, he had done an admirable job of shadow-graph mapping almost all the upper half of our original search box. As the SAR produced a sonar swath almost a thousand meters wide and Jean-Louis had been careful to keep his vehicle on precisely plotted survey lines so that the swathes overlapped, we could be confident *Titanic* did not lie in the area he had already searched—assuming, of course, that the huge hull had stayed reasonably intact.

But as we sailed back to the *Titanic* site, Jean-Louis and I discussed the somber possibility that *Titanic* might have been completely buried by mud slides following the massive Grand Banks earthquake in 1929, which broke several transatlantic cables. If in fact the wreck lay in Titanic Canyon, which cut diagonally through the central portion of our search box, or to the west of the canyon, it could well have been buried beneath millions of tons of bottom sediment dislodged from upper slopes by that earthquake. Neither the sensitive SAR system nor *Argo* could probe beneath the mud-choked bottom of a deep marine gully that might conceal *Titanic*'s grave.

The SAR search was scheduled to continue for another seventeen days, during which I would be more or less a supernumerary. I had no real role to play aboard *Le Suroit* other than to give encouragement and the occasional suggestion to Jean-Louis. Like so many professional French engineers, he was meticulous in his professional habits and tireless in his dedication to the mission.

But I frankly found the crowded little French research vessel claustrophobic. We certainly ate well, but there was a stiff formality about the meals, with the captain holding court at the head of the table. Despite the excellence of the *boeuf en daube* and the Burgundy and Bordeaux of fine vintages, I longed for the more spacious compartments of *Knorr* and unassuming burgers and fries from the galley. And when the weather inevitably turned rotten and we were forced inside, the overcrowded little ship seemed even more confining.

Discomfort, however, was the least of our problems. The IFREMER team plotted doggedly on, despite the rough seas and terrible currents, and managed to shadow-graph survey over 70% of our primary search box, a notable achievement given the weather. But late on the cold, overcast morning of August 6, when it was past time to reel in the SAR pod and head back to Canada, the normally loquacious French team was silent and downcast. Although the SAR shadow graphs had produced what seemed to be some intriguing images, reexamination showed the targets to be nothing more than crested sand ridges. For over a month, *Le Suroit* had carefully scoured the bottom.

But they had found no trace of *Titanic*. Now it was my turn, and I was less than confident that *Argo* would succeed where the sophisticated French sonar had failed.

Jean-Louis and I flew an interminable series of connecting flights from the island of Saint Pierre to Ponta Delgado in the Azores, where we joined *Knorr* on August 12, 1985, for the second half of the search. Stu Harris and his engineers were worn out from a combination of tension and frantic last-minute work. The huge reels of *Argo*'s long .68-inch coaxial cable had just arrived by air freight. The ship's crew and the *Argo* team had worked around the clock installing the cable on the squat take-up drum that stood on the starboard side of *Knorr*'s main deck next to *Argo*'s control van. If the cable hadn't arrived when it did, we would have lost precious days from the tightly budgeted three-week charter the navy had funded.

But before we could even steam west to the *Titanic* site, we had to pay our dues to Admiral Thunman and Op-23 by mapping *Scorpion*'s wreck site with *Argo*. This intriguing period in that summer's cruise remained highly classified until the cold war was officially declared over in 1993. As awkward as it was, I was forced to keep Jean-Louis and his two IFREMER colleagues, Jean Jarry and Bernard Pillaud, completely out of the loop as concerned our *Scorpion* search. This was tricky business: I didn't want to alienate my French colleagues, but the navy insisted only Americans with the proper clearances be allowed inside the control van while we searched for, then carefully videotaped *Scorpion* and its debris field in 11,500 feet of water south of the Azores.

I managed to keep the French reasonably satisfied with a vague explanation that the navy needed to test some secret equipment for a few days.

I brought the American team into the control van for a pep talk.

"If we're going to have any time left in this cruise to search for *Titanic*," I said, "we can't afford to make any mistakes over the next few days that might cost us *Argo* survey time on the bottom."

Earl Young and the other veterans of the ANGUS cruises

nodded grimly. They knew how easy such mistakes, and the resulting damage to equipment, were to make.

The Pentagon had sent three officers from the Office of Naval Intelligence to insure we thoroughly mapped the *Scorpion* and its debris before leaving the area and heading west to the *Titanic* site.

We installed a network of transponders around the classified sinking site of *Scorpion*. As soon as the transponders reached the bottom and their position logged, *Argo* was on its way to the bottom.

Just as in the *Thresher* survey the year before, we used *Knorr*'s powerful cycloidal thrusters to carefully maneuver *Argo* back and forth across the bottom. While each survey line was being run, we made a real-time record of its track on the large plotting table at the center of the control van.

Our job was to completely delineate the entire debris field surrounding the main pieces of wreckage. Unlike the *Thresher* debris field, which had few large pieces, most of the *Scorpion* was intact, composed of two large sections of the submarine's hull. Each big chunk was located inside a large impact crater formed by its high-speed crash into the soft deep-sea sediment.

Once again, the debris field was not circular in shape but an elongated trail laid down by the undersea currents, which had deflected the lighter debris away from the vertical path the heavy hull sections had followed.

We worked quietly and intensely, around the clock, driven by our mutual desire to do an excellent job and to finish the mission as quickly as possible. Finally, after four hard days, Lieutenant George Rey, the senior naval observer, gave us an A-OK and permission to terminate this phase of the cruise.

With *Argo* still dripping from its final run across *Scorpion*, and the crew still busy securing the camera sled in its deck cradle, Captain Richard Bowen ordered full speed ahead.

"*Titanic,* here we come," I said, as the helmsman spun the wheel and *Knorr* turned west.

*   *   *

We arrived on the *Titanic* site on the warm evening of August 24. The sunset sea was flat calm, the sky cloudless. We now had twelve days to complete the second phase of the hunt for *Titanic*.

En route from the Azores, I had carefully explained to Jean-Louis and his IFREMER colleagues the search strategy I intended to follow. Because the meticulous SAR sweeps had failed to locate *Titanic* in the most likely sectors of the original search box, I intended a radical departure from the northwest-southeast overlapping sweep pattern the French had employed. I outlined the winnowed-grain theory of a sunken vessel's debris trail that I had formed mapping the wreck of the *Thresher*.

The plausibility of this theory had been reinforced by our recent survey of the *Scorpion,* but I wasn't free to talk about it.

With this approach in mind, I told my French colleagues, "I've decided not to search for the hull of *Titanic,* but rather for the debris field."

Jean-Louis and the two other Frenchmen were at first skeptical but quickly became adherents to the plan as I revealed its underlying logic.

Taking a blank sheet of paper, I sketched a diagram showing how debris that had entered the water when *Titanic* broke up would have fallen toward the bottom. The depth at the position where *Titanic* reportedly sank was 3,700 meters (12,025 feet). *Carpathia* and the other nearby liner, *Californian*, reported a southeast-flowing current of just over 1 knot. This would render a debris field between half a mile and 1 mile in length.

"That's a lot bigger target to search for than a three-hundred-meter-long hull," I said.

Jean Jarry looked at his two colleagues and nodded. "*Oui, d'accord*. You are right, Bob."

Argo, I added, was the ideal vehicle for this debris field search. What I couldn't tell them was that I had already carefully tested this theory the year before, while mapping *Thresher*'s debris field, and just days earlier on the *Scorpion* site.

The farthest extension of *Thresher*'s trail consisted of very light debris strewn across a gently rolling countryside scattered with glacial boulders. The human eye, with the aid of *Argo*'s low-light-level video cameras, could easily distinguish between glacial boulders and man-made objects. But after mapping *Thresher*'s long debris trail, I conducted a sonar run parallel to the trail to see if I could make out the man-made objects on the sonar trace. I could not. All the sonar showed were the glacial boulders; the gloves, insulation, and lighter debris were transparent to the sonar. When it came to light debris, even the best sonar—SAR included—was blind as a bat.

In the French SAR search of the original area, they had done vital but thankless groundwork, which allowed me to shift my own hunt farther to the east. Now it was even more important to take into consideration the position at which *Titanic*'s lifeboats were found drifting on the calm morning after the tragedy. It was logical to assume that debris wafting from the sinking ship beneath the surface would have drifted toward the bottom in the same direction followed by the lifeboats on the surface—south-southeast from the sinking vessel. So it was also only logical that *Titanic*'s wreck *had* to be to the north of where her lifeboats were found.

This meant that the long comet trail of the debris field swept generally north to south somewhere in a box extending to the east from the line of icebergs and north of the position where *Carpathia* had retrieved the lifeboats. But how far east and how far north? In my new strategy, that factor was not critical. *Titanic*'s lightest debris—the equivalent of *Thresher*'s torn insulation and the rubber gloves and boots from the reactor room—would have been carried farthest by the underwater current and had to lie at the southern end of the debris field, while the bigger pieces, including the massive hull—assuming it was intact—would form the northern boundary of the debris trail.

I planned to lay down my search lines in an east-west pattern to intersect the debris field at right angles. In order to save time, we would run our *Argo* lines 1 mile apart, which obviously meant we'd miss whole swatches of bottom. But we were searching for a trail of debris, not the hull of a ship. If we missed the wreck on this first ladderlike set of east-west passes, we'd double back with runs halfway between the first set of rungs, which would mean we'd have surveyed the entire bottom of the search area at half-mile intervals. If there was a debris field down there, *Argo*'s sensitive video eyes would find it. Or so I hoped.

We would begin our *Argo* sweeps at the southern end of the new box, near the spot where *Carpathia* had first encountered the lifeboats.

But first we would make a brief sweep of Titanic Canyon to be certain the SAR hadn't missed any major wreckage shielded from the sonar beams by the steep walls and side gullies. As a geologist, I knew submarine canyons collected debris like big vacuum cleaners; deep currents swept across the surrounding countryside, dumping light debris down the axis of the canyon. By towing *Argo* up the canyon axis, I hoped to find any light debris that might indicate that the *Titanic* lay somewhere nearby, within the surrounding "drainage system" of the canyon.

Jean-Louis's SAR had mapped a major landslide in the canyon. It didn't take us long to lay down a transponder net, which we coordinated with precise fixes from navigation satellites, so that we knew our exact position. Our navigation resources were infinitely more advanced than the sextant, compass, and chronograph that *Titanic*'s officers had relied on. But I instinctively warded off the sense of invincibility that this modern electronic technology offered. Even though I was convinced *Argo* was a much better search tool than Deep Tow or *Sea MARC,* Fred Spiess and Bill Ryan were every bit as qualified to find the wreck as I was. And they had failed.

Once we began to search Titanic Canyon, the center of life aboard *Knorr* became *Argo*'s control van perched on the starboard stern. The interior of the van was about as spacious as a midsize mobile home. The center was occupied by a wide chart table and a plotting desk, while along the far side the consoles of the principal operators were arrayed beneath banks of television monitors.

I usually sat at the plotting table at the center of the van so I could observe each of the seven-member crew. The day was divided into six four-hour watches, each manned by one of three crews who worked four hours on and then had eight hours off.

In front and to the left of me was the flyer station where the person operated the controls of the winch that maintained *Argo*'s altitude above the bottom. Our three flyers were our most skilled technicians, Earl Young, Martin Bowen, and Emile Bergeron.

The navigator sat to the flyer's right at a computer console that processed the signals from the acoustic transponder network and matched them with Loran and satellite navigation fixes. Steve Gegg, Tom Crook, and Cathy Offinger were the navigators.

Farther right, down the rank of consoles, sat the driver, the person who steered and controlled the ship using the cycloidal thrusting propellers on the bow and stern. *Knorr*'s captain, Richard Bowen (no relation to Martin), was the most experienced driver. He'd con the vessel if we actually found *Titanic.* But for routine sweeps, the three watch leaders, Jean-Louis Michel, Jean Jarry, and Bernard Pillaud, would oversee the operation and insure that the coverage I had laid out for each four-hour watch was completed before turning it over to their replacements.

The computers of the *Argo* engineer workstation were arrayed in the right-hand corner. Stu Harris, Tom Dettweiler, or Bob Squires was always on duty with one of the watches. As things worked out, Stu Harris, *Argo*'s chief architect, spent hours on end in the van troubleshooting so that he solved any hardware problems before they arose. This was no small achievement, since he was prone to chronic seasickness and wore a circular transdermal dramamine patch behind his ear throughout the cruise.

The sonar operator's station was near the engineer's computers. Navy Lieutenant George Rey, a submariner with extensive experience in deep submergence, was assisted by Terry Snyder from the Klein Sonar Company, which had built *Argo*'s equipment. The third sonar operator was Jim Saint, on loan from Colmek, the company that had provided *Argo*'s sensitive cameras.

And each watch had a member of the documentation team standing by to photograph and videotape any important discovery. Veteran photographers Emory Kristof and Ralph White were augmented by Billy Lange, a kid I had met on the streets of Woods Hole years before and who was now working as a technician for the graphic arts department. Billy had no formal education but had a driving desire to be on our team.

The last member of each watch was probably the busiest, the data logger, who had to continually move from one workstation to another collecting data. This task reminded me of the exhausting slapstick logging routine Al Uchupi and I had suffered through during my first expedition on *Chain*. But Sharon Callahan, Georgina Baker, and Lisa Schwartz certainly had clearer handwriting and sunnier dispositions as they went about this demanding but thankless task than either Al or I.

Dana Yoerger, a new Ph.D. in robotics from MIT, was

on this cruise as an observer. He was *Jason*'s chief designer and proved invaluable in upgrading *Argo*'s tracking software, which was being overloaded by the demands placed on the vehicle.

These large *Argo* watches were indicative of the vehicle's complexity compared to ANGUS, the dope-on-a-rope that needed only three people to operate it. *Argo*'s control van always felt crowded and was usually thick with cigarette smoke, much to the annoyance and discomfort of the nonsmokers. But the mood was generally relaxed, with a truly eclectic variety of music, ranging from reggae to chamber quartets, playing softly on the stereo. And I always made sure there was plenty of hot buttered popcorn available in the galley.

Argo's first search sweep in Titanic Canyon ended quickly. A short had grounded out the telemetry system so that the TV monitors in the van were a chaos of static. We hauled the white steel-tube sled back on deck, and the engineers swarmed around the vehicle like combat medics treating a casualty. Only twenty-two minutes later, the fault was corrected, and *Argo* was on its way back to the bottom. The depth in Titanic Canyon was 12,690 feet, and Earl Young expertly maintained *Argo* at an altitude of only 30 feet above the canyon floor. The video images revealed a typical deep-sea bottom of gray mud sediment, traced by the occasional faint track of a sea slug, but otherwise lifeless.

Over the next two days, we towed *Argo* throughout the length and breadth of the canyon, investigating several "bomb craters," which had appeared on the SAR shadowgraphs and could have marked the impact site of heavy *Titanic* debris. Most of the craters were empty, but we did find one 20-foot-high glacial boulder surrounded by a perfect circular crater. How ironic, I thought, if this boulder had been carried out to sea by the same iceberg that had sunk *Titanic* and been jarred loose from the ice by the collision.

We were all aware of the ticking clock as we impatiently

scoured the canyon, even wasting time to search for Jack
Grimm's damned "propeller" site. But we never could find a
visual image to match his *Sea MARC* photographs.

All told, we spent three of our precious twelve days searching Titanic Canyon and other possible sonar and magnetic
targets from past expeditions. Now we had only nine days
before Captain Bowen had to turn *Knorr* back west toward
Woods Hole, where the ship would embark on another scheduled expedition.

As we began to lay out our new transponder net on the
afternoon of August 27, I began to feel the first cold edges of
pessimism. I had been unreasonably confident that we'd find
some piece of wreckage in the canyon, which would explain
why the detailed SAR shadowgraphs of the original search area
had revealed nothing. But the canyon was devoid of human
artifacts.

On the short run over to the new search site, *Knorr*'s
engineering department took the opportunity to repair *Argo*'s
vital winch system, which we planned to use nonstop for the
next nine days. We'd noticed that the big take-up drum, on
which *Argo*'s vital coaxial cable was stored, was shifting off
its axis. If that drum broke down in such a way as to sever
the cable, we'd lose *Argo* on the bottom with almost no chance
of retrieval.

By sunset on August 27, we had a basic transponder net
down, which we left open to the north to save time. We
launched *Argo* at 1:45 A.M., a calm, unusually warm night on
the North Atlantic. As I watched the white sled's jaunty Fiberglas tailfin dip beneath the surface, I felt both confidence and
alarm. We had less than nine days to survey an area of sea
bottom almost 100 square miles. We had enlarged the original
area covered by the French. But we would have to search this
new zone visually with *Argo* instead of by sonar. Using our
new search strategy, this would require ten or twelve east-
west, west-east passes, each a mile farther north than the one

before. If everything went perfectly, this preliminary search could take as much as six of the remaining eight-and-one-half days. And if we did strike out, there'd only be time for a partial double-back between the lines.

Once we had *Argo* flying stably across the bottom, I was pleased to see that the visibility in this search area was much clearer than the sediment-heavy water of the Titanic Canyon. The clear video images revealed a lifeless gray bottom of closely spaced sand waves, tight ripples, and larger sand dunes.

"It looks like a beach in Brittany," Jean-Louis remarked from the driver's console.

"An empty beach, Jean-Louis," I replied.

As always happened on a cruise, nicknames arose among the competing watches. Jean-Louis Michel's watch—midnight to four A.M., noon to four P.M.—declared they were the "Watch of Quiet Excellence," a friendly taunt to the rival "Zoo Crew," led by Jean Jarry. They were the ship's clowns, given to stunts like marching in lockstep while singing, "Hi-ho, Hi-ho," just like Snow White's dwarfs.

The third watch had not yet earned a nickname. But when they did become "The Crash Crew," the event almost marked the end of the expedition.

Just after breakfast on August 28, Bernard Pillaud was driving while Martin Bowen controlled the winch at the flyer's position. He was a veteran of ANGUS expeditions and a highly skilled flyer. Bernard slowed the ship and turned north to begin our next survey line a mile away, and Martin winched in cable as *Argo* stalled out and began to fall toward the bottom.

But Martin saw from the altimeter readout that the sled was still descending, so he threw the winch lever forward to take up cable fast. The winch traction unit mounted on the deck above the main lab dumped cable to the take-up drum below on the starboard deck. But none of us realized the recent repairs made the drum turn unusually slowly. The drum couldn't keep pace with the incoming cable. Fortunately, Martin shot a glance to one of the TV monitors, which displayed the take-up drum.

"Oh no!" Martin shouted.

I jumped up from the plotting table as I heard him yell. My eye shot to the monitor. A long loop of cable was spilling from the drum and across the main passageway. We watched helplessly as the now-slack cable rolled off the traction unit and fouled around the winch handle.

"Jesus," someone shouted beside me, "no. . . ."

The axle of the traction unit was chewing the precious cable in half. But, miraculously, the system stalled. We dashed from the control van and up the ladder to the traction unit. The cable was firmly jammed in the greasy machinery. Within a minute or two, the ship's momentum would put an unbearable strain on the cable as *Argo,* now sunk to the bottom, acted like an anchor. This was not only an emergency that would ruin the expedition; if the fouled cable snapped with so many of us crawling over the equipment, a person could be literally cut in half by the whipping severed cable end.

To make matters worse, we were at the farthest point from our transponders. If we lost *Argo* on the bottom here, we'd never be able to retrieve her.

"Let her drift," I shouted down through the open door of the van.

The worst thing we could do now would be to try to maneuver the vessel blindly.

In the control van, the watch monitored the cable strain gauge, which held at 17,000 pounds. If the tension increased much above 20,000 pounds, the cable would part, possibly dismembering or even decapitating anyone in its path.

I joined Earl Young and *Knorr*'s bo'sun Jerry Cotter as we and the deck crew worked frantically. We all knew the ship's northward momentum was inexorably building tension on the cable. The task at hand was a straightforward piece of seamanship: rig a scaffold on the stern below the piece of damaged cable, take the strain with a hitched stout line, then splice in an attach point so that *Argo* could be recovered. But we were acutely aware that the cable was a twanging, taut bow strung between the traction unit and the crane sheave.

As we worked, the crew spoke with terse commands and warnings.

"Watch the tension."

"Get me a braided line."

"Easy! Easy! It's slipping."

But twenty frantic minutes later, *Knorr* lay dead in the calm water, we had the strain relieved on *Argo*'s cable, and we were ready to winch the sled back on board.

My scraped hands covered with grease, I sat on the stern taffrail, head lowered despondently. Even if we got *Argo* back on board, I was sure the collision with the bottom and the damage to the cable would have permanently blinded the vehicle. There was no way anyone could airlift a replacement cable out here in the middle of the Atlantic before time ran out.

But as *Argo* was slowly winched from the bottom, Stu Harris went to his station in the van to assess the damage. To our amazement, the video pictures were sharp and clear. We scampered back up to the traction unit and studied the section of cable crushed by the axle. The armor exterior had been gouged, but the concentric woven sheaves of insulation and conductor had not been damaged.

Back at the plotting table, I frantically studied the depth charts of the search area to the north. Another reprieve: our search pattern ahead steadily moved into shallower soundings. We would not have to pay out *Argo*'s cable below the weakened section that had been crushed by the traction axle. This meant a simple electrician's tape bandage on the damaged portion would suffice and it could be carefully coiled on the take-up drum.

I came back out on deck as Bo'sun Cotter's able crew completed their work.

Maybe, I thought, *we might just pull this off.*

But our optimism over the cable's resurrection did not last long. For the next three days, we slowly bore along our search lines from east to west, shifted north, then from west to east. The sharp video images *Argo* transmitted to the van revealed only a dead, gray bottom of mud, ripply sand waves, and the occasional glacial boulder. If *Titanic*'s debris field lay along this north-south axis, we had not reached it yet.

To add to our mounting pessimism, there were the inevitable equipment glitches. On one late-night watch, the log-keeper wrote, "No GPS, no Loran, no ACNAV." A log-keeper on August 30 complained bitterly that our search line was less than precise: "Full speed against the wind, where are we?"

Such griping was inevitable, but the tone was now acquiring a sharp edge, as if in angry anticipation of failure.

That anger and frustration reached a peak on the four-to-eight evening watch on August 30. We had just over five days on station remaining, and *Argo*'s cameras had found no trace of *Titanic* or her debris field. Some members of the team were beginning to grumble, a discontent that formed into a quasi-mutinous cabal.

Its leader was Emory Kristof, my old colleague from *National Geographic* who was obviously chafing at the passive nature of his role. Emory wanted the *Titanic* as badly as I did, but since his skills were in photography and not in exploration, he couldn't move into action until *Titanic* was found. Patience and tact were not his strong suits. In fact, this side of his personality would lead to the termination of our long relationship one day. But aboard *Knorr*, he and fellow photographer Ralph White had been passing their idle hours reading *Titanic* literature and hatching their own theories about the location of the wreck.

When that evening's watch—the Zoo Crew—registered a sonar image of what they believed was a *Titanic*-sized object, Emory called for Jean-Louis and me to come to the van.

I studied the sonar shadowgraph intently, then handed it to Jean-Louis, who only shook his head. We'd seen scores of similar false-alarm images during the earlier SAR phase of the expedition: they were invariably sonar echoes from high sand waves with sculpted edges that formed an intriguing silhouette similar to the hull of a ship.

But Emory scowled when we explained that the "target" was just a sand ridge. He demanded that we break our search pattern and backtrack over the sonar anomaly, even though he had paid little attention to our search strategy up to that point.

"We're just not going to do that," I told him quietly.

But he would not be appeased. "By God," he threatened, "I'm going to radio Bill Garrett and have him *order* you to do it."

Garret was the *National Geographic* editor and partial sponsor of the expedition. The threat was ludicrous but typical of Emory's rebellious attitude. The problem did not rest with him alone. I could see there were others who shared his anger and frustration.

I nodded to Jean-Louis to join me on the fantail to discuss the problem. "What do you think?" I asked. "They're wrong, aren't they?"

Jean-Louis hunched in the suddenly cold wind, the harbinger of a predicted storm front. "Let's not begin to doubt ourselves now," he answered with his precise manner. "But we can't just proceed as if we did not hear them. They've all worked hard. A measure of respect is due."

He was right, and we quickly arrived at a compromise.

Without wasting time on an entirely new line, we could lay our next survey track between lines five and six, which would allow us to visually scan the target that had so intrigued Emory and the others.

"I like that compromise," Jean-Louis said. "We don't give in to mutiny, and they don't cast us off in a lifeboat like Captain Bligh."

I grinned. "If we're lucky."

We went back into the van and I walked silently past Emory to speak quietly to Steve Gegg, the watch navigator, giving him the instructions. Then I turned to leave, only to find my way blocked by Emory Kristof.

"What are you going to do?" he demanded, glowering.

I wanted to tell him to go straight to hell. Instead, I said, "Ask the navigator."

This incident reminded me of the incipient mutiny among Columbus's crew, who questioned his judgment just before he made landfall in the New World. Unfortunately, floggings were no longer in vogue.

While I was sleeping in my cabin, *Argo*'s seventh pass revealed the unmistakable image of a rolling sand ridge, its peaks weirdly sculpted into the contours of a large ship.

Over the next eighteen hours, survey line eight passed without revealing a trace of *Titanic*'s debris field. By the evening of Saturday, August 31, search line number nine was under way and proving just as fruitless. To make matters worse, the weather forecast for the approaching storm front now predicted a Force 8 gale with short, crashing seas and inevitably confused currents. Gales out here normally blew three days.

When I left the radio room after reading the gale warning, I made my way alone to the bow. Like a wounded animal, I needed time to take stock of my situation and prepare for defeat.

* * *

I gripped the briny stern rail, watching the last faint after-glow of sunset blacken as a thick stratus deck obscured the western horizon. The storm front was probably still ten hours away.

Shaking off the pessimism and lethargy, I went into the control van and made sure everything was all right with the Zoo Crew.

They were a quiet lot tonight, but I saw no signs of linger-ing animosity over the confrontation of the previous night.

After a sandwich and a beer in the galley, the pent-up fatigue of the past week hit me. But I stayed awake until midnight to be sure the Watch of Quiet Excellence understood their instructions for line number ten. Leaning over the plotting table, I noticed that the end of line nine would take *Argo* past the northeastern limit of the earlier SAR coverage. In an hour or so, we would be sweeping a section of sea bottom that Jean-Louis had missed, a sliver of territory 1 mile wide and 5 miles long.

It didn't take Jean-Louis's watch long to settle in, and they were living up to their nickname: the only sounds in the van were the habitually chirping computers, the whirr of data printers, and the metronome ping of the sonars. Then someone slipped a cassette into the stereo machine.

"Golden oldies," he said, scanning the plastic tape box.

"I'm going to grab some sleep," I told Jean-Louis, the watch leader.

As I left the van, "I Heard It Through the Grapevine" was playing on the stereo.

Up in my cabin, I felt the chill of the approaching weather and pulled on a pair of thick flannel pajamas. In order to purge my mind of the foundering expedition, I picked up Chuck Yeager's autobiography, hoping the tales of adventure in the sky would make me forget about failure.

*   *   *

Down in the control van, video-tech Bill Lange turned to Stu Harris.

"What are we going to do to keep ourselves awake to-night?" he asked.

The video monitors scrolled the same monotonous image: soft gray mud, low rippling sand hills. It was 0048 hours, twelve minutes before one A.M.

Stu did not answer. His eyes were fixed on the screen. "There's something," he said quietly, pointing at the monitor.

Everyone in the van was suddenly alert.

Stu flipped switches, changing the monitor view from the forward-scanning camera to the down-looking zoom. A moment later, Stu burst with excitement: "It's coming in!"

Bill Lange leaned close to the screen, then shouted, "Wreckage!"

Stu Harris gazed at the flickering gray image. It was angular, probably steel, clearly debris from a ship, but there was no way of knowing if it was from *Titanic*. In 1912, the liner had sunk in the regular trans-Atlantic shipping lanes, but over the intervening years, so had scores of other ships, particularly during World War II when German U-boats had prowled these waters searching for helpless cargo ships. It was more likely that *Argo* had found the debris from one of the wartime wrecks than from *Titanic*.

As *Argo*'s floodlights cast their full power, the crew in the van could distinguish twisted rusty pipes and fittings. The debris appeared considerably older than the wreckage at the *Thresher* and *Scorpion* sites. But how old was the question.

There was no doubt, however, that this material was large.

Lieutenant George Rey, the sonar operator, called out distinctly, "I'm getting a hard contact."

"Bingo!" cried Stu.

Argo passed beyond the metallic objects. The screen revealed only a few small glacial boulders.

The people in the van stared quizzically at each other, as

Stu was rewinding the video tape to the 0048 time hack. Had they all seen the same thing? Then, at 0058 hours, more metallic debris, including unmistakable sheets of riveted hull plate, slid across the TV monitors.

There could be no doubt. *Argo* was gliding 30 feet above *Titanic*'s debris field. Search line number nine had just entered the wedge of unsurveyed terrain that Jean-Louis Michel's SAR sweep had missed a month before.

Now all manner of metallic wreckage flowed across the video monitors.

"Someone should go get Bob," Bill Lange suggested.

But no one wanted to leave the van at this moment of triumph.

Then, at four minutes after one A.M., Stu Harris said, "Let's go get Bob." But still, there were no volunteers.

Finally, the ship's cook, John Bartolomei, who was visiting the van for the first time, volunteered to fetch me.

While the cook headed aft toward my cabin, the sketchy gray image of a circular object suddenly filled the screen. It was 0105 Hours. *Argo* flew at 14.6 meters above the bottom, at a depth of 12,230 feet. In the bright floodlights, three smaller circular shapes appeared on the larger metallic face.

"A boiler?" Jean-Louis mused.

Bill Lange was practically jumping up and down. "It's a boiler!" he yelled.

But Jean-Louis, ever the precise engineer, was cautious. He grabbed the book containing the 1911 *Shipbuilder* article on the construction of *Titanic* and her sister ship *Olympic*. After flipping to the pictures of the huge boilers in their Belfast foundry, then studying the image on the screen, Jean-Louis spoke with conviction.

"Yes. It *ees* a boiler."

John Bartolomei leaned into my cabin and spoke with a strange tone of suppressed excitement. "Uh, the guys think you should come down to the van."

There were only two things that would have caused them to interrupt my rest at this time: either we had a serious problem with the equipment, or we had found *Titanic*'s debris field.

I dragged on my jumpsuit over my flannel pajamas and scrambled down three decks, my boat shoes slipping on the damp stairs.

When I burst through the doorway of the van, Stu Harris rushed up to me, his face full of joy. The first word that registered was "boiler."

In the three minutes it had taken the cook to call for me, *Argo* had indeed passed over and videotaped one of *Titanic*'s twenty-nine gargantuan boilers, unmistakable from the three side-by-side circular vents on the top plate.

I was twanging with excitement, my eyes shooting around the van like a strobe, registering splintered images: the position of the plotline, the depth, the time, both here on the Atlantic and back in the States.

Stu was rewinding the videotape to replay the boiler image. Earle Young flew *Argo* steadily, his face neutral, determined to stay at his station, working well, while the others in the van exploded with our triumph.

Suddenly, the enormity of what had happened washed over me. The film crew was documenting this historic event, and I knew I should have some fitting words to say. But words failed me. All these years, dreaming of this moment. I turned to Jean-Louis and clapped him on the shoulder. His dark eyes were moist, brimming with pride. We had found *Titanic*.

"It was not luck," Jean-Louis said softly. "We earned it."

But I could only reply with stunned incredulity, "God damn . . . God damn."

Argo had found *Titanic*, the Golden Fleece of undersea exploration.

NINE

The voices in the control van rose to a loud babble, then subsided.

"Look at it," someone whispered. "Just look at all of it."

On *Argo*'s monitors we watched a procession of bronze portholes, twisted sections of railing, hull plating and small deck equipment stream by on the rolling gray mud of the bottom.

Most of us had forgotten how huge a ship *Titanic* had been, that she had been assembled from hundreds and thousands of these individual bits and pieces, now revealed to human eyes in the glare of *Argo*'s floodlights for the first time in seventy-three years.

Titanic had been an abstraction to us, a dream; we were not prepared for the mundane reality of the deck-lamp stanchion, bent like a shepherd's crook, the fragile old lightbulb still in place, or the clustered spouts of the ship's steam whistle, now forever mute.

Momentarily, we forgot the exhaustion and anxiety of the past weeks. This collection of light debris—stripped from the great liner by the violence of its long plunge to the bottom and winnowed by the currents to their final resting places on the soft deep-sea sediment—gripped us with absolute fascination.

But I snapped out of the near-hypnotic trance, realizing *Argo* might be in grave danger as we gazed like a herd of stunned deer at the images on the screen. *Titanic*'s massive hull could be looming in *Argo*'s path, only a few meters ahead. Worse, the ship's funnels, jutting cranes, and maybe even its mast-rigged radio antennae might still be intact but, made jagged by seventy-three years of rust, could act as scythes and sever the camera sled's umbilical cable like a stalk of dry grass.

"What's your altitude?" I asked Earl Young.

"Ten meters," he replied instantly.

"Take her up to fifty meters," I shot back, "fast."

Earl hit the winch lever, and we heard the cable whine above the roof of the van.

As we winched *Argo* to an altitude of 50 meters over the bottom, I tried to calculate if that would be adequate to clear the obstacles—provided the hull was intact and nearby—and still give us video coverage.

"Make it sixty," I said, just to be sure.

Even as *Argo* rose from its run across the debris field, we saw images of deck rails, the bronze frames of teak benches long ago consumed by worms, even tantalizing evidence of that final night at sea such as wine bottles and crockery.

Certainly the occasion called for champagne. If this had been *Le Suroit,* we'd be popping the corks on bottles of good Veuve Cliquot. But there was no champagne on board, just plenty of Budweiser and Wild Turkey. We toasted our victory with paper cups of warm sparkling Mateus we'd picked up in the Azores.

For some reason I glanced at the large electric clock on the bulkhead.

"Oh, my God," I exclaimed.

It was just after two A.M., local time. We had found *Titanic* almost at the hour of her death. She had sunk beneath the calm, cold surface of the Atlantic at 2:20 A.M. on April 15, 1912.

Suddenly, the debris strewn across the undulating gray sediment 2.5 miles below was no longer a fascinating Edwardian time capsule but the resting place of 1,522 fellow human beings.

I mumbled a few words to Steve Gegg and Cathy Offinger,

and they spread the word through the van. Most of the members of the expedition and the available crew joined me on the fantail. At exactly 2:20 A.M., Lieutenant George Rey helped me raise the red-white-gold-and-black flag of *Titanic*'s builder, Harland & Wolff, with the taffrail halyard.

I spoke only a few words. "I really don't have much to say, but I thought we might just observe a few moments of silence."

We bared our heads for a long time in respect for the souls of those whose remains rested in the icy black embrace of the deep-sea bottom below. The forecast storm front had stalled to the west and the weather was serene, better than in midsummer. The cloudless sky was velvety with stars, reflecting brightly from the flat surface. Except for the quarter moon overhead, the scene was almost identical to the night *Titanic* sank.

A few minutes later, I said, "Thank you all. Now let's get back to work."

I had to think beyond the jubilation that gripped the ship to somberly assess the reality of our situation. We had less than three days remaining before our time on the site ended. It didn't matter a bit that we'd just pulled off the exploration coup of the century; *Knorr* was chartered by other clients, who had paid good money in advance. So we had to "maximize our resources," in the jargon of modern expeditions. But we were all half dead with fatigue and giddy with spent adrenaline. Nevertheless, I conferred with the watch leaders to plan our tactics for the next few days.

Unfortunately, we'd discovered the debris field and one of *Titanic*'s distinctive boilers at the northern limit of our navigational coverage. Our network of acoustic transponders on the bottom allowed us to accurately follow *Argo*'s track lines across the ocean floor. Clearly, the main portion of the ship had to lie farther to the north. But before trying to find it, we had to recover the bottom beacons to our south and leapfrog them farther to the north.

Once the beacons had been recovered, their batteries replaced, and then dropped into their new northern positions, Jean-Louis and the navigators began to carefully survey them into position. To do this, *Knorr* was driven in a wide circle around the outer perimeter of the network of four transponders that formed a large parallelogram. At various points along the way, *Knorr* would come to "All Stop" and the navigators would listen for the faint echo of all the transponders. With this database, they could survey the transponders into position, and the search for *Titanic*'s main hull could continue.

While this operation was underway, I went to the radio room to notify the beach of our discovery. The first call was an attempt to reach Walter Cronkite, who had offered to help us in the documentation of the expedition, but I was unable to contact him. The second was to Woods Hole to tell our director, John Steele, that we had found the ship.

Unfortunately, it was early Saturday morning during Labor Day weekend and all I got was the guard on duty at the switchboard. I told him to find the director and inform him of our discovery. I would later learn that the message got through, but Dr. Steele decided he could wait until Monday morning before getting back to me for more details.

I returned to the control van disappointed that the world didn't seem to care that we had just found the greatest luxury liner of all time. As I was explaining the situation, Captain Richard Bowen interrupted us to announce that *Knorr*'s old-fashioned but powerful echo sounder on the bridge had just registered "a really big target" during our survey of the transponder network. While *Knorr* was drifting in the calm, quiet sea, listening for the faint echoes from the transponders, it had evidently drifted directly over the main portion of the ship. Although perfect conditions were needed for such an event to occur, it was ironic that, with all our sophisticated search equipment clustered on the fantail, a simple echo sounder would make the final discovery of *Titanic*.

With the survey complete and a possible target to look at, it was time to get *Argo* back into the water. Despite our apparent good fortune, I was not eager to fly *Argo* over the top of the target without knowing a little more about it. I was terrified of what might be waiting for us on the ocean floor. Was *Titanic* sitting upright on the bottom and were its funnels, masts, and rigging wires still intact, waiting to grab *Argo* as I flew over the top for a close visual inspection?

Initially, I planned to fly around the target and use our side-scanning sonar to size it up and see what it looked like. As Jean-Louis and I supervised this sonar survey, neither of us could avoid noting that the debris field leading to this large target lay just beyond the edge of the first SAR sweep he had made in July. But during that initial sonar run along the top of the original search square, the rough sea and currents had made it impossible for *Le Suroit* to keep the SAR unit on course. Jean-Louis's first sonar sweep had been pushed slightly west and south. He had missed *Titanic*'s hull and her debris field by less than 1,000 meters.

After that initial miss, his subsequent search lines inexorably took *Le Suroit* and the SAR further south and west, steadily away from the wreck. Staring at our plotting chart, I thought of the children's game "Hot and Cold." The French had been very hot, indeed, but there'd been nobody there to tell them.

I stumbled through an awkward effort to reassure Jean-Louis that our discovery was not mine alone, that the frustrating weeks of fruitless SAR searches had enabled the American team to search the second area farther east, which contained *Titanic*'s grave.

But he was not easily consoled. "Paris," he muttered, "will look at this as my failure."

By dawn on September 1, the sky had clouded over with

the approaching storm. *Knorr's* radar revealed that the small ship was surrounded by other vessels. Then the bridge shuddered with the thunderous vibration of a U.S. Navy P-3 Orion antisubmarine plane that roared over the ship, no doubt testing its magnetometer on our hull. A mottled gray fighter-bomber with a red Canadian maple leaf insignia roared by. *What the hell's going on?* I thought. Could word have leaked so soon that we'd discovered *Titanic?*

But then Captain Bowen told me that we'd blundered into a naval antisubmarine exercise. He quickly radioed the naval flotilla around us that *Knorr* was towing a deep research vehicle on a long tether. The NATO ships gave us a wide berth.

Some of the ships in the exercise were American, so I took the opportunity to try to reach the commanding officer of one of them in hopes of getting a message to the Secretary of the Navy, John Lehman. John and Walter Cronkite had hosted a send-off party for me on Martha's Vineyard, and John had asked me to call him the minute we found the ship.

I reached the commanding officer of the USS *Garcia* on the radio and told him to "tell the Secretary of the Navy we had found the ship." I didn't want to use the word *Titanic,* so he must have thought I was crazy. Ironically, John did finally get the message, but like the message to Pearl Harbor warning its commanding officers of a sneak attack by the Japanese, Secretary Lehman didn't get my announcement until after watching the news coverage on television.

After making several close sonar passing runs by the target with *Argo,* I still couldn't tell if *Titanic* was upright or lying on its side. More importantly, I couldn't tell if the masts and rigging wires were still in place. The only way to know was to make a direct visual run over the top of the ship and take my chances.

The metaphor of three-dimensional chess is often used to describe an extremely intricate spatial problem. In many ways, maneuvering *Argo* at the end of a 12,500-foot tether was more like a game of *four*-dimensional chess. This was because it took twenty minutes for changes in the velocity and direction of *Knorr* on the surface to be translated down the long cable to the camera sled kiting over the bottom. We could raise and lower *Argo* much more quickly, of course, but its direction and speed "across the ground" were purely a function of the ship's movement so far above.

As *Knorr* crept slowly north, I sat rigidly at the plotting table, my face wrinkled in a frown of concentration. In order to get clear video images of *Titanic*'s hull, we'd have to fly *Argo* only 10 or 15 meters above the wreck. However, the ship's diagram mounted on the control-van bulkhead showed that *Titanic*'s four huge funnels, as well as her fore and aft masts with the skein of guy wires and primitive old radio antennae, extended more than 15 meters above the superstructure.

But survivor accounts had suggested the funnels had toppled as the giant hull tilted toward vertical on its final plunge. Could the less sturdy mast and radio rigging have remained intact after the funnels had failed? I had to take a chance that the superstructure was relatively free of these vertical obstacles, assuming the hull lay upright on the bottom. Still, it was a hell of a chance to take. Shipwrecks were notoriously capricious disasters: one funnel and one mast might have failed, leaving intact a network of jagged obstructions that would kill *Argo* on the moment of contact. But the only thing we'd know in the control van was that the data uplink failed. Then there'd be the sickening drop on the cable tension meter, and we'd realize the *Argo* sled was lost in the wreckage, probably never to be retrieved.

The navy had given me explicit instructions not to endanger their expensive new technology. But, in order to fulfill my obligation as a scientist-explorer, I had to take the chance.

As I plotted the run, the van filled up with members of the off watches. All of us knew that I was going to take the risk. But no one warned me not to.

I looked around the suddenly crowded van, studying the faces of my teammates. Jean-Louis's expression was neutral, the precise, impassionate engineer, studying the computer displays. Earl Young, still at the flyer's station, leaned forward, his glasses perched loosely on his nose, his legs crossed casually, gazing at the video display with seeming nonchalance. It was only when I saw the taut tendons in his muscular right arm as he gripped the winch handle that I realized he was like a coiled serpent, ready to strike at the slightest danger—to yank back the winch-control lever in his hand and reel *Argo* in as quickly as possible.

We were coming up on the big echo-sounder target. The van became absolutely silent except for the monotonous sweet-toned ping of an outgoing sonar pulse followed by the duller incoming echo, the soft clacking of the data printers, and the higher-pitched whine of the winch as Earl maintained his altitude.

I rose from the plotting table and stood in the center of the van, my eyes automatically scanning the monitors: navigation fix, cable tension, wind speed, *Argo*'s altitude and depth, and compass heading. Then I studied the video images on the large television monitors in the control van. The main section of *Titanic* had evidently planed away from the stern and the other heavy objects making up the far end of the winnowed debris trail.

At the northern end of the debris field, slabs of hull plate were interspaced with several more cylindrical boilers and angular derricks ripped from the decks. This was heavy stuff. We were almost at the end of the winnowed chaff trail. Our sonar survey told us that the largest hull section was resting in a gently undulating countryside with only a few pieces of debris surrounding it.

I asked Earl Young to winch *Argo* up to an altitude of 50 meters.

"Fifty meters, on the button," Earl announced after a few moments. The video screens were now a blur of gray "fog," the backscatter of *Argo*'s powerful floodlights diffused by the marine snow falling ceaselessly to the bottom. At this altitude we were blind. The next image we saw would be the ship.

"Ship con," I told Captain Bowen in the driver's seat. "Let's begin our first pass. Try to maintain speed over the bottom of less than point-five knots."

He nodded acknowledgment, his eyes fixed on the navigation plot.

"Flyer," I said, turning to Earl again, "keep your eyes peeled for a sudden change in altitude. Let it come up. It should stop at an altitude of thirty to fifty meters."

If we had done our homework right, *Argo* would pass over the deck and deliver sharp images of the wreck.

This was against the flyer's standing orders, but Earl understood. "Roger that," he said without emotion.

The milky haze of backscatter filled the video screens.

Then Earl spoke. "The altimeter is beginning to flicker."

"I have a massive object off to starboard on sonar," Lieutenant Rey added. "We're about to cross it."

"Altimeter has just jumped," Earl said, his voice calm and precise. "The altitude is now twenty-five meters."

"Hold," I said, trying to inject confidence in my voice, which I certainly did not feel at that moment. "Don't take in cable."

None of the twenty people in the van made a sound as the first ghostly view of *Titanic*'s hull shimmered on the monitors. I strained, trying to make out the image. A faint vertical line was slowly advancing across the screen, but none of us recognized what portion of the ship we were seeing. And we were still too high to discern vertical obstacles such as funnels or rigging.

I knew that if we were to capture any recognizable images of *Titanic*'s hull, we would have to descend for a closer look.

I turned to Stu Harris. "Shift to real-time mode," I said softly. "We're going down."

Stu Harris, *Argo*'s chief architect and engineer on this watch, was fighting seasickness, but his response was immediate. He tapped in commands for *Argo*'s onboard computer. The periodic strobes shut down and the powerful incandescent lamps went on to illuminate a constant video transmission.

"Flyer," I said to Earl formally, so that later there would be no confusion as to who issued the command in the event of an accident, "down five meters."

"Roger that," Earl responded at once, tweaking the winch-control lever forward.

This 5-meter descent took *Argo* below the level of the funnels. If any still remained vertical, we had a problem.

As *Argo* kited down 5 meters, the confusing jumble of shapes slid into sharp perspective.

"It's the side of the ship," I said. "She's upright."

I could make out the boat deck, the uppermost level of the main superstructure. It was here the ship's inadequate roster of lifeboats had been lashed in chocks beneath davits along the rail. Despite the thin crust of sediment, it appeared that the once-spotless pine deck planks were still in place. *Argo* was passing over the starboard side, aft of *Titanic*'s proud bow. I saw a gaping dark void like the socket of a pulled tooth.

My eyes shot back and forth between the monitors and the schematic diagram of *Titanic* on the bulkhead. I still was not fully oriented. Was this dark gaping maw a funnel opening or was it the grand staircase, its leaded glass dome ripped away in the final plunge? Then I recognized the distinctive shape of a funnel opening. But which one was it . . . one or two?

The images on the video screens rippled. *Argo* began to stall, its forward progress failing. As the camera sled slipped into the distinctive falling-leaf motion, Earl tweaked the winch control to steady it. Twenty minutes earlier, we had slowed *Knorr*'s progress to a mere crawl on the surface, and that four-dimensional chess move now produced this result 12,500 feet below.

Argo glided off to the right, toward *Titanic*'s bow. Clearly, that dark hole had been the number-one-funnel opening. Now *Argo*'s cameras slowly revealed the section of superstructure where the bridge once stood, just forward of that funnel. But I saw no sign of the rectangular structure. Had the bridge been crushed in the fall to the bottom?

I thought of Captain Edward J. Smith, standing on that empty bridge as the bow slipped into the dark maw of the Atlantic and the deck tilted violently beneath his feet.

Now I saw the two large cargo cranes, folded inboard at the base of the superstructure like huge lobster claws. If the forward mast that held the lookout crow's nest was still in place, *Argo* was about to become tangled in its rigging, but I was now confident that that mast had fallen, swept away by the same relentless force that had ripped off the bridge.

As *Argo* glided farther to the right, I caught a glimpse of the toppled mast, still mounting the cylindrical crow's nest, midway up. It was from this perch that lookout Fred Fleet gave the warning, "Iceberg right ahead" at 11:40 P.M. on the night *Titanic* sank. I realized that the main wreck and the debris field would be virtually littered with such historic objects. It was as if we were visiting Gettysburg, seven decades after the battle, and the wreckage of war still lay untouched, unscavenged.

There were, of course, no bodies. I knew the mindless blind work of the albino crabs too well. They would have left no scrap of human remains intact.

Once we passed over the crow's nest and saw that the mast had toppled, the path ahead was clear. Slowly *Argo* inched forward toward the bow. But before reaching it, the sled began to drift farther to the right. There was nothing we could do as *Argo* slid past the starboard rail and the altimeter began to pick up a distant bottom echo. *Titanic* faded from view, replaced by a haze of backscattered particles floating just above bottom.

The entire run across *Titanic* had lasted less than six minutes, and *Argo* had survived intact. The van suddenly exploded in cheers and whistles.

At the center of the circle of people whooping, hugging, and dancing wildly around us, Jean-Louis and I stood silently, overcome by the significance of the moment. For just over five minutes, *Argo* and her team had surpassed all our previous underwater exploits, from the investigation of the Mid-Ocean Ridge to the discovery of the black smokers. Those important scientific achievements, we knew, would be viewed by the public as arcane precursors to this spectacular success.

Neither of us spoke. But we both understood that our lives had been changed forever.

The next two and a half days dissolved into a blur of exhaustion punctuated by adrenaline rushes, as we struggled to document as much of the *Titanic* wreck as possible before *Knorr* turned west toward Cape Cod and this summer's expedition ended.

Into that tight pocket of time, we somehow managed to squeeze in two more *Argo* passes over the wreck, each carefully plotted, each producing priceless videotape. One image captured by *Argo*'s cameras was particularly touching: a set of empty davits that once held a lifeboat, the big circular blocks now bearded with dripping rust. *Titanic* had gone to sea, confident of its own invincibility, carrying a token complement of lifeboats almost as an afterthought. That hubris had doomed 1,522 people.

During the second run, we learned that *Titanic*'s stern was, in fact, severed from the bow at a point on the hull about midway between the third and fourth funnels. The stern section lay nearly 2,000 feet south of the larger bow section. Again, the accounts of survivors—who reported tremendous snapping and shearing sounds as *Titanic*'s stern rose out of the water to an angle of more than forty-five degrees, then suddenly collapsed back near-horizontal before popping up to the vertical in a violent pivot, and finally disappearing. *Titanic*'s hull and keel had been strong indeed, but they could not withstand the immense stress forces as the ship became a giant water-filled lever, its fulcrum the point where the suspended stern section intersected the surface.

We now knew *Titanic*'s hull had fallen in two huge pieces, with massive cylindrical funnels, ripped sections of hull plate and deck, and all manner of light interior debris belching from both hull sections as they fell.

But that productive second *Argo* run was cut short by the arrival of the storm front that had stalled to the west just long enough to allow us to find the wreck. Now one squall after another lashed *Knorr,* and the sea became confused as gale-force winds ran counter to the surface current. We could not risk keeping *Argo* in the water.

It was time to fall back on our reliable, homely old friend, ANGUS, the dope-on-a-rope. It didn't matter if *Knorr*'s stern was surging and swooping 10 or even 15 feet between wave crest and trough. If ANGUS hit the bottom or even part of the wreck, it would probably give as well as it got. ANGUS, of course, was equipped for 35-millimeter still photography, rather than video. But this was well suited for our first target area: *Titanic*'s vast debris field.

Throughout the afternoon and evening of September 3, we towed ANGUS only 10 meters above the rolling bottom as her cameras captured thousands of sharp color images of the hemorrhaged lifeblood of the great liner.

When Martin Bowen developed the long rolls of film, we

were just as mesmerized a group around the projector as we had been viewing the first frames of the hydrothermal vent clam colonies on the Galapagos Rift in 1977.

Because the hull had ripped apart vertically from keel to boat deck, the wound cut through engine rooms, restaurants, kitchens, and both first- and second-class staterooms. The thousands of objects, large and small, in these diverse spaces spilled into the water during the long, probably spinning plunge to the ocean floor. The ANGUS pictures revealed white china chamber pots, gleaming copper kettles, space heaters, the head-board of a bed, a delicate porcelain teacup sitting upright near a silver serving platter, and what can only be described as an oenophile's dream or nightmare: a stream of wine bottles, still perfectly corked, identifiable as Bordeaux, Burgundy, Riesling, and champagne by their distinctive shapes. It was as if a large, luxurious Edwardian hotel had been picked up by a cyclone and dumped here on the ocean bottom.

Encouraged by these high-quality photos of the debris field, I ordered an ANGUS run across the hull. But this time I erred on the side of caution, and we wasted vital hours trying to photograph the larger bow section from too high an altitude. The resulting images were frame after frame of milky blue backscatter.

I was exhausted by this time, literally seeing pulsing neon spots whenever my eyelids snapped shut. But we had until 7:30 the next morning, enough time for one more ANGUS run across the hull. This was, after all, an exploration cruise, not simply a cautious voyage of discovery.

Relaunching ANGUS for the final time, after midnight on September 4, was a frightening experience that tested the strength and skill of *Knorr*'s crew. The wind was blowing at near-gale force, and the sea was building toward 20 feet. As soon as we winched up ANGUS from its deck mounts, the camera sled began to pendulum wildly, a 6,000-pound wreck-ing ball, even though the crew fought to hold it steady with multiple sets of block-and-tackle. Undaunted, Earl crawled like a monkey onto ANGUS's frame to activate the timers on the cameras and strobes. The night exploded with the dazzling flash as the twin strobes released 1,500 watts of illumination.

"She's working," Earl announced as his crewmates, Martin Bowen and Emile Bergeron, hauled him back off the bucking steel bronco.

Shucking off my wet foul-weather gear in the control van, I could see that Jean-Louis had gone past the point of dangerous exhaustion. If he didn't sleep at once, he might permanently injure his body.

"Get to bed," I told him. "There's no need for both of us to stay awake."

Jean-Louis nodded gratefully and dragged himself to his cabin. I wasn't in much better shape. While ANGUS dropped soundlessly toward the bottom, I also sank, crawling on my hands and knees beneath the chart table where I rested my head on a wastebasket. From this position, I could talk to the three key members of the team: Earl on the winch, Tom Crook at the nav station, and Captain Bowen at *Knorr*'s cycloidal thruster controls.

I must have dozed while ANGUS dropped toward the wreck. It was silent in the control room. All of us realized the maneuver I'd planned was downright crazy. From the blurred earlier images, I knew we had to get our cameras to within 6 or 7 meters (about 23 feet) of *Titanic*'s decks to get the clear color images I wanted. But *Knorr* was hobbyhorsing on the steep sea, a vertical movement of at least 10 feet with each passing wave crest and trough. This snapping motion was transmitted down the long cable to ANGUS. It was almost inevitable that we would either slam the camera sled into *Titanic*'s unyielding deck, or worse, down into one of the voids where a funnel had stood, or even into the jagged maw of the severed hull.

I dragged myself up and leaned heavily on Earl's right

shoulder to whisper commands as our ANGUS run neared the big bow section.

"Down to four meters," I croaked with exhaustion.

"Four meters?" Earl had never questioned a command before.

"Four meters," I repeated. If we were going to lose AN-GUS, this was as good a place as any for the accident to happen.

For the next three hours, we hardly spoke beyond terse, soft commands and acknowledgments. We made pass after terrifying pass over *Titanic*'s hull, each taking the camera sled less than 25 feet above the deck. But unlike real-time *Argo* runs, we were flying blind. If ANGUS snagged this late in the expedition, we would have to abandon it.

Throughout those long passes, Earl Young gripped the winch controls so tightly, his knuckles were literally white with strain.

At 5:56 A.M., the intercom from the bridge sounded with the message we all expected: "You have to start up now."

Earl snapped back the winch lever, and the traction unit whined above the van roof. Our first exploration of *Titanic*'s wreck was over.

Bringing ANGUS on board and developing the film was not my responsibility, although I wish it had been. I had other duties, among them dealing with the world news media.

As *Knorr* breasted the westerly swell and headed back toward Cape Cod, I had to untangle a mounting controversy about news coverage of our discovery that had begun the day we had found *Titanic*'s debris field.

Late that Sunday morning, a long-range helicopter carrying a television crew from the Canadian Broadcasting Company appeared over the search site. The CBC producer on board announced by VHF radio that he wanted to land his camera crew on *Knorr* and tape an exclusive report on the discovery.

My brain was still working fairly well at that point. And I answered emphatically, "No way."

Even though the Canadian network had contributed to our documentation budget and were welcome to film us from the air, I rebelled at the thought that any one network would have an exclusive on this historic event.

But Jean-Louis, Jean Jarry, and I decided the sudden appearance of the CBC helicopter could serve another useful purpose. All that morning we had heard shortwave news reports that there was an uproar on both sides of the Atlantic in response to the rumor that we were somehow dragging grapples through *Titanic*'s wreckage in a crude attempt to salvage artifacts. One account even stated that a protest had been lodged at the United Nations. It seemed that the tabloid *London Observer* was fanning the flames of this lurid rumor. We decided to send some of our own *Argo* footage out with the CBC crew when they left for Saint John's, Newfoundland, so we could set the record straight. In the canister lowered by the helicopter's winch, we sent back three copies of the videotape of the debris field's discovery, including the haunting image of *Titanic*'s boiler. One was addressed to Woods Hole, one to IFREMER headquarters in Paris, and one designated for the world press. All three of us signed an accompanying letter stating that the press tape was not for any one news organization's exclusive use but was to be shared.

A couple of hours later, I received an extremely agitated radio message from John Steele at Woods Hole. The Institution had apparently received a chorus of complaints from U.S. networks that had not yet received their copies of the tape and were threatening lawsuits against Woods Hole for "deliberately holding out."

Next Admiral Mooney, head of the Office of Naval Research, called in his congratulations but stunned me with the question: "Bob, did you give CBS exclusive news rights to the expedition?"

"Of course not," I answered. "And even if I'd wanted to, I couldn't have done it."

"Well, they've just broadcast your tape and told the viewers it was a CBS exclusive."

He explained that CBC in Newfoundland had uplinked the images to CBS in New York by satellite, which broadcast them while NBC was still waiting for its copy to arrive from Canada.

I felt like slamming my fist through the steel bulkhead of the radio room. No wonder NBC was angry. I put in a trans-Atlantic radio-telephone call immediately to a vice president at CBS, waking the man at home on a Sunday morning. Using clear, forceful language, I explained that his network definitely did *not* have an exclusive on the *Titanic* discovery story.

Then I called NBC to explain that they would have full access to the tape that had been sent ashore by helicopter.

"I'm sorry this happened," I told the NBC executive. "Is there anything I can do to make up for it?"

"Sure," the man replied over the scratchy single-sideband channel. "Give us some exclusive tapes."

"I'm sorry," I said, shaking my head at the machinations of network news, "but not that sorry."

With the first batch of ANGUS high-quality color pictures now available, I conferred with my French colleagues on the best way to distribute them. Another long-range helicopter was en route, this one chartered by the three big American television networks. We could send a selection of ANGUS stills back to Canada with that chopper. But just to make sure there was no "misinterpretation" of our intentions, we sent two of our team members, Steve Gegg representing the Americans, and Frenchman Bernard Pillaud, along with the pictures. The plan was for Pillaud to carry IFREMER's stills to Paris on board the Concorde so that they could be released at a press conference that would take place at exactly the same time I briefed the assembled press at Woods Hole and released the film.

This seemed like an excellent way to thwart the intrigues that were obviously standard operating procedure for ruthlessly ambitious news executives. But the plan fell apart soon after the helicopter reached shore.

WHOI director John Steele, an academic bureaucrat unused to handling the hungry press and already rattled by the networks' acrimony, went back on the Institution's promise to IFREMER and immediately released the packet of ANGUS images to the American media. The Concorde is fast but not as fast as the American networks. By the time IFREMER had the images in Paris, French television viewers had already seen the pictures, which their television networks had had to purchase from their American counterparts via satellite feed.

There is probably no more certain way to anger a Frenchman than to serve him American leftovers.

But I later discovered the IFREMER motives were hardly pure: one of their top managers had made a deal with a French newsman—reportedly a relative—who had offered an amazing $1 million for exclusive rights to the first ANGUS photographs of *Titanic*.

Despite this skullduggery in Paris, I couldn't blame my other colleagues in IFREMER for being furious with Woods Hole. Glory, *la Gloire,* was bread and butter to scientific institutions on both sides of the Atlantic. Success on such an historic discovery was equated to competence and worth on a national level. Discovering *Titanic* was an achievement of major importance for both IFREMER and Woods Hole. Now it appeared that the Americans were trying to steal this hard-won glory. Which I found ironic as hell, considering that John Steele had snubbed most of my efforts to mount this expedition.

Exhausted as I was, there was still the knotty problem of

keeping relations cordial between France and the United States, at least long enough for the public to savor the fruits of this high-technology exploration unblemished by the bitter acrimony that was already brewing.

But this new challenge looked impossible to solve. IFREMER had already responded to Steele's reneging on the simultaneous-release deal. The French were going to court to block the Washington news conference scheduled by WHOI, *National Geographic,* and the navy. I certainly sympathized with the French; we never would have found *Titanic* without the thankless SAR work during the first phase of the expedition. But I had to stand beside my American sponsors and colleagues when it came to lawsuits.

This was a far more serious and unpredictable dispute than the earlier academic infighting over who had first discovered volcanic pillars in the Pacific that had marred relations between my American and French colleagues in the late 1970s. Not only the prestige of academic institutions was at stake; national honor—with all the emotional baggage that entailed—had reared its head. I was an American, and expected to take my country's side.

But, again, John Steele tested my loyalty. I learned that he had been so snakebitten by angry news executives that he planned to release *all* the expedition's still photographs and videotapes to the news media the moment *Knorr* tied up at the Institution dock in Woods Hole.

I lay in my bunk as *Knorr* surged through the swell en route to Cape Cod, wondering how I could possibly buy time to head off Steele's action, which would no doubt cause an irrevocable breach between me and my colleagues. Then I saw an answer.

Because we had classified material on board related to our survey of *Scorpion,* the navy had made sure we had several strong steel safes to store the secret videotapes and bathymetric maps. If I put all the ANGUS images and *Argo* tapes into those safes, I reasoned, the press would have a hard time laying their hands on the visual images of our successful expedition.

But no, the Woods Hole security officer had a list of the safe combinations and could open them as soon as we tied up at the Institution dock.

Then I mentally scanned the haunting ANGUS images of the debris field once again. Among the crockery, dust pans, floor tiles, and other light debris, were poignant photographs of old-fashioned high-button shoes, some of them lying splayed side by side in perfect pairs. Obviously, two matched empty shoes had not fallen 12,500 feet—winnowed by the deep ocean currents—to arrive on the bottom as a pair. A human being had worn those shoes on the long fall to the sea floor. But in the seven decades since *Titanic* sank, all traces of the body had been consumed by crabs and worms.

Nevertheless, the ANGUS pictures were, in fact, strong evidence that human remains might be found in the two hull sections of *Titanic* or the scattered debris field. I knew, of course, that this was quite implausible, but navy regulations treated the possibility of finding human remains in a sunken ship with special sensitivity. If any member of a wreck survey team thinks he sees evidence of human remains, all the survey's data is classified Top Secret until it can be examined and that possibility eliminated and the material approved for release to the public.

Since *Knorr* was a navy vessel on permanent assignment to WHOI and I was the expedition leader, it was my decision to classify the images. I got out of my bunk and called Lieutenant George Rey, the ranking naval officer on board, to meet me in the control van, where the safes were located.

"I'm designating all the video footage and stills Top Secret," I told Lieutenant Rey.

He looked at me quizzically. "We'll have to change all the combinations on the safes," he said.

"Go ahead and do it," I replied.

Since all the civilians at Woods Hole only had Secret clearances, the contents of the safes would have to be transported to the Pentagon for review before they could be released. This guaranteed that the images would not be released to the press as soon as we reached Woods Hole, and the action bought time for saner heads to prevail.

On the morning of September 6, as we steamed up Martha's Vineyard Channel, John Steele and a delegation of VIPs came on board as our welcoming committee. I had also requested that my wife, Marjorie, and our two sons, Todd and Douglas, join me on the ship before pulling into Woods Hole.

For years, they had watched me go to sea for long periods of time with no real reward to them. This time I wanted my family to share our moment of glory, particularly since so many of their friends would be in the crowd standing on the dock.

These had been difficult times for two young boys growing up in a small community that expected them to succeed in everything they did, as their father always appeared to do. Todd and Doug reacted to this pressure in very different ways. Publicity seemed to roll off Doug's back. In fact, half joking, he wondered if my discovery of the *Titanic* would land him a cute girlfriend.

For Todd, my fame would soon become a heavier burden to carry. Perhaps it was because he was the older son. Whatever the reason, I felt at times the world was especially unfair to children of successful parents. I made a promise to myself that the next time I went on a high-profile expedition like the *Titanic* cruise, Todd would be a member of the team.

I had also requested that before the media were allowed aboard the *Knorr* to see our technology and meet with my team, the families of our crewmembers be first invited aboard to share in the excitement of the moment.

As the ship neared Woods Hole, I joined my wife and sons on the bridge. It was a great view. I could see John

Steele, suddenly very pleased with the expedition's glory he was receiving, an expedition he had tried so hard to ignore. Steele brought with him a group of WHOI security personnel intent on taking possession of the expedition images before we docked. I had insisted that a representative of the U.S. Navy join Steele's party. This turned out to be Hugh O'Neil, legal counsel to Navy Secretary John Lehman.

Steele was furious when he discovered my ploy. His eyes pulsed with animosity behind his thick, dark-framed glasses. Nonetheless, he had no choice but to allow the navy to pack up all the data, videotapes, and ANGUS pictures as we maneuvered for the assembled press cameras and finally tied up to the cheers of several thousand members of the Institution and other spectators. High school bands played nautical airs, ships' horns hooted, kids jumped and shouted, and a cannon even fired a salute from a nearby hilltop.

I was unprepared for this mass demonstration of joy and pride. Understanding *Argo*'s capabilities, I'd been reasonably confident that we would find *Titanic*'s wreck, provided we had enough time on the site to conduct an adequate search. But the cheering crowds on the Institution dock reminded me of the adoring mobs that had greeted the Apollo astronauts on return from the moon. It was as if we had restored everyone's optimistic faith in the powers of technology, a faith that had been painfully eroded that moonless night seven decades earlier when the technological achievement of the early twentieth century had succumbed to the invincible forces of nature and sunk to the bottom of the Atlantic.

John Steele was all smiles, his angular face visibly strained by the effort. During this hoopla, Hugh O'Neil and his navy officers marched unobtrusively down the gangplank, loaded the videotapes and rolls of film into the white navy sedan, and drove off to Otis Air Force Base for their flight to Washington.

I had certainly seen media circuses in which celebrities are buffeted by jostling photographers and TV camera crews as joyous crowds shouted praise, but I had never before had the experience of being at the center of such a human cyclone. The storm swept Jean-Louis Michel and me into the Redfield Auditorium, where we held a brief press conference.

I was careful to praise all the considerable contributions of the French, and in particular those of Jean-Louis Michel. For his part, Jean-Louis was gracious, noting that, "The work in the deep ocean between France and America will continue."

I ended my remarks with this unofficial epitaph.

"*Titanic* lies now in about thirteen thousand feet of water on a gently sloping, alpinelike countryside overlooking a small canyon. Its bow faces north and the ship sits upright on the bottom. There is no light at this great depth and little life can be found. It is a quiet and peaceful and fitting place for the remains of this greatest of sea tragedies to rest. Forever may it remain that way. And may God bless these newfound souls."

Later, when Jean-Louis and I said good-bye, we both felt a nagging sadness, realizing that politics and national pride were already driving a thin wedge between us, straining the bond of trust and respect that had built up over the years out on and beneath the open ocean, where national boundaries did not exist.

With the press conference over, I made a mad dash for our car, where Marjorie and the boys were waiting. Just as I jumped inside, a reporter tossed a note through the window. It was an invitation to be on a major network morning show the next day.

Keeping to my original agreement with the French, I retained possession of a small number of ANGUS still pictures and the same video footage that the French had agreed to release in two days during the simultaneous Paris and Washington news conferences. But when I arrived in Washington that night and showed *National Geographic* editor Bill Garrett what I planned to release to the press in the morning, he was appalled.

"Bob," he argued, "the press conference will be a disaster if we don't show them more than that."

"Well, Bill," I retorted, "I promised the French to release exactly what they have for their Paris press conference tomorrow, no more, no less."

It was hard to convey the sense of Gallic logic and personal honor that I believed lay at the foundation of this arrangement.

But Bill Garrett seemed exasperated by my position.

"What are you worried about the French for?" he asked. "They're taking all of us to court to try to stop our press conference."

I was still bone-tired from the expedition, but I tried to answer patiently. "Bill, John Steele may have broken his promise to the French, but that doesn't mean I have to break mine."

Then I asked him to assign me a good artist used to working on tight deadlines to make up some illustrations that would supplement the rather meager collection of images I'd kept for the press conference.

I worked all day and long into the night with Bill Garrett's artists, making up clear, attractive diagrams of *Titanic*'s bow section and debris field. Around midnight, we got word that the federal district court had just ruled that our news conference could proceed as scheduled.

The next morning, the slides still weren't ready half an hour before the ten A.M. press conference, but I was assured they would be. More importantly, no one seemed to know who was in charge of the press conference, Woods Hole, the navy, or the National Geographic Society. At a last-minute conference, we decided the navy's Public Affairs Office would be the official host. I raced down to the auditorium in National Geographic Society headquarters, where a dense throng of reporters were already jostling for position. The slides had not yet reached the projection booth, but before I could send out an alarm, a photo technician arrived with the slides, still dripping from the final rinse. He blotted them dry as he loaded them into the carousel following my directions.

I sidestepped reporters lying in ambush and made it backstage where the sponsoring VIPs had assembled. The atmosphere was grim. Navy Secretary John Lehman and a clutch of admirals sat together. Bill Garrett and National Geographic Society President Gil Grosevenor formed their own island to one side of the room, and WHOI's position was held by Chairman of the Board Guy Nichols and a visibly agitated John Steele. Everybody's nerves were shot over the trans-Atlantic acrimony and ongoing hassles with the American media.

"To hell with it," I muttered, leaving the room to fetch my blue expedition jumpsuit and baseball cap. The old adage about defeat being an orphan but victory having a hundred mothers had never been so true. But these VIP mothers still seemed convinced I was somehow going to disgrace the family.

I trailed my grim-faced superiors into the auditorium, and we were greeted by an explosion of photo strobes. After introductory remarks by Gil Grosevenor, John Steele, and the navy, I took the podium. As always, I preferred speaking informally, and today I was careful not to overdramatize in any way what we had accomplished. The discovery spoke for itself.

Apparently, I told a good story. The press listened patiently for an hour and a half as I took them through the stages of the expedition. Bill Garrett's fears about the "paucity" of visuals proved groundless. The haunting black-and-white *Argo* images of *Titanic*'s foredeck, the thick anchor chain stored neatly for the final voyage, and the blue-tinged ANGUS still photos of the crockery and wine bottles in the debris field captivated even the most cynical veterans of the Washington news media.

As I had at the Woods Hole auditorium, I noted that *Titanic*'s grave was a "quiet and peaceful place" and again voiced the plea that this grave not be desecrated by commercial salvagers determined to plunder the site for lucrative souvenirs.

I didn't mention the irresponsible rumors about safes full of jewels that had been swirling since news of our discovery flashed across the world the week before. In seven decades, no one had been able to verify if the wealthy Edwardian ladies who perished that April night in 1912 had died wearing their diamonds and emeralds, or if this virtual treasure trove had, in fact, sunk to the bottom in the first-class purser's safe. Now that we had found *Titanic,* one of my main responsibilities would be to rally public opinion to ward off high-tech grave robbers.

Our duty as scientists, I said, was to investigate *Titanic* but also to allow the souls of all those who had died with her to rest in peace. With the French legal offensive still a live issue, I was certain someone would raise the rift in the question-and-answer period that would soon follow my remarks. Today's news media took every opportunity to search out controversy in any story, no matter how harmless.

I was convinced that unless I provided some controversy for them, they would invent it themselves. Wanting to avoid our conflict with the French, I chose to resurrect an old one, namely Captain Lord of the *Californian*'s failure to respond to *Titanic*'s distress rockets. By precisely locating *Titanic*'s wreckage, we'd proven that Captain Lord could have easily reached the sinking ship before so many perished.

When the newspapers ran their stories the next day, it was the *Californian* controversy they chose to cover. The deflection tactic worked.

The piercing screech of an electrical alarm filled *Alvin*'s cramped pressure sphere.

I glanced nervously at Ralph Hollis, the chief pilot. He was hunched on his little doll's stool, eyes close to the center view port, oblivious to the nagging alarm as he drove the sub across the gently rolling bottom of gray mud. To Ralph's left, veteran pilot Dudley Foster scanned the instrument panel, his face taut with worry.

It was just after 11:00 A.M. on July 13, 1986. *Alvin* was on the bottom in 12,400 feet of water, somewhere very near *Titanic*'s bow section. Unfortunately, we didn't know much more than that; in fact, we were lost.

This first manned submersible reconnaissance dive of the second expedition had started well enough but had quickly gone to hell when Ralph's instruments registered a small but persistent seawater leak in one of the main battery bays. The large golf-cart-type batteries rested in large Fiberglas tubs filled with oil to protect them from the tremendous ambient pressure we were now exposed to. Every square inch of the submersible's hull was under 6,000 pounds of pressure. When seawater leaked into the battery bay through tiny gaps in the seals, it fell to the bottom, since it is heavier than oil.

As the leak continued, however, the level of seawater would slowly rise, tripping an ascending line of leak sensors on the way to the top of the bay. If seawater reached the top of the first layer of batteries, a hard ground would occur and the submersible would begin to devour its own electrical system through fused and melted battery cables. If that happened, not only was the dive over, but the entire expedition. A hard ground was not something to ignore, and the the warning buzzers told us we were headed for trouble if the leak continued.

To make matters worse, our dive navigator aboard *Atlantis II*, the modern tender that had replaced *Lulu* two years earlier, reported that one of the acoustic transponders in the net was sending him bad data, so he was unable to maintain his fix on *Alvin*. We would have to find the bow section ourselves.

But when Ralph Hollis dropped descent weights as we neared the bottom, we quickly discovered that our sector-scanning sonar—normally a reliable system, developed years before on navy submarines to search for mines—had also suddenly decided to pack up. We were not only lost but blind.

Then, as we bumbled across the bottom, searching vainly for telltale debris, the nagging battery-short alarm changed tone and grew louder. The leak was continuing; seawater was rising closer to the tops of the batteries. A hard ground could occur at any moment.

Very soon, Ralph would have no choice but to trip the ballast release, drop weights, and abort the dive. *Damn,* I thought, *it's taken me thirteen years to reach this point.* Now *Alvin,* normally the most reliable tool in my growing exploration inventory, had decided to break down.

Ralph drove blindly ahead, leaning close to his center view port, forcing himself to disregard the grating whine of the battery alarm. It certainly wasn't easy for me to ignore the screech, however. I could almost smell the choking, acrid smoke in *Archimede*'s cramped pressure sphere.

But Ralph had another reason to stubbornly persist when common sense and the *Alvin* Group's own stringent safety rules pointed toward an emergency ascent. My decision to use *Alvin* as the principal investigation tool on this second expedition to *Titanic* had brought a mixed reaction from some of the Drugstore old-timers, most notably Ralph Hollis. This was unfortunate but understandable. As my new Deep Submergence Laboratory, structured around the *Argo-Jason* system, grew and achieved international prominence after our discovery of *Titanic* the year before, the *Alvin* Group lost some of its popular glamour. And in press interviews, I'd certainly been forthright—tactless, according to my critics—in support of my new paradigm: the remotely operated vehicle (ROV), unmanned tethered robots, controlled in real-time operation by operators on the surface. In one regrettable interview in the *Cape Cod Times*, I'd noted how poor the visibility always was from *Alvin,* then added: "Manned submersibles are doomed."

What I meant, of course, was that advanced ROVs such

as the mature *Argo-Jason* system that I envisioned, would have much greater flexibility and unlimited duration search time. In short, ROVs were the new paradigm; thus, small manned submersibles like *Alvin* were, in fact, "doomed" as search and survey vehicles on missions such as the *Titanic* expedition.

But *Alvin*'s loyal supporters, especially Chief Pilot Ralph Hollis, saw this as a treasonous act by a formerly stalwart ally. It wasn't as if *Alvin* didn't have scientists around the world lined up to dive, and the old Drugstore team had their employment assured into the distant future. The investment in the modern vessel *Atlantis II* as *Alvin*'s tender was evidence of this. But they still insisted on seeing me as some kind of ingrate who had used *Alvin*, then abandoned her, only to come back sheepishly for the second *Titanic* expedition when I needed *Alvin*'s particular attributes again.

On the passage out from Woods Hole aboard *Atlantis II*, I'd done my best to smooth the feathers of the *Alvin* veterans. I'd even been a good sport when the ship's steward, John Lobo, baked a big layer cake decorated with the strawberry icing inscription, "Manned Submersibles Are Doomed." I gobbled down the first piece with relish, announcing to my colleagues: "Okay. I'll eat my words."

That public display of contrition had overcome most lingering bad feelings. Most, but not all. Ralph Hollis, a tough middle-aged ex-military type, who had gone to the school of hard knocks, still wanted to show me that *Alvin* was good as ever and her team not quaking in fear of little robots like *Jason Junior*. He had *Alvin*, and the DSL had JJ, and time would tell which performed the best.

That was the true reason behind the stubborn persistence he displayed driving *Alvin* blindly across the bottom.

None of us had a clue where the bow section lay. To make matters worse, particles kicked up by *Alvin* indicated a current of almost 1 knot from the south-southeast. So I figured we must have been pushed north.

"Let's search toward the south," I suggested.

Ralph agreed, and we swung around south, nose into the current, with *Alvin*'s single bottom runner just creasing the surface of the sediment. As we drove in this direction, I could only scan the swirling particles in our floodlights and try to ignore the shrill alarm. Without our sector-scanning sonar, we wouldn't know *Titanic*'s hull was there until we practically collided with it.

Then the navigator's voice echoed from the surface on the acoustic telephone: "*Alvin, this is A-II*. Tracking is now working. *Titanic* should bear fifty yards to the west of your present location."

I snatched the plastic-covered bathymetric map and held it under a small side lamp. We'd been just east of *Titanic*'s debris field and were near the long black steel cliff of the ship's portside.

Ralph swung *Alvin* neatly west, and we strained to catch sight of the hull. Through my view port, the crusted sediment rolled smoothly ahead. Then, suddenly, the even folds were creased sharply. The mud rose in a steep bank, too sharply to be a natural feature. It was as if we were coming up on a rugged berm that had been bulldozed by a huge blade.

"Ralph," I said, "come right. I think I see a wall of black just on the other side of that mud mound."

As soon as the nose swung around, we all saw a sight unlike any we'd encountered during hundreds of deep dives. Only a few feet from the submersible's view ports, a seemingly limitless black slab of steel rose from the bottom. The hull plates were blanketed with ripply sheets of dark-orange rust, but the neat, evenly spaced lines of rivets were clearly visible. We had made contact with *Titanic*.

Ralph had proved whatever point he was trying to make. He backed clear of the hull and dropped the last two descent weights. We rose inexorably toward the distant surface.

This ascent lacked the normal postmission banter and

relaxed camaraderie. Even after Ralph shut off the shrill battery alarm, he and Dudley seemed preoccupied with their submersible's mechanical problems. They knew they faced difficult and frustrating hours of troubleshooting and repairs once *Alvin* was hoisted up with the big blue A-frame crane and housed in her snug hangar aboard *Atlantis II*.

I knew the sub was in good hands, but my anxiety focused on another piece of equipment: the little *Jason Junior* ROV that we would "garage" in the science tray beneath *Alvin*'s chin and operate from inside the pressure sphere. JJ had never been tested in the deep ocean. In fact, the little ROV—a sky blue cube of pressure-resistant syntactic epoxy foam surrounding two linked pairs of vertical and horizontal thruster motors and a glass-domed titanium vessel with a color television camera, 35-millimeter still camera, and powerful strobe— had only been mated to *Alvin* for the first time three days before we sailed. And on the first shallow test dive in the Eel Pond, JJ refused to work at all. But Chris Von Alt, the robotics wizard we'd hired as JJ's chief designer, was confident he and his team could work out the bugs on the four-day cruise to the *Titanic* site.

I had to accept Chris's assurances on faith. The technical intricacies of fiber-optic remote operation, and advanced robotics in general, were beyond me. I was the expedition leader and had to have confidence in the people I'd assembled. So we sailed, with JJ ailing and untested.

In a way, these problems were emblematic of the overall situation. The year before, it was far from clear that I would lead a second expedition to *Titanic,* despite the resounding success of the first. Expeditions cost hundreds of thousands of dollars, and somebody had to pay. Over the winter I had worked closely with the French, hoping they'd be able to join us with IFREMER's *Le Suroit* and their new deep-diving submersible *Nautile.* Not only would French participation improve the atmosphere of mutual resentment between our two countries—it would also restore the sense of achievement and honor that the French so valued after their perceived embarrassment of the previous summer. On a practical level, French participation was even more important: it was very risky to dive so close to the snagging obstacles of *Titanic*'s wrecked hull sections without a backup submersible available to extract us in an emergency.

But at the end of the day, the French could not raise the funds necessary to participate. And this latest failure set a course of action that would ultimately widen the gulf between us into an unbridgeable chasm.

Without French support, I knew I could always rely on my old standbys: the U.S. Navy and *National Geographic*.

But winning navy support was a tricky matter. Almost as soon as we had discovered *Titanic* in September 1985, the irrepressible Jack Grimm had made a formal request to charter *Alvin* during the summer of 1986 to dive on *Titanic*—and plunder the wreck, according to his detractors. The *Alvin* Review Committee had rejected Grimm's proposal because his expedition completely lacked scientific merit.

My proposal to the navy was to continue field testing of the DSL's advanced ROV technology, specifically JJ. Everyone knew that I planned to couple these tests with the exploration of the *Titanic* wreck. And when the navy and the *Alvin* Review Committee approved the expedition—which also seemed to lack any scientific merit—there was audible grumbling among my professional peers. What I couldn't tell them, of course, at the time, was that *Jason Junior* was far more than a toy television camera built to pander to the popular entertainment industry and armchair explorers. The navy was deadly serious about developing ROV technology that could probe the dangerous and radioactive remains of cold war submarines. But the need for this technology was Top Secret.

So I had to take my licks from fellow scientists who groused about me selling out to "show business" instead of pursuing proper professional research. It was interesting that those censorious colleagues never said a negative word when Fred Spiess and Bill Ryan signed on with Cadillac Jack Grimm and his soothsaying monkey to search for *Titanic*.

All this unpleasant intrigue was part of the ongoing juggling act I conducted to support my ultimate goal of deep-sea exploration. Certainly JJ was not yet the fully mature ROV that *Jason* would one day become. JJ lacked the powerful mechanical gripping arms and sample storage containers planned for *Jason,* which would one day make the larger ROV an underwater research and exploration tool par excellence.

But JJ—our "swimming eyeball"—was a necessary intermediate test-bed prototype, designed to shake out the inevitable technical kinks and glitches on a smaller, less expensive scale than the full-size ROV.

Rising back to the sunlit surface after our first aborted *Alvin* dive on *Titanic*, I was preoccupied. Would JJ somehow perform in the black pressure maw of the deep ocean better than she had in the shallows of Eel Pond?

The answer to that worrisome question came all too early during the second dive the next morning. We launched *Alvin* with no problem on schedule at 8:15. Again, Ralph Hollis was the pilot, but Martin Bowen, JJ's operator, replaced Dudley Foster at the portside view port, while I kept my regular station on the starboard side of *Alvin*'s pressure sphere. The crew had worked all night, testing the batteries and sonar, so we were confident as the submersible sank through the darkening blue surface water toward the cold abyss.

Martin crouched with JJ's control panel balanced on his flexed knees, like a high school kid with an oversize Gameboy in his lap. He was still sensitive about the winch-drum mishap that had almost ended with the loss of *Argo* during the first cruise and was determined that everything go well on this dive a year later. As we sank into the cold darkness, Martin scanned his control board anxiously, monitoring JJ's systems. The squat blue cube of the ROV, nestled snugly in the science tray forward of our sphere, was getting its first taste of deep-sea pressure.

But after only a few minutes, an electrical indicator on Martin's instrument board gave the telltale signal that seawater was flooding one of JJ's motors. Martin had no choice but to shut down power to the system so that the isolated short would not spread and ruin irreplaceable circuits.

We were only ten minutes into the dive and could still abort, pop to the surface, haul *Alvin* back on board the tender, and spend the inevitable couple of hours resealing JJ's motor housings, then continue the dive. That would have been the logical way to optimize precious expedition time. But that was impossible. I clenched my fist in angry frustration. Ralph Hollis had made it clear that this cruise would strictly follow established *Alvin* regulations, which meant we had to leave the bottom each day no later than 3:00 P.M. so that the crew could be back aboard the tender in time for dinner. He was inflexible about this. It was easy to blame this intransigence on some lingering animosity, but I knew the rigid schedule also meant that both *Alvin* pilots and support crew would have adequate time for maintenance and rest between each day's diving schedule.

I also knew that we could never meet those rigid requirements if we tried to resurface to repair JJ's motor seals.

"Let's just press on," was all I said after Martin announced the problem and shut down power to JJ.

This second dive would be a preliminary reconnaissance for all of us. Ralph and I would have the chance to search out safe resting places for *Alvin* on *Titanic*'s deck, while Martin could assess his working conditions once JJ was back on line. I had already announced that I intended to send JJ down inside

Titanic's grand staircase, maybe even to the full length of its 250-foot tether, to demonstrate the ROV's capability to explore where manned submersibles dared not venture.

As we neared the bottom, Ralph got yet another failure signal on the sector-searching sonar. But the navigational transponder network was working well.

"Target bears one hundred-eighty degrees," the navigator announced from *Atlantis II*.

Our second view of *Titanic* was stunning. As we glided slowly across the bottom, the only sound was the faint whiplash click of *Alvin*'s sweeping sonar. Then the towering razor edge of the ship's bow suddenly loomed out of the darkness. I gulped with sudden alarm. The huge ship seemed to be steaming toward us through a sea of gray mud. My first impulse was to warn Ralph to turn away, but I kept silent.

Ralph delicately maneuvered *Alvin* until we could inspect the bow from only a few feet away. The ship's prow was buried more than 60 feet deep in the bottom sediment. Only 20 feet of dark hull-plate on the sharp-angled bow rose from the mud to the lifeline stanchions and short ensign mast at the forepeak. This massive section of *Titanic*'s hull had obviously absorbed the brunt of the impact. But both anchors still hung in place, the port one about 6 feet above the bottom, the starboard anchor almost resting on the mud itself.

As we maneuvered around the bow, *Titanic*'s hull seemed to be slowly melting away in the glare of *Alvin*'s floodlights. Sheets and torrents of ripply orange rust cascaded down the side of the ship. Some of the rust waves dropped the full height of the vertical hull and spilled across the bottom in wide ponds. The hue of these rust deposits varied from dull ochre to a sulfurous yellow-orange. Colleagues at Woods Hole had advised me that this type of rust deposit was different than the hard, caked oxidation we knew on land. Here in the deep ocean, iron-metabolizing bacteria had worked patiently over the decades, slowly building up these blanketing and dripping rust deposits.

"Bleeding rust," I muttered. "That's what it's doing, just bleeding rust. The whole ship is *bleeding* with rust. It's just incredible."

Hovering to probe carefully, ever wary of overhanging obstacles in the dark void above us, we inspected the forward section of *Titanic*'s bow. In places, the rust formed reddish brown stalactites that hung down like menacing daggers. Elsewhere, especially around portholes and lines of rivets, these fingers of rust were like stilettos. I called them "rusticles," a name that quickly caught on.

Despite their menacing appearance, these rust daggers were as fragile as cigarette ash and easily dislodged into a cloud of particles by the faint wash of *Alvin*'s thrusters. And beneath the seemingly solid crust, the original hull still gleamed like new. In effect, the cloak of bacterial iron oxides seemed to have preserved the ship's solid metallic integrity.

We searched in vain for *Titanic*'s name, which should have been painted in tall white letters on the first tier of black hull plates below the once-white deck scuppers. But all we found beneath the sheets of rust was the ghostly outline of the letter C on the port bow.

As we cautiously probed the open boat deck, searching for an area free of any obstacles so we could test the hull's weight-bearing integrity, I suddenly realized that the handsome pine planking we had observed in the ANGUS photographs of the previous year had been a cruel illusion.

"It's gone!" I said.

The neat parallel lines of indigestible caulking remained in the original pattern, but the planks themselves had been replaced by countless thousands of tiny, intertwined empty calcareous tubes, the shells of the long-dead wood-boring mollusks that had devoured the planking. Now I realized we would probably not find *Titanic*'s elegant mahogany and rosewood interior decorative woodwork intact. The mollusks and worms had probably digested every wooden door, staircase, armoire, and table on the ship.

We could only hope that the nubby, orangish rust on the horizontal steel decks that underlay the wooden planking had not weakened the metal. This was more than an aesthetic concern. Before the cruise, the navy had insisted that Ralph Hollis and I carefully work out safety rules for exploring this huge wreck. We were acutely conscious of the ever-present danger of entanglement in fallen guy wires, radio antennae, masts, and derricks.

Because we were diving without rescue backup from another submersible, *Alvin* would only "land" on carefully surveyed sites, and then only with extreme caution, pumping ballast in tiny increments so that the submersible's underwater weight being borne by *Titanic*'s deck would increase gradually. Nevertheless, there was always the danger that we would settle on what appeared to be a solid steel deck, only to have the surface shred like rotten canvas and *Alvin* tumble inside before the pilot had time to dump descent weights and regain positive buoyancy.

If that happened, *Alvin* would crash downward, below-decks. At best, the dive would have to be aborted. At worst, we'd be trapped in the collapsing cardhouse of rust-eaten steel. We were determined to treat the ship's seemingly solid decks with the same wary respect miners give a deep shaft after a cave-in. Landing *Alvin* on *Titanic*'s deck would be a feat of underwater flying only a few real masters like Ralph Hollis could dare to attempt.

We crossed the bow a few feet above the thick bronze-topped capstans and settled gingerly on the deck just forward and to the starboard of *Titanic*'s fallen foremast. Ralph's weather-beaten face was even more tightly wrinkled with absolute concentration as he delicately pumped ballast, decreasing

Alvin's buoyancy and increasing its weight only an ounce or so with each flick of the pump switch.

I crouched with my face close to the starboard view port, watching the sediment beneath our sphere for any sign of sudden movement. As the little sub settled, there was a muted crackling noise, like dry cereal shifting in a carton. But the deck held. A few minutes later, Ralph had pumped enough ballast so that we were convinced the underlying steel was solid enough to bear *Alvin*'s submerged weight.

Ralph lifted off into the increasingly strong current, and we maneuvered aft along the main axis of the bow section. This underwater "wind," together with the sediment we kicked up from the bottom, was bad enough today to create the blizzardlike illusion I'd seen on other dives. Luckily, we'd mounted a sensitive SIT video camera on *Alvin*'s belly, pointed straight down. I scanned this camera's tiny monitor to make sure we were clear of any obstacles that Ralph couldn't see in the swirling sediment.

We passed over the forward cargo hatch and the Well Deck. The forward cargo cranes, their crosshatched booms still folded neatly aft, remained chocked in place, just as they had after their last use when the ship left Queenstown, Ireland, its final port in the British Isles. This was in sharp contrast to the other cranes we'd seen strewn in the debris field, which bore mute testimony to the hull's violent rupture during the sinking.

"The bridge should be dead ahead," I told Ralph.

But the bridge had been swept away during *Titanic*'s final plunge. The only recognizable object left intact where the wheelhouse once stood was the bronze telemotor control that had once been attached to the wheel—an early version of robotic technology.

Once more we landed briefly to test the solidity of A Deck's steel surface. As we did so, Ralph's instrument board pinged with the initial warning of yet another seawater leak in a battery tank. We had only twenty minutes remaining on the bottom.

"Ralph, I want you to lift off from this site," I said, consulting the sketch of the bow section I'd had made from the mosaic of ANGUS photographs that my old mentor Dr. Al Uchupi had assembled over the winter. "Head directly to the grand staircase opening."

We skirted the jumble of torn sheet steel that marked the empty tooth socket of Funnel Number 1, and continued aft, a few feet above the uppermost surface of the superstructure. Ralph held *Alvin* neatly in the current flow as our floodlights illuminated the dark rectangular chasm of the grand staircase opening. This was where the ornate glass dome of the skylight had once stood. The staircase well itself dropped six decks to the lowest first-class staterooms.

"It's gigantic," Ralph said, leaning forward to gaze through his center viewport. "We don't need JJ. I can take *Alvin* down that opening."

"That's all right, Ralph," I said, knowing he was only half joking. "Let's stick to the original plan and land *Alvin* on the deck and let JJ go down that hole, not us."

We completed our first *Alvin* tour of *Titanic*'s bow section by dropping down the portside of the hull to peer through the windows of the enclosed first-class promenade on A Deck. We were sheltered somewhat from the current here, and Ralph had an easier time maneuvering. *Alvin*'s powerful floodlights easily penetrated the gloom inside the interior stateroom windows. It was bizarre to think that there were probably personal possessions of the wealthy passengers—at least objects not made of easily digestible organic material—still strewn about those cabins as the passengers donned their overcoats and life jackets.

As Ralph maneuvered *Alvin* vertically back toward the Boat Deck, the sub shuddered with a sharp clanging noise, and a cascade of roiling orange rust engulfed our viewports.

"Ralph," I shouted, "we've hit something. What is it?"

"I don't know," he said, his voice suddenly grim. "We should be clear of any overhang. I'm backing off."

I sucked in my breath and waited, glancing furtively at Martin Bowen on the portside. He was busy trying to trouble-shoot JJ's electronics and didn't understand the sudden menace as Ralph and I did. Invisible overhangs are the recurrent nightmare of deep-diving submariners. If *Alvin*'s open Fiberglas sail had become inextricably snarled in jutting wreckage, we would die here. Or if our blind ascent had dislodged unstable debris heavier than our descent weights and battery tubs, we would never be able to regain the surface. My mind flashed back to that huge volcanic boulder on the steep face of the Cayman Trough scarp.

Alvin's stern thruster whined in reverse, and we backed clear of the overhead obstacle. Ralph climbed in clear water, then inched forward with equal caution. The water was still turbid with rust particles, cutting visibility. The last thing we wanted to do was blunder too fast into some sharp obstacle jutting outward that might strike one of our recessed oval view ports, cracking the thick Plexiglas. At this depth, the pressure would instantly magnify a tiny crack, the view port would implode, and we'd be dead in a fraction of a second.

As we crept toward the Boat Deck, we saw a big steel davit block shrouded in rust. This oval pulley was attached to one of *Titanic*'s long, curved lifeboat davits that had toppled over and jutted out several feet from the hull. Had we bungled into this dangerous obstacle with any kind of closing velocity, we might have damaged *Alvin* or even crushed JJ, which was exposed on the chin tray between *Alvin*'s strong pressure hull and any obstacle we might hit.

I gazed at the block and davit, recognizing with a sudden chill that it had been rigged for Lifeboat Number 8. That was the boat the stout-hearted Mrs. Ida Straus had refused to enter when the cry went out, "Women and children first." Instead, she had died with her husband, Isidor.

On our last sweep across the top of the superstructure, the sub was buffeted by the full strength of the current, now moving at over one knot. Ralph had trouble keeping *Alvin*'s head into this deep-sea wind, and we were slowly swept aft along the axis of the bow section. Suddenly I saw a frightening sight: the graceful lines of *Titanic*'s superstructure disappeared in a tangle of shorn hull plate, portholes popped inside out, and crushed sandwiches of rusty steel that had once been entire decks. This was the pancaked midship section that marked the savage amputation wound that had severed the stern and bow sections.

"Swing back to the left!" I warned Ralph, my voice sharp. There were any number of things in that junk heap to snare us. "I have wreckage just out of my view port and it's getting close."

Still our nose swung left, despite the high-pitched whir of the thrusters at maximum amps.

"Swing left!" I warned again.

"It won't come around into the current," Ralph said, his voice strained.

"Then come up," I said. "Let's get out of here. It's too dangerous."

We rose clear of the obstacles and caught the full brunt of the current eddying over the superstructure. I directed Ralph to cross the hull and swing up the starboard side to the bow.

But our time on the bottom was almost over, given the slow seawater leak in the battery tub.

As much as I valued my time on the wreck, I wasn't displeased when Ralph punched off the descent weights and we began the long climb back to the world of sunlight and warmth.

Two and a half hours later, as we neared the surface, *Alvin* pitched violently forward, caught by a ragged wave.

"JJ is out of his garage," Ralph shouted.

I couldn't see from my view port, but I realized the squalls that had been forecast for that afternoon had arrived and the sudden chop had dislodged the little ROV from its perch in *Alvin*'s science tray. Without power to its thrusters, it sank beneath us, held only by its fiber-optic tether.

But that thin tether passed through the jaws of the emergency cutter we would activate if JJ ever became irretrievably tangled in *Titanic*'s wreckage.

Ralph called in vain over the VHF radio for the recovery divers to put a safety line on JJ. But his transmission was lost in the babble of competing calls among the recovery boats and the crew up on the stern of *Atlantis II*. Finally, as JJ was tossing beneath us like a runaway yo-yo, divers got the word and rescued our little robot. But in doing so, they had to cut the tether close to the sub.

Chris Von Alt's crew worked all night, reattaching the fiber-optic tether and carefully resealing all of JJ's key components.

In the morning, Martin Bowen and I were ready to climb aboard *Alvin* for our second attempt on the grand staircase. Our pilot today would be my old friend Dudley Foster. While completing the long prelaunch checklist, however, Martin was chagrined to discover that one of JJ's four thruster motors was jammed, the propeller striking its protective shroud.

I stood around in mounting disbelief for the next three hours as one problem led to another in a kind of nightmare domino effect.

We didn't launch until almost 11:30 A.M., and it was almost two by the time we neared the bottom. That left us just over an hour for JJ's tour of *Titanic*'s grand staircase, which was meant to be the centerpiece of the expedition. But, thankfully, visibility and current conditions were good on the bottom today, and Dudley didn't waste any time locating our landing spot just forward of the staircase opening.

Even moving quickly, I made sure we cleared any small, easily overlooked obstacles on the rust-carpeted deck. It took several minutes for Dudley to adjust the ballast, and with each sharp squeal of the pumps, I warily eyed the deck beneath our skids, watching for any sign of metal failure. We didn't have to be too heavy, just have enough negative buoyancy to stay in place while Martin deployed JJ.

I could see Martin was extremely nervous, not from the hazards of the dive but from the type of pregame butterflies any competitor feels before an important performance. Staring intently at JJ's control box in his lap, Martin operated the horizontal thruster joystick with his right hand and controlled JJ's vertical thrusters and tether with the pistol grip in his left hand. Martin's only visual reference came from the tiny Watchman monitor mounted in the center of the control panel and connected to JJ's video eye.

Martin eased JJ out of its garage on the science tray and let it flutter out directly ahead of the sphere to pirouette back and peer at us with its mismatched video and still camera eyes. JJ looked like the little movie robot R2D2's aquatic cousin, blinking at us from ten feet away. The ROV's floodlight cast an eerie glare through our view ports. In the TV monitor, we could see our own image, *Alvin*'s running lights looking like the glowing eyes of a mythical deep-sea monster.

Martin did not waste any more time but sailed JJ straight over to the staircase opening, then squeezed the trigger on his pistol grip to drop the little blue robot down into the dark shaft. As JJ disappeared from our floodlights, I glanced at the red safety cover on the emergency decoupling switch that would sever the tether. There'd been so many other equipment glitches today, I wondered if that device would work in an emergency.

"*Alvin*," I said, "this is *Atlantis II. Jason* is inside the staircase."

It was only after I'd spoken that I realized I had reversed call signs and described JJ as *Jason*. I guess I was more excited than I realized.

Martin hunched over his control panel, watching JJ's camera light flood the dark vertical shaft as the ROV descended cautiously, hugging the forward bulkhead where an ornate, bejeweled clock had once hung. In JJ's little backup monitor, no identifiable benchmarks appeared at first, only the crusty orange sheets of rust on the vertical bulkheads and the occasional line of rivets beneath the deposits. The massive oak staircase that had filled the shaft had all but disappeared. But we were able to identify some horizontal plating marking the spot where landings had stood. And the big rectangular openings to the public rooms on A Deck were obvious.

Martin swung JJ around for a closer look at some pillars, and we caught sight of something glimmering in the distance.

"Look at that," Martin whispered. "Look at that chandelier."

I shook my head in disbelief. "No, it *can't* be a chandelier. It couldn't possibly have survived."

I thought of the crushing forces involved with the impact of the huge bow section careening into the bottom at better than 30 miles an hour.

But as Martin maneuvered JJ even closer to the glittering object, I exclaimed, "My God, it *is* a chandelier!"

On close examination, however, the object proved not to be a chandelier per se, but rather a crystal-beaded light fixture still dangling from its electric cord, one of dozens of similar fixtures that had illuminated the grand staircase on its descent through the superstructure. This delicate fixture even sprouted its own quill-like sea pen, a rare species of deep-ocean corallike organism.

For the next twenty minutes, JJ probed deep into the staircase, with several adventurous side forays into ghostly empty public rooms.

Then Dudley reluctantly announced, "Bob, we are running short of bottom time."

I almost swore with exasperation at Ralph Hollis's inflexible rules. We had enough juice in the batteries to stay down here several more hours. Instead, I was forced to concede to bureaucratic inflexibility that was undoubtedly exacerbated by a good admixture of institutional jealousy. JJ was in the process of proving the superiority of ROVs over manned submersibles. But we had to surface so that *Alvin*'s crew could sit down to a prompt dinner before sunset.

I swallowed my annoyance on the way to the surface. JJ's majestic descent of the grand staircase had been much more than a media gimmick. That brief tethered flight of our little ROV had been exactly the field test of the fiber-optic telepresence robotic technology that I had promised the navy I would build and deploy less than four years earlier. Today I had kept that promise.

As with any new technology on its shake-down cruise, JJ's performance over the next several dives was a mixture of stunning success and inevitable glitches. Our dive on July 16 allowed Martin to fly JJ into some areas of *Titanic*'s bow section that were simply too dangerous for *Alvin* to investigate closely. This included the tangle of cables surrounding the collapsed foremast with its tublike crow's nest. JJ's unblinking video eye roamed up and down the toppled mast, peering intently. Again, I could almost hear lookout Fred Fleet announcing: "Iceberg right ahead," as he leaned against the curved lip of the crow's nest, bundled against the cold in duffel coat and watchcap. JJ's sharp video lens even discerned the heavy old telephone handset lookout Fleet had used to speak his futile warning.

Martin then flew JJ along a row of B Deck windows, and found a missing windowpane on a first-class cabin. Peering inside, JJ confirmed my earlier suspicions: all organic material—wood and fabric—had disappeared. All that was left was rusty steel.

On another foray along the Promenade Deck, JJ's tether

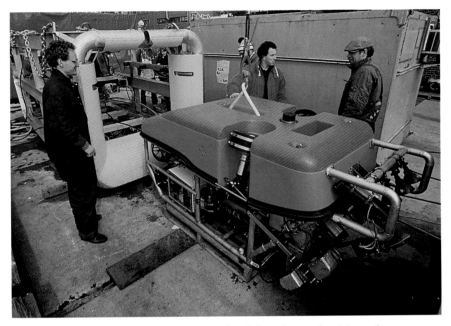

Jason resting inside *Hugo* prior to its fateful and near-fatal launch.
JASON Project

Rescue vehicle *Medea* appears to be suspended in air as *Hugo* crashes into the side of the *Star Hercules* during its recovery. *Joseph H. Bailey* © *National Geographic Society*

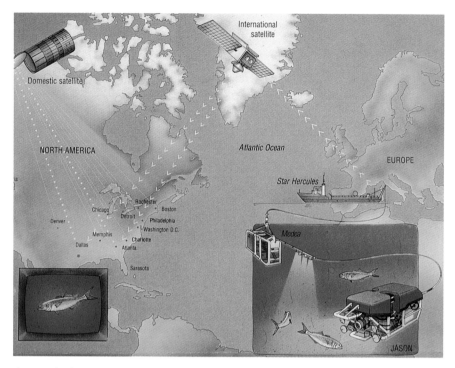

Artwork depicting technology used for "live" JASON Project broadcasts from the Mediterranean. *Madison Press*

Technician works inside portable television production studio aboard the *Star Hercules*, that was used by Turner Broadcasting for "live" JASON Project programs.
National Geographic Society

Jason hovering above an active hydrothermal vent on Marsili Seamount. *JASON Project*

Student Argonaut joins Jason team at control console during "live" broadcasts from the Mediterranean. *JASON Project*

Jason downlink site at National Geographic Headquarters in Washington, D.C., during *Jason IV*'s live broadcasts from Belize. *Mark D. Thiessen © National Geographic Society*

The author relaxes aboard the *Star Hercules* during a break in live broadcasting from the Mediterranean. *JASON Project*

The author with the Jason team in the control van during "live" broadcasts from Lake Ontario. *JASON Foundation/John Earle*

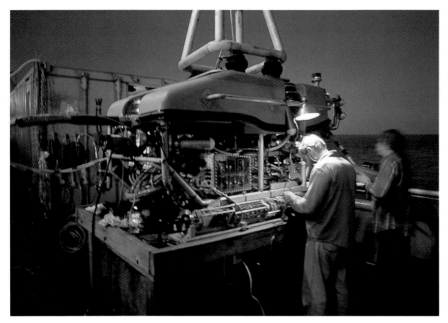

Bob Elder works into the night repairing Jason in preparation for another day of live exploration of hydrothermal vents during Jason IV broadcasts from the Sea of Cortez. *Robert Ballard*

The author with his son Douglas aboard a barge in Lake Ontario during Jason II broadcasts. *Robert Ballard*

National Geographic
Society downlink site during
Jason II broadcast from
Lake Ontario with figure-
head of *Hamilton* on screen.
Mark D. Thiessen ©
*National Geographic
Society*

The author with student Argonauts during Jason II.
JASON Foundation/John Earle

Student operating Jason from National Geographic downlink site while the robot is exploring shipwrecks from the War of 1812 in Lake Ontario during Jason II.
Mark D. Thiessen © National Geographic Society

The author's wife, Barbara, enjoys the friendly gray whales of St. Ignacio Lagoon in Baja California during filming effort in support of Jason IV broadcasts. *Robert Ballard*

Dr. Anna McCann holds a small terra-cotta lamp recovered from *Isis* wreck site. *JASON Project*

Member of Jason team removes large amphora from elevator. *JASON Project*

Barge anchored above warship *Hamilton* in Lake Ontario during Jason II.
Robert Ballard

Jason uses its mechanical arm to recover one of *Isis'* clay storage jars.
JASON Project

The author's wife, Barbara, and Andy Bowen stand their watch with other members of the search team aboard the *Restless M* during the first phase of the Guadalcanal project in Iron Bottom Sound.
Robert Ballard

With Savo Island in the background, a side-scan sonar is lowered over the side in search of the U.S.S. *Quincy*.
Robert Ballard

U.S. Navy support ship *Laney Chouest* on the calm surface of Iron Bottom Sound during 1992 diving program.
Robert Ballard/Odyssey Corp.

The long vigil pays off as the ghostly outline on a warship can be seen on the side-scan sonar record.
Robert Ballard

The search team aboard the *Restless M* during the first phase of the Guadalcanal project prepare a small camera system to photograph sonar targets on the bottom of Iron Bottom Sound.
Robert Ballard

The submersible *Sea Cliff* is lowered into the calm waters of Iron Bottom Sound to investigate a sonar target thought to be the U.S.S. *Quincy.* *Robert Ballard*

The remotely operated vehicle *Scorpio* on its way down to investigate sunken warships in Iron Bottom Sound.
Robert Ballard/Odyssey Corp.

Research team aboard the *Laney Chouest* review videotapes collected by *Scorpio* of the Australian heavy cruiser H.M.S. *Canberra. Robert Ballard*

Chris Raney confers with his *Scorpio* support team before launching the ROV to inspect the Japanese destroyer *Yudachi*. *Robert Ballard*

Bert Wayne, a survivor of the H.M.S. *Canberra*, holds a bronze plaque to be placed on his ship while Stewart Moredock, a survivor of the *Atlanta*, looks on. *Robert Ballard*

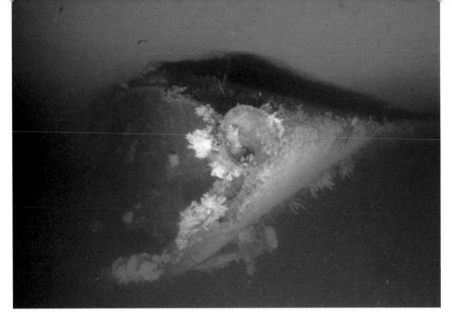

The bow section of the U.S.S. *Barton* lies quietly on its side as seen from the ROV *Scorpio. Odyssey Corp.*

Anti-aircraft battery on the stern of the heavy cruiser U.S.S. *Quincy*, sunk in Iron Bottom Sound during the 1942 Battle of Savo Island. *Odyssey Corp.*

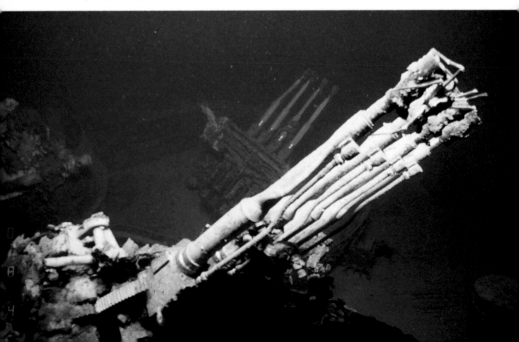

Afterbridge section of U.S.S. *Quincy*. *Odyssey Corp.*

Bridge of U.S.S. *Quincy* on the floor of Iron Bottom Sound. *Odyssey Corp.*

The Navy's nuclear research submarine *NR-1* resting on the surface while the author transfers aboard for a long reconnaissance dive. *Robert Ballard*

NR-1 glides beneath the waves like a leopard seal. *Emory Kristof © National Geographic Society*

The author and a member of *NR-1* crew look out of the submarine's viewports during its dive on the Rekyjanes Ridge south of Iceland. *Emory Kristof © National Geographic Society*

almost became snagged in a ripped hook of steel plating. But Martin skillfully extracted the little ROV.

We used JJ to inspect the tangle of deck plates near the Lifeboat Number 1 davit still standing well forward on the starboard side of the Boat Deck. As the ROV fluttered and turned like an inquisitive blue hummingbird, I thought of the human tragedy that had been enacted on these steel deck plates the night *Titanic* sank.

Here young Alfred Rush, who had celebrated his eighteenth birthday two days out from Queenstown, had refused to board a lifeboat with women and children. He was a man, he said, and died with the others when the ship sank.

But J. Bruce Ismay, the shipping magnate whose firm owned the White Star Line, had climbed aboard a half-full collapsible lifeboat, one of the last to be launched, and had survived to be rescued. The popular press crucified him as J. "Brute" Ismay. After becoming a recluse, Ismay died in lonely disgrace, a victim to the Edwardian concept of masculine honor, which itself did not survive the carnage of the muddy trenches of the Western Front a few years later.

While JJ remained on the surface undergoing repairs and maintenance, I dived with *Alvin* pilot Jim Hardiman and trainee copilot John Salzig to explore the full extent of the debris field between *Titanic*'s bow and stern sections. Al Uchupi—ever the meticulous field geologist—had drawn up a detailed map of the major debris based on ANGUS photographs.

Today Jim flew *Alvin* just over the bottom as we videotaped and photographed the seemingly endless procession of porcelain plates, gleaming silver salvers. It was on this run that I realized that nonferrous metal objects such as the silver trays and copper kettles, and the bronze gears and capstan crowns we'd seen on the bow section had retained their sheen by the ceaseless polishing action of the currents.

As I studied the parade of chamber pots, bathtubs, and leather suitcases, I also discovered that well-tanned leather—including several haunting pairs of high-button shoes—had survived the voracious worms and mollusks, the only organic material besides galvanized rubber to do so. And once more, I pictured the silent, relentless march of white crabs that I had seen during my first dive off Palm Beach, so many years before. There were certainly fewer scavenging crabs out here in the deep ocean, but they were just as relentless.

So it was clear to me then we would never encounter human remains—even a recognizable scrap of bone—in this resting place of 1,522 souls.

But this reassuring conclusion was suddenly shattered. Without warning, I found myself gazing into the eyes of a delicate, white smiling face. For a fractured second, I thought I'd encountered a corpse, somehow preserved by a bizarre mummifying alchemy. Then I released my stunned breath, realizing I was looking at a ceramic doll's head, its elaborate hairdo and silk dress gone forever. My shock gave way to a deep sadness. What little girl had owned this doll with the beautiful, wistful face of a high-society lady? Had the child survived? She had probably been from a wealthy family, and almost all of the first- and second-class passenger children had, in fact, been rescued the next morning from the lifeboats. I realized that this carefully crafted porcelain doll's head was probably much too expensive a toy for any child among the third-class immigrants to own. They had died by the hundreds, falling to this eternal night without the comfort of such dainty toy companions.

Just after our lunch of peanut-butter-and-jelly sandwiches, Jim continued our tour of the wide debris field. Suddenly, I spotted the distinctive shape of a safe, its brass handle and combination wheel polished bright by the current. My first impulse was to simply photograph the safe; after all, I had been one of the most vociferous public critics of those who proposed salvaging—I often said "scavenging"—the *Titanic* wreck site.

But curiosity took hold, as it so often did. Why not try to open the safe with *Alvin*'s mechanical arm and lay rest to the rumors of sunken treasures and Edwardian jewels? I was torn with indecision. The U.S. Congress would soon pass a bill making it a crime to pillage this wreck, however, I certainly didn't need a federal law to keep the promise I had made to Jean-Louis Michel and the world that I would never remove a single object from the *Titanic.* Taking something was one thing, but taking a peek into a safe was another. Finally, I used *Alvin*'s mechanical arm to twist the safe handle to see if the door was unlocked. Surprisingly, the handle turned easily; then it jammed, the door flanges rusted shut.

I was still curious, of course. One of the few artifacts of significance, a bejeweled illuminated edition of *The Rubaiyat of Omar Khayyam,* being shipped to New York, was known to have been stored in one of *Titanic*'s safes. What the hell. . . . I tried to lift the safe from the bottom to test its weight. It rose easily in a billow of sediment, feather-light. Twisting the mechanical arm's wrist, I saw that the entire back of the safe had rusted out.

So much for sunken treasure.

Ralph Hollis took backup JJ flyer Ken Stewart and me to the jumbled, chaotic wreckage of the stern section on July 21. I intended to put to rest forever Jack Grimm's questionable "propeller" sighting from his last expedition. We planned to land on the bottom beneath the towering, curved battlement of *Titanic*'s stern and use JJ to search for the three huge bronze propellers.

But when Ken launched JJ from its perch, the little ROV spun in confused circles; one of its thrusters had shorted out. After we retrieved JJ, I sat glumly at my view port, once again frustrated by the ROV's glitches on this overly demanding shakedown cruise.

I was startled to realize that Ralph Hollis—the stickler for rules and regulations—was creeping *Alvin* steadily ahead, directly under the overhanging steel cliff of *Titanic*'s stern. The stern section's structural integrity was probably just as good as the bow section's . . . probably. But if this battered mound of wreckage, half buried in the mud, was precariously split and rusted, it was certainly possible for *Alvin* to provoke a sudden avalanche of steel plate that would smother us.

After a very long and cautious approach, *Alvin*'s floodlights revealed the massive vertical slab of *Titanic*'s rudder. The trim marks were cloaked in rust, but we could see that the stern section was buried at least as deeply as the bow.

"I see the rudder, Bob," Ralph announced, proud of *Alvin*'s ability as a close-up explorer, "but I don't see any propellers."

I craned my neck to gaze out the view port up and down, left and right. Only about 16 feet of rudder was exposed above the crusty gray sediment. The propellers had to be buried beneath us. But I had no way to prove that. I could almost hear Jack Grimm's nasal chuckle at our failure.

Before we left the stern, I deposited an etched metal memorial plaque honoring my friend Bill Tantum that his widow Ann had given me before this cruise. The plaque was also a tribute to the members of the *Titanic* Historical Society who had worked so long to keep the memory of the great ship alive. Using *Alvin*'s arm, we slipped the plaque onto the open poop deck, where so many of the victims had clustered before the ship's final plunge beneath the surface.

After several minutes, Ralph lifted off, dumping the descent weights clear of the stern, and we began rising toward the surface. I kept the large color video camera we'd mounted on *Alvin*'s superstructure focused on the plaque as long as possible. As we glided up, the plaque dimmed and diminished in the viewfinder. Because our free ascent was so smooth and silent, I felt no motion. I was gripped by the optical illusion that the little sub was standing still and it was *Titanic*'s stern that was sinking beneath the glow of our flood lamps until it was swallowed in the eternal gloom.

I found my throat choked with sudden, unexpected sadness. In my mind's eye, I pictured that pathetic, doomed cluster of victims who had gathered close for the warmth of human contact as the cold sea sloshed up the tilted hull. They had jammed together against the curved stern rail as the deck tilted relentlessly beneath their feet.

Although I dived twice more on the wreck before the end of the expedition, that sight of the empty stern sinking from view was the haunting image of *Titanic* that stayed in my mind long after we returned to shore.

Part Five

GAINING TRUTH

TEN

I made my way aft along the heaving deck of the *Star Hercules,* grateful for the protection offered by the jumble of shipping vans that housed the expedition's science lab, technical support units, and television studio. The bow plunged into a steep swell, and cold seawater sloshed through the narrow walkways among the vans. With the deck suddenly flooded, I saw why my team had dubbed these clustered steel containers "Venice" on their stormy passage down from Britain to the Mediterranean.

It was Monday, April 24, 1989. The big oil-field support ship was two days out of Gibraltar, eastbound toward Sicily. And the "sunny" Mediterranean was becoming downright nasty. The sky was completely gray now, curdled with multilayered cirrus and high stratus decks that marked the approach of a strong storm front. Aft of the sheltering vans, stinging spray lashed the exposed stern.

Andy Bowen, the JASON Project's engineer, was hunched over the awkward, bulky shape of *Hugo,* our new principal Remotely Operated Vehicle.

An acronym for "Huge *Argo,*" the massive welded aluminum-girder framework was basically an elaborate garage for *Jason,* the robot explorer that was finally ready for its first expedition, almost ten years after I'd made my detailed plans for a deep-diving ROV tethered by fiber-optic cable during my Stanford sabbatical year. Out of habit, I patted *Jason*'s curved Fiberglas flanks nestled snugly within *Hugo*'s wide maw.

I loved everything about the gleaming blue cubical ROV.

Jason was a long-held dream that had actually materialized, despite years of technical problems. A quantum improvement over the trouble-plagued little JJ test vehicle that had nevertheless done yeoman service on the *Titanic* wreck, *Jason* was about the size of a Volkswagen Beetle and weighed 2,500 pounds "dry." But it really was the state of the art in underwater exploration robots. The ROV was equipped with side-scan and forward sonars and two high-resolution color video cameras. *Jason*'s seven computer-controlled thrusters allowed the remote operator to fly the vehicle with the precision and delicacy of a hummingbird. When fitted with agile and robust mechanical arms, *Jason* could retrieve objects weighing up to a hundred pounds from as deep as 20,000 feet.

A 500-foot fiber-optic tether connected *Jason* to *Hugo*, which in turn was connected by the long fiber-optic umbilical to the surface ship. We'd designed the *Hugo-Jason* system to work from a modern vessel such as *Star Hercules*, which had a dynamic positioning system that kept the ship precisely on station above a chosen spot on the deep ocean bottom. The images transmitted up *Jason-Hugo*'s long fiber-optic umbilical could be processed and rebroadcast worldwide via satellite from our onboard television production studio in one of the converted shipping vans that crowded the ship's flat, open deck.

This telepresence lay at the heart of the JASON Project. Although I'd developed this innovative hardware to meet specific deep ocean survey needs of the U.S. Navy, I'd always kept the system's civilian exploration and educational potential firmly in mind. And in four days, *Jason* would make its global television debut. On April 26, we would broadcast live exploration programs to twelve museums in the United States and Canada, where 250,000 students would assemble in classes to participate in our expedition. This would not be a canned and edited precis of the explorer's work replete with stirring background music but rather a real-time direct observation of ocean explorers practicing their profession. The students would see and hear exactly what we did.

Our plan was to take these students half a world away down to the rugged slopes of the Marsili Seamount, an active underwater volcano northwest of Sicily. After a week on the seamount, we would shift to Skerki Bank, the long shoals that lay between Tunisia and Sicily, one of the major shipping graveyards of the Mediterranean. There we would thoroughly explore the wreck of the *Isis,* a Roman trading vessel we had discovered the year before on an *Argo* search and named in honor of the classical goddess who protected seafarers.

As I had hoped, the JASON Project combined both serious educational goals—students enrolled in the project had to study both physical and life sciences as well as history and archaeology—and the exciting elements of mystery and expectation unique to deep-sea exploration. Because all our shows would be live with two-way satellite feeds, the students would be participants, not just spectators. They were free to ask questions in any phase of the operation. We had television coverage from our production studio and main control van. If all went well, the students would forget they were high and dry in a museum in Illinois or British Columbia and actually feel they were aboard ship with us, seeing the *Jason* images for the first time just as we did. To heighten this effect, the project had constructed replicas of our onboard control van at each of the twelve museum sites. Our plan was to upgrade these control vans in coming years so that students could actually fly the ROVs from these distant sites.

I believed strongly that once students experienced this direct connection between their theoretical classroom work and the practical reality of an exploration cruise, many of them would be channeled toward careers in science and technology.

But before any of these grandiose and intricate plans could reach fruition, the *Hugo-Jason* system had to work as advertised under difficult conditions.

Andy Bowen was bent over *Hugo*'s massive aluminum framework, making final adjustments to a chafing guard on a cable bridle. With the wind and spray, he didn't hear me approach. Andy (no relation to either Martin Bowen or *Knorr* captain Richard Bowen) was one of the most important members of the team. In matters nautical and mechanical, he was truly a master. Andy Bowen came from an English family, was raised in the Maritime Provinces of Canada, and ended every phrase with a habitual "eh?" He could shift from well-reasoned and politely accented Establishment English to some of the most imaginative combinations of curses and expletives that I've ever heard. Above all, Andy was a self-starter with an unbreakable work ethic who accepted any challenge without grumbling. He was skilled and fearless on deck in the worst of weather. But his true talent lay in bringing disparate members of an expedition together to work as an integrated team. I had come to consider Andy Bowen my "Number One," the resourceful and dedicated executive officer that every expedition leader needs.

I only regretted that Andy had not been aboard the previous summer's Mediterranean survey cruise, which had been one of the most bitter and frustrating experiences of my professional career. That summer, still flush with our victory on the *Titanic*, I'd opted for a team that was heavy on technical talent but definitely lacking in leadership among the designated watch chiefs. I had planned a combination of geological survey and exploration, using *Argo* to search for underwater volcanic activity in the central Mediterranean, as well as for evidence of ancient shipwrecks, both types of sites being targets for this year's JASON Project.

But these objectives lacked the concrete focus of a single sunken ship such as *Titanic*, and I wasn't able to convey to my team the intuitive reasoning that drove much of my search strategy. After days of unproductive search—the *Argo* monitors filled with the sterile, ugly scars of trawler nets that had virtually swept the bottom clean—rebellious factions formed and rose to challenge my decisions. The 1988 summer cruise was the only expedition I ever terminated early because of bad chemistry among the team.

I'd endured another, more private disappointment during the 1988 cruise, with my oldest son Todd. He had seemed eager enough to join the expedition crew that summer before his first year at college, and I was certainly happy to have him on board, although I was determined that he would receive no favoritism and had to haul his weight as the most junior member of the expedition party. To me, the chance for a young guy who had just turned nineteen to not only cruise the Mediterranean and Atlantic aboard a research vessel but to also learn the exacting yet fascinating craft of deep-sea robotic exploration, was a marvelous opportunity.

But Todd's performance in 1988 had been lackluster, even sullen on occasion. And there were times—especially when he seemed to deliberately sleep through his watch rotation—that he almost seemed to be challenging my authority as both the expedition leader and his father.

This led to simmering bad feelings, even a few hot exchanges between Todd and me. In retrospect, such a conflict was inevitable. Late adolescence, when a boy teeters on the frightening brink of manhood, is a difficult time, especially for a kid like Todd who was big, strong, and good-looking, seemingly mature beyond his years. In reality, Todd was anything but self-confident that summer. And I mistook his self-consciousness, which seemed to express itself through indolence, as a form of passive defiance.

But the 1988 cruise was far from a total washout.

We did manage to find a collection of distinctive terra-cotta amphorae on Skerki Bank, which we tentatively identified as the wreck of a Roman merchant vessel from the third or fourth century A.D. We also found unmistakable evidence of the first hydrothermal vent site in the Mediterranean on the slopes of Marsili Seamount.

Mindful of the near-mutiny the year before, I'd made sure this 1989 expedition team contained my ablest and most experienced veterans, including Andy Bowen, Cathy Offinger, Martin Bowen, Dana Yoerger, Skip Gleason, and Bob Elder.

When I boarded the ship in Gibraltar, I realized my decision was well founded. On the passage from Britain to the Mediterranean, the *Star Hercules* had encountered a savage storm in the Bay of Biscay. *Hugo,* lashed securely to the exposed deck among the cluster of vans, had been pummeled by a monstrous rogue wave that swept the ship from bow to stern. The all-important electronics van had been flooded and its floor had collapsed, ruining hundreds of thousands of dollars in vital computers. *Hugo* and *Jason* were damaged, although salvageable, but the technicians, already exhausted by the terrible week at sea, had to work around the clock as we steamed from Gibraltar to the central Mediterranean to meet our fast-approaching transmission schedule.

Our first test transmissions would be from the *Isis* site on Skerki Bank. This would give the producers and technicians at Turner Broadcasting in Atlanta, one of our main sponsors, and at the museum downlink sites in North America, the chance to work out the inevitable glitches before we scheduled our first system-wide student broadcast from Marsili Seamount.

I was reasonably confident that the hard-pressed technical staff had salvaged and revamped as much of the storm-damaged equipment as they could, and that their complex side of this intricate electronic ballet would be ready in time. But I had definite qualms about launching *Hugo* in this kind of weather.

As if these nagging worries were not enough to drive me

bonkers, the present expedition was only one of the multiple balls I had to juggle.

After the JASON Project phase of this cruise aboard the *Star Hercules,* we would return to the deep Atlantic southwest of the British Isles and resume our frustrating search for the wreck of the German battleship *Bismarck,* which had been sunk in one of the epic sea battles of World War II.

The previous summer I had hunted hard for *Bismarck,* but had come up empty-handed. The sponsors for the *Bismarck* search, the Quest Group, led by two duck-hunting friends from southern California, Don Kol and Marco Vitulli—as well as *National Geographic* and Turner Broadcasting—were among my most important patrons. The year before, I had spent a lot of their money searching for *Bismarck* which I had overconfidently stated would be a simple task to find, but I had only managed to locate the wreckage of a nineteenth-century sailing schooner after almost two frustrating weeks on the search site.

My professional reputation as an ocean explorer now rested on the success of both the Mediterranean and Atlantic phases of this year's demanding cruise.

I clapped Andy Bowen on the shoulder and pointed up at the angry gray cloud deck slashing across the sky.

"It looks bad."

Andy nodded and wiped some drying spray from his face. "Yeah. It's going to blow pretty hard, eh?"

The ship plunged into the mounting easterly swell, and we both ducked a cloud of stinging spray.

This was the forerunner of a notorious Genoa Front, a tightly organized low-pressure system that sweeps across the Mediterranean, especially in spring and autumn when the temperature differential is greatest between northern Europe and North Africa. These cyclonic storms—often called siroccos because of their strong southeasterly gales—had been the nemesis of Mediterranean shipping since prehistoric times.

Launching and operating *Hugo* with the *Star Hercules* pitching like a hobbyhorse in the storm swells could easily overstress our tow tether. Although our new fiber-optic cable was the same .68-inch thickness as *Argo*'s coaxial cable, it was slightly stronger, with a break strength of 20,000 pounds. But any cable has its breaking point. And even though I wasn't a professional engineer, my years at sea had taught me to expect the unexpected menace when you combined new equipment with bad weather.

I tapped *Hugo*'s massive aluminum-girder framework, which rose above the level of my head.

"I still don't like it," I told Andy. "This thing is a monster. It's going to cause us problems with this weather."

Andy glanced over *Hugo*'s massive form, then up at the thick yellow beams of the ship's hydraulic A-frame crane perched over the stern. *Star Hercules* was designed to deliver bundles of drill pipe and other bulky equipment five times *Hugo*'s mass and weight. He was confident that we had the right ship and the right crane for the job.

"Don't worry, Bob," Andy reassured me. He stroked *Hugo*'s gleaming aluminum girders like a proud father. "Our new baby will do just fine."

I studied the A-frame crane again, then *Hugo*'s stout frame. Finally, my eyes rested on the gray fiber-optic cable that ran through the big round sheave lashed beneath the A-frame center span.

"I hope so," was all I managed to reply.

"Dr. Ballard," the voice from the Turner Broadcasting control room in Atlanta sounded in my headset, "we have you on camera. All museums have signed on. Countdown to air: five, four, three . . ."

I gazed into the lens beneath the glowing ruby active-camera light a few feet away in *Jason*'s control van. From my position, I could watch the monitors that displayed the A-frame at the stern of *Star Hercules* where the launch crew had assembled.

"Good morning from the Mediterranean," I said cheerfully. "You've tuned in just in time to see a live launch of *Hugo* and *Jason*."

In the same cheerful tone, I noted that the weather was not ideal but that our crew was very experienced. Despite the director's instruction to keep my gaze focused on the camera and to avoid the inevitable "shifty" appearance that comes from glancing sideways, my eyes instinctively turned to the monitor that displayed the A-frame with the thin fiber-optic cable running through the sheave as the crew struggled with the guy lines to control the combined mass and weight of *Hugo* and *Jason* swinging from the stern. Although the worst of the storm had passed, the swell was still rolling in from the southeast, and the *Star Hercules* was pitching badly.

"We've got the vehicle in the water now," I continued, struggling to keep the nervous strain from my voice. "As you can see from the video screen behind me, the cable is going out smoothly." Following stage directions, I turned slowly and pointed to the video monitor, mindful that my eventual audience on this project would be eager youngsters for whom all this technology was mysterious, perhaps even frightening. "It will take about thirty minutes for *Hugo* to make the descent to the bottom, a distance of roughly half a mile."

I braced my legs against the studio chair as the ship smashed into an especially steep swell and plowed bow down, only to pitch up, bow high, a moment later. This was the worst of the hobbyhorse movement that I dreaded because of the snap-loading strain it placed on the cable. With the stern down in the trough, the cable went slack, only to snap overtaut again as the bow dipped and the stern rose on the wave crest.

Still smiling benignly with confidence, I turned to face the camera lens. Out of the corner of my eye, I saw the cable go slack and braced myself for the inevitable strain as the ship rose from the trough to the next crest. Suddenly the screen went black. An electric surge of adrenaline ran through my body. In that instant, I knew the cable had snapped.

"Oh my God!" I shouted, oblivious to the hundreds of television technicians in North America who were watching this live performance.

I ripped off my headset and sprinted from the production van, leaving the Turner Broadcasting producers in Atlanta to explain to the downlink museum sites what had happened.

As I pounded across the wet deck between the clustered vans, my heart thudded, and my mouth was dry. Over $2 million worth of advanced hardware, unique in the world, which had taken years of painful effort to design and build, was sinking to the bottom of the Mediterranean, 2,600 feet below.

But my first thought was not on the sinking *Hugo* and *Jason* but on the safety of the deck crew. My mind flashed back to the jammed winch traction unit aboard *Knorr* during the *Argo* search for *Titanic*. When a cable snaps under strain, the resulting whiplash can cut a man in half. When I cleared the vans, however, I saw that the crew, under Andy Bowen's leadership, had wisely taken shelter when they saw the cable go so slack. Now they were milling about the stern, gazing stricken at the severed end of the cable curled on the rough plank deck beneath the A-frame.

A dozen competing options and orders raced through my mind but were pushed aside by the terrible image of *Hugo*'s big girdered box sinking like a ballast weight into the black depths. *Hugo*, of course, was basically an expendable assemblage of welded aluminum and batteries. But *Jason*, the gleaming red-and-white Fiberglas ROV sheltered in that aluminum box, was literally irreplaceable. If *Jason* was not retrievable, I would probably never be able to fund a replacement. My ambitious dreams of robotic human exploration of the deep ocean were sinking with *Hugo*.

Suddenly, I began giving orders, some of them pointless, but my words had the desired effect of snapping people from their shocked immobility. Even as I spoke, part of my mind searched for a concrete solution to the specific problem at hand: how would we ever get *Jason* back in time for the television shows scheduled in just four days?

I had already decided to mothball *Hugo* if we did retrieve it from the bottom. That ungainly vehicle was just too heavy to deploy with our precious fiber-optic cable. I was now convinced that *Jason* was robust enough to operate without this elaborate garage. Instead, I'd modify a small sled we had used the year before to test our new fiber-optic cable. More importantly, this sled was all we had left aboard. Everything else was on the bottom of the ocean.

The crew had jokingly named the test sled "Anus," since most of our other vehicles had names that started with an *A*. Clearly, this would not do, not with 250,000 students about to learn its name. Fortunately, we had an archaeology student from Harvard aboard named Betsey Robinson, who quickly came to my rescue. She suggested we name the sled "Medea," who was Jason's wife. Medea had rescued him from her father when Jason stole the Golden Fleece.

Medea it would be, I said, but as I walked away, Betsey added one more fact. "But remember Bob," she said, "Medea did kill her children."

(I didn't give this arcane tidbit from Greek mythology much thought until two years later, when our barge sank off the Galapagos Island during *Jason III*, and *Jason Junior* was lost forever in 9,000 feet of water.)

Medea, I realized, could be fitted with lights and a sensitive television camera to search for *Hugo*, provided the big sled had not completely buried itself in the bottom mud. I wasn't yet sure how little *Medea* would retrieve its huge relative, but I knew we had a chance.

I turned to Bill Hersey, my top electrical engineer. "Bill," I shouted over the wind, "get *Medea* over here."

As Bill and his team hunched over *Medea*'s small tubular framework, I explained the equipment I needed mounted: two cameras, floodlights, a sonar transponder—and the vital, but often overlooked, control circuitry to integrate these components.

Right there on the spray-swept deck, Bill took out a sketch pad and began to design the upgraded *Medea*'s wiring and camera circuits. Andy Bowen joined this improvised war conference and suggested a practical means of converting *Medea* to a salvage vehicle. We could hang a stout grapple on a chain bridle beneath *Medea*'s tubular frame. When the *Medea* found *Hugo* on the bottom, the grapple could be deftly lowered until it snagged *Hugo*'s four-strand chain bridle. Then the entire assemblage could be safely hoisted back to the surface.

Less than ten minutes after the accident, Bill Hersey and Andy had basically designed a salvage vehicle.

"How long have I got, Bob?" Bill asked.

I thought of all the work that lay ahead and calculated the distance to Marsili Seamount. "Twenty-four hours," I answered, knowing full well I was asking the impossible.

That night few of us slept. And when day came, the sky to the west and north was again a gray jumble of another approaching front. The swell was building again. I made my way to the electronics van where Bill Hersey and his team had worked through the night. Their JASON Project jumpsuits were smeared with grease, and they looked queasy from standing all night in the closed, smoke-filled van. Snippets of cable and cartons of electronic components littered the steel floor. Mounted on its stand outside the van, *Medea* looked like a half-butchered animal as technicians worked on her.

I shook my head. "What do you think, Bill?" I was almost ready to concede defeat and cancel the expedition.

Bill smiled wearily. "No problem, Bob. She'll be ready on time." He looked up at the approaching squall line. "But there's no way we can launch her in this storm."

I slapped Bill on the back and grinned with admiration at his skill and confidence. "You just get her ready. We'll handle the weather."

In the main control van, Dana Yoerger, my DSL robotics expert, and chief navigator Tom Crook greeted me with a broad grin.

"You'll be happy to hear that we know exactly where *Hugo* and *Jason* landed on the bottom," he announced proudly. "Both transponders are working, and I can even tell you which way *Hugo* is oriented."

Tired as I was, it took me a moment to digest Dana's good news. If both transponders were beaming out coherent signals, which Dana had managed to triangulate so precisely, *Hugo*'s framework could not be buried very deep in the bottom mud. This meant locating the lost ROVs would not be a particularly difficult challenge. And it was just possible that *Jason* had not been damaged by bottom impact.

As if reading my thoughts, Dana produced a pad with calculations made from the transponder logs. "By the way, Bob, I can tell you exactly how fast *Hugo* fell. Four miles an hour."

I sighed with gratitude. "Saved by the drag."

Hugo's massive size had the unexpected advantage of unusual water resistance. A smaller, heavier, and more streamlined ROV would have fallen much faster and might well have buried itself in the bottom mud after suffering severe impact shock.

For the next twenty-four hours we suffered through the battering passage of the second storm front and were finally forced to take shelter in the lee of the Trapani Peninsula of Sicily. But this frustrating respite gave Bill Hersey and his team time to complete and debug their improvised modifications to *Medea*.

On the morning of April 29, just two days before our first scheduled broadcast, we pounded back through the swell to the site on Skerki Bank where *Hugo* had sunk. With the front blown past, the warm spring sun returned, but the residual swell was still sloppy. We couldn't wait, however, for the sea to calm before attempting to recover *Hugo* and *Jason*. Even if we succeeded in the first attempt, we'd still have to make tracks to cover the 70 miles to Marsili Seamount and get a transponder net deployed so that we could launch *Jason* in time for the scheduled May 1 JASON Project broadcasts.

With this heavy sea still running, we'd face the same snap-load problem that had severed the cable in the first place. So I assembled the best team from the three watches in the risky grapple attempt. Dana Yoerger was on the navigation computer, fine-tuning the *Star Hercules* dynamic-positioning system to hold the vessel directly above the sunken ROVs, despite the lingering swell. Martin Bowen, who had flown JJ from inside *Alvin* on the *Titanic* wreck, took the flyer's console. Even though *Medea* had no thrusters, we were able to control our horizontal motion by maneuvering the entire ship through Dana's fine tweaking of the dynamic-positioning system bow and stern thrusters.

I stared nervously at *Medea*'s television monitor as the little vehicle dropped straight toward the bottom. If Dana's Nav calculations were accurate, we should soon get a glimpse of *Hugo* through *Medea*'s downward-looking camera. At an altitude of 200 feet above the bottom, a tiny faint rectangle appeared smack in the center of the screen.

"All right," Dana whispered, his fingers hovering above the computer keyboard, ready to engage his thrusters like a

space shuttle astronaut attempting a delicate orbital rendez-
vous.

As Martin slowed *Medea*'s descent with the winch handle,
the image of *Hugo* grew steadily on the monitor. There it was,
with *Jason* still garaged snugly inside. *Hugo* rested upright on
the flat mud bottom and was only slightly embedded in the
sediment.

Dana tapped his keyboard, and the entire assembly of
ship, fiber-optic cable, and *Medea* with her grappling chain
slid in a tight rectangular pattern, giving us a good reconnaissance of the floodlit target. *Hugo*'s chain bridle was splayed
across the top of the aluminum-girder framework. If Martin
moved deftly and was lucky, the grapple dangling on the length
of heavy chain beneath *Medea* would snag the bridle on the
first pass.

When I judged we were in the proper position, I gave the
order: "Okay, let's go and get it."

Martin eased the winch handle forward, and *Medea*, with
her grappling hook dangling below, plunged toward *Hugo*.

But the surface swell was snatching *Medea* up and down
like a slow-motion yo-yo. Martin's eyes seemed to burn a
hole through his video monitor as the image of *Hugo* pulsed
drunkenly in and out of focus with the motion of the ship.

Martin's hand fluttered back and forth on the winch joystick, then hauled back to winch in cable quickly. As the monitor clouded with milky roiled sediment, we saw the bizarre
image of *Hugo* twisting beneath the grapple chain like a hypno-
tist's spinning watch. The grapple hook had snared *Hugo*'s
frame, not the chain bridle. Martin made a quick attempt to
lower the big spinning ROV back to the bottom but then
checked himself as the turbulence increased, kicking up an
even larger mud cloud. There was nothing we could do but
haul up on the cable, hoping the precarious grapple purchase
held.

I successfully fought the urge to give nervous, superfluous orders. Watching that ascent was hair-raising. I gripped the edge of the navigational console, gazing in stricken silence at *Medea*'s video monitor. Twice, as the *Star Hercules* heaved through large swells and the cable went momentarily slack, the grapple hook dropped free, only to miraculously snag *Hugo*'s frame again a moment later as the stern rose with the next swell. My eye shot to the cable-tension meter, half expecting to see the sudden snap load pass the maximum breaking strength of 20,000 pounds.

But Dana and Martin kept their cool, slowly but steadily hauling the bizarre tandem load of three vehicles, back to the surface. As the precious cargo passed up through 500 feet, I made my way to the fantail where the deck team under Andy Bowen's supervision had already assembled. I insisted on taking the exposed position in the "hero bucket," a narrow mesh cage suspended from the stern that gave me the best shot of attaching a safety line on *Hugo* the moment it broke free of the water.

Dana was holding the vessel in a good position to the passing swells as little *Medea* came up through the creamy surface, followed by its taut grapple chain, then a moment later by the huge gleaming bulk of *Hugo*. The second the big ROV garage cleared the surface, and it began to careen wildly as the ship rose and fell.

"Throw me a line," I shouted, as the chill sea surged up past my waist.

Leaning forward, I managed to clip a snap link to *Hugo*'s bridle and hand the line back over my shoulder to a crewman who passed it up even higher to the top of the A-frame. I quickly attached two more lines, and we snugged the surging aluminum cage against the stern.

But no sooner had we secured *Hugo* than *Jason*, which had been crashing around inside its garage like a 2-ton bowling ball, rolled out of its cage and plunged under the ship.

I turned wildly in the hero bucket and shouted a desperate order: "Prepare to launch the Zodiac."

Crewmen scrambled around the big inflatable rubber boat, attempting to launch it, despite the swell surging against the hull. *Jason* bobbed up on the port side of the stern, her tether floating dangerously close to the *Star Hercules*' thrusters, which we were using to hold station. If the thrusters caught the cable, they could draw *Jason* in and slice it into small pieces in a matter of seconds.

With *Hugo* being winched aboard the *Star Hercules*, I bolted for the Zodiac, which was being launched as fast as possible. I jumped aboard and was quickly soaked by a wave crashing over the small rubber boat. Fearful of cutting the cable, the captain could not turn the ship into the wind to give us a lee for launching. If we wanted to use the Zodiac, we had to launch it into the oncoming waves. The outboard was immediately flooded, and we found ourselves slamming against the hull. Pushing the Zodiac away from the ship with the wooden oars, we were able to grab hold of the bobbing *Jason* and secure it with handling lines.

I clambered back onto the stern, my soaked jeans cold against my legs, my shoes squishing. But I grinned happily. Against all odds, we had managed to rescue our lost robot explorers from the sea bottom in the middle of a spring gale.

As I watched the deck crew strain to secure *Hugo* to the deck, I was reminded of the struggling Gulliver being subdued by the Lilliputians.

"Well, you were right, eh, Bob?" Andy Bowen said. "That thing is just too damn big."

The crewmen lashed *Hugo* down and gingerly reeled in *Jason,* with the Zodiac hovering protectively nearby until the jaunty blue-and-red ROV was safely on deck.

As the *Star Hercules* heaved north through the queasy swell toward Marsili Seamount, I lingered on the fantail, relishing both the Mediterranean spring sunshine and our hard-won victory.

"Hello, I'm Bob Ballard," I said into my headset microphone, gazing into the camera eye. "We're in a special control room aboard the research vessel *Star Hercules*. For the next forty minutes we want you to share in an exciting undersea adventure using advanced robot systems. . . ."

I didn't need the script for my introductory comments. I knew the words by heart. This was the fifth day of live broadcasts from Marsili Seamount, our twenty-seventh show.

But to the thousands of primary and high school students assembled by classes at museum "control rooms" across North America, I knew my comments did indeed mark the beginning of an exciting undersea adventure. *Medea* and *Jason* hung on their tender a thousand feet below, delicately negotiating the rough terrain of an active undersea volcano, which had never been seen by human eyes until our discovery of it the year before.

As Martin Bowen, flying *Jason,* and navigator Dana Yoerger, controlling the ship's dynamic-positioning system thrusters, worked intently at their consoles, *Jason* hovered like a bumblebee among jutting cylindrical chimneys on the upper slopes of the seamount. The improvised composite *Medea-Jason* vehicle was working better than I'd dreamed possible the week before.

Bill Hersey and his crew had done an incredible field renovation of *Medea*. The little vehicle that had simply been a tubular-framework test bed for electronic components was now fitted with its own floodlights, sensitive SIT video cameras, color camera, and electronic package. *Jason*'s 500-foot fiber-optic tether was now connected to *Medea*. As we had hoped, there really was no need for a big, clumsy garage like *Hugo*;

Jason was perfectly capable of working without the support of an elaborate infrastructure.

But even as robust as *Jason* had proved to be, we still had to be extremely careful working among the jagged chimneys of hydrothermal mineral deposits on the slopes of the seamount.

"We're in very rugged terrain," Martin Bowen commented to our audience half a world away.

I hoped the kids didn't note the edge of tension in his voice as he eased *Jason* closer to a ragged outcropping of reddish-yellow sulfide deposits. But everyone in the control van was aware of the dangerous situation. The hydrothermal vents on the top of the Marsili Seamount were more difficult to work on than their counterparts in the Pacific. Instead of resting down inside an axis rift, which forms a long, linear trench, the sulfide chimneys here stood on the summit of a steep-sided volcano. We had to negotiate among tall chimneys of sulfides and steep lava flows.

In effect, we were exploring the natural equivalent of the *Titanic* wreck's tangled obstacle zones. This feat demanded the concentrated coordination of Dana, Martin Bowen at *Jason*'s flyer station, and Bob Elder on *Medea*'s winch control. Although the kids in North America might have viewed *Jason*'s exploration as a straightforward exercise in modern technology, all of us in the control van held our collective breath while the vehicle negotiated the savage terrain.

"Look at this!" Dana called. "We've got shimmering water."

On *Jason*'s forward camera video monitor, a rippling plume of hot water rose from a gnarled vent. Martin cautiously brought *Jason* close enough to the shimmering vent to measure the water temperature.

As the readings came in, I explained in accurate but straightforward language, devoid of baffling jargon, the hydrothermal process at work. "Seawater seeped down cracks in the volcano, and as it neared the magma chamber, it became superhot and absorbed great quantities of minerals. . . ."

Delivering this brief geology lecture, I had visual aids no teacher in the world had ever enjoyed: a live robotic television eye that could reveal each feature of the vent system as I described it. In developing the JASON Project, I'd spent a lot of time with primary and high school science teachers. Many shared a common complaint: their books and other teaching materials were dry and static, overly theoretical, devoid of the color and motion a generation of students weaned on *Sesame Street*—not to mention various "transformers" and assorted Mighty Morphin Power Rangers—were accustomed to. At its pedagogic core, the JASON Project played the television long suit, providing movement, color, and exotic locale. But our shows were in fact hard science, not slapstick or mindlessly violent children's entertainment. In one forty-minute lesson alone, the students would be exposed to enough geology and chemistry concepts to keep them busy the rest of the semester.

Moreover, they got to see attractive people not much older than themselves, such as our young student Argonauts, wearing "cool" expedition jumpsuits and operating all kinds of advanced hardware. I was convinced that none of the students that participated in the JASON Project would ever again characterize science with the ultimate pejorative of American youngsters: "bor-ing."

A week later, *Medea* and *Jason* were poised to explore the wreck of the Roman merchant vessel we had named *Isis*. Again, we had the elaborate television link-up active to the twelve museums and research centers in North America so that the participating students could share with us either the thrill of our rediscovery of the wreck or our disappointment and frustration if we failed to find the clustered amphorae we had located with *Argo* the year before.

History and archaeology, of course, were the dominant

scientific themes of this phase of the expedition. And we had on board one of the world's pioneers in underwater archaeology, Dr. Anna McCann from Trinity College, who was an expert on Roman trade and artifacts. She and Mary-Lou Florian, an artifact conservation scientist from the Royal British Columbia Museum, could identify for our North American students the contents of *Isis*'s cargo and its historic relevance.

Again, there was definite pedagogic purpose to this exercise. An understanding of history was unfortunately one of the weak points of many of today's students; there was widespread anecdotal reporting that many otherwise bright kids weren't sure whether the American Civil War happened before or after the Middle Ages. As in the physical sciences, history and geography were often taught as bloodless abstractions with which the students felt absolutely no empathy.

But watching *Jason* glide down through the bright cone of *Medea*'s floodlights toward the gray sediment of the bottom, the kids in North America were gripped by the immediacy of practical exploration. Searching for *Isis* was anything but abstract. To make this connection even firmer, I'd assigned Louise Jones, one of the student Argonauts on the expedition team, to *Medea*'s controls. This was her first chance to handle the big fiber-optic cable winch, and she was squeezing the joystick so hard her knuckles were bloodless white.

I had just finished my introduction when *Jason*'s camera zoomed in on a single cylindrical tan amphora. Then the camera panned right and detected two more. Panning further, *Jason*'s camera revealed a cluster of amphorae, some perfectly intact, others caved in like rotten teeth.

"I think we're coming in on the target," I said, fighting to keep my voice reasonably calm. Then the screen filled with a jumble of large and small amphorae, the upper layer of the ancient vessel's cargo hold. "We've got it! Bingo!" I yelled, hardly the dispassionate professor. "Fantastic!"

"The mother lode!" Dana Yoerger shouted.

The van filled with whoops, whistles, and shouts of, "All right!"

I regained my composure long enough to quip to the student audience, "Now you know just how professional we are when we make our discoveries."

I later learned from the teachers at the downlink sites that our enthusiasm was literally contagious, that students who had previously considered it uncool to show emotion, stood and cheered as *Jason* fluttered across the amphora bed of the *Isis* wreck.

As we began our more disciplined preliminary archaeological survey of the site, Anna McCann told the audience, "Just imagine, you are seeing what no one has seen for almost two thousand years."

As she spoke those words, the mood in the control van shifted from adolescent exuberance to a focused and respectful concentration. *Jason* was exploring the deepest ancient shipwreck ever discovered, more than 2,000 feet beneath the sea.

For years, I had preached the theory that the deep ocean was the world's largest museum, the ultimate archive of seafaring mankind's historic record. The deep sea floor around the world held archaeological treasures every bit as appealing as the *Isis* wreck. And with *Jason,* we not only had the tool to explore these archaeological treasures but also to share the passion of discovery with a global audience of students.

Over the next several "live" broadcasts, we completed the site survey, flying *Jason* in precise grid patterns across the area of the wreck. Had *Isis* lain in shallow water, scuba divers would have placed a search grid of staked-out twine. Instead, we constructed an electronic grid pattern and made do with videotape from *Jason*'s close-up camera, not direct human observation. I was especially proud of the student Argonauts' work as data loggers during these surveys. This is a vital but unglamorous part of science. They performed the demanding, repetitive tasks patiently and accurately.

Anna McCann had predicted that almost all the vessel's wooden structure exposed above the mud line would have disappeared centuries earlier, consumed by voracious wood borers. But our survey photos and videotape revealed the unmistakable tear-drop overhead outline of a classic Roman merchantman's hull, approximately 100 feet in length overall. And using *Jason*'s thruster wash to blow away sand and sediment, we even managed to expose the top posts of the hull ribs. It was from such hull details and the close examination of the dozens of amphorae strewn across the wreck site that Anna McCann reached her tentative conclusion, dating *Isis* from the third or fourth century A.D., the commercial and military zenith of the Roman Empire.

After two days of careful mapping, we were able to use *Jason* for an approximation of the hands-on artifact recovery familiar to land archaeologists. For this delicate task, we fitted *Jason*'s mechanical arm with a pair of curved tongs, nicknamed "Knuckles," which were designed to grasp an amphora or a fragile piece of hull without crushing it. A fine-netting "scoop bag" hung beneath the tongs to hold the artifact in place while *Jason* transported it across the seabed to our other innovation, the "elevator."

This was an ingenious system designed and built by Skip Gleason, one of our *Jason* pilots who came to us from the *Alvin* submersible group. Skip had a great deal of seagoing experience and knew that the first axiom in design is "KISS"— Keep It Simple, Stupid. The elevator was of tubular construction with attached anchor weights for sinking it to the bottom and large Fiberglas floats to lift it back to the surface. The heart of the system was the spherical electronic "brain" of one of our standard navigation transponders. This was surrounded by a welded tubular framework, holding two large red mesh nets, the elevator's cargo bins.

It was amazing to watch this system in operation through *Jason*'s camera eyes. The ROV gingerly lifted a big terra-cotta amphora from the wreck site, moved smoothly across the sea bottom with its burden, then deposited the amphora in the suspended elevator net. When *Jason* was clear, we sent an acoustic signal to the transponder, which released the anchor weights and carried the elevator and its cargo back to the surface. After the elevator surfaced, it was taken aboard the *Star Hercules,* emptied of its precious artifacts, outfitted with a new anchor weight, and sent back to the bottom for another load.

Using this system, we recovered more than fifty artifacts of all sizes from the *Isis* site without so much as scratching a single object. Anna commented that in shallow water excavations using divers, objects often were damaged. But this was not a problem with *Jason*.

Unfortunately, the clay and wax seals of the amphorae had not survived sixteen centuries on the sea bottom and neither had the wine, grain, olive oil, or *garum* (fermented fish sauce) that the amphorae had contained on this vessel's final voyage. Nevertheless, Anna McCann was able to determine a great deal about this voyage from the mute testimony of the amphorae, which we submerged in a seawater "swimming pool" among the vans to slowly pull out the salt water impregnated in the terra-cotta. Had we let the artifacts simply dry out, salt crystals would form and crack the clay jars.

The *Isis* carried two basic types of late–Roman Empire amphorae: Africana Piccolo and Africana Grande ("little African" and "big African"). Since both were made at kilns in the Roman province of Mauretania Caesariensis, which included ancient Carthage and present-day Tunisia, it was almost certain the vessel was en route from a North African port to mainland Italy when it foundered.

Our videotape and photographic survey of the buried hull's outline revealed *Isis* had been a rather large Roman merchant ship, with a gross weight of around 200 tons, capable of carrying as many as 5,000 amphorae, stacked densely in wooden racks all the way down to the keel. So it was probable that the bottom sediment covered hundreds of the surviving big terra-cotta jugs, some possibly still sealed with their contents preserved.

It was the smaller, more personal artifacts that *Jason* recovered, however, that truly stimulated our imaginations and gave *Isis* an evocative sense of human presence. Among these were a small round millstone from the galley, probably used to grind grain into flour for bread. A pottery cup and small pitcher found close by had no doubt once contained the tarry wine that was the staple drink of the classical era. But it was not until our last day that *Jason* delicately recovered the smallest and most exciting artifact, a flat terra-cotta Roman lamp. The open lamp spout was still blackened from the soot of the flame that had no doubt burned on the vessel's final voyage, perhaps lighting the galley while a crewman prepared the last meal those ill-fated sailors ever ate.

Anna McCann proudly cupped the small clay lamp in her hands and spoke eloquently to our audience of North American students, explaining that the lamp's distinctive heart shape dated it from the second half of the fourth century A.D.

As she spoke, I was almost overcome with astonishment at the significance of our accomplishment. That fragile little clay lamp—the throwaway equivalent of today's lightbulb—had somehow survived the sinking of a deeply laden 200-ton wooden merchant vessel, probably in the type of gale that *Star Hercules* had weathered in late April. Then, after sixteen centuries on the deep-sea bottom, a bizarre titanium and Fiberglas robot had appeared out of the eternal darkness to scoop up the tiny lamp in a net and carry it to a robot elevator for the ride back to the world of air and sunlight. There a professor who had spent her career studying these obscure artifacts, used the lamp, still dripping deep-sea water, as a teaching aid for an unseen class of students clustered before television screens in museums on the other side of the planet.

Some of my more traditional colleagues had grumbled that the JASON Project, my latest detour from "serious science," was even more tainted by the pollution of popular entertainment than the *Titanic* expeditions. Watching Professor McCann teach a lesson in archaeological site dating with that soot-streaked little clay lamp cupped in her hands, I couldn't have cared less about my hide-bound peers' criticism. I was certain that somewhere in the unseen television classroom we had just ignited intellectual sparks that would kindle and one day grow into mature archaeologists and ocean explorers.

The shipping-container village of "Venice" seemed like a ghost town tonight.

I wandered restlessly from the fantail through the clutter of vans that had housed the bustling television crews and technical support team for our ambitious JASON Project. Now the vans were deserted, half-empty storage bins for unused equipment. It was almost midnight on Sunday, June 4, 1989, and the *Star Hercules* had been on the *Bismarck* search site 300 miles west southwest of Ireland for six and a half days.

In that time, we had swept over 80% of this year's designated search area, trailing *Argo* across the bottom 16,000 feet below with long, relentless visual sweeps. And in this time, we had encountered only a few insignificant and barely recognizable human artifacts. I eased past the dark padlocked van that had housed a technical support section for the television broadcasts from the central Mediterranean. The big white Fiberglas igloo protecting our satellite transmission dish was still in place, an almost taunting reminder that this portion of the summer cruise seemed destined to be an anticlimactic failure.

Going to the rail, I stared out at the faint moonlight glinting on the black face of the Atlantic. This northern sea had been the site of my greatest triumphs and my most bitter frustrations. And it now seemed inevitable that the search for the *Bismarck* would end in failure.

I clenched my fist involuntarily, then forced myself to relax. Somewhere down in the vicinity of a massive and rugged volcanic seamount rising from the flat mud of the Porcupine Abyssal Plain lay the wreck of the German battleship *Bismarck*, the pride of Hitler's Kriegsmarine. One of the Third Reich's largest and most powerful warships, *Bismarck* was also among the heaviest armored vessels ever built.

She had stayed intact through a protracted and savage naval artillery barrage, the climactic scene in the fiercest surface sea battle in the Atlantic during World War II. According to German reports, it was only when *Bismarck*'s crew set off scuttling charges and opened her seacocks that the battered but still seaworthy battleship rolled over and sank. Throughout my exhaustive preparations for both the previous year's and this summer's expeditions, I had worked on the logical assumption that the hull of such a strongly built warship would have remained in one piece on the long plunge to the bottom of the Atlantic.

I stared back aft to the stout yellow A-frame from which *Argo*'s thin coaxial cable trailed into the faint wake. If *Bismarck*'s hull, 823 feet long with a beam of 118 feet, lay in this search area, our meticulous, yet frustrating "mowing the lawn" with *Argo* the previous summer and for over six days this year should have detected such a huge target, either with sonar or with the upgraded sensitive SIT video cameras.

But all we had found the year before was a jumble of rigging wire and a tall teak rudder from a nineteenth-century sailing schooner. This year, we had so far discovered even less than that. Moreover, as on any expedition, the clock did not stop running. My charter of the *Star Hercules* ended in just over five days. In many ways I was in the same stymied position I'd been in on the night of August 31, 1985, just hours before

Argo's video cameras swept over the distinctive triple-vent boiler and we located *Titanic*'s debris field.

I watched the dark Atlantic roll sluggishly by. At least the weather, which had been vicious for several days on the search site, had finally calmed. But I could muster no confidence from my recollection of the successful *Titanic* expedition. Instead, that world-famous triumph now seemed to mock me. Part of this discomfort was my own damn fault. The year before, I'd been stupid enough to go on record stating that finding the *Bismarck* would be a relatively simple and straight-forward task, given the ship's huge size. But for several hours that night, as I pored over the navigation plot with Cathy Offinger, Al Uchupi, and one of my new watch leaders, retired navy captain Jack Maurer, I desperately wished that I could go back and retract that brazen prediction.

The search boxes of the two summers' expeditions had been based on careful computations that encompassed the three disparate *Bismarck* sinking positions as reported by the navigators on three of the British warships that fought the final battle, the Royal Navy battleships *Rodney* and *King George V,* and the cruiser *Dorsetshire.* As with *Titanic*'s reported sinking position, I was all too aware that the historical record from that savage sea battle on May 27, 1941, could have been flawed by insurmountably large navigational errors. This was only one of the demons haunting me, but it was never far from my thoughts. The sinking position by HMS *Rodney,* for example, had *Bismarck* sinking well to the west of the steep multiridge seamount. But the *Dorsetshire,* the cruiser that had been closest to *Bismarck* when she sank, had reported a position well east and slightly to the north of *Rodney*'s position, while the other battleship in the final fight, *King George V,* compounded the confusion by recording a position well to the south of *Dorsetshire*'s. I was also well aware that these recorded positions were hardly the product of precise navigational plotting. At the height of a battle with a wily and deadly foe like *Bismarck,* the officers of the British warships would have been preoccupied with gunnery and defensive maneuvering, not with logging a meticulous dead-reckoning track from which they could estimate the distant position of the sinking *Bismarck* with any degree of certainty. Further, the weather was terrible that glowering spring morning, with a near-gale blowing and a low, scudding overcast that had precluded taking celestial fixes all day.

The practical offshoot of this confused situation was that *Bismarck*'s wreck might lie anywhere within a rectangular box measuring 150 square nautical miles. This gave us a combined two-season search box 50% larger than the area we'd scoured for *Titanic* before finally discovering her debris trail just before our allotted time on the site was about to expire. Despite the size of this search box, I was plagued with the worry that all three Royal Navy positions had been grossly miscalculated and that *Bismarck* lay serene and intact on the flat mud bottom of the Atlantic 20 miles to the east . . . the west . . . maybe to the north.

Dwelling on that worry was a good way to lose sleep and grow an ulcer.

I had tried to make the most of my resources the year before by spending most of my time on the search site, using *Argo*'s powerful side-scanning sonar to sweep the bottom to the north of the seamount, a basically flat abyssal plain on which a target the size of *Bismarck*'s hull would have been readily detected. And with this method, we'd found debris from the sailing schooner much smaller than even *Bismarck*'s light-caliber antiaircraft guns but discovered not a single recognizable piece of debris from the German battleship.

This frustrating experience had provoked our self-deluded conclusion that the schooner debris was actually light wreckage resting on the surface of the mud that had somehow completely buried *Bismarck*'s massive hull. But over the winter, careful analysis of the detailed *Argo* electronic photographs had revealed with painful certainty that the debris—including the distinctive teak rudder—was from an old sailing vessel, not a modern battleship.

Sitting with Al Uchupi in my Woods Hole office that winter, I cut the final emotional strings attaching me to that impractical theory. Al, still the consummate geomorphologist, had run a complex calculation that proved that it was impossible for the sediments on the abyssal plain and on the slopes of the seamount to be deep enough to completely bury an object the size of *Bismarck*'s hull, even if the wreck had impacted the bottom at speeds in excess of 50 knots.

That grim conclusion led me back to an even darker speculation. Maybe *Bismarck*'s crew had not scuttled her after all, and their report of the action had merely been a face-saving wartime expedient to protect the families of the survivors from the stigma of defeat, no small consideration in Nazi Germany. This meant that *Bismarck* might have sunk only partially flooded, her hull pierced in only a few critical locations by British shells and torpedoes. I knew from my survey of the *Thresher* wreck that a vessel with as many strong, water-tight compartments as the *Bismarck* would be ultimately shredded by powerful implosions if the ship sank with those compartments unflooded. This theory raised the specter that *Bismarck* had sunk basically intact to a depth of perhaps 1,000 feet, only to be ripped into thousands of torn chunks and fragments by the horrendous imploding pressure of the deep ocean. And if that catastrophic scenario was valid, then the bottom sediment certainly was deep and spongy enough to hide all but a few traces of the wreck.

But in theory, there still had to be a trail of lighter debris— the thin-gauge piping, crockery, and other mundane housekeeping items—just as *Titanic* and the *Thresher* had laid down. Those vessels, however, had sunk in shallower water and I couldn't be certain that *Bismarck*'s light debris trail would have winnowed into a telltale arrow pointing toward the main wreck, not at this depth, not with the steeply gullied slopes of the seamount rising to the south, which could have hidden a vast collection of debris from the smallest teacup to a 380-millimeter naval gun from one of the battleship's four giant turrets.

Clouds covered the tilted wedge of the moon, extinguishing the last light on the surface. The darkness matched my mood. I had just over five days to find the *Bismarck*. And if I returned to England aboard the *Star Hercules* emptyhanded, I'd be forced to publicly announce defeat. I could see the headlines now: "*Bismarck* Eludes Ballard." The news media would have a field day throwing my overconfident predictions of an easy search back in my face.

I could certainly weather that temporary humiliation. But for an explorer, the long-term effect of failure could be much more destructive than hurt feelings. Patrons backed winners, not losers. Failure to find a giant sunken battleship after first predicting an easy expedition, then rashly crying wolf with the schooner wreckage—shades of Jack Grimm's phantom propeller—would be a tacit admission of gross incompetence. Just as the expedition leader was unjustly awarded the laurels of success, I would have to personally bear the burden of defeat. My West Coast backers in the Quest Group would not gamble again after I squandered their generous investment.

Worse, *National Geographic* and Turner Broadcasting would have gambled even more but have completely missed the gleaming brass ring: a popular television show that would capture the drama of the search and the ultimate prize of discovery. No discovery, no show! Television executives in the future would be loath to gamble on a loser. In ocean exploration, the challenge, "What have you done for me lately?" was a way of life, not a cynical joke.

With these cheery thoughts in mind, I entered the control van, which was lit by the familiar rosy glow of the red lamps, and went silently to the plotting table to consider our options.

A wide Plexiglas sheet crosshatched with a grease pencil gridwork of our search lines was mounted beside the chart table. We had covered just over 80% of the combined two-year search box. Those thick grease-pencil lines represented hundreds of hours of sonar and visual search. Yet all we had found was some rusted galvanized rigging wire and a teak rudder from an old sailing vessel.

Flipping through the tall ledger book of the control van log for the previous several days, I found a series of entries typical of our mounting frustration: "1221 hours—fish (1); 1303 hours—octopod; 1442 hours—rock (black)."

Similar entries were dotted randomly through the pages. But one from earlier that evening epitomized the search: "2227 hours—mud (what else?)".

Over the course of this expedition, I'd reminded some of the newcomers to deep-sea exploration of a truism sacred to marine geologists, but little known outside the profession: most of Planet Earth's surface was mud. The dry continents took up less than a quarter of the sphere; the rest was sea bottom, and almost all of that was soft, relatively featureless gray sediment. The pale rippled mud drifting slowly beneath *Argo*'s bright cone of floodlight was typical deep sea bottom. The scene could have been the equatorial Pacific or the floor of the Arctic Ocean beneath the permanent ice pack. The ocean floor was a near desert, frigid and black—above all, unimaginably vast.

And our tools for searching this black abyss were pitifully inadequate. Even if I had been able to afford a long enough fiber-optic cable to use my new ROV *Jason* on this search site, I still would have relied on *Argo*. This tough imaging sled had been steadily upgraded with sensitive side-scan sonar and could now probe a swatch of ocean floor 2,400 feet wide when flying high above the bottom. This sonar was ideal for scanning the flat western portion of the search area.

But to enter the rugged slopes of the seamount in the

eastern portion of the search area, *Argo* would have to be lowered to an altitude of only 15 to 20 meters. Using its ultra-sensitive silicon intensified target (SIT) video cameras, it would conduct a visual search for *Bismarck*'s debris trail. No other vehicle in the world could match *Argo*'s visual search capabilities. The Deep Submergence Laboratory could be rightfully proud of this tool.

But, as I frankly admitted to the news media and my sponsors, searching for a target the size of *Bismarck* at this depth with *Argo* was the equivalent of hunting for the proverbial needle in a haystack—at night, in a blizzard, using a penlight with weak batteries.

The plotting sheet on the chart table showed that the midnight-to-four watch was following a long search line eastward that led across the southern slopes of the undersea volcano. This was rough terrain, a jumbled massif with innerlock ridges, each bisected with deep gullies—definitely not the smooth-sided Fujiyama-type volcanic cone people often pictured when I discussed undersea volcanoes. This volcanic seamount was similar to the chaotic terrain I'd encountered along the Reykjanes Ridge. The deep gullies and steep scarps on the slopes would create sonar "shadows" and visual obstacles that could completely mask *Bismarck*'s hull, despite its size. For this reason, my search strategy for the remaining five days of the cruise would be low-altitude visual search, the most painstaking, exhausting mode in our inventory of operations. Once more the image of searching an immense haystack for the lost needle, a few inches at a time, came to mind.

Jack Maurer, the eight-to-twelve watch leader who had remained in the control van after the end of his shift, joined me at the plotting table. He was a stocky retired Navy captain with a jet-black brush haircut, new to oceanographic expeditions, but a veteran of countless months at sea. Jack brought a quiet, disciplined sense of purpose to his watch. I was always glad when the demanding chore of calibrating our entire linked navigation network with updates from the passing Global Positioning System satellites came during Jack's watch. I could be confident that this complex electronic web—which included the *Star Hercules* dynamic-positioning system, our navigational computer, and the sonar transponder network—was properly tuned, one less concern for me to worry about.

I tapped the transparent plotting sheet that overlay the detailed bathymetric map of the ocean floor. "We'll be right in the middle of these gullies during your watch tomorrow, Jack," I said. "We're going to have to keep *Argo* right down in that bad terrain to get any decent visual coverage."

Jack scanned the map slowly, his eyes noting each feature. "We'll be ready," he said with quiet confidence.

That was reassuring. I knew that I'd managed to assemble a team as good as those talented men and women who'd discovered the *Titanic*. Now, as the search phase moved away from the featureless abyssal plain to the jumbled countryside of the seamount, I also knew this team's dedication and skills would be tested to their limit.

Back out on deck, I went to the stern to verify that *Argo*'s cable was running true and free as the ship crept across the surface. The sky was completely overcast and the wind was freshening from the east.

This was *Bismarck* weather, dark and foreboding.

It was on a black night like this, May 19, 1941, that the newest and most powerful battleship in Nazi Germany's Kriegsmarine slipped its moorings in the naval port of Gotenhafen near Danzig. Off Rügen Island, *Bismarck* rendezvoused with its consort heavy cruiser *Prinz Eugen* and headed west through the Baltic toward the North Sea.

Bismarck was an impressive sight: almost 300 meters long, its rakish but thickly armored hull displacing over 50,000 tons.

Despite its massive size, *Bismarck* could maneuver nimbly at speeds exceeding 30 knots.

And in naming this powerful vessel of war after Imperial Germany's first "Iron" chancellor, Otto von Bismarck, the Nazis clearly hoped to forge a link of legitimacy between their fascist dictatorship and the untarnished glory of the first German Reich.

But it was the battleship's devastating arsenal that was most impressive—especially to the British Admiralty. *Bismarck* carried eight 15-inch (380-millimeter) guns mounted in four twin turrets. These rifled naval cannons could hurl a 1-ton high-explosive shell almost twenty miles. And the warship's new radar and stereoscopic long-range fire-direction equipment assured that those devastating salvos would strike with unprecedented accuracy. *Bismarck*'s big guns were augmented by scores of other cannons in descending caliber, most having dual antiship-antiaircraft capability.

The battleship's topsides, deck, turrets, and superstructure were clad in the strongest tempered armor plate German foundries could produce, which ranged in thickness from 5 to 14 inches and could withstand direct hits from all but the largest caliber shells the British navy could deliver. *Bismarck*'s vital innards, including its high-pressure steam turbines and magazines, were located in a heavily armored citadel, protected by armored transverse watertight bulkheads fore and aft. The welded double hull could absorb and disperse the impact of torpedo hits, minimizing damage. Elsewhere belowdecks, the ship was partitioned into twenty-two watertight compartments that could be completely sealed off in the event of battle damage, unlike similar compartments on the *Titanic*.

Launched in 1939, and now ready for its first operational cruise, the *Bismarck* epitomized the ideal warship that had long been the goal of German naval architects: "an unsinkable gun platform."

Now this devastating new weapon was outbound on its maiden voyage from the Nazi sanctuary of the Baltic, en route to German-occupied Norway, where it would take on provisions for its final destination. As the two warships zigzagged through the dark Baltic, *Bismarck* captain Ernst Lindemann announced the task force's mission over the ship's public address system: *Bismarck* and *Prinz Eugen* would slip undetected into the North Atlantic and sink as much British shipping as possible over the next several months.

The mission was one of the most audacious in the history of naval warfare. In effect, *Bismarck* was throwing down a gauntlet, challenging the entire Royal Navy's Home Fleet, which protected the British Isles and the vital convoy route from North America.

But the challenge, as hubristic as it seemed, was not hollow arrogance. *Bismarck* and its consort would not operate alone but in coordination with long-range Luftwaffe bombers and reconnaissance aircraft, as well as U-boat wolf packs. Any Royal Navy ships hunting *Bismarck* and *Prinz Eugen* would themselves be hunted by Nazi planes close to occupied Europe and by submarines on the open ocean.

The destructive potential of *Bismarck* and the heavy cruiser, which could maneuver hidden beneath the horizon and destroy an entire convoy of lumbering merchant ships with a few well-placed salvos of their heavy guns—guided by the reconnaissance float planes the warships carried—was like a dagger poised above Britain's heart. In mid-1941, Britain and its Empire stood alone against the victorious Axis, which had occupied all of western Europe from Norway's north cape to the Aegean. Field Marshal Erwin Rommel's Afrika Korps had already entered Egypt and threatened the Suez Canal. And two hundred Nazi divisions were poised to plunge into the steppes of Russia.

If the Nazi navy and air force led by *Bismarck* managed

to sever the North Atlantic convoy route, the British Isles would starve, and England would be forced to sue for peace.

These were the incredibly high stakes at play as *Bismarck* and *Prinz Eugen* dodged through the constricted waters of the Danish archipelago. If the two ships managed to make the open Atlantic undetected, the British Navy would have no clue they were running loose.

And the battle plan of Admiral Gunther Lutjens, who commanded the task force from aboard *Bismarck,* was meant to keep the British in the dark until the Nazi ships drew their first blood from unsuspecting convoys far to the west. Lutjens planned to sail northwest from Norway, skirt the polar ice pack above Iceland, then use Greenland's late spring ice pack as a shield to slip south and pounce on British convoys steaming east from Canada's maritime provinces.

But as so often happens in elaborate, grandiose plans, mishaps occurred. While trying to slip out to sea, *Bismarck* and *Prinz Eugen* were spotted by British spies as the ships left the Baltic. Alerted, the British sent RAF reconnaissance Spitfires aloft. One found the two Nazi warships through a break in the clouds above Norway's Grimstadfjord. Now the British Admiralty knew the *Bismarck* was free of the Baltic.

While the ships were in the fjord, Lutjens ordered *Prinz Eugen* refueled but inexplicably did not replenish *Bismarck*'s fuel tanks because the cumbersome operation was not in the printed orders of the day and the overconfident admiral was certain he'd be able to refuel the battleship from a tanker in the Norwegian Sea.

But the reconnaissance photos snapped by the Spitfire had sparked an aggressive British response: warships and bombers streamed from Scottish bases toward Norway. On the night of May 21, 1941, the two Nazi ships had barely cleared the fjord when RAF bombers pounded the now empty moorings in the narrow waterway.

Lutjens and his task force were lucky with the weather: fog and low overcast clouded the Norwegian Sea. The ships continued northwest toward the Arctic ice pack and their long, looping track above Iceland.

Over the next three days, the overcast weather shielded Nazi ships. But on the evening of May 23, just as *Bismarck* headed through the narrow gauntlet between a British minefield stretching seaward from Iceland and the Greenland ice pack, the weather cleared. At the southern end of that constricted corridor, British warships, including the heavy battle cruiser *Hood*—the modern pride of the Royal Navy—were maneuvering to intercept the Nazi ships.

Just after dawn on May 24, the British sprang their ambush. The Royal Navy attack was led by the *Hood* and the other new heavy battle cruiser *Prince of Wales*. But as the ships began to exchange salvos in the milky iridescent light of the near-Arctic dawn, disaster struck the British. A plunging 15-inch shell fired by *Bismarck* at extreme range crashed through a lightly armored point on *Hood*'s aft deck, penetrated deeply, and ignited an ammunition magazine. The ship erupted in a horrendous fireball. *Hood*'s back was broken, and the severed hull sank within a minute. There were only 3 survivors among the crew of 1,419.

In an exchange lasting less than twenty minutes, *Bismarck*'s guns had killed the equivalent of a full army regiment. Now outgunned, the *Prince of Wales* turned southeast and sped out of range of the *Bismarck*'s devastating salvos.

The news of *Hood*'s catastrophic loss stunned Great Britain. However, Prime Minister Winston Churchill, a former First Lord of the Admiralty, learned that *Bismarck* had also suffered heavy damage during the vicious long-range exchange. Almost alone among British leaders, he realized the seemingly invincible Nazi juggernaut would proudly head back toward occupied Europe for repairs before resuming the Atlantic operation.

Now weather again favored the Germans with squalls and occasional fog banks blowing off the Greenland ice pack. But the small British task force shadowing *Bismarck* stayed doggedly on the trail of the Germans, just out of range of the 15-inch guns. *Bismarck*'s disciplined crew worked steadily, repairing the moderate battle damage suffered in the exchange with the British ships.

Near midnight on May 24 in the eerie northern twilight, obsolete Swordfish torpedo planes flying from the aircraft carrier *Victorious* attacked *Bismarck*. The British were certain the aerial torpedoes had seriously damaged the German battleship. Lutjens, however, used the exchange to double back on his course, circling north, and completely evaded the pursuing British warships. *Bismarck* was now free of pursuit but low on fuel from battle-damaged tanks. Lutjens headed southeast through the open North Atlantic, making for the French port of Saint-Nazaire. The admiral ordered *Prince Eugen* south as a diversion, while *Bismarck* traveled back toward Europe at flank speed. By the night of May 27, the battleship would be under the protective umbrella of long-range Luftwaffe bombers flying from French bases.

But German aircraft were not the only planes aloft searching for *Bismarck*.

On the morning of May 26, an RAF Catalina flying boat, co-piloted by a young American volunteer, spotted *Bismarck*. Although battered by a devastating flak barrage, the plane managed to transmit an accurate sighting report. That night, lumbering Swordfish biplanes from the carrier *Ark Royal* dropped torpedoes from just above the storm-tossed wave crests. While two torpedoes impacted without serious damage on *Bismarck*'s hull, one exploded in the warship's Achilles heel, its vulnerable twin rudders.

With the rudders jammed hard to starboard, the battleship could only turn to port. All night Captain Lindemann attempted to free his rudders and maneuver using variable thrust

ROBERT D. BALLARD, PH.D.   360

on the propellers. But *Bismarck* turned inexorably northeast toward Ireland, away from the protection of the Luftwaffe's bomber umbrella. On the morning of May 27, 1941, the British Navy closed in for the kill. This time, the Admiralty brought more than battle cruisers to the fight. The first line battleships *Rodney* and *King George V* closed on *Bismarck* in a vicious northwest gale, 300 miles west southwest of Ireland. In a long-range exchange of heavy naval cannon that began at first light, *Bismarck* was struck by scores of heavy shells, which blew thinly armored sections of its superstructure off the ship. Over the next two hours, the British ships pounded *Bismarck* mercilessly. Her superstructure ablaze but several turrets still firing blindly, *Bismarck* slowed and went dead in the water.

As the heavy cruiser *Dorsetshire* closed in to deliver a coup de grâce torpedo attack, hundreds of *Bismarck* crewmen fled the blazing forward compartments toward the stern, where they launched liferafts or simply dove into the oily water.

At 10:39 A.M. on May 27, 1941, the British vessels watched *Bismarck* sink steadily at the stern, then roll over to port, its dull red bottom paint glinting briefly in the weak sunlight, and disappear forever.

The cold, oil-choked water was thick with *Bismarck* survivors, many terribly burned or wounded. *Dorsetshire* and the destroyer *Maori* steamed slowly into the clot of German survivors and began hauling them on board. But when only 115 German sailors had been rescued, a U-boat alert was flashed by radio. Had the wolf pack everyone feared now assembled to protect *Bismarck*? The two Royal Navy captains had no option but to zigzag away at high speed from the sinking site, leaving behind several hundred horror-stricken German sailors bobbing in the cold Atlantic. There the German survivors died, some linked together in a line bridle clipped to their life jackets.

Bismarck's casualties were even greater than the *Hood*'s. Only 115 survived from a crew of over 2,206. Admiral Lutjens,

Captain Lindemann, and most of the senior officers died with their ship.

The British had reaped revenge for the loss of the *Hood*.

More important from a strategic perspective, the Nazi navy never again posed a serious surface threat in the Atlantic. The fragile convoy lifeline from North America survived, despite mounting losses from U-boat wolf packs. The Battle of the Atlantic was far from over. But one of its most critical engagements had ended with the British victory.

I stayed at the rail late that night, gazing at the freshening swell, my mind filled with images of crashing gunfire, exploding shells, and terrified young men floating in the icy clotted oil as they watched their "unsinkable" ship roll over and slip beneath the waves.

There were so many ironic parallels between the *Bismarck* and the *Titanic*. Both ships had been heralded as technical paradigms of their day. Both were on their maiden voyages. Both were under the command of overconfident, audacious officers. Both had sunk with horrendous loss of life.

I had discovered and thoroughly explored *Titanic*. But now it seemed *Bismarck* would indeed elude me, just as Admiral Lutjens had eluded the pursuing British ships south of Iceland.

And I knew that there were those in both Europe and America who would be pleased to see our search fail. Already there'd been grumbling that this expedition was a misguided attempt to glorify a warship that had flown the swastika battle flag of the most despicable dictatorship in world history. Among some Germans, finding and exploring *Bismarck*'s wreck would reopen the unhealed wound of World War II; others would be forced to face their own ambivalence about the Nazi era and weigh their pride at German military achievements with their guilt at wartime atrocities and the lingering shame of defeat.

But I certainly did not intend to glorify a Nazi ship. The epic sea battle that led to *Bismarck*'s sinking was as much a British endeavor as it was German. *Bismarck* was a piece of history. And I was now firmly convinced that the ocean bottom was, in fact, a museum belonging to all the nations of the world. Finding *Bismarck* and photographing the wreck with *Argo* would be proof that this sea-bottom museum contained much more than simply the evocative Edwardian time machine of *Titanic*'s wreck.

In order to search the "Museum of the Sea" for classical wrecks like *Isis*—or perhaps the artifacts of Polynesian explorers, seagoing Chinese junks of the Ming Dynasty, slave ships of the notorious Middle Passage, and all the other historically important shipwrecks I knew rested in that ubiquitous gray deep-ocean mud—I would need sponsors. I was already beginning to plan for the creation of a new institute once I retired from Woods Hole, an organization that would be dedicated to widening understanding of human history preserved beneath the sea. This new institute would require major funding from the private sector, and raising money would be a continual concern. Credibility as an ocean explorer was my only true asset. Finding *Bismarck* would bolster that credibility.

I snatched a couple of hours' sleep, then woke before dawn and went back to the control van to check on our progress across the gullies of the seamount's lower slopes. Entering the van, it was as if no time had passed since midnight. The four-to-eight watch was bathed in the eerie red light, music played softly on the stereo, competing with the usual electronic chimes and pings of the instruments.

I went to the chart table to check the plot. Then my eyes instinctively went to the flyer's console where my son Todd hunched intently over the winch control joystick, his gaze fixed on the flickering gray monitor of *Argo*'s forward camera. I grinned. If nothing else came of this cruise, my pleasure at sailing with Todd would have been worth the price of admission.

Trying not to be obvious, I studied Todd as he deftly flew *Argo* across the rolling hillocks and steep gullies of the mountainside 15,000 feet below. He'd grown a bit in the last year and filled out through his chest and shoulders. But there was more than just physical maturation evident. Todd had shed the tentative, vague lack of confidence that had so aggravated me the previous summer. He was lively, responsive, and eager to do his share of the work no matter what.

Now, hunched at his watch station, Todd was too preoccupied to sense me gazing at him with a strange mixture of pride and regret at the uneven nature of our past relationship.

My being Todd's father had not been easy for either of us. First, I was away on expeditions for a good part of his adolescent years. And just when he was old enough to become an interesting companion, I was catapulted into international fame by the *Titanic* discovery.

Celebrity on this scale is awkward enough in world capitals, but it completely transformed our lives in the small world of western Cape Cod. The *Titanic* expeditions were only the culmination of a series of successes that elevated my reputation in the local community to unrealistic levels. I was the Brilliant and Daring Dr. Ballard, and everyone expected my oldest son to naturally follow in my footsteps.

This put unfair pressure on Todd, who at the time was daring enough but certainly had not demonstrated scholastic brilliance. This hurt because I had almost-ingrained high expectations for my first son. In my family, a myth had evolved that Ballard men were all smart and successful. My father had always led my brother Richard and me to believe that he had struggled hard to earn an engineering degree during the Great

Depression. Only later did I learn that this had been a relatively harmless deception: although he worked successfully as an aerospace engineer during and after World War II, he had actually never earned a degree.

But because both Richard and I had completed Ph.D.s, we naturally assumed our sons would do well in school. In fact, Richard's son, Jeff, was a brilliant student. But Todd definitely was not, much to my chagrin and misplaced sense of pride. I'd been determined that Todd would excel academically, an unreasonable goal that probably had more to do with my own self-image than Todd's happiness. Even when I was a struggling graduate student, I'd hired private tutors to work with Todd at home after school. Later, I sent him to a private academy for a year before entering him in high school, a strategy that did not work well at all.

Todd was interested in practical things, not scholastic theory. His abiding hobby was auto mechanics. And his consuming passion was to rebuild an old Mustang that sat under a tarp in our barn, not to become a world-famous ocean explorer. He certainly did not want to study any more science than was needed to earn his high school diploma. Todd wanted to become a very good auto mechanic and couldn't understand why that wasn't good enough for me.

In fact, Todd was quietly consumed by the frustrating desire to please me. But he simply was not cut out to fill the unrealistic chip-off-the-old-block mold I clung to unreasonably.

Love was never an issue between us. In fact, our deep bond transcended petty issues like school grades and career choices, and often made our inability to communicate even more painful.

Only later did I realize that Todd had simply tried to live true to his own identity and that I was the one clinging to illusions. Above all, Todd clung stubbornly to his own goals. One of the most important was to play on the Falmouth High

School's hockey team. When Todd and his younger brother Doug had first approached me about playing ice hockey, I'd responded negatively. I didn't understand hockey, having grown up in southern California. My only exposure to the game was watching the occasional television match. I found it chaotic and, above all, violent. To me, hockey was a street brawl on ice, totally lacking in finesse. I didn't want my sons' faces smashed and scarred on a hockey rink. And I didn't want them to become brutal.

Then I went away on a long expedition and returned to find that Marjorie had given in and allowed Doug to try out for the Youth Hockey League. I was furious. How could we have said no to Todd when he wanted so badly to try out for the team, then turn around and say yes to Douglas?

That night I sat down in our living room with Todd. "If you still want to play ice hockey," I said, "I won't stand in your way."

"Thanks, Dad," Todd said. "I want to try."

We both knew that his chances of making the high school team were poor because he had missed more than eight years of competitive ice skating. He would be a novice going up against pros.

But I promised to help in any way I could.

For the next several years, I lived and breathed hockey with my two sons, driving thousands of miles to ice rinks all over New England. We spent thousands of dollars sending the two boys to every summer hockey camp that would accept them. Not only were Todd and Douglas competing against boys who had worn ice skates since they could walk, but I, too, was competing against parents who were passionate about the sport and pulled every old-boy-network and political trick they could to see their kids on the team.

I never liked the sport, and my initial assessment of hockey as a poor builder of character never changed. What especially disappointed me was that, after years of working with Todd, he ended up in the hands of a nasty, aggressive, and manipulative varsity hockey coach, a man who, in my opinion, had no business molding the character of young students. This coach taught his team some valuable hockey skills, but he also exposed them to favoritism, petty politics, and the crueler aspects of the sport. I was powerless to balance this negative impact on Todd at a critical point in his life.

From age fifteen on, Todd was one of the biggest and strongest kids in his class. Once he made the varsity hockey team, it was assumed by everyone that he was also one of the toughest. Todd was, in fact, a tiger on the ice and overcame his fundamental lack of skating skills with a fearless heart. In defense, he had an incredibly powerful but somewhat wild slap shot from point. And when you were bodychecked by Todd Ballard, you were sometimes literally knocked off the ice. But when Todd was not on the rink, he was a very mild-mannered, even tender kid who deplored violence, more a throwback to a 1960s flower child than a product of the ambitious and ruthless 1980s.

Todd's nonviolence was seen by many of his peers as weakness. In fact, Douglas would sometimes even comment that his older brother was a "sissy." Todd was also bedeviled by the acute embarrassment of being an occasional bed wetter, a problem I had suffered as a young kid but which seemed especially painful for Todd.

Beset by this emotional pain, Todd sought me out one day for advice. He knew I was opposed to fighting and prided myself on having never been in a fight, even though I had played football and other contact sports. I had always taught Todd to walk away from a fight and try to convince others to use reason instead of violence to resolve problems. But being a big kid on the varsity hockey team, walking away from a fight was not always easy.

"Look, Todd," I finally advised him, "if walking away from a fistfight becomes completely impossible, then and only then should you use violence to defend yourself. But never start a fight."

Only a few nights later, the phone rang at one in the morning, shaking me from sleep. It was Todd.

"I've been in a fight, Dad," he said. "And I think the other guy's in really bad shape. Can you come and pick me up?"

I found Todd standing on the beach road west of Falmouth. As he climbed into the car, I was overcome with conflicting emotions and thoughts. Had this been my fault? I'd advised him to fight only if necessary, but just two days after that advice, he'd been involved in a serious brawl. Was he all right or badly hurt?

I examined his face in the car light. Todd seemed fine. But down the road we saw the flashing red lights of a police car and an ambulance.

"My God," I said, "what happened?"

As we drove home, Todd slowly and methodically explained. He and two of his hockey buddies had been sitting in their car, staring out at the moonlit sea. A carful of football players pulled up beside them, and the taunts began. When one of Todd's friends left the car to urinate, the football players began to push him around. This kid was small, and Todd was always one to back the underdog, an image he no doubt had of himself as well. When Todd intervened to pull his friend to safety, one of the big football players began jabbing Todd in the chest, a challenge to fight. Following my instructions, Todd backed away, one step at a time. Finally, he stood with his back to the edge of a steep bluff. There was a sheer drop to sharp boulders on the beach below. Todd could back away no farther. But the football player continued to prod and taunt him. With no other recourse, Todd clenched his fist and came up with one solid punch to the other kid's head. The boy fell to the ground, knocked completely unconscious. When Todd tried to arouse him, the football player lay still, seemingly not breathing.

"My God," Todd whispered in the car, "I think I killed him. What am I going to do?"

I told Todd to call the police as soon as we got home. He picked up the phone with stricken dread, then exhaled a deep breath of relief. The police and ambulance had recovered no casualties from the beach road. Apparently the football players had revived their friend and driven home before the ambulance arrived. The next day at school, kids in the corridor began to hum the tune from *Rocky* when Todd walked by. Doug was very proud of his older brother, but Todd was anxious, waiting for the other shoe to drop.

Within a day, it did. The football player, one of the team heroes, was demanding a rematch. But agreeing to such a premeditated fight was completely counter to the advice I'd given Todd. If he didn't fight, however, Todd would be branded a coward, an unacceptable stigma for an adolescent boy at a small high school.

Again Todd came to me for advice. Analyze the situation, I told him. The other kid had just been hit harder than any blow he'd ever received in a football game. Did this guy really want to face that kind of punishment again? His call for a rematch was merely a desperate attempt at saving face.

I advised Todd to pass the following word to the friend of the football hero who was acting as a second: "Todd doesn't really want to fight. But if your friend confronts Todd and leaves him no choice, he will fight. But your friend has to make one promise, that he will swing first. Because if Todd really hits him this time, he might well kill him, and he doesn't want to be responsible for his death."

Todd passed the word.

There was no reply. And there was no rematch. Whenever Todd saw the football player in the school halls after that, the boy looked away with embarrassed chagrin.

That painful encounter had taught Todd a valuable lesson in maturity.

I had sent Todd off to Brewster Academy after graduating from Falmouth High School. He thrived on the experience, and had done well in school. After a semester at Brewster, Todd entered Northeastern University at Boston and managed to earn respectable grades, even with a demanding class schedule. Buoyed by this experience, Todd wanted to try for a better school, the University of Colorado. I advised him to stay on at Northeastern, but Todd still had a stubborn streak. He went off to Colorado, had a great time skiing, but bombed academically. Now Todd was enrolled for the fall semester back at Northeastern.

I was hardly one to cast aspersions at his changing from one school to the next, having bounced around more than my share of graduate schools. My main satisfaction now was that Todd seemed comfortable in his own identity and mature enough to profit from the good, solid education he would undoubtedly receive at Northeastern.

I had hoped that joining me on the second *Bismarck* expedition would further bolster his maturation. Todd certainly did seem receptive to all the positive new experiences this cruise had to offer. I planned to continue challenging Todd and the two buddies from our summer home in Whitefish, Montana, who'd joined him on this year's cruise, Billy Yunck and Kirk Gustafson. They were bright, agile youngsters who'd cut their eyeteeth on high-speed downhill skiing. They were my steadiest *Argo* flyers on this long search expedition.

Confident that the watch was working smoothly, I slipped out of the control van to steal another hour's sleep.

Late that night I was in the mess hall, wedged into a Naugahyde booth, killing a sleepless hour in a four-handed game of Trivial

Pursuit. When I'd left the control van an hour earlier, *Argo*'s monitors revealed nothing more interesting than a multifingered gully of dirty white mud halfway up the slopes of the volcano.

Then I felt Al Uchupi's hand on my shoulder.

"Bob," Al said in his Bronx accent, "we've encountered some debris I think you should have a look at."

Even though Al's tone had been as flat and dispassionate as if he had been commenting on an abstract geomorphology article, his words sparked an explosion of adrenaline. I was out of the booth like a jack-in-a-box, scattering potato chips and Trivial Pursuit tokens. My mind echoed with the words of John Lobo, the cook aboard *Atlantis II*, when he had announced the discovery of *Titanic*'s debris field.

With Al Uchupi pounding down the corridor behind me, I raced to the van. The watch crew stared at a clump of small black objects moving diagonally across the monitor. These were definitely artifacts. It was 2352 hours on June 5, 1989.

Cathy Offinger, the watch navigator, wrote neatly in the log, "Debris."

I scanned the VCR playback monitor to note the pattern of debris *Argo* had encountered a few minutes earlier. The hazy images were nondescript, scattered chunks of small pipe, shards of metal. But I felt they were definitely of twentieth-century origin, not more debris from an old sailing ship.

On the real-time monitor, the light debris kept streaming past.

"Looks like we've got something this time," Jack Maurer commented. He was not one to cry wolf.

"Absolutely no doubt about it," I replied. "But what is it? If it's *Bismarck*, we've got two choices. Either this stuff was shot off during the battle, or this is part of the debris field."

Indeed, I'd been expecting to encounter shell-blasted debris scattered from *Bismarck*'s superstructure during the final two-hour battle at some point during the search. But locating this type of light battle-damage trash would not help us find the main wreck.

As if to confirm my suspicion, Mel Lee, the sonar operator, reported, "We're not picking up any sonar contacts on the side-scan."

Then a larger, rectangular piece of debris slid across the video screen.

"Zoom in on that," I told Jim Saint, the *Argo* watch engineer.

The sharp-edged object cast a definite shadow in *Argo's* floodlights. It had to be a human artifact.

As the watch changed and the van grew crowded and stuffy, we kept *Star Hercules* at dead slow, creeping eastward, with *Argo* trailing far below across the southern flanks of the seamount. The debris trail was intermittent, much to my chagrin. A long stretch of rolling gray slope would give way to a scrap of metal, then a larger square object or a twisted piece of pipe. This was definitely not an evenly winnowed trail with debris sorted in a predictable light-to-heavy hierarchy. After half an hour, I was convinced we had simply encountered showers of *Bismarck* superstructure debris that had been dispersed by the exploding British shells.

Around one A.M., the bottom scape abruptly changed, becoming mottled and patchy. The smoothly rippled dirty snow-drift texture of the mud gave way to a very disturbed pattern of mixed rock and sediment that looked like roughly ground hamburger. Was this the edge of an impact crater? If so, it had been one hell of an impact because the strange, patchy bottom rolled on and on.

But there was no debris in this plowed-up ground. Then suddenly we were back on the smooth, featureless mud slope. Instead of continuing on our easterly search line, I ordered a course change back south and west to intercept the broken ground again.

After a while, the pieces of the jigsaw puzzle began to mesh. As we doubled back to the west, we again encountered light debris. When we passed beyond it to a smooth sediment bottom, I had *Argo* turn north, cross over the initial discovery line, and then double back to the east. We slowly followed the debris trail to the northeast until we finally crossed a small drop off. As *Argo* kept close to the descending bottom, we entered what looked like an impact crater, expecting the wreckage of *Bismarck* to appear at any second. Tension mounted as we prepared ourselves for a thrill that never came. Before we knew it, we cleared the lip of the crater and returned to a gentle, sloping countryside without seeing a single piece of debris.

We quickly doubled back. Over the next several hours, a fascinating picture began to emerge. We were able to close the crater to the east, west, and north, but not downslope to the south. Just as we had tried to close *Thresher*'s debris trail years before, we were unable to find closure on this giant impact crater.

As we continued our lines back and forth, Al Uchupi's trained eye recognized the disturbed bottom as the path of an underwater landslide, a wide tongue-shaped avalanche of sediment that had cascaded from the seamount's upper slopes. But what had caused this huge landslide? I was confident I knew the answer.

An object as massive as *Bismarck* impacting the seamount's upper slopes at high speed would have dislodged just such a wide avalanche. And if the landslide continued long enough, it would also partly bury the typical winnowed trail of lighter debris found on wrecks that sank to a more horizontal sea bottom.

Somewhere on this slope the heaviest wreckage, maybe *Bismarck*'s intact hull itself, was hiding in the icy dark. Since the landslide seemed to be oriented from southeast to northwest and I believed *Bismarck*'s hull lay along this axis, I decided to "mow the lawn" in a narrow ladder of *Argo* sweeps back up the avalanche track toward the northwest. But this decision was the equivalent of a coin toss. I had no way to know where on the landslide the hull lay because, as Al noted with his usual geological insight, the collision of *Bismarck*'s heavy hull with the slope would have triggered an avalanche both above and below the point of impact.

The night became timeless, with no obvious clue of the passing hours in the eternal rosy gloom of the control van. I was surprised when Jack Maurer appeared beside me to take up the morning watch. I told him we were halfway up the avalanche area and advised him, "Keep your eyes peeled. I'm just worried about burial."

Jack nodded and took his station. Despite Al Uchupi's calculations about sediment depth, most of us believed there were enough acres of loose mud down there in the avalanche to have completely buried even an object the size of *Bismarck*'s hull.

The watch crew was completely focused now, oblivious to my presence. Todd's young friend Kirk Gustafson was flying *Argo* beautifully over the rough terrain of the landslide.

Suddenly Mel Lee sang out from his station, "I'm getting a forward sonar contact."

I snapped from the haze of exhaustion that had settled over me. "Go down, Kirk," I said. "There's something right in the middle."

Kirk flipped the winch joystick forward, "Going down."

"Stop! Stop!" I ordered loudly, certain he was about to crash.

But the kid had sharper coordination than any adult. He checked *Argo*'s descent expertly a few meters above the bottom.

"Thar she blows!" I shouted, staring at a big chunk of riveted steel, dangling a narrow naval ladder.

Cathy Offinger logged the time and position.

But then, just as suddenly as we'd found the wreckage, the shotgun spattering of debris gave way to jumbled avalanche mud. We spent the rest of the morning in seemingly endless frustration, slowly looping back and forth across the landslide track. Finally, just before noon, we encountered a lonely leather boot lying on the disturbed sediment. The van went silent for a moment at the chilling image. Had a young German sailor Todd's age or younger worn that boot on the final long plunge to the sea bottom?

Through long hours that afternoon, we slalomed across the axis of the avalanche, descending now. My body ached, and my mind was numb with fatigue. I hadn't slept for twenty-four hours. Everyone was tense. Each sonar target seemed like the main wreckage; every stretch of chaotic mud became the primary impact crater. Once more, small factions of opinion coalesced. People began to grumble that we should change course to zero in on this or that tempting target. I welcomed their comments, but resisted a major course change, reminded of the phantom sonar silhouette of *Titanic*'s "hull" that had almost led to mutiny aboard *Knorr*.

Then, halfway down the avalanche in midafternoon, a scattered belt of metallic chunks—possibly spent shrapnel—gave way to a stunning image: a field of empty leather boots.

Again the humming banter in the van ceased abruptly. There were boots everywhere, most scattered randomly, but at least one pair stood perfectly matched, and I thought I saw shreds of trousers still attached. What we were witnessing was the final resting ground of a large group of *Bismarck*'s sailors, who had probably drowned in the same life raft or perhaps had died, lashed together in life jackets, on the oily surface. They had sunk—still bound together—all the way to this black slope. In the five decades since the war, the deep sea and its creatures had claimed their bodies, leaving behind these indigestible tanned leather boots as their final memorial.

The afternoon passed to evening. I subsisted on cans of Coke and dozed periodically in my chair at the chart table.

Then, near ten that night, Kirk Gustafson's voice rang out from the flyer station, "Oh, wow, look at that!"

I shot upright in my chair, gazing at the video monitor. The image was unmistakable, a ring of gear teeth, probably the exposed turning mechanism of one of *Bismarck*'s four main gun turrets.

Someone handed me a plastic ruler and I held it to the monitor screen to get a measurement. After a brief calculation—that seemed unbearably plodding in my exhausted condition—I announced that the circular object on the bottom measured 8 meters in diameter. "That's a main turret."

"They didn't have those on nineteenth-century sailing ships," Cathy Offinger announced wryly.

She was right, of course. This was the first irrefutable evidence that *Bismarck*'s grave did lie on this volcanic slope. More important, the sight of the huge, heavy turret, probably lying upside down, well above the mud level of the avalanche was a reassurance that the heavy wreckage had not been buried.

Bismarck's main hull, either intact or in sections, had to lie nearby.

A good leader delegates. And I had a capable crew. So, despite the excitement of the endgame, I dragged myself to my cabin for a few hours sleep. But lying in my bunk, a repeater video monitor from the van propped above the couch, sleep evaded me. My mind rippled with hypotheses. Had *Bismarck*'s sleek armored hull planed away from the plunging circular turrets after the ship turned turtle and sank—just as *Titanic*'s bow section had slipped away from the severed stern? Had the battleship's hull contained enough air-filled compartments to implode? Was Al wrong in his assessment of the sediment depth? And was that 8-meter-diameter geared circle perhaps the gaping turret barbette that marked the buried upper deck of *Bismarck*'s buried hull?

I found no answers in my sleep. But I did recover my strength. Late that night, I rejoined the watch in the control van, well rested and alert. All day *Argo* had relentlessly swept back and forth, locating several large pieces of wreckage, including a shattered chunk of superstructure complete with portholes. But now another night bore on with no sign of other large targets. Again exhaustion hit, and I retreated to my bunk. The next morning, June 8, 1989, I lay groggily on my cabin coach gazing at the streaked gray image on the repeater monitor, debating whether to eat breakfast or to shower.

Then the all-too-familiar image of roiled gray mud on the monitor suddenly changed. I saw the unmistakable shape of a naval cannon—no—two gun barrels jutting from an angular turret. And that knife-edged line on the screen's left side was not just another scarp face. It was the edge of *Bismarck*'s armored hull.

"We've got it!" I shouted, pounding from my cabin, still in my stocking feet.

I threw open the door of the control van just as *Argo* was passing over the central portion of the ship, a few meters aft of the bridge. Kurt pulled back on the winch control as hard as he could, hoping *Argo* would not crash into the side of the ship. Fortunately for *Argo*, the pounding *Bismarck* received from the British had blasted off the radio antennae and the upper superstructure, otherwise we might have lost *Argo* right then and there.

Al Uchupi was hunched over the chart, studying the coffee-colored sonar trace of the landslide, and did not immediately see the images on the screen. "It's a scarp," he announced flatly.

"That's no scarp," Cathy burst out as the gun barrels came into view on the down-looking camera monitor.

Tired cheers filled the narrow van. We had found the *Bismarck.*

At 0900 hours, Cathy logged the time and scrawled across the log page in thick block letters: "GOT IT."

For the next ten minutes, the control van became crowded with chattering people as *Argo* glided silently across the remarkably intact decks of *Bismarck,* the sunken pride of Nazi Germany.

I sat beside *Argo* flyer Billy Yunck, gripping the big plastic model of *Bismarck* the *National Geographic* crew had earlier assembled from a kit in anticipation of this discovery. The sensitive SIT cameras glided only a few meters above the battleship's shell-scarred superstructure. This was our first detailed camera run across the wreck, and we were all almost speechless at the silent spectacle.

Fifteen thousand six hundred feet below the surface of the Atlantic, *Bismarck* lay upright and almost completely intact on an open, gently sloping saddle of the sprawling seamount. Her sharply raked bow pointed southwest, turned forever away from the sanctuary of occupied France. The four big turrets were missing, leaving the gaping circular maws of their geared barbettes, reminiscent of but much larger than the chasm of *Titanic*'s grand staircase. The multiple smaller gun turrets, however, were still in place. Without question, *Bismarck* was a ship of war and could never be mistaken for a foundered merchantman.

"Does somebody have an X-Acto knife?" I asked. I was handed a penknife and grinned at the look of horror on the faces of the camera crew as I began to hack off pieces of the model *Bismarck*'s superstructure to match the scene of destruction *Argo*'s cameras were slowly revealing.

But even with the twin stacks, the main turrets, and the

jutting fire-control towers missing, *Bismarck* still looked remarkably battle-ready. The most damage we found was on the port decks amidship, where at least one of *Rodney*'s big 16-inch shells had pierced the armor.

Most of the teak-planked decks were surprisingly intact and much freer of sediment than the worm-ridden remnants of *Titanic*'s pine decks. The overall effect of the *Bismarck* wreck was ghostly preservation. Gazing at the image of each sharp-edged shell hole and every flak gun still shielded in its armored tub, I could almost hear the insanity of battle, hoarse young voices crying in anger and fear, lost in the mindless, chaotic thunder of exploding shells.

As *Argo*'s cameras crept past the empty mouth of the final gaping barbette where Turret Dora had stood, we saw another large shell hole, probably the one into which so many survivors of the initial barrages had reportedly fallen as they sought the safety of the stern. The downward-looking zoom lens moved steadily across the teak planking, stealing slowly aft. But what were those dark angular markings on the planks? I'd seen similar discolored patches near the bow, straight edges undoubtedly paint on wood.

An electric chill shot up my spine. We were gazing at a huge swastika—an air recognition insignia—meant for Luftwaffe bombers, that had been painted over when the ship left German-controlled airspace for the open Atlantic. But five decades of seawater had dissolved the masking paint. Here was the arrogant, pagan symbol of Nazi superiority, resting forever on the deep ocean floor.

Suddenly the swastika sheared away as if severed by a guillotine. The last 15 meters of the stern were missing. This hull rupture probably marked the impact point where the wreck collided, stern-first, with the upper slopes of the seamount, triggering the massive avalanche.

British witnesses and German survivors had all reported that *Bismarck* had sunk stern down before rolling over, so it was probable the aft compartments had been completely flooded. But because the hull showed no other signs of impact damage and both the deck and topside plates were smooth and unbuckled—except for obvious shell damage—it was almost certain that the internal compartments had been flooded before *Bismarck* reached great depth.

The battleship had not imploded. Here was proof that the German survivors had told the truth: *Bismarck* had been scuttled and not sunk by British guns.

As *Argo* glided forward on another pass across the starboard side of the huge dead battleship, I pondered the significance of this discovery. The military honor of the German Navy had been vindicated.

But what true significance had a concept such as "honor," when weighed against that ghostly field of boots that lay in eternal silence just up the slope from the ship?

As our camera sled swept back and forth across the huge wreck, capturing a precise historical record of the ultimate chapter of a brutal but exciting naval battle, my mind's eye returned often to that phantom parade ground of empty boots.

We had not come to glorify the military might of Nazi Germany. Rather, we had assembled stark and impressive archival evidence, as if any were needed, of the cruel and complete futility of war.

On the return trip to England, the mood aboard *Star Hercules* was both triumphant and reflective.

The spontaneous eruption of joy at the discovery and the unexpectedly well-preserved condition of *Bismarck*'s hull quickly gave way to an undercurrent of discontent among some members of the team, who believed our visual record of the sunken battleship might indeed be seen as an attempt to glorify Nazi military prowess. This grumbling reached an angry pitch when I gave graduate student Hagen Schempf, the only German national on board, the task of preparing a suitable memorial for the dead *Bismarck* sailors. The *Star Hercules* second engineer, Rick Latham, an enthusiastic Englishman, welded up a metal cross and wrapped it carefully with a strand of polypropylene line from a fishnet *Argo* had snagged near the wreck. But the idea of dropping a Christian cross onto a sunken Nazi ship was anathema to some team members.

Hagen, an insightful young man mature beyond his years, did not rise to the incipient German baiting. Instead, he consulted the entire team and reached a suitable compromise. We would drop a nautical rope wreath onto the Atlantic waters during a memorial service that transcended a single ship and honored the brave young men who had died aboard both the *Hood* and the *Bismarck*.

As we sailed away from the site of the *Bismarck*'s grave, Derek Latter, captain of the *Star Hercules,* led the service. His comments were forthright yet tender, exactly what I expected from a professional British seaman. He asked us to remember the young men who had lost their lives in the "tragic sea battle," and to use the opportunity of this ceremony to "put to rest all those souls lost at sea" during that savage, desperate week in May almost fifty years earlier.

I used the ship's rickety old telex to send brief messages to Woods Hole, the Quest Group, and *National Geographic,* announcing our discovery. But I was careful not to divulge the precise coordinates of the wreck at this time. *Bismarck* was a war grave, just as the field of phantom boots so starkly revealed. I did not want scavengers on this site plundering the somber wreck or its scattered debris field for valuable souvenirs.

My concern was not an empty worry. Only a year after our second *Titanic* expedition, a consortium of American investors under the umbrella of France's IFREMER had formed with the declared purpose of salvaging artifacts from the *Titanic* site. The French provided their deep-diving submersible, and in August 1987, they recovered a total of eighteen hundred objects from the sea floor. But as I had feared, this rapacious scavenging had done serious damage to the wreck, where rigging wire and even fixed lamps had been cut away. And completely counter to the spirit of historic preservation, the submarine salvagers had also ripped apart the cylindrical crow's nest in order to snatch the old Bakelite telephone that seaman Fred Fleet had used to issue his famous warning: "Ice, right ahead."

I was determined that uniform buttons, belt buckles, and those leather boots worn by the burned and bleeding young German sailors on their way to their deep-sea grave would not be hawked as trinkets to the highest bidder. Nor did I want any piece of *Bismarck* displayed in a circuslike television special as had the artifacts in the *Return to the* Titanic . . . *Live* broadcast, hosted by Telly Savalas.

I was especially proud that we had carefully surveyed and visually recorded the entire *Bismarck* wreck without damaging it or disrupting the scattered debris field. And my pride was bolstered by the fact that Todd had been the *Argo* flyer during some of the most demanding close-in sweeps across the hull. To me this was dramatic affirmation that Todd had stepped with both feet across the threshold of responsible manhood, leaving the sometimes sullen adolescence of the previous summer's cruise behind him.

But just to show that my judgment was a peg or two below perfect, the scene I encountered at sunset after the memorial service reminded me that Todd was still a high-spirited youngster. I was strolling along the open deck toward the stern when I spotted his Montana buddies, Billy and Kirk, leaning on the rail near the hero bucket. They did not look happy to see me, and I knew something was up. As I neared the fantail, I spotted Todd, hanging completely outside the bucket with only his feet locked into the cage, bent over backward like a trapeze daredevil beneath the big top. A wild grin gripped his face; his splayed arms arced down toward the churning wake of the ship's propellers. I'm sure this must have been exhilarating. But the dangerous act almost gave me cardiac arrest.

I yelled harshly, the outraged parent, not the thoughtful expedition leader. Todd had reverted from manhood to a boy caught in an act of mischief. At the time, I just didn't realize how much these high-spirited risks were a part of his life.

But no anger remained between us as I made sure Todd joined me at the triumphant press conferences in England and at *National Geographic* headquarters in Washington. This indulgence was not unfair patronage. Todd had earned his place in the sun.

After the media blitz cooled, my entire family headed for our vacation home in the mountains near Whitefish in northwestern Montana. The secluded log cabin was exactly the kind of refuge I always needed after the hectic pace and claustrophobic conditions of sea expeditions.

I enjoyed several days of trout fishing and waterskiing with the boys before being drawn away for a quick business trip. Flying back to Montana after a scouting trip for our next live *Jason* broadcast from Lake Ontario, I looked forward to another two weeks in the wilderness with my sons before Todd had to return east to begin his second year of college.

But when I reached Whitefish, Marjorie had unexpected news. Todd had left suddenly two days earlier, driving his Ford LTD all the way back to Cape Cod. She'd been able to piece together the reason for Todd's precipitous departure.

Todd had girlfriend problems. The girl's name was Jen and she was his high school sweetheart, a cheerleader he had met when he was playing varsity ice hockey in his senior year at Falmouth. Jen had made it clear that she was not satisfied with a proxy romance. First, Todd had gone off to Colorado, leaving her behind, then he had gone off to sea with me for most of the summer, and finally, he had gone off to spend the remaining weeks of August with his family in distant Montana.

She had told Todd that their relationship was over. He

reacted predictably, driving all the way across the continent in a futile attempt to patch things up with his girlfriend.

I was angry and disappointed when I first heard the news. But then I softened. Todd *had* behaved maturely and responsibly on the expedition. And he was only missing a few days with the family. So why make a federal case out of his impulsive act? I settled in for some serious trout fishing with Douglas.

A few nights later, I was roused from sleep by a sheriff's deputy from nearby Whitefish pounding on the cabin door. I pulled on a robe and shook the sleep from my head.

The young man's face was pale and constricted. "Dr. Ballard," he said, "I'm sorry to tell you that your son is dead. And so is his friend."

The words struck like invisible, pummeling blows. Mercifully, the first human reaction to such news is denial. I was sure Douglas was asleep in his room and brusquely informed the deputy of this.

He looked even more stricken. "It's not Douglas Ballard, sir," he said. "It's your son Todd."

I found myself sitting, my chest gripped in a frozen vise. Clutching Marjorie's hand tightly, I heard the deputy's words as if echoing from a long distance, through a chill fog.

The Whitefish sheriff's department had received a sketchy report from the police in Falmouth on Cape Cod. Todd and his friend had died instantly in a car crash on a winding, rain-slicked secondary road.

Over the next several hours, we assembled the grim details by telephone. At first, I had assumed Todd had been in a car accident with his boyhood friend, Greg Depunte. But then I learned that the other kid in the crash had been Chad Dalton, his old roommate from the Brewster Academy. And they had not died in the Ford LTD Todd had been driving for years. Todd had somehow found the keys to his mother's new Ford Thunderbird, the car that we had refused to let him drive. He and Chad were coming home late at night from a friend's house, driving too fast around a slippery curve. Todd had lost control of the high-performance sports car, and they slammed into a tree sideways. Their safety belts did them no good. Both boys were killed instantly, their necks broken.

Writing the details on a legal pad, the phone like a lump of ice in my fist, I could picture all too well those "quaint" Cape Cod side roads, which were simply paved nineteenth-century carriage lanes with no shoulders to provide a margin of safety from the stately old hardwoods that guarded each turn like unforgiving sentinels.

Todd had learned to drive five years before on these narrow roads. If he'd only been in his own car instead of that powerful new Thunderbird. . . . But there was no way to alter the events of that horrible night. Death was final. There could be no revisions, no appeals.

The interminable flight east the next day was a trip through hell that I never imagined could be so agonizing. When I closed my eyes, I saw Todd clearly again, his face pulsing with excitement as he leaned over the *Argo* flyer station during those last dangerous low runs across the *Bismarck*'s shell-torn superstructure. Then I saw him once more hanging from the hero bucket, an adolescent daredevil, his eyes animated, forehead streaked with spray from the ship's wake.

I had heard that the burden of burying a child was the cruelest pain an adult would ever face. That pronouncement had meant nothing until Todd's funeral on that sunny September morning three days later.

Still bound by icy numbness, I took refuge that fall in the solitude offered by a scheduled navy expedition. Working on a highly classified project in the Central Atlantic, I performed my duties with the dull movements of a robot. Normally a voracious eater at sea, I now had to force myself to nibble. Sleep, when it came, was a tangle of nightmares.

I found solace in reading the comparative mythology of Joseph Campbell. In particular, his book, *The Power of Myth*, struck a resonant chord. In the mythology of many cultures, Campbell explained, the epic journey was a metaphor for life's voyage. Just as Ulysses and Jason had gone out on their voyages of exploration and discovery, to be sorely tested, then to return triumphant, so, I realized, did some of us travel through life toward hard-won maturity and knowledge.

But others, like Todd and those brave young sailors on the *Hood* and the *Bismarck,* were cut down even before they had fairly set sail.

Campbell's insights and Todd's death brought home a vital lesson, a truth that I had felt for years but had not yet consciously embraced. Life was too precious a gift to squander. Those of us lucky enough to survive into seasoned maturity had an obligation to live the invaluable gift of the years, months, and days they were given to the fullest of their potential.

Alone in my cabin as the navy research vessel rolled through the autumn swells, I had to face the somber assessment that my life was far from complete.

Todd's death had come during another, less sudden personal crisis. For years, I'd tried to evade the fact that my marriage of twenty-one years was coming to an end. Marjorie and I had married when we were both very young and inexperienced. In many ways, the partnership of our marriage had mirrored that of my parents. I had undoubtedly been looking for someone very much like my mother, a woman content to be a housewife who stayed at home and raised children.

But in the decades since the 1960s, so much had changed. Perhaps unfairly, I had expected Marjorie to automatically change with the times. But she was both unwilling and in many ways unable to deal with this situation.

My career as an academic had kept me in the forefront of change, closely involved with people excited by revelations such as plate tectonics, deep-diving submersibles, and robotic exploration. All around me in the professional world, I encountered partnerships between intelligent, thoroughly involved young men and women.

But even as my world expanded and became more rich through the professional opportunities I encountered, Marjorie's world remained static and seemed to diminish in my eyes. For years, I had tried to encourage her to expand her horizons, to go back to college, to start a career. But she had resisted.

In a way, seeking out the wilderness sanctuary in Montana had been an unconscious attempt to return to simpler times, where men and women's roles were more traditional.

Todd's death, however, had stripped away the self-protective cloak of illusion I had drawn around our marriage. I recognized the only course of action open to me if I were to live the remainder of my life as fully as I now intended. Still battered and raw from the funeral, I told Marjorie my intention to file for divorce. Certainly it would have been kinder to wait for the first emotional scars to heal, but when you lose a child, it is impossible to return to "normal" life as if nothing had happened. I felt compelled to make dramatic changes in my life so that some good would come out of Todd's death.

These personal cataclysms were also coupled with similar upheavals in my professional life. While I was at sea that fall, the Berlin Wall fell. The Soviet Empire was crumbling, and with it the cold war. For over twenty years, that murky global conflict—so much of which involved submarine warfare—had formed one of the legs of the triad of science, exploration, and military research that made up my professional life. Now, with the end of the cold war, I had to recognize that my involvement in highly classified navy research projects would taper off and end.

My position as a senior scientist at Woods Hole was also reaching a natural conclusion. I'd been fortunate enough to be in the vanguard of some of the most exciting moments of modern marine science, from Project FAMOUS to the astounding discoveries of chemosynthetic ecosystems on the sea bottom. But it's a professional truism that young scientists make the most innovative discoveries. It was time now for me to leave marine geology to my younger colleagues.

Numbly fulfilling my duty on that fall navy expedition, I turned repeatedly to Campbell's archetype of the epic voyage as a guide to assess my past life and find direction for the future. Campbell tells us that this mythological voyage through life is often rendered in stages.

First comes the dream. For me, that had been my childhood spent on the Pacific shore of California, my head filled with visions of Captain Nemo's world beneath the sea.

Next comes the preparation. This had been my training as a scientist that culminated in the epic discoveries of Project FAMOUS.

Then the voyager assembles his crew. Mine had been the team that coalesced around the Deep Submergence Laboratory at Woods Hole.

These voyagers then go forth and are tested. My colleagues and I were certainly tested by *Titanic,* the Cayman Trough, the Galapagos Rift, and the East Pacific Rise.

And like Campbell's voyagers, we overcame and gained truth, on Marsili Seamount, Skerki Bank, and on *Bismarck*'s somber grave.

Now, if my own life were in fact to parallel the mythical epic voyage, it was time for me to return and share the truth I had learned.

I realized that I had the perfect tool in the JASON Project to share that hard-won knowledge. As I returned to shore from the autumn Atlantic, I knew the future course my life's voyage would take.

EPILOGUE

"Surface Control, this is *Sea Cliff*," I called on the acoustic phone. "Depth two-six-one-seven, and descending. No target on the sonar."

The cramped pressure sphere of the submersible was still almost as hot and humid as it had been when we sealed the hatch in the blood-red tropical dawn an hour earlier. I was in *Sea Cliff*, a younger sister of *Alvin*, which the U.S. Navy has operated for twenty years. We were 2,617 feet beneath the surface of Iron Bottom Sound, the channel separating Guadalcanal and Tulagi in the Solomon Islands of the Southwest Pacific.

It was Sunday, August 9, 1992, almost exactly fifty years since U.S. Marines had landed on the north coast of Guadalcanal and seized the unfinished Japanese airstrip in the first American offensive operation of World War II.

To my generation, who had grown up after the war, the very name Guadalcanal evoked equal measures of anguish and pride. The Battle of Guadalcanal lasted for six months, from August 1942 until February 1943. In a vicious series of sea, land, and air engagements, tens of thousands of Americans and Japanese were killed in this remote and rugged volcanic archipelago 10 degrees south of the equator, which marked the zenith of Japanese expansion in the Pacific.

The most savage naval battles had occurred in Iron Bottom Sound—named for the scores of ships and airplanes that litter the bottom of a 3,000-foot deep trough bounded by the rugged coast of Guadalcanal to the south, Tulagi 18 miles to the north, with the circular volcanic hump of Savo Island, standing like a sentinel at the sound's western end.

On the night of August 8, 1942, only a day after the First Marine Division had landed near the half-built airstrip on the north coast, which they named Henderson Field, a powerful Japanese task force ambushed the U.S. Navy invasion fleet— its strength ill-advisedly split into two sections, north and south of Savo Island—sinking four heavy cruisers in the most humiliating defeat ever suffered by the U.S. Navy.

This initial Japanese victory left the small, beleaguered marine contingent ashore virtually without naval protection and allowed the Japanese to reinforce their garrison on Guadalcanal almost unopposed.

Stripped of their naval support, the marines fought valiantly to defend their small beachhead, a fan-shaped wedge of coastal jungle that included a steep knife-edged bluff, Bloody Ridge, against which the Japanese threw repeated fanatical, but ultimately futile banzai attacks. Unable to dislodge the marines—whose strength was sapped by hunger, dysentery, and malaria—by land attack, the Imperial Japanese command tried to blast them from their grip on the airstrip with some of the heaviest barrages of naval gunfire of the war. Over nine hundred 14-inch shells from Japanese battleships pounded Henderson Field in a single night. But the marines clung stubbornly to their beachhead.

Three months later, in the naval Battle of Guadalcanal— savage, close-range night engagements fought from November 12 to 15, 1942, in the narrow waters of Iron Bottom Sound— scores of American and Japanese battleships, cruisers, and destroyers were lost. The Japanese attempt to reinforce their troops was repulsed at terrible cost in ships and lives.

The land and sea combat on and around Guadalcanal was some of the most vicious of the war in the Pacific. Japanese and American warships, whose captains did not trust the newly installed innovation of radar fire-control, used searchlights to fight ferocious close-in engagements, with heavy cruisers, even battleships, firing their powerful naval artillery into their opponents at ranges of less than a mile. Huge, heavily armored warships were literally blown to pieces and sunk in a matter of minutes. Other crippled ships drifted, burning on the surface, their crews fighting desperately to save them, until they were sunk at dawn by torpedoes or aerial bombs.

Ashore, Marines and Japanese soldiers fought barbaric hand-to-hand battles in corpse-choked mangrove swamps and along the banks of sluggish coastal rivers. Men killed each other with bayonets, grenades, machetes, and entrenching tools. Often the combat was more like an atavistic massacre than modern warfare. Inhuman hatred ruled the battlefield. Men on both sides, driven almost insane by fear, disease, and the incessant tropical heat, gave in to acts of hideous bloodlust. Neither side took many prisoners.

Over two dozen major and minor American and Japanese warships litter the floor of Iron Bottom Sound, the densest concentration of sunken warships in the world. I led a two-season expedition to survey the sound and to produce a visual record of this lost fleet. The previous summer, we had overcome seemingly intractable equipment problems to conduct a sonar survey of the warship graveyard, locating a dozen of the most historically important wrecks. This year, sponsored by the U.S. Navy and the National Geographic Society, our exploration was part of a larger fiftieth anniversary commemoration of the Guadalcanal campaign.

I was proud to participate in this endeavor. Certainly, as in my *Bismarck* expedition, I didn't intend to glorify the ghastly struggle that had made these isolated tropical islands synonymous with the horror of war. When I learned that survivors of the sunken ships and veterans of the land battle—both American and Japanese—planned to return to Guadalcanal for the fiftieth anniversary ceremonies, however, I realized our effort to photograph and videotape the lost ships of Iron

Bottom Sound offered the opportunity for these veterans to finally put the war behind them and perhaps to find some measure of reconciliation.

But as if in mocking replication of the chaotic conditions of fifty years earlier, both the 1991 and 1992 phases of the Guadalcanal expedition were nearly crippled by chronic equipment failures. Our main exploration tools this summer were the navy's *Sea Cliff*—the slightly heavier sibling of *Alvin*—and *Scorpio,* a close cousin of my ROV *Jason.* Both the navy's manned submersible and ROV, however, spent more time stripped down in the workshop aboard our tender, the *Laney Chouest,* waiting for spare parts to be airlifted from the States, than exploring the wrecks of Iron Bottom Sound.

Despite these disappointments, we did manage to videotape several of the principal warships, including the U.S. cruisers sunk near Savo Island in August 1942 and several of the important Japanese vessels that went down in the November melee.

And today, as we neared the bottom in 3,000 feet of water, midway between the steep slopes of Savo and Tulagi Islands, I was confident we'd be able to closely inspect and videotape the wreck of the U.S. heavy cruiser *Quincy,* which was sunk with great loss of life on the early morning of August 9, 1942.

The monotonous swish and click of our sonar suddenly changed pitch as the instrument acquired bottom, 400 feet below.

I stopped musing about the bloody sea battles fifty years before and concentrated on the task at hand. To my right, Navy Lieutenant Jerry Peterson, *Sea Cliff*'s pilot, was preparing for our landing on the mud bottom. I was copilot today, and Mark Shelley, *National Geographic*'s underwater photographer for the expedition, was observer.

As Jerry Peterson checked his systems, preparing to dump descent weights, I completed my own checklist. One of the items to verify was the function of our life-support air system. But when I shined my flashlight on the gauge of the carbon dioxide–level meter, I was shocked to see the needle creeping steadily from the black digits of the safe levels into the bright red danger zone.

Despite the cloying trapped humidity we'd brought with us from the surface, my mouth went suddenly dry. Carbon dioxide poisoning was the insidious nightmare every submariner dreaded. Aboard submersibles such as *Sea Cliff*, we "scrubbed" carbon dioxide from the cramped personnel sphere with a large lithium-hydroxide canister, normally a simple and reliable system. But for some reason, today the carbon dioxide level in the sphere was rising steadily with every breath we expelled. Even as I watched, the level rose to 30 millimeters of mercury. We couldn't see or smell the gas, of course. But if we didn't do something soon, we'd be overcome.

"The CO_2 is going up," I said flatly, tapping the gauge above my head in the crowded rack of instruments. I tapped again, and the needle rose higher into the red zone. "Yep, it's going up."

Jerry Peterson was a well-trained naval officer, who seemed determined to maintain the unflappable sangfroid that submariners were expected to display in such emergencies. He took the handheld backup carbon dioxide meter from its rack and set about to test the cabin air with laborious slowness.

I found myself breathing shallowly, an involuntary response to the thought of asphyxiation. After what seemed like a long, long time, Jerry and Mark nodded their concurrence that the portable gas meter agreed with the primary instrument. We were poisoning ourselves with our own spent breath.

Following emergency procedures, we changed the lithium-hydroxide canister with a fresh one and made sure the air was flowing normally through the unit. But still the needle on the meter climbed higher in the red danger zone.

Jerry punched off all our weights, and we began a maximum-speed emergency ascent.

"Donning EBS," Jerry called on the acoustic phone to our surface controller aboard the *Laney Chouest* as we reached for the Emergency Breathing System masks.

I felt a chill sense of déjà vu as Mark Shelley groped behind him in the cramped space to hand out the hoses and face masks. These rubber-and-Plexiglas face shields were eerily reminiscent of the unit I'd worn during the electrical fire aboard *Archimede*.

Once my mask was in place, I forced myself to take regular, normal breaths, half expecting to smell the acrid stench of burned insulation. Instead, the air entering the face mask was warm and slightly medicinal in scent.

Our ascent-rate meter was pegged out at 61 feet per minute, the maximum. We'd be on the surface in fifty minutes. With hundreds of deep dives aboard *Alvin* and other submersibles behind me, I hadn't thought too much about these relatively short junkets to the floor of Iron Bottom Sound. But I had more or less made up my mind that since I'd probably exhausted my lifetime supply of luck, I would not go out of my way to dive much in the future. Now here I was right in the middle of a full-blown emergency. If all went well, the crisis would be over in less than an hour. But I couldn't relax as I normally did during an ascent.

As if in response to my anxiety, Mark Shelley shook his head violently and swore. The double, intake-outlet hoses had just broken loose from the chin-fitting of his face mask. He gaped in disbelief at the accordion-pleated tan plastic hoses in his hand.

Suddenly the emergency had gone critical. Unless we quickly repaired Mark's breathing unit, the three of us would have to share two masks, thus increasing the risk of incipient carbon dioxide poisoning.

Jerry snatched down the tool kit, and I held the hoses while Mark gripped the mask. But it wasn't just simply a question of a loose spring clip. The tight flange that made the hose connection airtight had sprung loose.

As we worked frantically, we all recognized the maddening nature of the emergency. We needed both hands to manipulate the flopping mask and hoses in order to reseat the connection seal. However, we also needed our hands to pass the two masks back and forth among the three of us so that we could all breathe uncontaminated air.

The miniature fixed video camera on the sphere's interior dome was recording what probably looked like a Three Stooges slapstick routine. But our clumsy maneuvers were anything but funny.

No one is ever prepared for their death in an emergency. Nonetheless, I felt particularly vulnerable. It seemed so ironic, so patently *unfair* that I might die in the black waters of Iron Bottom Sound and join the ghosts of the thousands of young Japanese and Americans who had been killed here. Only that morning in the hot, crimson dawn, I had told my wife, Barbara, that I was probably getting a little too long in the tooth for these adventures in submersibles.

Now, passing the sweaty, flopping rubber face mask back and forth as we struggled to repair the third unit, I only wished I had listened to that inner voice and sent a younger man on this dive.

I do not *want to die,* a voice sounded faint and cold in my head. *Not here, not now.*

I had too much to live for.

Todd's death in 1989 had been an alarm bell, causing me to somberly, honestly assess my life. I wanted his death to have a profound impact upon my future. I simply could not say after a suitable mourning period was over, "Now where was I?"

My career had been extremely successful, but deep inside I was unhappy, and Todd's death only intensified this discontent. In fact, losing Todd made it intolerable.

When I married Marjorie in 1966, the world was still living in the '40s. A woman's place was in the home as a housewife and mother, her life totally subjugated to her husband and his career.

But by 1989, the world had been turned upside down. Women were emerging as equals to men in all the professions. As I began to question the value of continuing our marriage after Todd's death, I turned back to Joseph Campbell's *The Power of Myth*, which had consoled me on that lonely navy research cruise in the fall of 1989. I was deeply influenced by his discussion of "finding your other half." I took his comments to mean that a man looks at the world through one eye, while a woman sees it through the other eye. Each view is valid, but fundamentally different, and the only way an individual can view life in proper perspective, i.e. in stereo, is with the help of his or her other half. But for this partnership to work, each person, each eye, has to be equal.

I had spent a lifetime going through one adventure after another and had learned a great deal about myself and the world around me. But I still lacked the other perspective, Campbell's "other half." And suddenly I hungered for it.

I longed for someone who could be my equal, my lover, my companion and partner, and even possibly the mother of a new child.

Ironically, after separating from Marjorie and beginning the long process of divorce, the last thing I wanted to do was to remarry. I felt I needed time to decompress from twenty-one years of marriage, to carefully review what I had learned from that experience before seeking a new wife.

Then Barbara Hanford Earle walked into my life. Barbara was in charge of National Geographic Television Special Projects. When my old friend and the president of the National Geographic Society, Gil Grosevenor, joined the board of my new Jason Foundation for Education, the day-to-day interactions between the foundation and the society came under the wing of the Television division. Tim Kelly, who was in charge of that division, assigned Barbara to be their point of contact.

Barbara quickly became a member of Jason's "Kitchen Cabinet" and was extremely helpful in getting our new foundation under way. Her background was in television production, so she had an excellent understanding of the complexities associated with our "live" Jason broadcasts from remote sites. I was also hosting National Geographic's weekly television program, *Explorer,* on TBS. Sunday nights. But I was a true novice in television and found myself increasingly seeking Bar bara's advice.

Prior to my association with Barbara, I had never worked with a woman as an equal. Oceanography in its early years had been a male undertaking. Research ships and especially submersibles had been male bastions. The same held true for the military.

But the JASON Project and my expanding role with National Geographic put me in much greater contact with professional women. And working with them in general, and Barbara in particular, was extremely exciting.

Barbara was a wonderful mixture of all the ingredients I was looking for in a partner and lover. Besides being a beautiful woman, she was intelligent and very focused. Each of our strengths seemed to offset a weakness in the other. I was a risk-taker, willing to jump at opportunities; Barbara was organized and loved to deal with details such as making sure that my parachute was properly packed, with a reserve chute attached.

On January 12, 1991, we were married, and my life began to change in ways I never expected.

First and foremost, Barbara wanted to continue her career in the field of multimedia, where things were just beginning to take off.

Two years later, both my personal and professional lives were meshed in a way I had never dreamed possible. At age fifty, I felt as young and vital as I had three decades before.

As I struggled to repair the emergency breathing mask in the hot, cramped pressure sphere, I vowed that I would savor the rich potential of this new life . . . *if* we pulled off this latest Houdini escape. Finally, the three of us, short of breath and sweating, managed to repair the Emergency Breathing System mask. The rest of the ascent was tense, but uneventful.

An hour later, when I climbed out of *Sea Cliff*'s red sail after the submersible had been hauled aboard the *Laney Chouest,* I stood on the sub's Fiberglas deck, in the hot shade of the superstructure, breathing deeply. Across the shimmering water of Iron Bottom Sound, the lush green jungle ridges of Guadalcanal rose into a gray crown of windblown rain cloud.

"An interesting dive," I said, with unintended irony.

There was definitely something to the old adage that life was never so delicious as when you had tasted the dank breath of death lurking nearby.

Nevertheless, I dived again, unable to resist the lure of closely inspecting the sunken Japanese battleship *Kirishima.* This huge warship was one of the key vessels of the Japanese fleet in the South Pacific and the pride of the Imperial Navy, having often appeared in morale-boosting propaganda films after the military dictatorship in Tokyo launched Japan on its campaign of conquest in the 1930s. *Kirishima* was even larger and more heavily armored than *Bismarck*. But on the night of November 14, 1942, *Kirishima* was sunk by long-range barrages from the 16-inch guns of the battleship *Washington.*

Now, almost fifty years later, *Sea Cliff* crept up on the

huge sonar target of the sunken Japanese battleship. The scene we encountered was bizarre, completely unexpected. Instead of our floodlights revealing the normal image of a shell-battered but recognizable sunken warship, we saw a seemingly endless rusty, sponge-flecked expanse of curved steel.

Kirishima had turned turtle after sinking. Probably because her towering armored superstructure acted like a keel, she had failed to right herself on the final plunge to the bottom.

It was as if the monstrous ship had been extinguished, not merely sunk. *Kirishima* had become a long, hump-backed ridge of armor plate, hardly recognizable as the powerful warship that had once been the scourge of the Pacific. As *Sea Cliff* inched cautiously closer to the hull, I peered out the small recessed view port, searching for familiar shapes on the wreck.

"My God," I whispered, "look at that."

We were near one of the battleship's four huge triple-bladed bronze propellers. Our floodlights revealed that the propellers, now seemingly standing upright on their bearing braces like nightmare windmills, were in excellent condition, testimony to the skill of the Japanese foundrymen. The circumference of each propeller disk was greater than *Sea Cliff*'s length. Never before, not even during the dives on *Titanic,* had I encountered such a gargantuan wreck.

Yet this monster lay upside down, smashed and impotent, a dinosaur overturned, never to right itself.

Vanity, I thought, echoing the old passage of scripture. *All is vanity.*

On our last evening on Iron Bottom Sound, I witnessed a scene even more moving than my encounter with *Kirishima.* We had invited Japanese and American survivors of the naval battle to observe from the *Scorpio* control room as we videotaped the wrecks below with the ROV. Stewart Moredock, who had been wounded in the sinking of the light cruiser *Atlanta,* stood in the bow of the *Laney Chouest,* watching the sudden tropical sunset fade from lavender to indigo. Beside him stood Michiharu Shinya, whose destroyer *Akatsuki* had been sunk that same night in November 1942.

Naval historians indicated that the Japanese destroyer and the American light cruiser might have actually sunk each other. But during our brief cruise on Iron Bottom Sound, the two veterans, who had served their countries well as gallant young naval officers, quickly corrected one small point in the history books. Shinya told Moredock that *Akatsuki* had fired no torpedoes that night. The Japanese veteran did confirm, however, that it was probably *Atlanta*'s guns that had sunk his ship.

Since the war, both men had tried to put the terrible events of that night in 1942 behind them. Moredock had married and become a university professor, and had long refused to discuss the war. Shinya converted to Christianity while a POW and eventually became a minister in the United Church of Christ. Like the American, Shinya also had maintained fifty years of silence about the war.

But in one afternoon out on the sound, the two men broke their silence and recounted with voices choked by tears, still hot after five decades, the details of that terrible battle.

I watched them standing shoulder-to-shoulder on the bow as we crossed the calm water toward the green coast of the island. They were talked out. Then I saw Stewart Moredock, a tall, dignified figure with white hair, reach out and rest his hand on Shinya's shoulder. To me, witnessing this heartfelt gesture of reconciliation made up for all the frustrations and danger of the expedition.

Laney Chouest held station in a slight westerly chop on the glinting turquoise surface of the Sea of Cortez, between the stark tan peninsula of Baja California and the Mexican mainland. It was the first week in March 1993, near the end of the JASON IV expedition, the most complex and ambitious undertaking of my professional life.

Six thousand feet below, *Jason* worked at the end of its tether to *Medea,* exploring a field of strange, mushroom-shaped hydrothermal vents, a unique feature of this tectonic rift that marked the fault between the North American and the Pacific Plates.

As I stood in the control van, my eyes darting out of habit from the ROV's video monitors to the sonar plot, the Nav computer, and the all-important cable-tension meter, I was suddenly struck by the irony of the moment. In the past, when *Jason* or *Argo* had operated in such chaotic and potentially dangerous bottom terrain, the person at the flyer's console was the key team member in the van. But today, our pilot Will Sellers sat back in his chair, his hands free of the joystick.

Yet *Jason* maneuvered with its usual hummingbird precision among the polychrome sulfide crowns of these mushroom vents, lining up to make a series of temperature measurements of the superheated fluid that pooled beneath the yellow and crimson overhangs of the mineral deposits. The ROV's flyer was not in the van, not even aboard the *Laney Chouest.* For part of today's mission, a high school student in Washington, DC, was flying the ROV via an intricate electronic loop of telepresence.

As I watched, the unseen student guided *Jason* deftly into the measuring position, then paused while Dana Yoerger punched commands into his computer keyboard to operate the temperature probe gripped in the ROV's mechanical fist.

The rest of the procedure worked smoothly. After about fifteen minutes, Will Sellers thanked the youngster 2,000 miles to the north and took back control of the ROV for the transit to the next bottom station.

I completed my commentary to the video cameras, and we wrapped up the show, the third 90-minute JASON Project broadcast of the day.

In the previous two weeks, we had produced more than forty live broadcasts. Before this week was over, the total would be past fifty. More than 500,000 students and 12,000 teachers at twenty-five down-link sites in the United States, Canada, Great Britain, and Bermuda were participating in this year's program. A team of educators and project scientists led by the National Science Teachers Association had produced a 250-page curriculum to guide the thousands of teachers through our program. The students, ranging in age from ten to eighteen, were all enrolled in science classes geared toward our research.

Beyond the vital educational aspect of the expedition, we also incorporated for the first time the telepresence participation by shore-based scientific colleagues in marine biology, geology, chemistry, and geophysics. They, too, had the chance to "fly" *Jason* in their own experiments, even though they might be thousands of miles from the Sea of Cortez. Interest in our project had been keen among young scientists at institutions that had no research vessels of their own.

Although some of my older, more traditional colleagues, including several powerful figures who controlled the limited research funds available to young scientists, viewed this operation as another one of Ballard's show-business gimmicks, the young professionals who joined us were very serious about their projects. They took their key from NASA's space program, in which scientists in specially designed laboratories on the ground used telepresence satellite links similar to our own to operate experiments on the space shuttle.

And the interest among professional colleagues in the hydrothermal vents of the Guaymas Basin here in the Sea of Cortez was intense. This was because the vents' overhanging mushroom-capped sulfide deposits often trapped superheated hydrothermal fluids and created a unique chemosynthetic ecosystem rich in rare subspecies. Microbiologists were fascinated: the youthful speculation of my Galapagos Rift teammates who had suggested in 1979 that life on Earth might have begun in the churning hot cauldron of marine hydrothermal vents had become an accepted tenet of science now, fourteen years later. Indeed, research since the first Galapagos expedition had revealed that the sulfur-metabolizing bacteria common to these vents contained RNA patterns linking them to the oldest known species of microorganisms on the planet.

As this year's project neared its end, I told the students assembled in museums and university laboratories that actively participating in science was the best job in the world, a chance to maintain the sense of wonder at discovery that made childhood so magical throughout their entire life.

Then, addressing the hundreds of teachers watching that particular broadcast, I urged them to continue exciting their students about science. "You win or lose a scientist between the fifth and eighth grades," I said. I noted that after our *Titanic* expedition my office walls were covered with thousands of letters from kids basically asking the same thing, "Can I go?"

As I fielded questions from teachers and students that afternoon, I felt the physical distance separating this ship on the Sea of Cortez and their down-link sites fade, then disappear. All the participants on the JASON network were excited about that day's ROV runs through the exotic landscape of the vent field. Many were particularly eager to begin preparing for future expeditions, which would include the exploration of active volcanoes in the Hawaiian Islands. But they weren't satisfied to simply study volcanism; they wanted to qualify as *Jason* flyers at remote down-link sites.

For me this enthusiasm was immensely satisfying. A few of my more traditional colleagues had dismissed such hands-on student participation as expensive video-arcade game-playing. But I knew better. Children who had always known multichannel color television would simply not be adequately stimulated by the so-called Gutenberg technology of textbook and blackboard. Merely watching a video performance did not spark a child's imagination. As any parent can attest, the flickering screen of a color television set is hypnotic to children. They watch football games, hyperviolent cartoons, and deodorant commercials with the same unblinking passivity.

The JASON Project, however, was not simply another visual aid. The students had the chance to interact with the remote expedition. Certainly not every one earned the chance to fly the ROV. But specialized study groups investigated particular aspects of the project's research, and each group's representative had the opportunity to discuss the research with professional team members on the site.

And I was aware that in two weeks on the Sea of Cortez, I'd had the chance to personally teach many more students than most teachers ever reached in their entire careers.

After the day's hectic broadcast schedule was completed and the science and ROV teams were preparing for the next day, I relaxed on the stern with a cold bottle of Tecate beer.

The familiar rumble of ship's engines rose through the steel deck plates. I was suddenly reminded of that period of cold, lonely grief aboard the naval research ship out on the autumn Atlantic after Todd's death. It was then I had decided that, if indeed life was a voyage of exploration, it was time for me to share the truth that I had learned during that long voyage.

Now I was satisfied that I had finally begun to meet that obligation to pay that debt.

I push Ben's stroller across the cobblestones of the Mystic waterfront. My ten-month-old son's head bounces with every jolt of the wheels, and Barbara's hand grips my arm.

"He's okay," I try to reassure her.

But the protective instinct of a mother for her first child is strong indeed. Then Ben turns his face up toward us and breaks into his beguiling snaggle-toothed grin. He flings out his arm and points with delight at the seagulls wheeling above the topmasts of the square-rigged *Joseph Conrad* and the renovated 19th century whaler, *Charles W. Morgan* moored at the historic docks of the Mystic Seaport Museum.

"Bird, bird," he says happily. This is his favorite word, the first he learned to speak.

"He's going to be a sailor," I tell Barbara.

"That's all we need in the family," she replies with mock concern, "another sailor."

We move through the splendid early-winter sunlight in a buoyant mood, relishing the simple act of pushing our child in a stroller after months of hectic work. My older son, Douglas, who will graduate from college in a few weeks, has just called to announce that he's been offered a job.

And our own professional future looks bright.

Three years before, Barbara and I formed the Odyssey Corporation and presented National Geographic with a three-year plan to coproduce two television specials: *The Lost Fleet of Guadalcanal* and *The Last Voyage of the* Lusitania. Soon we were working on books, CD-ROMs, an IMAX film, and short television segments for Steven Spielberg's new NBC series, *SeaQuest DSV*.

With the end of the cold war, I stopped my military activities and hung up my navy uniform. My company, Marquest, which built specialized search equipment for the navy and mounted highly classified military expeditions, was not headed in the direction I wanted to go. It was time to close it down and begin moving my career in another direction.

The same was true of Woods Hole. After twenty-five years at WHOI doing basic research in marine geology and geophysics and developing the *Argo-Jason* system, all my goals had been reached and it was time to move on as well.

The changes in my life continued. On January 22, 1994,

William Benjamin Aymar Ballard was born. Our life together was clearly heading off in a new direction.

But our future course remained unclear. I definitely knew what I did *not* want to do but wasn't certain how to best use my experience.

I truly believed that change was possible only after you had totally abandoned your past. If you left the bridges intact, it was too tempting to go back to your old ways. Cortez burned his ships as did Fletcher Christian of the *Bounty*. So, with that in mind, I began burning all of my bridges. Then the long wait commenced.

Slowly, a new dream began to emerge, but I didn't know how it might manifest itself.

Then came the call from Hugh Connell, the new president of Mystic Aquarium, asking if I would join their board. Something told me to accept, which I did.

If I was going to leave Woods Hole, I knew I would need a new home, a place that was committed to educating students and the public in general about the true potential of the sea. And a place that would permit me to pursue my new love, maritime history and marine archaeology.

I was now convinced that the deep ocean contained more preserved history than all of the museums of the world combined, and I wanted to work with archaeologists to reveal that hidden history and make it accessible to people worldwide. I also wanted to use my expertise in telepresence technology to create the first in situ underwater museum.

Then a wonderful thing happened. Governor Lowell Weicker of Connecticut got wind of my dream and my discussions with Mystic Aquarium through his wife Claudia, who also serves on the Mystic Aquarium board. He invited Hugh Connell and me to Hartford.

"If you will promise to come to Mystic, I will help finance your new Institute for Exploration," the governor promised.

On December 6, 1994, true to his word, Governor Weicker signed into law a bill passed by the state legislature that committed $30 million in state grands and bonds—to match an additional $15 million from the private sector—to fund the creation of our new Institute for Exploration as part of an expansion of the Mystic Marinelife Aquarium.

The institute will be the capstone of my career as an explorer. Housed in its own building on the aquarium grounds, the institute will have an interactive museum called the World of Undersea Exploration, which will contain a multimedia theater, that serves as an experimental down-link site for the JASON Project. The creation of the Institute for Exploration will allow me to bring together under one roof my disparate publishing and filmmaking activities, the JASON Project, and my ongoing research on the technology of robotic undersea exploration.

Finally, after so many decades of complex and improvised fund-raising efforts, I will have a steady source of income to partially support my work.

Retiring from Woods Hole at age fifty-five in 1997 will not be easy. The Institution will have been my professional home for thirty years. But again, I believe my work in the forefront of important scientific research is behind me, and my main responsibility now will be as an educator, both of students through the JASON Project and of adults through the Institute for Exploration and the books and television documentaries its activities spawn.

But I certainly do not intend to abandon exploration. Indeed, now that my team has developed such useful robotic tools, I hope to conduct at least one major exploration expedition a year, sometimes in conjunction with the JASON Project.

As I recently told a reporter from the *New York Times,* "The public knows more about Mars and Venus than they do about the deep sea."

In the coming years, I hope to take an increasingly larger

segment of the public, both in the United States and abroad, with me through telepresence and video on my continuing voyage of exploration. Like many who have spent much of their life at sea, I am keenly aware that most of the planet is underwater.

I'm also aware that the world's population, which even by optimistic estimates will double in the next century, will inevitably place an increasing burden on the world's complex, interdependent ecosystem that supports all life.

And gazing past the ships' spars out the mouth of the Mystic River at the distant gray Atlantic horizon, I recognize that human beings may one day colonize the world's oceans; if not the deep, chill deserts of the abyss, at least the fertile shallows of the continental shelves.

As history teaches us, exploration must precede colonization.

So I will continue my voyage.